Montgomery County, Tennessee

Marriages

1838 – 1867

Byron and Barbara Sistler

Janaway Publishing, Inc.
2007

Montgomery County, Tennessee, Marriages 1838-1867

Originally published, Nashville, 1986

Reprinted for
Byron Sistler and Associates, Inc.

by

Janaway Publishing, Inc.
2412 Nicklaus Dr.
Santa Maria, California 93455
(805) 925-1038
www.JanawayGenealogy.com

2007

ISBN: 978-1-59641-134-0

MONTGOMERY COUNTY, TN MARRIAGES

1838-1867

Where two dates appear on an entry, the first one is the date license was issued, the second (in parentheses) the date marriage was solemnized. If only one date, it usually means that the date of execution was the same as the date of license issuance.

Sometimes the execution of the marriage was not reported to the courthouse, and occasionally the clerk failed to note in the marriage book that the license was returned. We would usually make a notation in the entry to indicate the non-execution of a marriage if the book so stated.

The marriages are arranged alphabetically, the first half of the book by groom--the second half by bride.

The records included in this book were transcribed by us directly from microfilm of the original marriage books. Error, where it occurs, may be attributed to us, or to the clerks of the period, many of whom obviously did an appallingly sloppy job of entering the information.

If the bride and groom were black, a B is placed at the end of the entry.

It should be remembered that this and other marriage books we have prepared are indexes, not including all the information to be found in the original marriage book. Such data as names of bondsmen, ministers, justices of the peace, churches etc. is omitted. Often such information is helpful to the researcher. Consequently the serious researcher, to obtain this additional information as well as to check on the accuracy of the transcriber, should examine the original marriage record if at all possible, or at least another marriage record book which may contain this data.

Byron Sistler
Barbara Sistler

Nashville, TN
December, 1986

Abbott, George to Hariet Caroline Lane 3-12-1846 (3-13-1846)
Abernathy, Andrew to Sarah G. Tally 2-20-1860 (2-22-1860)
Abernathy, Cary to Molly McCurdy 4-26-1865 [b]
Abernathy, George to Mariah Gueran 6-23-1866 [b]
Abernathy, Gilbert T. to Emily Tally 12-14-1853 (12-15-1853)
Abernathy, Gilbert T. to Louisa Baxter 1-2-1839 (1-8-1839)
Abney, Harman to Adeline Minerva Williams 11-30-1847 (12-2-1847)
Acock, Benjamin F. to Nancy R. Pendleton 9-3-1850
Acre, Horace M. to Caroline E. H. Allin 9-1-1857 (9-2-1857)
Acre, John C. to F. H. Ogburn 9-14-1859 (9-21-1859)
Acre, John R. to Mary L. A. E. Ross 12-22-1853
Adams, A. G. to Mary S. Adams 11-18-1862 (11-20-1862)
Adams, Ethanah P. to Rebecca A. Bryan 10-19-1855
Adams, James to Matild H. McGee 6-27-1852
Adams, Jessee G. to Agness Byless 2-8-1864 (2-15-1864)
Adams, Jessee G. to Elizabeth C. Harris 12-13-1857
Adams, Jessee G. to Martha J. Adams 12-19-1851 (12-23-1851)
Adams, John H. to Ellen Fletcher 9-17-1849 (9-19-1849)
Adams, John J. to Sallie B. Halyard 11-3-1863 (11-5-1863)
Adams, N. B. to E. J. Speer 8-30-1857 (8-30-1856?)
Adams, Oliver to Martha Adams 8-24-1856
Adams, Richard to Mattie Grady 12-27-1865
Adams, Thomas J. to Mary E. Thompson 3-3-1857
Adams, Thos. to Angeline Linsey 2-1-1847
Adams, Thos. to Susan M. Rives 4-29-1850
Adams, W. D. to Ann L. Rollow 4-2-1852 (4-4-1852)
Adams, William F. to Ermine P. Adams 12-11-1858 (12-12-1858)
Adams, William to Eunice McDaniel 1-18-1859
Adcock, H. M. to Mildred W. Williams 1-14-1853 (1-18-1853)
Adderhold, Henry W. to Ann Eliza Smith 3-7-1860
Addison, William F. to Serilda D. Shepherd 1-15-1860
Adkins, James to Susan Nesbitt 11-11-1850
Adkins, Lemuel K. to Sylvestie C. Morriss 7-25-1839 (7-27-1839)
Adkins, Robt. B. to Mollie M. Smith 11-30-1865 (12-5-1865)
Adkins, W. P. to Priscilla Council 2-14-1859 (2-15-1859)
Adkins, Wm. P. to Mary J. Reynolds 12-17-1851 (12-25-1851)
Adwell, Wm. to L. A. Clarke 1-8-1861
Ainsworth, Joseph to Mary A. Clinard 7-15-1848 (7-16-1848)
Albright, J. T. to M. G. King 1-7-1861 (1-15-1861)
Albright, Jacob P. to Elizabeth Hutcherson 3-27-1848
Albright, Thos. H. to Sarah A. Marshall 8-18-1852
Alexander, John N. to Mary W. Conley 4-11-1842
Alexander, John P. to Hellen M. Hiter 12-29-1841
Alexander, Maynham H. to Alice Sawyer 12-19-1859 (12-20-1859)
Alexander, William E. to Mary Sawyer 12-29-1857 (1-1-1858)
Allen, A. J. to Elizabeth S. Orgain 5-24-1852
Allen, Bailey F. to Mary Jane Osbourn 12-24-1845 (12-25-1845)
Allen, Daniel D. to Mary A. Rasey 1-18-1850
Allen, Danl. D. to Matt T. Lowe 3-14-1866
Allen, Donal J. to Mary J. Right 3-12-1849 (3-13-1849)
Allen, Drury to Perlina Bowers 7-11-1841
Allen, Henry to Cathrine A. Dycus 9-27-1847
Allen, James C. to Louisa A. Lyle 6-1-1852
Allen, John B. to E. P. McGowan 12-18-1866 (12-21-1866)
Allen, Joseph H. to Martha A. Smith 11-30-1861 (12-1-1861)
Allen, Nathan to Lucretia E. Brown 6-7-1843
Allen, R. A. to Mary Merrit 7-5-1851
Allen, R. C. to Mary Smith 9-23-1851 (9-22?-1851)
Allen, Robert to Martha Smith 10-4-1839 (10-10-1839)
Allen, Saml. F. to N. Virginia Organ 11-14-1863
Allen, Samuel F. to Mary Ann Daly 12-10-1844 (12-12-1844)
Allen, Samuel F. to Salina H. Steel 2-8-1860 (2-9-1860)
Allen, Thos. H. to Mary Smith 11-23-1861 (11-24-1861)
Allensworth, D. J. to Elizabeth P. Jones 8-17-1848
Allensworth, George P. to Jessie Landram 11-2-1863
Allensworth, Jackson to Joanna B. Fauntleroy 3-2-1854
Allensworth, John T. to Henrietta Hopson 5-8-1861
Allinsworth, P. Q.? to Elizabeth Thomas 6-23-1844
Allison, Lawrence to Nancy Jane Carneal 1-21-1858 (1-22-1858)
Allsbrooks, G. W. to Mary J. Hunt 9-25-1848 (9-26-1848)
Ally, R. H. to Amanda L. Watkins 1-23-1845
Alman, Robert J. to Delila T. Dilling 12-29-1853
Alsup, Asaph H. to Martha S. Manson 11-4-1854 (11-8-1854)
Alsup, J. F. to Eliza A. Trice 6-14-1858 (6-15-1858)
Altaway, J. W. R. to Mary B. Lyle 3-29-1858 (3-30-1858)

Anderon, B. J. to E. Starks 9-19-1841
Anderon, James W. to Eliz. B. Moseley 3-38-1844
Anderon, P. N. to Agniss Brame 3-23-1844
Anderon, W. H. to Margarett E. Smith 10-3-1843 (10-5-1843)
Anderson, Archibald M. to Amelia Sensing 11-24-1840
Anderson, Archibald M. to Virginia Apperson 9-29-1838 (9-30-1838)
Anderson, Charles Madison to Elizabeth Vaughn 1-27-1852
Anderson, Charles to Siloia Moore 7-28-1866 [b]
Anderson, Elijah to Harriet Burton 9-4-1848
Anderson, Jacob to J. S. Odoniley 1-4-1842
Anderson, Jas. to Matilda Johnson 5-21-1866 [b]
Anderson, Jessee J. to Elizabeth J. Shanklin 11-27-1863
Anderson, John to Sarah Ann Bonds 2-26-1847? (2-28-1848)
Anderson, Robert A. to Carian B. Love 7-29-1839 (8-1-1839)
Anderson, Samuel M. to Martha N. Kerr 4-24-1859 (4-26-1859)
Anderson, Thornsberry to Fredonia Toler 1-29-1848 (1-30-1848)
Anderson, William R. to Dicy Adaline Lewis 6-11-1853 (6-12-1853)
Anderson, Wm. to Lucy J. Rutherford 2-27-1844
Andrews, Berry W. to Sally Ann Barnes 12-16-1839 (12-19-1839)
Andrews, James to Ann E. Sleigh 10-6-1858 (10-7-1858)
Andrews, Jas. to Georg E. Slye 8-11-1865 (8-12-1865)
Andrews, W. H. to Margaret Trice 8-4-1858 (8-6-1858)
Anglin, John W. to Martha E. Harris 12-12-1855
Anglin, Thompson W. to Nancy J. Smith 6-10-1846 (6-11-1846)
Apperson, John B. to Susan A. Pollard 3-12-1846
Appleton, James to Mary Elizabeth Miles 1-8-1861 (1-9-1861)
Arminett, Wm. to Elmina Wind 2-5-1851 (2-6-1851)
Armistead, John Henry to Elizabeth(Frances?) Nesbit 12-17-1859 (12-18-1859)
Armonett, William to Mary Grant 7-16-1840
Armstead, Henry A. to Maggie G. Cook 1-24-1867 (2-6-1867)
Armstrong, David H. to Angaline C. Haynes 7-9-1853 (7-10-1853)
Armstrong, Geo. W. to Lucy A. Seray 6-1-1863
Armstrong, John E. to Caroline C. Swader 1-9-1861 (1-10-1861)
Asberry, Dudley E. to Emma Coleman 6-20-1865
Asby, Enoch to Rebecca Brackett 11-10-1849
Ashley, Alexander H. to Catharine Westzell 12-26-1856
Atkins, George S. to Mrs. C. E. Glass 11-27-1860
Atkins, Isaac S. to Lucie A. Randle 11-18-1863
Atkins, James T. to Virginia Carr 11-18-1840 (12-22-1840)
Atkins, John H. to Prussia Denney 8-17-1852
Atkinson, T. W. Jr. to Henrietta E. Trice 1-25-1847
Attaway, J. W. to Lucy J. Lyle 11-18-1865 (11-21-1865)
Audy, Richard to Martha Dyer 4-20-1856
Averet, Richard to Martha Shelton 9-16-1856 (9-17-1856)
Averet, Thos. H. to Rebecca Ann Lemay 9-11-1845
Averett, Elijah to Charlotte Edwards 3-19-1852
Averett, Jarret to Mary J. Shelton 12-18-1858 (12-21-1858)
Averett, Thomas H. to Rebecca Tyre 11-1-1853
Averitt, Francis H. to Demarius Gilbert 3-3-1843
Averitt, Peter J. to Eliza Ann Lay 8-27-1853
Bacon, Charles P. to Margaret Ratcliff 12-17-1844
Bagget, James to Elizabeth Powers 3-10-1852 (3-14-1852)
Bagget, James to Rebecca Ann Bridge 5-30-1860
Bagget, Josiah to Elizabeth Baggett 3-19-1860 (3-23-1860)
Bagget, Oliver to Liza Ann Hayes 2-21-1856
Bagget, William to Mary Hodges 11-17-1859 (11-18-1859)
Bagget, William to Sarah Underwood 4-9-1850
Baggett, A. to D. A. Baggett 7-30-1862 (8-3-1862)
Baggett, Abraham to Elizabeth Hodge 9-13-1865 (9-17-1865)
Baggett, Allen to America Gagle 8-15-1865 (8-16-1865)
Baggett, Benjamin to Elizabeth Bone 7-4-1849
Baggett, Harvell to Mary Powell 1-29-1844
Baggett, Henry to Malinda Powell 2-29-1844
Baggett, Henry to Mary Mowrer? 5-26-1851 (5-21?-1851)
Baggett, J. Westley to Laressa Smith 2-4-1856 (2-7-1856)
Baggett, James M. to Mary J. Wright 12-12-1865
Baggett, Jas. to Harriet Rainwaters 12-20-1862 (12-25-1862)
Baggett, Jessee to Leona Hodges 8-6-1860 (8-14-1860)
Baggett, John to Eliza Davis 10-1841 (10-7-1841)
Baggett, John to Mary Bane 8-17-1856
Baggett, John to Mary Underwood 12-17-1863
Baggett, John to Sarah E. Allen 7-11-1866 (7-12-1866)
Baggett, Thomas to Mary Black 11-1-1862 (11-17-1862)
Baggett, Thomas to Sarah Jane Sinks 8-11-1855

Baggett, Wesley to Caroline Powell 4-3-1839
Bagwell, G. P. to A. F. Adams 8-4-1840
Bagwell, G. W. to Mrs. Margaret Wheeler 5-3-1865
Bagwell, Jno. W. to Martha Brown 11-30-1843 12-1-1843
Bagwell, L.R. to Mary J. Wall 11-19-1859 (11-20-1859)
Bagwell, N. E. to Emma Patrick 10-18-1866
Bagwell, Nicholas E. to Elizabeth C. Burney 12-15-1858 (12-16-1858)
Bagwell, William M. to Mary Ann Brown 9-28-1852
Bailey, C. W. to Virginia Corney 11-26-1850
Bailey, Henry L. to Wilmuth H. Boyd 3-22-1843
Bailey, J. J. to Sarah Frances Morrow 4-17-1861 (4-18-1861)
Bailey, James C. to Mary C. Troville 3-20-1844
Bailey, John B. to Nancy Dortch 10-8-1845
Bailey, John to Elizabeth Lewis 10-9-1865
Bailey, Thomas B. to Sarah M. Ewing 7-20-1846
Bailey, W. H. to Mary Ann Pearce 11-15-1855
Bailey, William to Mary Brown 7-1-1839 (7-4-1839)
Bailey, Wm. to Amanda James 2-27-1866
Baily, Robert J. to Sarah R. Smith 12-13-1857 (1-7-1858)
Baily, Robert to Sarah Terrell 5-25-1858 (5-26-1858)
Baily, Wm. A. to Martha A. M. Johnson 8-3-1846 (8-22-1846)
Baine, Erastus to Eliza J. Collins 3-25-1853 (3-27-1853)
Baird, Rev. A. J. to A. H. Britten 5-8-1850
Baker, Diskin to Mary Ann Owsley 4-29-1865
Baker, Isham W. to Clarissa Ferguson 7-1-1853
Baker, John L. N. to Julia Gibbs 1-24-1843 (1-25-1843)
Baker, John to Marona Duncan 12-4-1839 (12-5-1839)
Baker, Jonathan S. to Martha H. Browder 4-11-1853
Baker, Major to Lucy Merriweather 8-31-1865 [b?]
Baker, Michael to Catharine Dolan 7-24-1854 (7-26-1854)
Baker, Richard to Elizabeth Scott 6-17-1854 (6-23-1854)
Baker, William to Sarah Jones 3-10-1848
Baldrey, Jake to Lydia Fort 9-15-1866 (9-22-1866) [b]
Ball, Emery S. to Mrs. Sarah Tucker 4-28-1865 (4-29-1865)
Ballard, John to Jane F. Peacher 3-20-1845
Ballentine, William to Amberlin? Jones 7-9-1853
Balthrop, Ferdanand E. to Elizabeth J. Harris 10-7-1864 (10-9-1864)
Balton(Ballow?), Charles H. to Octavia Lacy 7-25-1864 (7-27-1864)
Bancroft, Jones H. to Elizabeth J. Long 1-28-1860 (1-29-1860)
Banister, H. to Hester An Harkman? 3-27-1851
Barbee, Abner Cain to Mary Ann M. Trice 12-21-1846 (12-24-1846)
Barbee, Augustus to Sarah Wynn 10-21-1845 (10-24-1844?)
Barbee, Bartley to Emily E. Darnel 1-21-1850
Barbee, George to Jane Smith 8-30-1855
Barbee, John to Hester Ann Wilson 5-9-1853 (5-10-1853)
Barbee, Robt. to Ellen F. Taler? 2-24-1851
Barbee, S. W. to Lizzie A. Gold 6-3-1865 (6-6-1865)
Barbee, W. J. to Ally J. Fields 12-27-1856 (12-28-1856)
Barbee, W. J. to Bettie Ann Fields 10-23-1862 (12-4-1862)
Barbee, W. J. to Malord? Trice 1-2-1849
Barbee, William J. to Frances M. Trice 12-20-1854
Barbee, William P. to Susannah Trice 12-21-1844 (12-23-1844)
Barbee, Young to Martha J. Greenhill 10-20-1859 (10-21-1859)
Barber, John R. to Piety Yancy 2-8-1867 (2-12-1867)
Bardes, Calvin? to Ruthey Bailey 12-27-1866
Barker, E. Walton to Mary W. Barker 11-14-1860 (11-15-1860)
Barker, Harbard to Mary Clark 12-25-1866 [b]
Barker, Lemial to Edline Carter 12-24-1866 [b]
Barker, Therston to Phebee Allen 6-19-1865
Barker, Thos. M. to Mary L. Morris 12-28-1866
Barker, Watson to Rena Marable 12-1-1866 (12-18-1866) [b]
Barksdale, W. C. to Josephine Tally 10-17-1853 (10-20-1853)
Barksdale, Wilton C. to Araminda D. Martin 9-7-1852
Barnes, Joseph to Sally Lisenby 9-10-1855 (10-10-1855)
Barnes, Mathew A. to Clarrinda F. Lee 4-5-1859 (4-7-1859)
Barnes, R. A. to Fannie Trigg 1-16-1861 (1-17-1861)
Barnett, Benjamine to Eveline Maar? 10-26-1849 (10-29-1849)
Barnett, George S. to Henrietta M. Robertson 9-13-1858 (9-16-1858)
Barnett, William H. to Luticia Morrison 5-12-1861
Barnum, Charles to Bella Waller 8-16-1860
Barnwell, Jno. to M. E. Taylor Little 12-27-1843
Barons?, Joseph to Louisa Mann 9-7-1846 (9-8-1846)
Barrett, Chas. to Dora Mabry 11-24-1866 [b]
Bartee, A. J. to Luisa Elliott 4-3-1854 (4-4-1854)
Bartee, G. W. to Susan A. Moore 8-4-1852

Bartee, Jessee W. to Lucy Ann Bullock 2-7-1852
Barten, Leon? to Ann Sidner 1-3-1867 (1-4-1867) [b]
Bartlett, Benjamin F. to Mary King 4-14-1845 (4-15-1845)
Barton, John to Elizabeth Coon 11-17-1847
Barton, William to Lilevant Crown? 9-6-1854
Basford, Jacob B. to Ann Eliza Bethune 10-14-1854 (10-19-1854)
Basford, James to Charity Isbell 7-6-1846 (7-23-1846)
Basford, Jas. to E. Starkey 8-25-1862 (9-2-1862)
Basford, Joseph J. to Mary Ann Alley 3-13-1854
Basford, Thomas to Eliza Wright 12-19-1853 (12-22-1853)
Basquit, Abraham to Martha Ann Warden 8-20-1850
Batsford, C. H. to Rebecca W. Hudson 12-28-1860 (12-30-1860)
Batson, Stephen C. to A. M. Williams 12-8-1840 (12-11-1840)
Batson, W. B. to Virginia Morris 9-20-1854 (9-21-1854)
Batterman, August to Ellen Sutton 3-29-1854
Battle, J. W. to Mary G. Fort 7-23-1856 (7-24-1856)
Batts, Benj. to Sarah Gepton 1-3-1851
Batts, John to Nancy Nanry 5-16-1846 (5-17-1846)
Batts, Thomas to Martha Pool 1-7-1855
Bayer, Wm. D. to R. W. Wisdom 7-10-1847 (7-13-1847)
Bayless, B. to N. J. Hogan 8-12-1848
Bayless, Thomas to Mary Ellen Wilkins 5-20-1859 (5-23-1859)
Bayless, Wm. to M. Fritts 10-14-1862 (10-16-1862)
Baylis, Samuel to Mary E. Brickle 11-11-1847
Bayliss, Joel to Susan Niblett 11-20-1847
Bayly, Fredrick jr. to Susan Woodson 1-3-1855
Beacun?, Thomas L. to Eliza Mildred Madison 5-20-1845
Bead, J. C. to Annie H. Cooper 12-11-1858 (12-12-1858)
Beam, R. S. H. to Mary Jane Mason 8-21-1855 (8-22-1855)
Bear, John W. to Frances E. Miller 12-16-1845
Bearden, Alford to Frances Little 3-11-1839
Bearden, Benjamin B. to Nancy Maxey 8-24-1853 (8-25-1853)
Bearden, Haywood to Elizabeth Weakley 6-7-1850
Bearden, Thomas to Elizabeth Farmer 5-18-1844 (5-21-1844)
Bearden, William to Sally Farmer 5-19-1845
Beardin, John to Prudence Majors 12-13-1841 (12-15-1841)
Beardune, Isaac to Elizabeth Sutton 9-2-1849
Beaumont, E. H. to Lucy J. Ellis 10-17-1858 (10-19-1858)
Beaumont, Franklin S. to Laura E. Conrad 11-21-1854
Beaumont, Sterling F. to Mattie P. Conrad? 5-24-1853
Beaumont, Tom to Mary Jane Steel 6-26-1866 [b]
Becley?, John to Mary Dority 12-11-1858
Beech, H. E. to Fannie J. Bourne 12-15-1859 (12-22-1859)
Been, Benjamin H. to Eliza Jane Gossett 3-11-1847
Belamy, Peter F. to Margaret E. Morrow 10-1-1858 (10-7-1858)
Belcher, N. H. to Adline Hutchings 5-8-1842 (5-23-1842)
Bell, Darwin to Mary Walker Merriweather 12-28-1857
Bell, Henry to Ellen Stovall 8-29-1865 [b?]
Bell, J. Q. A. to Mary R. Wright 3-23-1846
Bell, Jim to Chaney Smith 8-24-1866 [b]
Bell, Thomas to Rosa Ann Harris 1-10-1850 (1-17-1850)
Bell, Thomas to Sarah M. Truax 6-4-1846 (6-10-1846)
Bell, William to Fannie Rogers 11-22-1866 [b]
Bellemy, Isaac to Mary A. Sanders 1-6-1866 (1-15-1866) [b]
Bellemy, John T. to Elizabeth D. Wimberly 7-24-1861
Bellemy, Nelson to Amanda Vance 1-6-1866 (1-15-1866) [b]
Bellemy, Robt. D. to Sally Ann Northington 10-28-1839 (10-30-1839)
Bennet, John W. to Holly Baggett 7-8-1865
Bennet, Michael to Bridget Leonard 7-16-1859 (7-17-1859)
Bentley, D. A. to Mollie E. Osburn 12-17-1866
Bergie, James S. to Mary Harvey 1-28-1849 (1-30-1849)
Berk, John T. to Mary Ann Fips 5-13-1861
Berniss?, James M. to M. F. Lockert 10-16-1849 (10-19-1849)
Berpo?, Wm. T. to Lucy Ann Vaughn 11-4-1865 (11-7-1865)
Berry, Daniel to Mary Abbott 3-2-1844 (3-6-1844)
Biggs, Mathew to Paulina Shaddock 4-3-1847 (4-18-1847)
Biggs, Mathew to Paulina Shaddock 5-3-1848 (5-5-1848)
Billingsley, Joseph H. to Ophelia Fowlkes 5-14-1866 (5-10?-1866)
Bingham, Francis G. to Elizabeth J. Dean 6-4-1853
Binkley, A. J. to Elizabeth Jones 1-10-1861
Binkley, F. M. to Catharine Crocket 2-25-1846 (2-26-1846)
Bisby, John to Sarah Scale? 2-27-1847
Bishop, Prestly to Polly Weakly 9-26-1848
Bishop, T. L. to M. E. Mills 6-27-1852
Biter, W. A. J. to Lucy J. Harvey 10-18-1864

Black, Alfred to Janie White 2-7-1855
Black, Alfred to Sarah Ann Cawsey 10-4-1855
Black, Dock to Juddie Johnson 4-14-1866 [b]
Black, James H. to Lucy Ann Lee 10-16-1846 (11-5-1846)
Black, John to Elizabeth C. Hunter 3-30-1844 (4-3-1844)
Black, Michael to Martha Causey 7-6-1840
Black, Michael to Prudence Stewart 5-23-1846 (5-24-1846)
Black, W. G. to Nancy Billingsly 3-11-1851
Blackford, Benjamin to Elizabeth Wickham 9-13-1838 (9-18-1838)
Blackford, Josephus N. to Rebeca Mariah Mathis 3-1-1861 (3-6-1861)
Blackman, Samuel to Martha E. Seebree 6-21-1847 (6-23-1847)
Blackwell, R. W. to Mary Harriss 1-17-1851 (1-22-1851)
Blackwell, William to Sarah Tariann 2-4-1852 (2-5-1852)
Blair, Daniel R. to Sarah E. Bartlett 6-19-1865
Blair, Evan B. to Winniford Fletcher 12-17-1840
Blair, Henry to Rachael McDougle 1-21-1853 (1-28-1853)
Blair, J. H. to Sarah Ann Elliott (no date; with 3-1852)
Blake, Albert E. to Mary J. Nickle 9-9-1855
Blake, J. R. to E. A. Rye 12-16-1862
Blake, John R. to Susan F. Hancock 10-22-1851 (10-23-1851)
Blakemore, T. F. to Susan P. Bailey 12-18-1849 (12-19-1848?)
Blaksey, Robt. J. to Zilpha Donaldson 6-13-1850
Blane, John to Martha E. Thomas 4-22-1861 (4-25-1861)
Blankenship, John C. to Mary Catharine Senserey 9-11-1844
          (CTF says 1845)
Blankenship, L. T. to Virginia Ross 11-9-1852
Blankenship, Samuel R. to Sarah A. Toone 6-22-1856
Blanks, Wm. D. to Narcissa W. Horn 9-23-1849
Blanton, James J. to Clarinda Black 3-10-1851
Blanton, John W. to Lucy B. Buck 12-4-1851
Blaw(Balaw?), John to Marthy Ann Foster 5-22-1857
Bledsoe, Alford G. to Phebe Ann Welker 12-25-1839
Board, Hardin to Elizabeth Hobbs 10-18-1860
Boardman, Thomas M. to Mary Gray 1-6-1859
Boardman, Thomas M. to Mildred S. Ware 11-19-1861
Boatwright, B. W. to Z. H. Donaldson 9-24-1860 (9-28-1860)
Bodine, Thomas to Harriett Searcey 3-34-1843
Boid, Henry to Mary Jane Wilson 11-28-1866 (12-2-1866) [b]
Boles, S. H. to Mary R. Parham 7-12-1848 (7-13-1848)
Bolin, Sam to Virginia McNeal 12-18-1866 (12-26-1866)
Boller, George T. to Martha Moore 9-1-1839
Bolton, Samuel to Bell Booth 1-24-1861
Bond, Francis W. to Eliza Smith 6-17-1852
Bond, Wm. G. to Irene J. Pennington 11-24-1866 (11-25-1866)
Bonds, John to Mary Damron 5-31-1851
Bonds, Thornbury A. to Margaret Jane Roark 10-6-1841 (10-7-1841)
Bonner, Thomas to Lucinda D. Carr 8-19-1840
Booker, G. W. to Frances D. Duke 10-22-1839 (10-23-1839)
Boon, John to Vicey B. Williams 9-25-1847 (9-26-1847)
Boon, L. B. to Sally Ann H. B. Brodie 6-8-1841 (6-15-1841)
Boon, S.? B. to Mary M. Foster 3-31-1843
Boothe, W. D. to Mary Conly 10-3-1852
Borden, Joseph C. to Mary Ann Page 5-18-1844 (5-19-1844)
Bose, Aron W. to Martha J. Rose 1-2-1867 (1-8-1867)
Boston, George P. to Mary M. Pollard 9-16-1844 (9-18-1844)
Boswell, John H. to Mary A. Dilling 8-14-1863 (8-16-1863)
Boswell, John to Lou Bradshaw 8-7-1866 [b]
Bourland, M. S. to Sarah A. Vaughn 6-2-1852
Bowe, Levi to Mary Collins 12-20-1841 (12-23-1841)
Bowe?, John to Julian Kinies? 1-31-1846
Bowers, James D. to Frances J. Mallory 9-9-1850
Bowers, James D. to Nancy C. Dilling 6-9-1856 (6-10-1856)
Bowers, John C. to Cordelia H. Lewis 11-15-1853 (11-20-1853)
Bowers, John M. to Mary C. Harris 10-10-1851 (10-12-1851)
Bowers, Joseph J. to Frances E. Wall 1-7-1845
Bowers, K. C. to Elizabeth C. Bowers 12-19-1849 (12-24-1849)
Bowers, Kinchen C. to Elizabeth C. Bowers 12-19-1850 (12-24-1849?)
Bowers, Sanford to Emily Collier 10-14-1853 (10-18-1853)
Bowling, B. P. to Ann Swingle? 10-1-1844 (10-2-1844)
Bowling, James H. to Jane S. Grant 3-17-1852
Bowling, John P. to Lucy B. Forston 11-3-1859 (11-8-1859)
Bowling, P. to Mary M. Sale 10-29-1866
Bowling, R. P. to Mary A. Philip 4-10-1850
Box, Jerry to Amanda West 10-29-1866 [b]
Boyd, David L. to Malissa E. Williams 3-15-1859 (3-17-1859)

Boyd, George E. to Mary Adaline Adkins 8-16-1853 (9-28-1853)
Boyd, James A. to Susan Brodie 1-23-1849 (1-25-1849)
Boyd, Joseph M. to Mary F.? Pratt 8-14-1851
Boyd, Marcus D. to Sarah Balentine 2-9-1850 (2-10-1850)
Boyd, William to Susan E. Moe? 1-17-1848
Brackingberry, John to Easter Cross 8-21-1865
Bradberry, Geo. to Sarah Oneal 1-17-1846 (1-18-1846)
Bradberry, William to Ann Ragsdale 11-19-1839
Bradbury, R. S. to Elizabeth Ford 12-23-1846 (12-24-1846)
Braddus, Joseph E. to Harriet J. Whittaker 3-21-1853 (3-22-1853)
Bradley, Adam to Nancy Smith 10-4-1866] (10-5-1866) [b]
Bradley, Enoch to Polly Gibbs 10-12-1839 (10-20-1839)
Bradley, George W. to D. P. Wisdom 9-22-1845 (9-24-1845)
Bradley, John to Emily Baird 1-16-1845
Bradley, Larkin to Mary Ann Baird 2-29-1844 (3-1-1844)
Bradley, Sam to Silvy Jarrell 3-31-1866 (4-14-1866) [b]
Bradley, Walter L. to Margarett E. Samford 1-7-1852
Bradley, William to Jane Baird 3-5-1838
Bradly, Joihn to Emily Baird 1-16-1845
Bradshaw, George to Fanny Bernan 4-21-1865 [b]
Bradshaw, James to Mary Ann Ford 12-20-1847
Bradshaw, Samuel to Georgeann Jeter 7-13-1856
Bradshaw, Samuel to Mary Jane Jeter 6-30-1852
Brake, Thomas to Melissa Duncan 6-3-1856
Brame, James E. to Olevia Hutchins 12-19-1859
Brame, Jas. Henry to Nancy F. Bumpass 1-11-1866
Brame, Joseph to F. Wall 3-18-1863 (3-25-1863)
Brandon, Stephen to Mary Reynolds 8-21-1855
Branham, Albert G. to Elizabeth S. Furgerson 3-1-1848 (3-2-1848)
Brantley, Charles to Margarette Shelton 9-14-1838 (9-18-1838)
Brashears, Thomas to Mary L. Moore 2-24-1858
Brawner, Lemuel S. to Semanthia L. Winn 2-8-1864
Brazer, Abraham to Margaret M. Council 5-17-1855
Brazier, Isaac to Nepsiarm McComac 7-27-1860
Breeden, Isham to Martha Elizabeth Powers 12-10-1852 (12-14-1852)
Breeden, J. C. to Nancy Clark 9-23-1848 (9-17?-1848)
Breeden, Joseph to Martha J. Powers 7-9-1864 (7-13-1864)
Breeden, L. O. to Rhoda Caroline Breeden 3-25-1858
Breeden, Wade to Lurana(Susanna?) Jarman 6-28-1859 (6-29-1859)
Breeden, William H. to Mary B. Breeden 11-22-1855 (10?-22-1855)
Breedin, George to Adelia Ann J. Breeden 3-25-1858
Breedin, J. O. to Secile Dean 12-19-1863
Breedlove, Dudley to Sally Pace? 1-2-1855
Bresner?, Jessee to Nancy A. Latham 8-24-1847
Brewer, Sterling to Agnes J. Saunders 10-3-1839
Brewer, Sterling to Virginia G. Glenn 9-4-1844 (9-5-1844)
Briant, Burrel to Rebecca Elizabeth Lyle 7-16-1853 (7-17-1853)
Brickell, B. N. W. to Mary Parkerson 6-21-1859 (6-23-1859)
Brickle, William M. to Nancy C. Brockman 11-10-1864
Bridges, James to Louisa Mockbee 5-4-1861 (5-8-1861)
Bridgewater, Chesley to Julia Ann Johnson 4-20-1849
Bridgewater, Richard to Fane A. Goley 11-11-1847
Briggs, Charles M. to Elizabeth M. Rogers 1-19-1848
Brigham, David to Sarah Mixan 7-15-1852
Bright, James L. to Mary Ann Pool 7-20-1844 (7-31-1844)
Bright, Wm. J. to Nancy H. Thorn 9-25-1851
Brillane?, R. L. to Mary E. Meyers 3-21-1860 (3-23-1860)
Bringhurst, William R. to Virginia Manlove 1-17-1867
Brisendine, Jehu R. to Catharine M. Evans 6-8-1854
Bristoe, Nicholas to Huldy Clifton 2-24-1848 (SB 1849?)
Britt, John M. to Eliza Ann Powers 7-20-1849 (7-22-1849)
Britt, John M. to Lucena Williams 7-9-1841 (7-11-1841)
Brittan, Edward H. to Florence Beaumont 6-26-1865
Britton, Chas. to Allis Davis 7-28-1866 (7-19?-1866) [b]
Britton, Z. to Lucy M. Quarles 6-9-1866 (6-17-1866) [b]
Broadbent, William to Sarah F. Harris 5-1-1849
Broaddie, Bill to Emerline Smith 2-7-1866 (2-18-1866) [b]
Broaddus, Elijah to Martha A. Broaddus 5-31-1838
Broady, Tom to Lily Broady 1-1-1867 (4-14-1867) [b]
Brock, John to Tabitha Miles 11-14-1848
Brockman, Oswell to Elizabeth W. Pitman 10-7-1844
Brockman, Saml. to Angie Buck 8-26-1857 (8-21?-1857)
Broddie, Stephen to Ann Wood 7-27-1866 (8-1-1866) [b]
Brodie, C. A. to S. L. Neblett 6-21-1842 (6-23-1842)
Brook, Owen to Ellen Jarman 9-12-1859

Brooks, John jr. to Mary Staley 12-27-1847 (12-29-1847)
Brooks, Wm. to Mary Ann Ellis 9-26-1838 (9-27-1838)
Broom, Francis to Pamela Rye 1-29-1839 (1-30-1839)
Broom, J. W. to Marya Allen 1-7-1867
Broom, W. F. to Martha Bagget 1-1-1867 (1-3-1867)
Broom, Wm. H. to Permelia F. Harris 11-17-1863
Broomfield, Obadiah to Mary E. Hancocke 1-21-1840 (1-23-1840)
Broomfield, William J. to Ann C. Fortner 5-3-1854
Browder, George R. to A. E. Warfield 9-5-1850
Browder, Thomas E. to Virginia S. Warfield 12-23-1856
Brown, Benj. H. to M. A. Humphreys 8-1-1843 (8-5-1843)
Brown, Bob to Manie McComes 12-8-1866 (12-24-1866) [b]
Brown, Charles M. to Madosa C. Howard 4-15-1858
Brown, David M. to Louiza J. Grant 8-26-1857
Brown, G. E. to Elizabeth Rives 4-12-1849
Brown, Green Shelton to Mary Marisee? Grant 6-12-1857 (8-2-1857)
Brown, Henry M. to Jane B. Morrow 9-11-1844
Brown, Jacob to Nancy Funk 10-28-1846
Brown, James H. to N. Morrison 12-20-1866
Brown, James M. to Martha Jane Wynn 9-16-1851
Brown, James to Mrs. Ann Jarman 7-27-1865
Brown, Jas. A. to M. L. Allen 8-27-1862
Brown, Jas. W. to Gabriella Dunning 12-31-1866
Brown, John C. to Dicy Kinser 2-22-1845
Brown, John to Ann Roggers 12-26-1866 [b]
Brown, John to Winna Southwood 12-19-1855 (12-20-1855)
Brown, Joseph D. to Emerline C. Hooper 8-29-1864 (8-30-1864)
Brown, Josiah H. to Jennie L. Morrison 10-13-1866 (10-18-1866)
Brown, Rily to Nancy Smith 7-19-1849
Brown, W. R. to Amanda Stephens 12-15-1859
Brown, W. R. to Sarah J. Welker 2-7-1852 (2-9-1852)
Brown?, Jno. to Louvina Southard 12-20-1855
Browning, Wm. to May Lovicy 2-14-1848
Bruce, Joel to Phenaty Ward 1-2-1843 (1-5-1843)
Bruce, William H. to Mary Jane Baily 6-20-1857 (6-25-1857)
Bruce, William to Elizabeth Frazier 6-19-1845
Bruden, William to Sarah Terry' 7-22-1857 (7-23-1857)
Bruer, Daniel to Jinnie Fort 12-26-1866 (12-27-1866) [b]
Brumbaugh, A. C. to Jane Sheridan 10-26-1854
Brunt, William to Mrs. Anni Maria Wilson 8-26-1865
Brunty, James to Eliza Long 6-5-1848
Bruster, L. W. to Mrs. Martha Ann Clark 6-9-1864
Bryan, A. J. W. to Virginia C. Tate 1-13-1850 (1-15-1850)
Bryan, Arthur to Margarett Kirk 10-26-1850 (10-1?-1850)
Bryan, B. F. to Elizabeth Jones 1-13-1855 (1-16-1855)
Bryan, Calep to Nannie Campbell 9-21-1865 [b]
Bryan, Christopher to Mary T. Bryant 3-1-1847
Bryan, Jack to Martha Grady 12-8-1866 (12-9-1866) [b]
Bryan, John H. to Jane A. Brickle 1-3-1842 (1-4-1842)
Bryan, Martin W. to Susan M. Jones 4-30-1866 (5-1-1866)
Bryan, Wm. T. to Tennessee H. Bryan 10-31-1864 (11-1-1864)
Bryant, Arthur to Frances Cordle 7-21-1841
Bryant, Jefferson to Nancy C. Gilbert 2-26-1842 (3-1-1842)
Bryant, John to Elizabeth W. Monroe 1-19-1852 (1-22-1852)
Bryant, John to Nancy Monroe 5-1-1847 (5-9-1847)
Bryant, W. S. to Eliza G. Richardson 8-4-1845 (8-6-1845)
Bryant, Wm. M. to Susan White 11-5-1846
Buck, James M. to Queen Victoria Chiles 5-19-1859 (5-20-1859)
Buck, John H. to Elizabeth Brantly 4-8-1857
Buck, Patric to Mary Sheridan 7-2-1857 (7-15-1857)
Buckhanan, Charles to Mary McCauley 12-6-1866 (5-9-1867)
Buckhannon, David D. to Lucinda Shepherd 11-22-1852 (11-25-1852)
Buckhannon, John W. to Nancy Hardin 3-28-1858
Buckhannon, Peter to Elizabeth Ham 9-14-1855 (9-15-1855)
Buckhannon, Samuel D. to Susan H. Moss 10-13-1846 (10-22-1846)
Buckhannon, Wm. to Mariah T. Thomas 7-13-1846 (7-14-1846)
Buckingham, James W. to Mrs. Nancy L. Cathey 7-17-1865 (7-26-1865)
Buckle, Henry? J. to Maney Mills 12-17-1845 (12-18-1845)
Buckly, Samuel to Mary Ann Jones 8-8-1857 (8-9-1857)
Buckly, Washington D. to Rebecca E. Farmer]8-10-1857
Buckner, John J. to Melvina Whatley 5-6-1855
Buckner, Wm. S. to Caroline S. Morm 4-28-1849
Bucks, James M. to Caroline Beaime? 11-25-1845 (11-29-1845)
Bullard, William E. to Sarah E. Cummins 8-13-1855 (8-14-1855)

Bumpass, George W. to Mary Ann Price 1-12-1854
Bumpass, H. O. to Jane Yarbrough 12-19-1844
Bumpass, John to Mary J. Jones 12-19-1850 (12-18?-1850)
Bumpass, Joseph to Elizabeth N. Jones 12-31-1850
Bumpass, Samuel to Lucy D. Jones 12-10-1845
Bumpass, William to Martha Blount 10-26-1857 (10-29-1857)
Buntin, Theodore to Maria Tally 8-27-1854
Bunting, Thomas W. to Sarah Vaughn 2-9-1847 (2-11-1847)
Buras, Wm. to Lucy Fort 1-5-1867 (1-6-1867) [b]
Burchett, Burwell R. to Henrietta Walthal 2-10-1857
Burchett, William C. to Cindarella Gillis 4-11-1839
Burchett, William C. to Mary Ann Gilbert 2-14-1843
Burden, Robert A. H. to Mary M. Phillips 12-15-1857
Burgess, Gillam W. to Martha A. Brantly 6-19-1856
Burgess, Gilliam W. to Amanda Dycus 9-20-1859
Burgess, Joseph to Mary A. Allen 3-11-1843 (3-12-1843)
Burk, J. T. to Mary Ann Phipps 11-11-1862 (11-12-1862)
Burkes, Wm. Martin to Mary Ellis 11-25-1844
Burnes, Waner to Adaline Goodman 1-2-1867 [b]
Burnett, John to Demarius Jourdon 3-13-1846 (3-15-1846)
Burney, John C. to Nancy Brown 12-29-1847
Burney, Joseph Davis to Amanda Hogan 12-6-1858 (12-8-1858)
Burnley, H. R. to M. J. Young 8-15-1866
Burns, Eli to Susan Mitchell 4-11-1838 (4-12-1838)
Burns, Hughy to Elizabeth Baggett 1-22-1844
Burton, Dempsey to Louisa Smith 11-3-1856 (11-6-1856)
Burton, Isaac to Bittie Gardner 9-8-1866 [b]
Burton, Joseph W. to Susan E. Justis 12-28-1850 (12-30-1850)
Bush, George B. to Sarah E. Hill 12-25-1852 (12-30-1852)
Buster, Green to Mildred Johnson 8-10-1865 [b]
Butler, George W. to Eliza C. Butler 8-5-1860
Butler, George W. to Nancy Outlaw 11-18-1865
Butler, James to Susan Lad 7-31-1856
Butler, Thomas to Winny Carney 4-5-1856
Butterworth, K. A. to Mary J. Brockman 10-31-1850 (10-5-1850)
Byars, Alexr. to Hariett Edmington 4-3-1843 (4-6-1843)
Byrd, John C. to Elizabeth Herring 2-25-1839 (2-26-1839)
Byrd, John to Virginia Nichols 4-18-1854
Cachett, J. M. to Sarah M. Bayliss 2-17-1846 (2-19-1846)
Cage, Thomas to Nancy Pickering 4-1-1844 (4-2-1844)
Cahal, Joseph to Hannah Marrymire 5-6-1848 (5-8-1848)
Cain, A. W. to P. N. Price 12-8-1854
Cain, John B. to Arinda Hale 1-23-1850
Cain, John B. to Arinda Hall (no date; SB 1-20-1851?)
Cain, Robert J. to Catharine Adams 11-16-1838
Cain, Robt. T. to Hester Ann Harrison 9-16-1849
Calder, Wm. A. to Margaret J. Langston 11-7-1839
Caldwell, James T. to Elizabeth F. Laughran 11-8-1850
Caldwell, S. A. to M. A. Neblett 4-27-1858 (4-28-1858)
Calesham, John H. to Sarah Elizabeth Baker 2-28-1854
Calesham, Joseph A. to Sarah A. Riggins 1-12-1854
Calhound, John C. to Mariah M Prince 11-16-1859
Calisham, William D. to Sarah J. Powers 6-16-1856 (6-17-1856)
Calvert, Bluford to Catharine Kirtley 11-20-1846
Calvin, Edward to Eliza Ann Simons 1-3-1848 (7-3-1848)
Campbell, G. W. to Rebecca Cooksey 5-3-1840
Campbell, John W. to Margarette —— 10-18-1838
Campbell, L. L. to J. B. Wade 4-2-1866
Campbell, Wm. G. M. to Manerva Ann Norfleet 4-20-1843 (4-26-1843)
Campbell?, W. B. to Lucinda Simmons 6-27-1847
Cannell?, John to Catharine Dalton 12-12-1857 (12-13-1857)
Canseter, Samuel H. to Susan E. Dunning 9-21-1856 (9-26-1856)
Capps, L. C. to Arabella A. Smith 10-4-1858
Carless, Henry C. to Nannie R. Cocke 3-1-1862
Carlin, Wm. D. to Martha Harper 10-14-1847
Carlisle, C. C. to Mrs. Nannie Wood 8-4-1866 (8-7-1866)
Carlyle, Saml. to Susan Littlepage 9-6-1843
Carmack, G. W. to Amanda Fortson 8-11-1849
Carmack?, Joseph to Pennina Allen 8-6-1854
Carnal, William to Martha Jane Chester 1-22-1858 (1-24-1858)
Carneal, Charles to Rincy Massey 4-30-1866 (5-3-1866) [b]
Carneal, Frederick to Mary Tolliver 4-3-1866 [b]
Carneal, John to Mary Jane Tally 2-27-1854
Carneal, Josiah to Lucy Jane McQuery 8-13-1853 (8-16-1853)

Carneel?, John D. to Elizabeth Dorety 5-6-1854 (5-7-1854)
Carnell, William F. to Terrell Tally 10-5-1857
Carney, C. N. to Margaret C. Lynn 5-6-1848 (5-7-1848)
Carney, Daniel to Bridgett King 1-24-1859 (1-25-1859)
Carney, David to Josephine Sims 8-6-1866 (8-7-1866) [b]
Carney, Harrold P. to Elizabeth Ellebrue 4-9-1838
Carney, Lewis to Martha Poindexter 10-6-1866 [b]
Carney, Marion G. to Mary Tate 1-5-1846 (1-16-1846)
Carney, R. H. to M. E. Carney 3-9-1861 (no return)
Carpenter, James S. to Janie Goggins 9-25-1840 (9-27-1840)
Carpenter, James S. to Lucy Furguson 4-14-1838
Carr, John S. to Nancy B. Whitledge 5-9-1844
Carr, Robert C. to Mary E. Pritchett 2-15-1855
Carrier, William to Mary Clark 12-20-1858 (12-24-1858)
Carroll, Ellington A. to Sally Collins 2-21-1853 (2-24-1853)
Carroll, Isaac to Lucinda Kerr 5-21-1839
Carroll, John L. to Margaret F. Pollard 7-31-1852 (8-1-1852)
Carroll, John to Caroline Counsell 12-9-1840
Carson, Daniel A. to Elizabeth J. Shelton 12-30-1846
Carter, Alexander L. to Levita A. Baird 5-27-1861 (5-30-1861)
Carter, Henry F. to Mary J. Hester 5-3-1842 (5-5-1842)
Carter, James Y. to Mattie J. Balthrop 6-15-1858 (6-17-1858)
Carter, Jessee to Emiline —— 5-11-1843
Carter, Jno. M. to Frances J. Killebrew 11-2-1841
Carter, Junius to Lucy Palmo 5-15-1865 [b]
Carter, Wm. C. to Frances J. Graham 10-12-1848
Cartland, Dennis to Hellen McCarty 7-21-1860
Cartwright, Jehu N. to Lutitia F. M. Allender 10-14-1856 (10-16-1856)
Carver, James to Jane Thomas 12-3-1838
Cassel?, W. R. to Catharine Greenwood 11-15-1854
Castello, Patrick to Mary Cary 2-5-1859 (2-13-1859)
Castner, Dr. W. J. to Mrs. L. A. Parrish 12-26-1865
Castner, W. J. to Mary Ann Beaumont 6-9-1842
Cathey, Wilie to Nancy L. Hancock 10-12-1859 (10-13-1859)
Catlutt, John A. to Alatha A. Simery 3-28-1839
Catron, George W. to Elizabeth G. Bell 5-6-1839 (5-7-1839)
Caudle, James K. to Cora G. Collins 10-9-1858 (10-13-1858)
Caudle, John to Fredonia Oharram 12-28-1859 (12-29-1859)
Cavanah, Charles W. to Elizabeth Lacy 11-16-1847
Cavellur?, P. T. to Eliza Beach 2-8-1840
Cavitt, N. Y. to S. A. Bailey 9-18-1854 (9-19-1854)
Cayce, Thomas to Sarah Thomas 5-12-1851 (5-15-1851)_
Cayce, William to Mary S. Killebrew 4-11-1839
Cellighan, Philip to Mary Ann Carroll 8-29-1848
Center, H. H. to Mary Campbell 9-19-1860
Cevils?, John to Fredonia Heathcock 6-17-1854 (6-18-1854)
Chambless, M. M. to Lucy H. Teasley 12-19-1843 (12-21-1843)
Chance, Robert C. to Julian Birdwell 1-13-1846 (1-14-1846)
Chandler, Thomas W. to Mary M. Smith 1-1-1856
Chandler, Wm. C. to Susan Lemons 5-6-1865 (5-7-1865)
Channel, Wm. to Allena Smith 1-6-1851 (1-9-1851)
Channen, Thomas F. to Harriet F. McNeil 4-22-1854 (4-25-1854)
Chapman, William to Amanda Griffin 3-25-1859 (3-26-1859)
Chappel, Asahel to Martha Woodruff 7-28-1849
Charles, Albert to Sarah Elizabeth Walker 5-5-1865
Charlton, James W. to Mary Elizabeth Harvey 2-23-1847 (2-25-1847)
Charnell, Elisha J. to Manerva Powell 1-22-1849 (1-23-1849)
Chaudron?, Andrew to Mary Ann Shepherd 1-2-1839 (1-3-1839)
Cheatham, W. C. to Elizabeth Rutherford 2-26-1858
Cherry, A. L. to Frances E. Darnell 1-3-1867 (1-11-1867)
Cherry, C. B. to M. C. Thomas 11-13-1860
Cherry, Geo. B. to Viola Grimes 12-22-1866 (12-23-1866)
Cherry, George to Susan Mildred Helling 2-11-1848
Cherry, Lemuel to Julia Ann Harris 12-22-1855
Cherry, Silas M. to Elizabeth J. Tally 12-17-1846
Cheshire, John L. to Martha Ann Sanderfer 7-8-1853
Chester, Dan to Charlotte Chester 5-2-1866 [b]
Chester, George Washington to Susan Jane White 2-4-1858 (2-6-1858)
Chester, John to Sarah Tubbs 12-22-1858 (12-23-1858)
Chester, Levi to Lennia Davie 7-23-1842 (7-26-1842)
Chiles, A. C. to Luella Parish 1-17-1864
Chiles, Garland to Frances Head 4-16-1847
Chilton, Joseph to Dorothy A. Dennison 2-22-1850
Chilton, L. F. to Sarah W. Killebrew 10-15-1851
Chilton, Wm. L. to Annie Dortch 4-27-1847

Chisenhall, George M. to Ellin Frances Toler 2-12-1861
Chisenhall, John Reuben to Lucintha Riggins 10-20-1858 (10-21-1858)
Chisenhall, Leigh to Sarah Jane Hambleton 3-11-1852
Chisenhall, William to Martha Shepherd 3-15-1856 (3-16-1856)
Choate, Edward to Mary Elizabeth Collins 10-29-1856
Christian, B. F. to Caroline Carr 11-17-1839 (11-21-1839)
Christian, John S. to Mary C. Roberson 10-17-1851
Chumbles, Wilson to Sarah Brown 1-20-1855
Cigar?, Jacob Wesley to Carrenia Travis 7-3-1855 (7-4-1855)
Cipe, Salem P. to Rebecca L. Gant 5-12-1852
Clackston, James L. to Bridget Muller 1-23-1861 (1-24-1861)
Clanton, George W. to Sarah A. Mickle 10-24-1854
Clardy, Henry to Sophy Moore 5-21-1866 [b]
Clardy, Jas. to Sarah Ann Clardy 5-21-1866 (1-16-1867) [b]
Clardy, Joseph B. to Emily Shamwell 10-7-1841
Clardy, W. D. to M. L. Oldham 2-1-1847
Clark, Ambrose to Georgian Liggon 12-27-1865 (12-29-1865)
Clark, Beverly to Quintella Atkinson 8-29-1846
Clark, Charles G. to Virginia T. Clark 1-14-1858 (1-16-1858)
Clark, E. M. to Catharine Covington 4-20-1843 (4-25-1843)
Clark, Gholston to Eastes Smith 12-25-1866 (12-26-1866) [b]
Clark, James to Mrs. Nancy E. Grimes 12-2-1861
Clark, Jno. D. to L. J. Davidson 9-15-1849 (9-16-1849)
Clark, John to Elizabeth Wray 4-13-1848
Clark, Joseph J. to Mary E. Sutor 3-9-1850 (3-10-1850)
Clark, M. H. to Elizabeth W. Kerr 7-29-1861
Clark, Robert to Frances Pass 9-29-1863
Clark, Samuel to Sarah H. Coleman 9-9-1851
Clark, Thomas H. to Martha Ann Hale 1-12-1853
Clark, Thomas R. to Elizabeth Burnes 8-18-1848 (8-21-1848)
Clark, Thomas to Elizabeth Pierce 11-30-1857 (12-1-1857)
Clark, Uriah B. to Elizabeth H. Jones 8-22-1861
Clark, W. F. to Caroline M. Prince 10-22-1862 (10-23-1862)
Clark, Wm. F. to Mrs. Elizabeth W. Todd 6-6-1866 (6-7-1866)
Claxton, D. C. to Eliza Taylor 8-1-1849
Claxton, J. H. to Mary M. P. Mosure 6-15-1864 (6-27-1864)
Clayton, A. M. to Barbary Ann Barker 1-10-1839
Clifer?, Abner to Jane Self 3-27-1856
Clifford, John to Mary Dorne? 4-19-1858
Clifton, Asbure to Jane McFarlin 8-23-1843 (8-25-1843)
Clifton, B. M. to Mary Ann Wells 7-28-1853 (7-25?-1853)
Clifton, Henry to Huldy Hott 5-4-1840 (5-7-1840)
Clifton, Joseph J. F. to Martha W. Chamless 1-20-1841 (1-21-1841)
Clifton, Samual A. to Mary C. Adkins 5-10-1856
Clifton, William to Dilly Everette 9-2-1854
Clifton, Wm. to Elizabeth Pardue 9-10-1849 (9-11-1849)
Clymer, William to Darcus Bristow 3-21-1846 (3-26-1846)
Clynard, Robert H. to Rebecca Nelson 7-14-1855 (7-16-1855)
Cobb, Joshua to Maina D. Dortch 1-18-1843
Cobles, E. H. to Abigil Matilda Gray 9-3-1848
Cochran, James R. to Rebecca Harney 10-18-1853 (10-20-1853)
Cocke, C. C. to J. A. Yarbrough 12-11-1855
Cocke, John to Margaret J. Fouste 9-1-1853
Cocke, Plesant E. to Mary Starkey 12-6-1860
Cocke, Stephen to Elizabeth Ransdale 11-30-1853 (12-7-1853)
Cocke, Stephen to Rebecca A. Thompson 6-13-1839
Cocke, Thomas to Maranda Miller 10-23-1857
Cocke, Thos. J. to Ann E. George 11-17-1845 (11-18-1845)
Cockran, James to Louisiana Parker 7-25-1844
Cockrul, John W. to Catharine C. Settle 11-30-1842
Coe, James to Sarah C. Blake 10-29-1855
Cofer, Thomas J.? to Sarah S. Witty 7-26-1858 (7-29-1858)
Coffey, R. T. to Elizabeth Gilcres? 12-24-1840
Coffman, T. J. to Sarah C. Geeler? 6-3-1856
Cole, Henry A. to Elizabeth C. Garland 11-11-1846
Cole, John to Amanda F. Williams 10-30-1865
Coleman, Alexander to Lucy Yancy 7-5-1866 [b]
Coleman, Ambrose to Sophie J. Nolen 11-30-1866 (12-16-1866)
Coleman, B. F. to Mrs. Matilda H. Parrish 6-13-1865 (6-15-1865)
Coleman, Daniel to Sarah Higgins 1-23-1853
Coleman, Elliott to Prissilla Brantley 6-29-1839 (7-1-1839)
Coleman, George H. to Mary A. Wilie 2-23-1859 (2-24-1859)
Coleman, James Braxton to Piety Rebecca Jones 11-27-1860
Coleman, Jo. C. to Amanda Dickinson 5-7-1866 (5-8-1866) [b]
Coleman, R. J. to Mary Henderson 10-28-1860

Coleman, Richard H. to Susan Ann Wetherford 10-12-1852 (10-19-1852)
Coleman, Tom to Edie Edington 12-26-1866 (12-29?-1866) [b]
Coleman, Wm. D. to Mary E. Seay 10-21-1850
Colesham, John H. to Lucy Ann Powell 1-4-1855
Colley, Wm. H. to Sarah E. Howard 6-9-1849
Collier, Charles J. to Nancy Stewart 9-13-1839
Collier, Hugh to Martha Jane Turner 1-4-1854
Collier, J. to Elizabeth Brewers 1-20-1851
Collier, Joshua to Maria E. Morris 7-1-1856 (7-4-1856)
Collier, Thomas to Mary Alley 1-25-1866
Collins, Demsey to Susan Trigg 7-31-1866 [b]
Collins, James to Eliza Hill 12-23-1844
Collins, John to Amanda Collins 11-7-1859
Collins, Josephus to Jane Jones 7-11-1864
Collins, L. S. to Marth L. A. Workman 1-16-1865
Collins, Lorn to Harriet Bull 2-28-1855
Collins, Thomas to Sarah F. Parchment 4-8-1855
Combs, John N. to Columbia Ann Atcherson 1-11-1861
Combs, William to Margaret Gray 10-20-1858 (10-23-1858)
Comer, John E. to Mary E. Collins 2-8-1843 (2-10-1843)
Commins, Saml. to Jane C. Bullard 5-22-1848 (5-24-1848)
Comparee?, John to Rebecca Anderson 10-20-1840 (10-21-1840)
Connally, Rizen to Ivy J. Manning 2-4-1844 (Blve SB 1842)
Connel, Benjn. to Ann Baxter Young 8-15-1866 (12-1-1866) [b]
Connors, John to Sidney Ford 1-27-1859 (1-28-1859)
Connors, Peter to Bridget Hennessy 9-1-1855
Conrad, Jackson Munroe to Julia Ann Malone 12-25-1854 (12-27-1854)
Conroy, John to Hannah P. Murray 9-6-1864
Cook, Cyrus to Mary Curtis 1-30-1866 [b]
Cook, David? to Elvira Dicks 1-14-1867 [b]
Cook, John to Mary Bradly 6-9-1857
Cook, Sam to Siller Levell 2-24-1866 [b]
Cook, T. L. to F. E. Long 2-21-1859 (2-22-1859)
Cook, Willis to Sarah D. Oldham 5-21-1858
Cooksey, John to Charlotte Grant 5-2-1838 (5-3-1838)
Cooksey, William H. to Melvile Jett 7-5-1854 (7-6-1854)
Coon, G. W. to Mrs. C. Blanton 12-20-1863
Coon, James to Martha J. Gupton 1-11-1856 (2-11-1856)
Cooper, David to Rebecca Fowler 11-19-1843
Cooper, George W. to Martha McCrae 4-4-1859 (4-5-1859)
Cooper, Levi to Pricilla H. Stearn 2-22-1851 (2-23-1851)
Cooper, William to Caroline Smith 9-4-1850
Cooper?, A. H. to Elizabeth Frazier 6-1-1849 (6-3-1849)
Cope, John A. to Sarah Ann Williams 9-11-1849
Cope, Thomas to Sally Ann Waggoner 9-10-1845
Corban, Burrell to Sally Ann Andrews 8-21-1851
Corbin, Billy to Jemima Jackson 9-20-1866 (10-6-1866) [b]
Cordal, Henry to Peggy Broady 12-12-1866 (12-16-1866) [b]
Cordle, Bob to Enerline(Emily?) Cordle 1-6-1866 (10-20-1866) [b]
Cordle, Payton to Julia Overton 5-14-1866 (5-20-1866) [b]
Corkieff, Madison W. to Martha Ann Walthall 1-31-1854
Corlew, Thomas W. to Susan P. More 10-3-1844
Corlew, William to Eliza Pritchard 2-14-1842 (2-16-1842)
Corneal, Allen to Nancy(Mary?) Price 6-25-1857
Cornell, Hamilton to Bettie Hester 3-29-1866 (4-3-1866)
Cornell, Jeff to Sumira Chesten 7-7-1866 [b]
Cornell, John to Jane McComes 12-8-1866 (1-3-1867) [b]
Costello, Edward to Bridget Branigan 4-21-1859
Cotton, James A. J. to Mary Jane Doss 9-3-1851 (9-4-1851)
Cotton, Thos. L. to Louisa A. M. Buckner 5-4-1854
Couget?, Frank to Rebecca H. Felden 4-20-1865
Coulter, Benjamin F. to Mary Isabella Moore 5-7-1856
Council, James W. to Mary Elizabeth Brown 10-26-1858 (10-27-1858)
Council, Joseph W. to Eliza Redd 11-12-1838 (11-16-1838)
Counsell, David to Prissilla Hunter 2-15-1841 (2-18-1841)
Covington, Albert M. to Martha M. Johnson 1-4-1855
Covington, T. H. to Kate L. Hancock 5-30-1864
Covington, Thelbert to Eliza Marian Grant 1-26-1860
Cowans, Andrew to Ann McLane 3-27-1850
Coward, Albert to Harrett Hellem 12-27-1866 (12-31-1866) [b]
Coward, B. W. to Nannie S. Dunlap 4-18-1864 (4-20-1864)
Cox, Henry Clay to Mary E. T. Abbott 12-24-1857
Cox, John to Maria Butler 1-13-1860 (1-15-1860)

Coyle, John to Clarissa Chasteen 10-12-1850 (10-17-1850)
Coyle, Wm. R. to Martha E. Scudder 3-27-1848 (3-30-1848)
Crabtree, James M. to Laurana J. Trice 8-5-1847
Craft, James R. to Angelina Bashar 11-20-1855
Crafton, Joseph to Sarah Moor 7-12-1852
Crame?, Martin to Mrs. Mary Murphey 6-13-1864 (6-18-1864)
Cravens, Gersham to Zerilda Darnell 10-14-1845
Cravens, James R. to Mary E. Lyle 12-5-1865
Cravens, Richard to Rebecca Darnell 1-8-1846
Creamer, Jeremiah to Catharine Simons 5-9-1846
Crews, Pleasant to Mary Tinsley 11-21-1848 (11-23-1848)
Crews, Robert to Elizabeth Broddis 5-18-1846
Criner, Henry to Mary Dabney 8-18-1866 [b]
Crocket, Jas. M. to Ellen Brock 10-7-1848
Crocket, Liftnot? to Huldy Davidson 8-2-1849 (8-5-1849)
Crockett, Leftridge to Eliza Jones 9-15-1844
Crockett, Robert M. to Ann Tinsley 10-2-1854 (10-4-1854)
Cromwell, A. H. to Catharine F. Rocke 2-8-1842 (2-9-1842)
Cromwell, C. J. to Susannah King 10-11-1843
Crosier, James to Mary C. Johnson 11-3-1849 (11-4-1849)
Cross, Clay to Milly Moore 11-16-1865
Cross, George T. to Cordelia Carney 3-1-1855
Cross, James B. to Louisana Parker 2-5-1856 (4-5-1856)
Cross, John B. to Louisanna Claxton 12-7-1866
Cross?, William to Lucy Ann Morris 9-1-1853
Crotzer, Aaron to Margaret Powers 10-21-1843 (10-22-1843)
Crotzer, Jas. to Rachel Smith 1-11-1849 (1-18-1849)
Crotzer, Jessee L. to Mahala Brown 7-28-1842
Crotzer, Joshua to Nancy J. Myres 2-6-1851
Crotzer, Leander W. to Martha C. Brown 11-13-1856
Crotzer, Phillip to Mrs. Annet Nevell 5-27-1864
Crotzer, Solomon to Eliza McNeil 2-13-1855
Crotzer, Wiley F. to Mary Brown 10-29-1844
Crouch, David F. to Harriet Angeline Ferrell 9-14-1859 (9-15-1859)
Crouch, William H. to Margaret J. Rudolph 8-18-1846
Crow, Joshua to Sarah Ann Rinehart 9-8-1859
Crowder, B. J. to Rebecca M. Elliott 10-8-1845 (10-9-1845)
Crowder, Joseph H. to Frances Peacher 7-2-1866 (7-3-1866)
Crowder, William H. to Ann Rebecca Peaches 1-17-1854
Crozer, Moses to Aliney E. Poore 4-27-1843 (5-4-1843)
Crunk, John M. to Sarah J. Armstrong 11-28-1853
Cummins, James F. to Elizabeth H. Thomas 11-15-1855
Cunningham, James W. to E. M. Yates 9-3-1843
Current, Hugh A. to Elizabeth G. Halliburton 3-31-1859
Curtis, Wm. to Jane Harden 12-22-1866 (12-23-1866)
Curts, John F. to Adaline W. Poston 11-17-1842
Cushman, Abial to Elizabeth Ann Bryant 12-11-1848 (12-12-1848)
Cuthbertson, Jos. to Claussa Scudder 1-6-1842
Dabney, E. R. to Ellen V. Manson 12-18-1856
Dabney, Louis to George Frances Dabney 1-20-1853
Dailey, James G. to Elizabeth H. Taylor 9-17-1853 (9-18-1853)
Dailey, Josiah P. to Catharine A. L. Myatt 3-13-1843 (3-15-1843)
Dailey, Thomas F. to Susan Chester 11-24-1852
Dale, Jas. M. to Emma M. Jenkins 9-4-1866
Dancy, Charles M. to Amanda W. Moore 7-11-1855
Dancy, John A. to Elizabeth Johnson 2-16-1857 (2-17-1857)
Daniel, John L. to Elizabeth Mathis 12-6-1847 (12-9-1847)
Daniel, John to Sarah Jane Tap 8-22-1859
Daniel, Richard to Martha Allan 1-22-1841 (2-4-1841)
Daniel, W. B. to Jenny Bradly 7-6-1855
Darden, J. T. to M. Weatherford 4-10-1862
Dargan, Thos. to Catharine Murphy 9-10-1860
Darnal, John J. to Malinda J. Abney 4-13-1852
Darnel, Geo. W. to Martha Barbee 7-23-1850 (7-24-1850)
Darnell, Alford to Louisa Tolar 2-28-1843 (3-2-1843)
Darnell, James to Fanny? Bayless 7-24-1841 (7-31-1841)
Darnell, Jessee to Lynda Hardy 11-3-1856 (11-6-1856)
Darnell, John to Mar. Elizabeth Prewitt 8-23-1866 (8-24-1866)
Darnell, Wm. to Elizabeth Smith 4-1-1844
Dashner, Joseph to Tennie A. Hasley 1-6-1866
Daugherty, James to Tabitha A. Vance 10-17-1865 (10-21-1865)
Dauson, Jno. T. to Mary A. Luke 11-8-1843
Davidson, Benjamin F. to Mary J. Lemons 10-28-1858 (10-29-1858)
Davidson, Benjamine to Huldy Clark 6-28-1842 (6-30-1842)
Davidson, J. W. to S. E. Lacy 11-16-1863

Davidson, James to Tamilin Scale 12-24-1845
Davidson, Jno. S. to Sarah W. Comer 2-27-1844
Davidson, William to Luana Potter 2-18-1841
Davie, A. F. to Saphrona A. Davie 5-13-1850
Davie, Buck to Sarah Davie 1-6-1866 (10-20-1866) [b]
Davie, Jackson to Harriett Barber 9-15-1866 (10-20-1866) [b]
Davis, A. J. to Mary Mulcaster 3-13-1848 (3-19-1848)
Davis, Andrew to Mary Ann Cassey 5-14-1852
Davis, Benjamin to Amanda F. Carter 4-24-1844
Davis, David to Martha Baggett 2-21-1849 (2-22-1849)
Davis, Dominerkous L. to Sarah Shuff 6-4-1858 (6-6-1858)
Davis, Edward J. to Mary A. W. Witt 4-4-1866
Davis, Elijah to Mary Ann Jackson 9-12-1842
Davis, Gabriel J. to Sarah F. Reeves 2-13-1860 (2-14-1860)
Davis, George W. to Catharine Maham 8-24-1854
Davis, George to Mary Frances Bradshaw 4-9-1852 (4-11-1852)
Davis, H. J. to Ann Herring 11-1-1838
Davis, Hiram to Elizabeth Wyatt 2-12-1850
Davis, James M. to Jane Holt 11-15-1847 (11-18-1847)
Davis, Jas. C. to Nannie Bradley 4-18-1865
Davis, Jos. H. to Julia Ann Shuff 12-28-1863
Davis, Kendal Burgess to Mildred Jane Carnell 9-8-1856
Davis, Nelson to Rebecca Frances Harvey 7-15-1856 (7-17-1856)
Davis, Oliver to C. Marsh 8-23-1862 (9-4-1862)
Davis, Orlander E. to Gracy L. Lander 1-31-1852
Davis, Robert to Cordelia A. Rose 4-15-1865 (4-16-1865)
Davis, Thomas A. to Judith B. Brunson 2-24-1848
Davis, Thomas E. to Amanda M. Reasons 4-15-1847 (5-6-1847)
Davis, Thomas W. to Margarett Ann McBride 5-14-1856
Davis, Thomas to Amanda J. Donalson 7-3-1852 (7-4-1852)
Davis, Thomas to Lucretia Vaughn 12-22-1840 (12-26-1840)
Davis, Tom to Betsey Parmer 8-2-1866 [b]
Davis, William to Anna Averett 7-11-1842
Davis, William to Hulda Black 8-13-1851 (8-14-1851)
Davis, Wm. H. to Mary E. McMordie 1-23-1849
Davis, Wm. W. to Harriett Clifton 7-20-1840 (7-22-1840)
Davis?, Jarvis? B. to Nancy Jane Oneel 4-13-1859 (4-15-1859)
Davison, Absalom to Margaret Stephens 3-23-1847 (3-25-1847)
Davison, Absalom to Martha Ann Whitworth 10-13-1840 (10-18-1840)
Davison, Joseph to Susan Powers 1-20-1860 (2-1-1860)
Davison, Wilie to Sarah Ann Rye 5-30-1846
Dawson, Ambrose to Silla Kendrick 3-5-1866 (3-8-1866) [b]
Dawson, Rewben N. to Catharine H. Dycus 12-21-1844 (12-22-1844)
Day, Chas. M. to Mary C. Bell 12-4-1851
Dayly, William to Eliza Newel 4-24-1857 (4-25-1857)
Deadman, Jas. B. to E. S. Terrell 2-8-1844
Dean, E. H. to Nancy Jane Bailey 7-4-1854
Dearing, Jas. N. to Julia Ann Eison? 8-22-1860 (8-23-1860)
Delany, Samuel D. to Sally V. McCutchin 12-15-1838 (12-19-1838)
Delp, Henry to Mahaly Elizabeth Davis 12-29-1860 (12-31-1860)
Dennis, Marmaduke O. to Mary E. Bailey 9-22-1840 (9-23-1840)
Denny, G. W. to Marthy Ann Smith 1-5-1867 (1-8-1867)
Derrick?, Zebedee F. to Ellen Pettus 7-20-1859
Derrit, Robert to Kizie Slaughter 1-1-1867 (1-5-1867) [b]
Deshong, Isaac R. to Elizabeth Wells 3-9-1865
Diamond, James L. to Augusta R. Foster 3-11-1856 (3-13-1856)
Dick, John to Easter Harris 12-16-1866 [b]
Dickerson, Henry to Robert A. V. Bryan 12-8-1840
Dickinson, David S. to Mary Ann Rollow 12-19-1851
Dickinson, S. H. to Sallie Watts 5-14-1866
Dickson, Adam to Matilda Nolen 11-13-1844 (11-14-1844)
Dickson, Thomas Y. to Cara T. C. Marable 1-9-1854
Diffenderffer, Lewis A. to Christina G. Dicks 1-17-1854
Dillard, Wm. L. to Virginia C. Neblett 1-22-1848 (1-27-1848)
Dilling, F. M. to Virginia Thomas 2-9-1866
Dilling, James B. to Harriett Rogers 6-11-1841 (6-13-1841)
Dilling, John J. to Mary Ann Almon 8-1-1857 (8-6-1857)
Dilling, John to Catharine Crimmins 6-17-1845 (6-18-1845)
Dilling, P. K. to Sarah P. Bullard 7-25-1848
Dillins, Wm. H. to Elizabeth Cummings 11-10-1846 (11-11-1846)
Dilworth, Isaiah B. to Mira A. S. Woodward 8-20-1855
Dingman, D. J. to Nannie Myers 5-3-1866
Dinneen, John to Catharine Harney 7-29-1865 (7-30-1865)
Dinnen?, Anthony to Elizabeth E. W. Patterson 3-27-1838
Dinning, Anthony to Elizabeth Patterson 9-20-1848 (10-1-1848)

Dinnun, Cornelius to Margaret Hayes 3-12-1860
Dismukes, William S. to Louisa F. Clayton 2-20-1860 (2-23-1860)
Dist, Jackson to Manerva Trice 12-26-1866 (1-5-1867) [b]
Dittner, Jacob to Catharine McCool 9-20-1838
Diver, Anthony to Ellen Agen 5-15-1861
Dixon, Thomas Y. to Mary E. Ramey 11-17-1857 (11-18-1857)
Doak, Henry M. to Maggie Lockhert 8-28-1866
Dockry, Watson to Martha Burton? 1-31-1850 (2-5-1850)
Dodd, John to Mary Jane Clardy 2-2-1847 (2-4-1847)
Dodson, J. A. to Mary A. E. Laird 9-20-1849
Dolan, John D. to Elizabeth Reynolds 6-8-1852
Donaho, A. B. to Mary L. Brown 10-4-1855
Donaldson, Jas. C. to Bettie V. Homen 10-25-1865 (10-26-1865)
Donaldson, W. A. to Annie Parker 11-22-1865
Donley, John to Theresa Sampson 10-23-1862 (10-24-1862)
Dorch, Robt. to Catharine Waters 12-23-1865 (12-25-1865)
Dorety, Thos. to Mary E. Stone 7-21-1851
Dority, John to Fredonia Easley 9-21-1865
Dorrington, Allen to Frances E. Latham 3-17-1848
Dorris, David M. to Charlotte Reynolds 9-28-1865
Dortch, James N. to Lucy Ann Garland 12-16-1841
Dortch, John to Cathrine Williams 12-25-1866 (12-26-1866) [b]
Dortch, Wm. T. to Ellen P. Galbreth 12-11-1860
Dougherty, Geo. to Lucretia Bowers 1-29-1866 (1-31-1866)
Dougherty, John to Emily Tolar 2-28-1843 (3-2-1843)
Dougherty, Saml. to Julia Ann Carter 10-13-1843
Doughson, Malden to Martha Ann Warden 9-22-1845 (9-24-1845)
Doughton, Charles T. to Sarah W. Hodges 12-29-1846
Doughton, William to Sarah E. Thornton 12-26-1843
Dougton, Franklin to Julia Lyle 7-29-1844
Doward, Benjamin W. to Bettie H. Lacy 6-17-1861 (6-20-1861)
Dowdy, James G. to Martha Powers 4-10-1848 (4-12-1848)
Dowdy, W. T. to Arlean Allbright 9-22-1856
Dowdy?, John C. to Lucinda Martin 7-28-1849 (8-2-1849)
Downs, Peter to Frances E. Glay? 4-26-1855
Drake, Francis M. to Martha L. Scott 7-20-1857 (7-21-1857)
Drake, James W. to Virginia Bagwell 7-27-1859 (8-30-1859)
Drane, Dock to Kate Kennedy 5-18-1866 (5-28-1866) [b]
Drane, Phillip E. to Harriett Williams 4-17-1839
Drewry, A. to Nancy B. Morris 9-2-1845
Driscoll, Denis T. to Isabella Platt 8-12-1861 (8-13-1861)
Driskell, G. W. to M. H. Driskell 8-26-1849
Drummond, M. to Keziah Smittoe 7-24-1866
Drummonds, James M. to Susannah McCauley 9-8-1841 (9-9-1841)
Dudley, Henry M. to Susan Neblett 9-13-1843
Dudly, N. R. to M. A. Ross 12-12-1849 (12-13-1849)]
Duerson, A. L. to Mary L. Leach 1-29-1852
Duff, John E. to Northana Hansborough 1-22-1859 (1-28-1859)
Duguid, Jacob to Joyce P. Warfield 1-18-1858 (1-19-1858)
Duke, Welkins E. to Louisa Yarrell 11-15-1853
Duke, William H. to Mary D. Mockbee 11-30-1858
Duncan, Daniel H. to Mrs. Margaret J. Caulder 6-10-1852
Duncan, Elijah to Eliza Jane Lewis 12-10-1853 (12-12-1853)
Duncan, Elisha to Mary Keats 1-12-1858
Duncan, Hezekiah to Lucy Ann Hatsell 10-9-1858 (10-12-1858)
Duncan, John to Mary E. Johnson 11-21-1861 (11-27-1861)
Dunlap, Jas. M. to Pemelia R. Hester 2-1-1867 (2-6-1867)
Dunlavey, Jno. to Sarah Cocke 6-5-1844 (6-6-1844)
Dunlavy, John to Hannah Cahill 4-16-1855 (4-17-1855)
Dunlop, Alfred to Addie Staton 12-22-1866 [b]
Dunlop, Hugh to Mattie Williams 5-15-1865 (5-17-1865)
Dunlop, Hugh to Rebecca P. Talley 2-17-1852 (2-18-1852)
Dunn, C. H. to Arabella A. Jenkins 12-7-1859 (12-8-1859)
Dunn, James C. to Jane McGowan 5-30-1860 (6-4-1860)
Dupree, Eli G. to Sarah Ford 8-26-1844
Dupree, James W. to Frances Haflin 10-15-1840
Durham, James to Margaret Durham 10-10-1860
Durrell, Isaac to Sarah Coon 8-24-1847
Durrett, J. M. to Frances C. Fortson 1-21-1839 (1-24-1839)
Durrett, Jas. W. to Elizabeth Lambuth 10-23-1849
Dwyer, William L. to Mary Barton 11-26-1856 (11-27-1856)
Dycas, E. C. to Atalantus G. Duncan 4-30-1849 (5-1-1849)
Dyce?, Joseph M. to Sally Ann Williams 1-27-1854
Dycus, G. B. to Susannah Tine 9-22-1841
Dycus, John T. to Lora J. Trice 3-3-1866 (3-6-1866)

Dye, Benson W. to Rebecca A. Smith 2-24-1852 (2-26-1852)
Dye, Jack to Laura McNeal 9-15-1866 [b]
Dye, Joseph M. to Elizabeth A. Bobo 5-11-1840 (5-12-1840)
Dye, W. T. to Sue N. Allen 4-23-1861
Dyer, George H. to Mary Luella Ferrell 10-19-1858 (10-21-1858)
Dyer, George J. to Shelton Payne 2-21-1850
Dyer, Jas. H. to Emily L. Purkerson 1-23-1861 (1-24-1861)
Dyles, William to Mary Jane Odam 4-9-1851
Dyson, William to Catharine Petty 3-11-1847
Eades, Samuel to Elizabeth Rainwaters 12-30-1847
Eagily?, Henry to Liziebeth McFall 12-18-1866 [b]
Eaker, M. H. to Mary Ellison 5-28-1848
Easley, Drury to Mary Jane Wells 9-1-1846
Easley, Ira E. to Hannah C. Russel 10-31-1839
Easley?, Rhodeham to Frances Tatum 9-11-1838
Eatherly, Alford to Martha McCormick 7-29-1843 (8-17-1843)
Eatherly, Alfred to Lucinda Harris 12-12-1848
Eatherly, Johnathan to Indiana J. Read 3-19-1844
Eatherly, T. E. C. to C. M. Steward 7-28-1845
Eaton, Adam to Frances A. Joiner 9-23-1843 (10-24-1843)
Edds?, L. B. to Drusilla Lake 5-9-1853
Edes, James to Mary Milam 4-30-1840
Edes, Jessee to Martha Martin 3-31-1842 (3-30?-1842)
Edgar, Joseph R. to Jemima J. W. Yates 5-11-1846 (5-13-1846)
Edger, Josiah R. to Sarah E. Gooch 5-31-1865 (6-6-1865)
Edlin, James to Sarah Francisco 12-29-1842
Edmondson, Benjamine to Minerva E. Orgain 5-13-1851
Edmondson, Ephraim to Ann Rogers 12-23-1865
Edmondson, John to Beedie H. Roberts 12-1-1846 (12-2-1846)
Edmondson, Josh to Matilda Martin 9-22-1866 (9-23-1866) [b]
Edmondson, Robert to Lucy Ann Roberts 10-19-1842
Edmondson, Thomas F. to Louisiana McGee 11-29-1854
Edmondson, Thomas to Elizabeth Thacker 7-3-1859
Edmondson, Upton to Martha A. Rice 9-14-1853 (9-17-1853)
Edmondson, William H. to Mary J. Foster 1-19-1859 (1-30-1859)
Edmondson, William to C. V. Neblett 12-23-1846 (12-24-1846)
Edmonson, Robt. H. to Elizabeth Crowder 11-12-1864 (12-1-1864)
Edmonson, Robt. H. to Susan Morrow 2-7-1862 (2-9-1862)
Edward, Isaac to Rebecca Bruce 5-1-1847 (5-2-1847)
Edwards, Bazel to Mary Smith 12-24-1839 (12-15-1839)
Edwards, Charles to Della Hester 12-28-1866 [b]
Edwards, E. J. to Barbara Ann Allen 8-22-1858
Edwards, E. J. to Barbara Ann Allen 9-8-1858
Edwards, Edward to Solila Walker 3-23-1849
Edwards, George A. to Jane P. McFadden 3-6-1841 (3-7-1841)
Edwards, Lewis T. to Virginia J. Collins 9-11-1865 (9-12-1865)
Edwards, Orrin to Lucy Melvina Calhoon 1-22-1861 (1-24-1861)
Edwards, William A. to Nancy Caroline Eberly 2-3-1846
Edwards, William to Mary A. Shepherd 2-11-1843
Edwards, Wm. D. to Mariah L. McDaniel 3-9-1840 (3-10-1840)
Elam, A. V. to Sarah A. Venable 1-6-1842
Elbert, David jr. to Arminda Davis 1-25-1844
Elder, Anthony to Chanie Galbraith 1-14-1867 (1-19-1867) [b]
Elder, Bartlett to Ann Turner 9-25-1866 [b]
Elder, Henry to Elizabeth Leavell 12-11-1865
Elder, Joshua to M. M. Martin 11-27-1849
Eldridge, Aristotle to Bettie M. Eldridge 5-10-1859
Eldridge, Edwin H. to Elizabeth M. Haynes 10-26-1854 (10-27-1854)
Eldridge, Granderson to Lacy Bellemy 1-6-1866 (1-15-1866) [b]
Eldridge, Rolf to Susan E. Blake 3-14-1859 (3-15-1859)
Eldridge, W. H. to Martha Crowder 11-25-1862
Eldridge, William H. to Mary Laird 1-5-1858 (1-6-1858)
Elkins, Nolley W. to Elizabeth Menefee 11-1-1857 (11-8-1857)
Elleatt, Joseph J. to Sarah Ann Taler 11-9-1851
Elliott, Claborn to Emelia Tucker 10-6-1866 (10-18-1866) [b]
Elliott, D. A. to Susan Ann Durrett 9-11-1858 (9-16-1858)
Elliott, David jr. to Lutitia Davis 1-13-1846
Elliott, Geo. to Judy C. Pickering 7-9-1841
Elliott, George W. to Elizabeth Sneed 4-3-1865 (4-11-1865)
Elliott, J. W. to Arabella Wall 11-23-1866
Elliott, Wm. G. to Mary F. Pickering 10-5-1865 (10-6-1865)
Ellis, Lewis to Jane Proctor 12-3-1839 (12-4-1839)
Ellis, Thomas to Malissa Fips 11-24-1852 (11-25-1852)
Ellis, Thomas to Maria F. Black 5-15-1866 (5-23-1866)
Ellis, William E. to Eliza Calisham 8-23-1853

Ellis, William to Julia Doughran 1-8-1845 (1-9-1845)
Ellis, Wm. H. to Mary J. Seay 12-28-1864 (12-30-1864)
Ellitt, Wm. to Mary M. Lewis 1-17-1866
Elloitt?, David A. to Ann M. Adams 11-2-1853 (11-3-1853)
Elmire, Charles J. to Sadie J. Bird 12-15-1859
Emmery, James to Amanda J. Spurrier 3-15-1854
Emmery, James to Mary Russell 5-17-1847
Emmet, Isaiah R. to M. A. Gibbs 12-13-1840
Ennis, J. T. to Mary H. Jordan 4-1-1865
Enniss, Demsey to Sally Bright 8-25-1838 (8-26-1838)
Enniss, Saml. to Mary S. Frazier 4-27-1842 (5-5-1842)
Ensly, E. jr. to Laura E. Martin 10-10-1860
Epley, Bartley to Sallie Ann Graham 6-20-1866
Epley, Fletcher to Dosia Kyle 12-6-1866
Epperson, Ben C. to Fannie Scott 10-4-1866 (10-5-1866)
Epperson, Edward to Sarah M.' Lane 12-2-1852
Erwin, John J. to Nancy A. Mackelroy 10-22-1864 (10-23-1864)
Estes, A. F. to Mattie E. Boatwright 5-9-1859 (1-10-1859)
Estis, David C. to Mary E. Carney 12-6-1856 (12-7-1856)
Etherly, T. H. to C. M. Stewart 7-25-1845 (8-11-1845)
Evans, A. E. to Louisa Adams 6-13-1864 (6-15-1864)
Evans, Ambrose to Nancy J. Dycus 4-8-1839
Evans, Finney? L. to Sarah Ann Hutcherson 3-17-1853
Evans, George W. to Mrs. Julia V. A. E. Johnson 11-2-1866
    (11-6-1866)
Evans, Jos. J. W. to Harriet F. Hackney 12-20-1856 (12-21-1856)
Evans, L. W. to Frankie Shephard 1-1-1859 (1-2-1859)
Evans, Lewis E. to Mrs. Harriett V. Page 5-12-1865 (5-23-1865)
Evans, Samuel W. to Mariah Fritt 10-11-1853
Evans, Spelward? P. to Elizabeth M. Calesham 1-9-1860
Evans, William L. to Hardin Cherry 9-19-1855 (9-17?-1855)
Everett, Asa to Susanna White 9-15-1859
Everson, Michael to Virginia A. Williamson 11-29-1857
Ewing, Andrew H. to Harriett E. Hiter 11-14-1858 (11-15-1858)
Ewing, Finis to Delinia M. Wimberly 10-14-1858
Ezel, Absalom to Malinda Mathews 8-16-1851
Falkner, John to Eliza Ratliff 11-16-1866 [b]
Fambrough, Johnathan to Sarah E. Miles 12-20-1853
Fambrough?, Adam? H. to Rutha A. Owens 9-9-1853 (9-11-1853)
Fane, Terry(Tyree) to Martha Jane Claxton 2-14-1859 (2-16-1859)
Fane, Tery L. to Betsey A. Tinsley 2-28-1865
Fanning, A. J. to M. A. Black 10-27-1855
Faren, James M. to Susan Hollist 8-19-1863
Faris, John W. to Sarah F. Cardin 3-30-1864 (3-31-1864)
Farley, J. H. to Sarah R. Young 9-4-1856 (9-8-1856)
Farley, Jos. M. to Mary Skinner 2-19-1851? (yr omitted)
Farmer, Gerry to Elizabeth Hewett 12-7-1846 (12-8-1846)
Farmer, J. H. to J. C. A. Izer 1-8-1847 (1-9-1847)
Farmer, Jacob to Sarah Tuck 2-27-1847
Farmer, James R. to Elizabeth A. Mosier 9-18-1861
Farmer, T. Y. to Sarah Mumford 1-23-1851
Farquehar, Wm. to Jenett McCleral 1-2-1849
Farrell, Wm. A. to Elizabeth A. Moss 1-4-1865 (1-5-1865)
Faulkerson, Charles T. to Virginia G. Laird 10-6-1859
Faulkner, Charles B. to Mary Elam Jones 8-5-1856
Fauntleroy, Joseph M. to Mary R. Vance 6-17-1857 (6-18-1857)
Faxon, John W. to Florence Herring 2-22-1866
Faxon, Leonard G. to Martha Wilkinson 11-25-1854
Felts, Benjamin C. to Sarah R. Allen 12-29-1852
Fergason, A. E. to Sarah A. Young 9-13-1849
Ferguson, Robt. F. to Nancy M. Barker 8-19-1842
Ferrel, Charles to Catharine G. Wood 2-10-1855 (2-11-1855)
Ferrell, Wm. F. to Nancy A. Leigh 3-24-1860 (3-29-1860)
Ferrels, Charles J. to Arabella Zellers 1-16-1853
Ferrill, Benjamin to Nancy Ellis 8-6-1842 (8-7-1842)
Ferrill, John to Martha Ellis 8-24-1852 (8-26-1852)
Ferrill, S. F. to Virginia P. Keats 3-1-1865 (3-5-1865)
Ferriman, Jas. to Ada Miller 12-5-1865 (12-6-1865)
Fielder, William S. to Rebecca Justice 3-5-1853
Fields, Nicholas to Elizabeth Moor 7-?-1851
Figuer, M. to Lizzy Nash 2-11-1848
Finley, Wm. M. to Ann L. Dortch 4-3-1849
Finly, William M. to Virginia C. Boyd 9-20-1859
Fite, A. to Delila Crotzer 4-16-1845 (4-17-1845)
Fite, L. B. to Mrs. Martha Mann 8-13-1866 (8-15-1866)

Fitz Gerald, A. D. to Nancy G. Davidson 12-26-1866 (12-29-1866)
Flack, James H. to Mary Ann Leigh 3-3-1842
Flannigan, Hugh to Mrs. Margaret Coffee 4-9-1861 (4-13-1861)
Fletcher, A. D. to Medora Broaddie 12-3-1861
Fletcher, Andrew J. to Eliza R. Wooten 12-22-1857 (12-23-1857)
Fletcher, Drew S. to Mary Ann Walls 3-10-1846
Fletcher, Elijah to Martha A. Hill 11-9-1859
Fletcher, Henry to Patsey Harrison 9-8-1866 (9-15-1866) [b]
Fletcher, J. J. W. H. to E. C. P. Horn 12-10-1850 (12-12-1850)
Fletcher, J. R. to A. L. Wilson 6-5-1866
Fletcher, James to Henrietta Moore 3-6-1843
Fletcher, John T. to Elizabeth Dycus 1-14-1856
Fletcher, S. G. to Mary E. Seay 12-22-1863 (12-23-1863)
Fletcher, William E. to Elizabeth Ann Coleman 11-3-1847
Flinn?, John to Ellen Morrison 11-11-1854 (11-16-1854)
Flowers, Joseph E. to Angeline Davis 1-27-1848
Flowers, Thomas H. to Henrietta C. Parham 6-29-1859 (6-22?-1859)
Flyn, Alfred M. to Mary Hambleton 11-19-1840
Forbes, William A. to Mary E. Garland 12-26-1853 (12-29-1853)
Ford, Andrew Jackson to Rachael Smith 8-24-1854
Ford, Andrew Jackson to Rachel Smith 8-24-1854
Ford, F. S. to Margarett Kacy 3-25-1843 (3-29-1843)
Ford, George W. to Mary Oneal 12-10-1853 (12-11-1853)
Ford, Moses C. to Malinda Adelina Oldham 1-17-1859 (1-18-1859)
Ford, T. F. M. to Virginia E. Ogg 12-20-1858 (12-23-1858)
Ford, William R. to Sarah Childers 12-8-1848
Forgerson, Robert to Clara Shepherd 4-27-1844
Forsythe, J. to Sarah Cain 7-24-1850
Forsythe, Jerry to Caroline Carroll 9-2-1857 (9-27-1857)
Forsythe, John F. to Sallie Miller 5-16-1864
Fort, Frank to Isabella Hooper 8-17-1866 [b]
Fort, Ilas? M. to Charlotte M. Dancy 12-4-1854 (12-6-1854)
Fort, Joseph H. to Jack Ann Fort 11-3-1849
Fort, Josiah W. to Eliza P. Dancy 10-1-1853
Fort, Robert to Eliza Jane Tompkins 1-29-1855
Fort, Wiley to Harriett Fort 10-22-1866 [b]
Fort, Wm. H. to Mary G. Ligon 8-30-1847
Fortner, Andrew J. to Virginia Seay 12-27-1853 (12-28-1853)
Fortson, Henry to Elizabeth Mash 12-10-1844
Fortson, Jas. to Margaret Barker 1-24-1867 [b]
Fortson, Richd. D. to Mary Glenn 9-6-1843
Fortsone, Henry to Jane Crouse 10-31-1866 (12-24-1866) [b]
Fortune, Stephen T. to Mary J. Baguel 8-14-1857
Foster, Hugh L. to Virginia C. Thacker 11-24-1846
Foster, J. W. to Mary A. Avritt 5-25-1848
Foster, John S. E. to Sarah C. Davis 9-11-1865 (9-14-1865)
Foster, William Thomas to Jane Hampton 6-1-1857
Foster, Wm. L. to Caroline Thompson 3-10-1842
Foust, R. N. to Nancy H. Smith 11-20-1866 (11-22-1866)
Foust, Thomas to Eliza B. Hutcherson 9-21-1850 (9-26-1850)
Fouste, John T. to Sarah A. Hurt 1-4-1855 (1-5-1855)
Fowler, Jack to Nannie Morrison 2-8-1866
Fowlkes, Henry A. to E. A. Chilton 9-21-1839
Fox, Ferdinand F. to Amanda Ely 5-9-1861
Fox, Henry to Alitha Maning 8-25-1864 (8-24?-1864)
Fox, Henry to Eliza Fox 1-19-1867 [b]
Fox, Isah L. to M. E. Sisk 8-16-1851
Fox?, B. F. to Elizabeth Jackson 1-2-1843 (1-3-1843)
Frambrough, Edward to Lucy Thackston 2-12-1840 (3-5-1840)
Franklin, Benjamin to Ferrid R. Catharine 5-18-1860
Franklin, Charles W. to Arieller S. Harding 12-16-1854 (12-18-1854)
Franklin, James E. to Frances Dudley 6-4-1840
Franklin, Jas. E. to Nancy Carr 10-28-1847
Franklin, John M. to Cyntha Ann Clark 8-4-1843
Franziers?, James to Mary J. Driver? 7-17-1851 (7-27-1851)
Frasier, M. E. to C. A. Hester 7-18-1859 (7-17?-1859)
Frazer, James to Aquilla Teasley 7-16-1842 (7-21-1842)
Frazier, James to Hester Ann Teasly 12-21-1846
Frazier, Overton to Paptice Carney 12-27-1866 (12-29-1866) [b]
Frazier, R. H. to Josephine Smith 4-23-1860 (4-24-1860)
Frazier, William to Harriett Pinson 1-14-1840 (1-17-1840)
Frederick, C. to Mahala Bailey 8-5-1841
Free, William to Martha Phillips 2-11-1839 (2-14-1839)
Freil, Francis to Martha Laird 7-30-1857
Frick, Jacob to Rebecca Langston 1-5-1852 (1-6-1852)

Frick, Peter to Emily F. Langston 12-14-1847 (12-15-1847)
Fritt, Jehu P. to Maria A. Donnolly 1-31-1858
Fry, John to Martha Anderson 4-4-1842
Fulcher, Wm. W. to Unity W. Fulcher 10-30-1848 (11-2-1848)
Fulkerson, Abram to Selina Johnson 1-28-1862
Fulkerson, Thos. E. to Siscia B. Hunley 9-29-1852
Fulkerson, William to Lucy Bayliss 8-28-1860 (8-29-1860)
Fuqua, Samuel to Margaret J. Toler 2-18-1858 (2-19-1858)
Fuqua, Washington L. to Nancy Mary Hobbs 9-15-1847
Furgerson, John D. to Zilphia Ann Vuaghn 3-16-1857 (3-17-1857)
Furgerson, W. T. to Mary Meacham 5-31-1851 (6-1-1851)
Furgerson, William to Deny Barker 1-1-1866 (4-1-1866) [b]
Furguson, John C. to Martha Giles 12-21-1840
Furguson, John D. to Nancy M. Merriweather 3-1-1848 (3-2-1848)
Furguson, Luke H. to Charlott Grant 11-4-1845
Gafford, William to Frances Smith 9-1-1859
Galey, John to Mary Meacham 9-1-1850
Gambel, John W. to Nancy C. Henderson 4-11-1858
Gamble, J. R. to Nancy L. Russell 1-10-1861
Gamble, Nathan to Susan R. Terrell 10-24-1857 (10-25-1857)
Gamell, Henry N. to Virginia F. Hunter 5-3-1852
Ganes, Jerry to Jennie Weatherford 7-28-1866 [b]
Gardiner, William Louis to Mancy M. Buckly 5-3-1856 (5-4-1856)
Gardner, J. C. to Mrs. Amelia Dolan 4-29-1863
Gardner, Richard C. to Lucy S. Copeland 2-7-1849 (2-8-1849)
Gardner, W. B. to Charlotte M. Bobo 12-7-1847
Gargus, William to Martha Ann King 7-12-1865
Garland, Antony to Vilet Oneal 8-26-1865 [b?]
Garland, F. L. to Catharine J. Mayfield 2-9-1852
Garland, Hugh S. to Mary E. Brinson 11-12-1839
Garland, J. M. to C. F. Powers 12-15-1845 (12-17-1845)
Garnett, A. to Lucrecia Barnett 12-18-1857
Garnett, J. T. to Mary E. Fauntleroy 1-8-1844 (1-16-1844)
Garnett, Jackson to Clarinda Anderson 7-?-1860 [b]
Garrard, S. L. to Mary J. Young 12-4-1843 (12-12-1843)
Garrell, David F. to Ellen Reynolds 4-4-1853
Garret, Antony to Mary Henry 10-27-1866 [b]
Garrett, Isaac to Patsey Baker 11-3-1866 [b]
Garrett, Sam to Vene Allensworth 12-27-1866 [b]
Garvin, W. S. to Mary Bunghurst 10-20-1842
Garvis?, John to Sarah L. Holt 9-15-1850
Gay, James M. to Mary Kissebech 9-8-1852
Gee, Joseph to Louiza King 1-18-1854
Gelay, William H. to Elizabeth B. Jourdan 2-12-1859 (2-15-1859)
Geleen?, Thomas to Winny Malone 4-2-1858
George, Richard C. to Martha J. Bullifin 3-5-1838
Geter, Calvin L. to Elizabeth Farmer 8-21-1856
Gholson, John A. to Dora Lyles 5-21-1860
Gibbons, Robert E. to Nannie S. Wheatley 12-18-1858
Gibbons, Thomas to Bridget Dalton 11-9-1857
Gibbs, Joseph to Amy Golsen 12-25-1865
Gibbs, Mark P. to Mary C. Adams 10-20-1863
Gibbs, Parin T. to Mary Jane Snellings 1-6-1847 (1-8-1847)
Gibbs, Stephen to Malinda Harris 1-15-1840 (1-20-1840)
Gibson, Thompson to Martha Tucker 12-29-1845
Gilbert, Felix G. to Elizabeth Maning 3-6-1851
Gilbert, Felix G. to Lockey C. Bradley 6-18-1850 (not endorsed)
Gilbert, Jessee to E. H. Johnson 2-21-1863 (2-22-1863)
Gilbert, Joel to Mary Z. Shelby 1-26-1863 (1-29-1863)
Gilbert, Nathan to Mary Jane Corlew 12-15-1839
Gilbert, William H. to Ellen McDaniel 11-2-1857
Gill, Henry to Rody Killebrew 9-25-1865 (10-28-1865)
Gill, James M. to Lizza V. Bagwell(Bagett?) 11-18-1856 (11-26-1856)
Gill, Samuel H. to Margaret Wilcox 11-30-1861
Gill, Spencer to Rosann Herring 12-25-1866 [b]
Gill, W. P. to Lucy B. Allen 11-26-1845
Gillam, Elisha D. to Cynthia B. Vaughan 3-13-1851
Gillaspie, Gabriel to Eliza J. Campbell 11-11-1856 (11-16-1856)
Gillaspy, David to Mary Evans 5-29-1840 (6-4-1840)
Gilliam, A. M. to Isabella J. Robinson 5-29-1847 (5-31-1847)
Gillum, Frederick to Elizabeth Baugh 3-10-1845
Gillum, John C. to Tennessee B. Jenkins 8-11-1863 (8-12-1863)
Gilmore, John W. to Mary Goggin 11-13-1866 (11-14-1866)
Gipson, Henry to Henrietta Parks 6-1-1866 [b]
Gipson, Wm. A. to Martha Glenn 12-1-1845 (12-2-1845)

Gitt, James to Susan Scott 11-25-1840
Givans, Charles to Frances Dickson 1-16-1867 (1-26-1867) [b]
Glascock, James M. to S. E. Jones 3-22-1845
Glascock,, James to Lucy Alice Faxon 2-25-1858
Glass, F. to Caroline E. Barker 1-9-1845 (1-15-1845)
Glenn, Lemuel C. to Mary M. Tomerlin 2-4-1858
Glover, Wm. C. to Jane Trammel 11-17-1863
Godsey, John to Harriet Beckham(Beshears?) 11-15-1855 (11-25-1855)
Goff, John to Bettie Luck 8-1-1865 (8-3-1865)
Goggin, William to Jane Cobb 3-23-1854
Gold, Benj. K. to M. J. Oldham 9-17-1860 (9-18-1860)
Gold, Daniel to Sarah A. Davie 11-5-1858
Gold, Henry to Phebe Morse 1-4-1866 [b]
Gold, John to Clarrissa McDougle 3-24-1845 (4-15-1845)
Gold, Joseph C. to F. M. Hinson 9-4-1855 (8?-12-1855)
Gold, R. to Manerva Williams 10-23-1866 (10-24-1866) [b]
Gooch, Wm. C. to Martha Buckle 9-16-1841
Good, Edward to Dilila A. Ellesson 7-18-1840 (7-23-1840)
Goodall, Joel to America Lynn 7-2-1853
Goode, John H. to Elizabeth Jane Goode 2-11-1850
Goolder, John S. to Lucy M. Chiles 8-5-1844 (8-7-1844)
Gordan, Harry to Mollie E. Gibson 9-5-1865
Gordan, William O. to Elizabeth Caisley 2-18-1843 (2-23-1843)
Gordin, James to Josephine Thomas 5-8-1849 (5-13-1849)
Gordon, Robt. B. to Sarah Ann Ogburn 9-19-1840 (9-27-1840)
Gordon, Wm. O. to Elizabeth Causby 2-18-1843
Gorham, Thornton to Mary Rogers 9-14-1865 (10-15-1865) [b?]
Gosset, G. W. to Nancy J. Mosely 12-18-1851 (12-23-1851)
Gossett, Jas. H. to Margarett Martin 8-31-1861
Gossett, Jonathan to F. J. Ventress 8-22-1856
Goughf, John to Minerva Riggins 3-28-1858? (3-28-1859)
Gowans, William to Margarette Johnson 11-21-1839
Gowans, Wm. to Elizabeth S. Vanhook 5-16-1848
Grace, Albert to Mary Jane West 2-25-1858
Gracy, Francis P. to Irene (Frances?) Cobb 11-9-1857 (11-10-1857)
Gradey, James T. to Martha Johnson 3-1-1861 (3-5-1861)
Grady, James R. to Ann B. Warfield 1-9-1839 (1-16-1839)
Graham, George to Sarah Lindly 12-29-1852
Graham, William E. to Ellen Warring 5-19-1844
Graham, William J. to Mary A. Allen 5-18-1854 (5-8?-1854)
Grand, Hector M. to Sarah C. Griffin 3-4-1847
Grant, Aquilla to Maria L. Cherry 2-24-1848
Grant, B. F. to M. J. Lee 8-9-1862 (8-13-1862)
Grant, Chas. M. to Mildred W. Williams 1-9-1850
Grant, D. H. to Elizabeth Fortson 10-16-1858 (10-19-1858)
Grant, David to Lucinda Bobo 7-20-1840 (7-21-1840)
Grant, Edwin H. to Sarah J. Allison 10-11-1856
Grant, Geo. W. to Tennessee Hutchinson 1-8-1848
Grant, George to Catharine Kestner 8-21-1860
Grant, George to Sarah M. Byrus 10-31-1839
Grant, Hart to Ellen Neblett 10-13-1866 (10-14-1866) [b]
Grant, Henry to Elmira E. Cage 12-26-1866 [b]
Grant, James A. to Frances E. Roberts 6-26-1850 (6-27-1850)
Grant, James B. to Virginia A. Bowling 2-7-1854
Grant, Jas. A. to H. M. Adams 5-12-1862
Grant, John E. to Nancy Jane Kistner 10-28-1854 (11-1-1854)
Grant, Saml. to Nancy Cooper 8-27-1840
Grant, Washington to Henrietta Bryan 10-20-1841
Grant, Wm. T. to Mary J. Holt 10-24-1849
Graves, R. N. to Mariah Bacules? 5-13-1846
Gray, H. W. to G. A. Jones 12-13-1864 (not executed)
Gray, John W. to Margaret Brake 1-5-1843
Gray, John to Mary Atkerson 12-25-1866 (12-27-1866) [b]
Gray, Jones to Sarah G. McCauley 1-6-1849
Gray, Mathew T. to Nancy Walker 10-2-1845
Gray, R. D. to Hester Ann Maddox 5-22-1854
Gray, Vincent to Martha McDaniel 7-27-1843
Green, B. N. to Narcissa Grant 2-1-1842 (2-3-1842)
Green, Chas. to Easter Killebrew 10-20-1866 (10-27-1866) [b]
Green, Edward H. to Martha House 1-24-1860
Green, Elisha P. to Matilda Duncan 7-11-1839 (7-26-1839)
Green, James P. to Tennessee Gilbert 12-11-1845
Green, Robert E. to Elizabeth Green 4-5-1849
Greene, James P. to Elizabeth C.? Kendrick 5-21-1851 (6-3-1851)

Greene, Marcus M. to Martha L. Dean 1-31-1852 (2-1-1852)
Greenfield, Cyrus W. to Nancy A. Barker 9-9-1856
Greenfield, Wm. to Jane Shepherd 9-1-1845
Greenwood, James to Elizabeth Strader 11-15-1854
Greenwood, William F. to Martha J. McCraw 4-1-1849
Gregory, John G. to M. V. Madden 7-9-1855 (7-8?-1855)
Gregory, John T. to Virginia Mitchell 12-31-1856
Gresham, F. C. to Martha Cooper 2-24-1844
Gresham, Joel to Martha C. Long 1-9-1852
Griffey, Aaron to Margaret Elizabeth Vaughn 10-13-1857 (10-14-1857)
Griffey, David S. to Louisa Frances Dinwiddie 1-16-1854
Griffey, George D. to Catharine V. Rives 11-12-1861 (11-21-1861)
Griffey, John to Mary J. Bryant 12-19-1864 (12-21-1864)
Griffey, Jordan to Harriett Rutherford 5-19-1866 [b]
Griffey, Marcellus to Sarah F. Halliburton 8-24-1865
Griffey, William to Mary D. Smith 1-14-1858 (1-16-1858)
Griffey, Wm. M. to Mary Ann McBride? 2-18-1848
Griffin, Edward J. to Amanda Ezel 10-13-1853
Griffin, James W. to Sarah M. Primm 6-19-1860 (6-21-1860)
Griffin, James to Margaret Buckhanon 7-7-1845
Griffin, John K. to Sarah Wickum 3-20-1851
Griffin, Joseph L. to Ethalinda Harrid 3-1-1852 (3-2-1852)
Griffin, Obediah B. to Sophia Ann Bell 1-31-1859 (2-4-1859)
Grigg, John to Caroline M. Moody 1-10-1852 (1-11-1852)
Grimes, Frederick to Supprana Jane Stephens 5-5-1851
Grimes, Granderson to Ellen Parson 9-19-1849 (9-18?-1849)
Grimes, Henry to Sally Rebecca Mallory 12-18-1855 (11?-11?-1855)
Grimes, J. L. to Nancy A. Mockibee 11-6-1848
Grimes, Thomas to Elizabeth Powers 3-11-1840
Grimes, William N. to Martha P. Harvey 9-25-1852 (9-29-1852)
Grinson?, William to Nancy Davis 10-5-1840 (10-8-1840)
Grinstall?, Richard to Sarah E. Pettus 5-8-1839 (5-9-1839)
Grinsted, Anderson to Celia Ann Cox 4-27-1866 [b]
Grizzard, Wm. H. to Mrs. Lou Grizzard 11-22-1864
Groom, Cyrus to Malindy Petree 1-?-1867 [b]
Groom, Wm. W. to Elizabeth Lasetter 9-9-1848 (9-10-1848)
Groves, Geo W. to Sevanna Groves 10-17-1859
Grymes, Zumroll to Sarah Rudolph 9-14-1843
Guardner, Josiah S. to Caroline M. Cook 9-19-1848
Gunning, Thomas to Elizabeth Tidwell 5-23-1861
Gupton, Abner J. to Mary Crow 7-12-1866
Gupton, Abner to Jane Batts 5-18-1844 (5-19-1844)
Gupton, Abner to Martha A. Power 9-14-1841 (10-5-1841)
Gupton, Abner to Mary Nicholson 2-7-1846 (2-12-1846)
Gupton, Berry to Kitty Hatcher 5-30-1866 (5-31-1866) [b]
Gupton, C. J. to Henrietta Duke 9-17-1866 (12-20-1866)
Gupton, Cooper to Mary Hunter 8-4-1845 (8-6-1845)
Gupton, E. N. to Lidia Page 6-15-1844 (6-20-1844)
Gupton, Jas. to Martha Makes 1-5-1851
Gupton, Oscar to Elizabeth Batheny 1-7-1840
Gupton, Solomon to Fanny Woodward 1-29-1866 [b]
Gupton, Thos. to Harriet A. Jones 12-15-1851 (12-18-1851)
Guren, Jas. G. to Rusia A. Smith 12-27-1865 (12-28-1865)
Guthrie, W. P. to A. V. Bagwell 2-1-1864
Guynn, Joseph G. to Virginia A. Parham 10-20-1856
Guynn, Thomas H. to Martha Ann Sadler 9-5-1859 (9-8-1859)
Hackney, Benjamin B. to Drusilla Hackney 4-1-1855
Hackney, David W. to Martha A. Watts 12-11-1856
Hackney, Geo. to Dianah Leavell 8-29-1866 [b]
Hackney, Joseph to Bettie Allen 1-9-1866 [b]
Hackney, Wm. V. to Almetia Brickell 8-2-1850
Haddock, Wm. to Ellen Dodd 2-21-1850
Hagan, Wilis J. to Mary E. Myers 4-23-1856
Hagart?, John N. to Margaret Wright 2-14-1853
Hagewood, Jessee B. to Angeline Bull 8-20-1858 (8-22-1858)
Hagood, Elijah T. to Mrs. Sallie F. Morrison 12-28-1865
Hagood, John J. to Jerusha R. Dicks 12-13-1856 (12-14-1856)
Hagwood, Dabney to Cynthia Fain 1-2-1841 (1-3-1841)
Hagwood, James P. to Lucrecia Teasley 8-1-1854
Hagwood, John R. to Mary Gamble? 7-15-1840 (7-16-1840)
Hagy, Archibald N. to Jane Rose 11-22-1860
Haigue?, Wm. to Susan Batson 1-13-1851 (1-15-1851)
Hainsworth, John P. to Mary E. Harris 1-24-1857 (1-25-1857)
Hair, James to Sallie Carr 8-1-1859

Hairston, Wm. to Elizabeth Nicholson 1-2-1847 (1-7-1847)
Halay, Edmund P. to Mary Waters 5-21-1853
Hale, B. W. to Eliza Ann Harris 3-8-1849
Hale, James M. to Paralee A. Hale 7-10-1856
Hall, A. F. to Rebecca Jones 7-20-1850 (7-21-1850)
Hall, Bardett H. to Minerva Hardwick 12-8-1853
Hall, Chas. W. to Eliza J. Edwards 2-28-1866 (3-1-1866)
Hall, Francis J. to Fanny H. Hill 1-12-1852 (1-13-1852)
Hall, Joseph G. to Mariann Cox 5-28-1847
Halliberton, W. D. to Mrs. E. A. Jett 1-28-1861 (1-29-1861)
Halliburton, David to Margaret A. Hamlet 9-21-1865 (10-21-1865)
Halliburton, George C. to Mary Grant 12-16-1840
Halseel, John B. to Martha Adams 7-7-1841 (7-8-1841)
Halsel, E. B. to Mary Ann White 9-15-1853
Halsiel, Certain T. to Martha A. Jones 2-25-1840 (2-27-1840)
Halsul, Edwd. B. to Ruth A. Manning 9-25-1842
Halyard, James B. to Zilpha Holliway 1-22-1842
Hambaugh?, P. C. to Virginia B. Burgess 10-5-1852
Hamid, J. W. to Mary S. Harris 12-27-1858 (12-29-1858)
Hamilton, Nicholas Thomas to Jeraldine Payne 7-21-1856 (7-22-1856)
Hamilton, William A. to Leanie Harris 3-5-1853 (3-6-1853)
Hamins?, George to Matilda Patterson 6-8-1854
Hamlet, Andrew Jackson to Rachael Winniford McNeil 2-13-1855
     (2-14-1855)
Hamlett, James J. to Susan Elizabeth Morrison 2-1-1855
Hamlin, Allen to Lucy Jane Lee 9-13-1860 (9-15-1860)
Hammond, Chas. B. to Harriett C. Hammond 8-4-1866 (8-5-1866)
Hampton, William P. to Narcissa E.? Wicks 8-3-1860
Hamrick, A. J. to Mary Powers 9-10-1860 (5?-12-1860)
Hancock, John P. to Rebecca E. Tilman 9-30-1852
Handlin, John N. to Georgian P. Shelton 3-12-1864 (3-15-1864)
Handy, Thomas to Sarah Campanie 5-7-1858 (5-9-1858)
Hankins, A. to Jane Rudolph 3-14-1862
Hanna, Isaac to Nancy Swasey 9-14-1842
Hannah, Sidney to Henrietta Rollins 5-16-1866 [b]
Harbin, Saml. to Katy Norflett 5-5-1866 [b]
Harding, Robert C. to Sallie Morris 8-30-1859 (9-7-1859)
Harding, William L. to Ann E. Kelly 1-9-1856
Hardis, James to Sarah Leet 11-11-1863 (11-12-1863)
Hardison, Phillip S. to Mary E. Hardison 12-6-1858
Hardwick, Frank E. to Sarah V. Barksdale 6-23-1859
Hardy, Willis to Margaret Faro? 10-8-1845 (10-9-1845)
Harelson, J. C. to Mary Settle 7-24-1848
Harelson, William C. to Louisa L. Massey 11-10-1853
Hargrave, W. T. to H. M. Lynn 10-6-1851
Hargrove, Jehu to Fredonia Allen 12-1-1857 (12-3-1857)
Hargrove, Thomas G. to Susanah W. Whitenton 12-5-1851
     (12-7-1851)
Hargrove, Washington to Susan Bailey 12-13-1856 (12-18-1856)
Haris, Thos. H. to Tabitha E. Tyre 2-24-1847 (2-25-1847)
Haris, William to Rebecca D. Morris 2-11-1847 (2-25-1847)
Harned, James to Susan Crunk 3-21-1858
Harned?, Enos to Mary Allman 3-1-1851 (3-7-1851)
Harnell?, J. W. to Elizabeth —— 8-17-1855
Harney, Joel to Mary Ann Porter 5-6-1854 (6-1-1854)
Harney, Leander to Lucy Bagget 2-4-1860 (2-6-1860)
Harnon, Berton to Tennessee A. Patterson 8-2-1865
Harole?, G. W. to Margaret G. Martin 6-24-1845
Harper, Benjamin to Mary Cocke 10-4-1850 (10-7-1850)
Harper, David H. to Elizabeth Harris 12-22-1853
Harper, Jas. S. to Matilda H. Hogel 8-4-1849 (8-10-1849)
Harper, Thomas to Mary W. Collins 12-28-1858 (12-29-1858)
Harper, William B. to Catharine Vicks 6-26-1845
Harrell, Leroy S. to Elizabeth A. McAddams 11-2-1848
Harrelson, D. G. to F. J. Gillam 11-20-1862 (11-23-1862)
Harrelson, James to Laura A. Witherspoon 4-7-1845
Harris, Allen M. to Louvany Newson 1-1-1859 (1-2-1859)
Harris, Arthar to Elvirie W. Walker 4-26-1842
Harris, Benj. F. to M. E. Neblett 1-17-1860 (1-18-1860)
Harris, David A. to Sarah E. F. Wyatt 2-7-1858 (2-4?-1858)
Harris, G. L. to Sarah Ann Goodman 4-4-1856
Harris, George R. to Isabella W. Adkins 11-24-1855 (11-28-1855)
Harris, Henry to Matilda Sampson 1-4-1856
Harris, Henry to Matilda Sampson 9-29-1852
Harris, Isham to Eliza Yarborough 5-18-1864

Harris, James M. to Mary L. Bull 12-21-1854
Harris, James M. to Sarah Jane Harris 12-14-1858 (11?-14-1858)
Harris, James to Lurana A. Cromwell 11-5-1847 (11-7-1847)
Harris, Jas. H. to Sarah M. Curtis 9-12-1848
Harris, Jas. R. to Martha A. Mathews 4-20-1865
Harris, John J. to Darthuna Haggard 3-27-1856
Harris, John M. to Martha Ann Carsly? 1-3-1852
Harris, John R. to Sarah Vaughn 2-21-1860 (2-22-1860)
Harris, John to Martha C. Jones 4-8-1856 (4-6?-1856)
Harris, Mathew to Ann Terrell 5-25-1841
Harris, Miles to Rebecca Clifton 12-23-1839 (12-26-1839)
Harris, R. A. to C. M. Chiles 1-12-1847 (1-13-1847)
Harris, Richard Washington to Mahala Jane Alexander 1-24-1853
Harris, Sampson C. to Eliza J. Mathus 4-4-1849 (4-5-1849)
Harris, Thomas to Elizabeth A. Stegall 8-1-1858
Harris, W. T. to Martha Ann Hunter 1-12-1850 (3-27-1850)
Harris, Westly Tally to Mary Ann Hunter 2-5-1845 (4-2-1845)
Harris, Wiley to Margaret Thacker 8-19-1865 (8-20-1865)
Harris, William Weldon to Mary Lucy Kelly 2-7-1855 (2-8-1855)
Harris, William to Easter Knight 3-21-1859
Harris, William to Susan Ritter 10-27-1866 [b]
Harris, Zak to Lucinda Everett 4-25-1845
Harrison, A. B. to Jenette J. Chilton 3-9-1849 (3-10-1849)
Harrison, Adam M. to Sarah Ann Farmer 2-19-1849
Harrison, David A. to Rutha Hankins 1-2-1860 (1-5-1860)
Harrison, David H. to Mary J. Harrison 5-19-1844
Harrison, David to Elizabeth Hall 12-13-1843
Harrison, Elbert H. to Edith N. Collins 5-31-1838
Harrison, Elisha B. to Delphina A. Heflin 2-5-1851
Harrison, Elisha R. to Elizabeth A. Davidson 4-3-1850 (4-4-1850)
Harrison, George S. to Sarah Ann Peacher 6-11-1860
Harrison, George W. to Mattie Fantelroy 12-23-1865 [b]
Harrison, M. to Missourie Niel 3-16-1845
Harrison, Reuben to Agness Heflin 5-14-1846
Harrison, W. J. to Sarah L. Davidson 1-23-1851
Harrison, Wm. to Catharine Wade 1-4-1848
Harriss, Goin to Mary E. Burns 12-30-1843 (12-31-1843)
Harrisson, James D. to Sally V. Neblett 11-28-1839
Harrold, John to Janetta Dobson 3-24-1840
Hart, Edwin T. to Martha Brown 12-29-1853
Hart, Hesakiah Pagril? to Julia Ann Ashford 8-30-1850 (9-5-1850)
Hart, Hezekiah P. to America Ann Monys? 11-26-1845
Hart, Hezekiah P. to Elizabeth Morris 6-23-1842
Hart, John M. to Mary J. Leigh 3-11-1844 (3-14-1844)
Hart, John S. to Martha A. Miller 7-27-1843
Hart, Sampson to Eliza Burgess 2-15-1843 (2-16-1843)
Hart, W. J. to Arabella Bayless 5-1-1848 (5-4-1848)
Hart, William J. to Priscilla Jane Fletcher 10-25-1844 (10-29-1844)
Hart, William to Martha C. Farmer 8-3-1844 (8-4-1844)
Hartman, M. to Julia A. Johnson 12-31-1862 (1-3-1863)
Harvey, G. to Sallie Baggett 9-17-1864
Harvey, J. M. to G. A. Powers 4-27-1860 (4-20?-1860)
Harvey, Thos. D. to Mrs. Louisa Brock 1-26-1865
Hase, Jacob B. to Mary Banes 2-19-1844 (2-21-1844)
Haslett, Wm. H. to Mary Rensils(Walthal?) 1-15-1867 (1-19-1867) [b]
Hatcher, Benjamin to Eliza Ann Neblett 9-15-1842
Hatcher, James to Amanda Orenduff 6-11-1865
Hatcher, Joseph to Mary Grinsted 7-21-1865 (7-25-1865)
Hatcher, Richard N. to Mary Ann Buckley 7-29-1846 (7-30-1846)
Hatcher, Richd. A. to Elizabeth C. Hackary? 4-12-1842
Hatcher, William to Mary Malinda Fox 11-7-1853 (11-8-1853)
Hatsell, Stephen J. to Lucy Ann Sydnor 11-12-1850
Hausben?, Ephram S. to Martha N. Gustin 12-12-1850
Hawkins, Olander to Lucy Ann Browder 3-25-1865 [b]
Hawkins, William to Amy Stocker 11-30-1866 (12-2-1866) [b]
Hay, William to Martha Ann Daniel 1-13-1859
Hayden, John to Sarah Frances Catlet 5-15-1859
Hayes, Thomas S. to Mary Elizabeth Johnson 2-17-1856
Haynes, Henry to Martha Albright 10-29-1850
Haynes, Isaac to Tennessee Thorn 5-4-1856 (5-2?-1856)
Haynes, Jim Meredy to Milly Nichol 12-28-1866 (12-30-1866) [b]
Haynes, Thomas A. to Mary J. Elliott 5-9-1850 (5-14-1850)
Haynes, William A. to Elizabeth A. Tyson 11-1-1858
Hays, D. J. to Margarett C. Alman 7-24-1851
Hays, Jno. J. to Narcissa J. Taylor 12-2-1856

Hays, John to Sarah Shepherd 2-28-1866 (3-4-1866) [b]
Haysley?, Thomas to Sally McGehee 8-1-1839
Haywood, William to Susan Patterson 4-14-1838
Heal, Luke to Mary Baggett 9-11-1858 (9-12-1858)
Heart, Saml. to Emeline Leigh 2-15-1843 (2-24-1843)
Heathcock, John to Harriett Harris 7-9-1849
Heathman, James to Elizabeth Lynn 10-4-1841 (10-6-1841)
Heathman, John H. to Caroline T. Davison 1-21-1854
Heathman, William H. to Frances Smith 1-4-1855
Heel, John B. to Mary Holloway 1-16-1840
Heflin, David to Nancy Ann Foust 9-20-1845 (9-25-1845)
Heflin, Jas. K. Polk to Mary Ann Kistnor 2-27-1861
Heleighty?, Lewis P. to Jane Brooking 8-28-1847
Helm, J. B. to R. Buck 12-15-1862 (12-16-1862)
Helm, Jno. B. to Martha L. Blakemore 5-26-1842 (6-2-1842)
Hemet?, James to Mary Eads 11-20-1845
Henderson, J. R. to K. M. Word 11-23-1851
Henderson, James Robert to Kitty M. Word 11-23-1851 (11-24-1851)
Henderson, John W. to E. A. Whuldom 12-18-1845
Henderson, John W. to L. J. Martin 5-11-1854
Henderson, Liland B. to Miriam H. Price 9-1-1852
Hendrick, A. B. to M. C. Bell 12-18-1862
Hendrick, J. T. to Mary A. Cooke 11-11-1852
Hendricks, Jeremiah sr. to Angeline Hardeman 11-23-1854
Henitsman, Adam to Nancy Mosely 12-9-1846 (12-11-1846)
Hensler, L. J. to Martha T. Council 12-16-1854 (12-21-1854)
Hensley, J. J. to Mary J. Custer 11-3-1854
Henson, Jas. L. to Selia Dilmoth Eason 6-8-1865
Herndon, Abraham to Lizzie Rollins 12-15-1866 [b]
Herndon, Thos. to Sallie B. Dinwiddie 1-11-1866 (1-14-1866)
Herndon?, William H. to Virginia R. Cabaniss 3-15-1853
Herrin, A. B. to Lucy A. Head 1-22-1852
Herring, Barrett to Margaret Edwards 1-2-1866
Herring, E. R. to S. H. Killibrew 6-28-1855 (7-1-1855)
Herring, Edmond to Fancis? Broadmax 12-8-1866 [b]
Herring, Joseph L. to Henrietta A. Rudolph 12-18-1854 (12-21-1855?)
Herring, Owen W. to Catharine Ross 1-20-1840
Herring, Peter G. to Emeline Feelix 12-20-1840
Herring, Simon B. to Virginia G. Wilcox 6-2-1853
Herrington, John C. to Mahala Scholds 6-22-1854 (6-28-1854)
Herrington, John to Mary Langston 10-8-1845 (10-9-1845)
Herter?, Charles M. to Gertrude H. McDaniel 2-18-1854
Hesler, Abner N. to Mary J. Galey 10-20-1853
Hester, James C. to Sarah Dawson 12-6-1858 (12-9-1858)
Hester, James H. to Elizabeth Culbertson 7-14-1842
Hester, James to Mary Stagner 1-27-1841 (1-28-1841)
Hester, Jessee to S. A. McCallister 12-24-1862 (12-25-1862)
Hester, John P. to Cathern Fletcher 12-18-1855 (12-25-1855)
Hester, John W. to Sallie Dillard 6-8-1857
Hester, Nathan to Elizabeth Mallory 1-18-1844 (1-21-1844)
Hester, William O. to Virginia Fletcher 12-29-1855 (1-3-1856)
Hester, Wm. N.? to Nancy Stone 12-6-1841
Hewlett, Augustus E. to Eliza Adams 9-11-1865
Hews, John F. to Almyra R. Dabney 8-8-1838
Hiatt, Peter J. to Nannie C. Moore 7-14-1863
Hickerson, William J. to Emily Jane Johnson 11-17-1856 (11-18-1856)
Hickison, Henry to Mary C. Brantly 7-27-1855 (7-31-1855)
Hickman, E. W. to Penelope J. Brunson 9-4-1845
Hickman, Edwin C. to Letitia L. Downing 8-18-1864
Hickman, Edwin W. to Parnelope J. Brunson 9-4-1845
Hickman, George to Mrs. N. Mear? 11-13-1866 (11-15-1866)
Hicks, William to Mary Martha Mickle 1-19-1856 (1-20-1856)
Higgie, William to Nancy M. Walker 10-8-1845 (10-9-1845)
Higgins, Benjamin to Nannie Pettus 10-19-1866 [b]
Higgins, James to Nancy Hutcherson 3-28-1853 (3-30-1853)
Higgins, Jno. to Mahulda Roger 12-30-1843
High, John W. to Eliza F. Cooksey 12-18-1844 (12-19-1844)
Hightower, A. J. to Eveline Stokes 10-14-1855
Hill, Green B. to Ann Eliza McKean 1-5-1848 (1-6-1848)
Hill, Jessee E. to Mary A. Tally 12-13-1841
Hill, John M. to Lafayett Ann Dawson 5-27-1852
Hill, John W. to Mary E. Stephens 1-17-1859
Hill, Thomas B. to C. T. Farley 3-18-1841 (3-8?-1841)
Hill, William to Elmira Akins 11-17-1864
Hilman, Danel to Ann J. Marable 4-14-1840 (4-16-1840)

Hilton, Jas. M. to Rebecca J. Holcomb 8-11-1863
Himes?, Wilson H. to Elizabeth J. Vaughan 2-4-1851
Hinch, G. G. to E. J. Grant 9-27-1845 (9-28-1845)
Hinley, James H. to Mary C. Broom 9-30-1865
Hinly?, Jeremiah to Matilda Watson 10-22-1847
Hinson, Henry to Sarah Speed? 8-20-1840
Hinson, James E. to Sarah Taucker 6-12-1842
Hinton, Jno. H. to Frances Lynes 10-1-1840
Hinton, Presley to Susan Norwood 8-28-1844
Hirch, J. H. to Ada B. Kelly 1-23-1863 (2-3-1863)
Hiser, Charles to Elizabeth Liles 7-9-1853
Hite, Samuel to Mary Thomas Garnet 9-22-1856
Hiter, C. J. to Sarepta A. Lyle 2-15-1866
Hiter, Osbern to Susan Warfield 8-31-1865 [b?]
Hobbs, Benedict H. to Ann Harrison 12-19-1839 (12-25-1839)
Hobbs, Samuel to Margaret Wills 4-24-1865 [b]
Hobbs,, Zachariah to Sarah E. Turner 7-11-1842
Hobson, Henry to C. H. Woodson 3-25-1841
Hodges, C. S. to Sally Ann Albright 6-30-1838 (7-9-1838)
Hodges, Charles G. to Frances E. Broom 6-17-1854 (6-22-1854)
Hodges, Charles S. to Fredonia R. Britt 7-8-1848
Hodges, Daniel to Elizabeth Black 2-1-1840 (2-2-1840)
Hodges, Marcus to Sarah E. Blair 12-24-1866 (12-26-1866)
Hodges, Maxwell to Mary Stailey 6-3-1850 (6-4-1850)
Hodges, P. M. to Telitha E. Hodges 4-1-1865 (4-2-1865)
Hodges, Saml. P. to Sarah A. Lee 12-14-1865 (12-20-1865)
Hodgson, Saml. to Julia Carney 10-1-1853 (10-4-1853)
Hoffman, George to Belle M. Jones 7-21-1862
Hogan, Bannister W. to Elizabeth Driskell 10-30-1840
Hogan, Jacob to Ann Burton 4-4-1842 (4-5-1842)
Hogan, James to Margarette Morgan 12-10-1838
Hogan, John M. to Sarah S. Bruton 4-16-1850
Hogg, Harvey to Prudence J. Alcorn 4-24-1855
Hogwood, Hartwell D. to Mary B. Mackley 3-24-1853 (3-30-1853)
Holcomb, William to Eliza Bircham 11-24-1854
Holeman, Jessee W. to Nancy Jane Morehead 11-7-1857
Holland, James F. to Margaret V. Hoskins 10-27-1858
Holland, Leroy to Mary Smith 10-2-1844 (10-3-1844)
Holland, Milton W. to Maranda Brownfield 10-16-1842 (10-17-1842)
Holland, Robert to Eliza Litteral 11-11-1855
Holland, Thomas to Manerva Willis 5-11-1848
Holland, U. J. to Almira G. Yates 6-10-1843 (6-13-1843)
Holliday, Andrew J. to Sally M. Allen 12-19-1854
Holliman, Chas. to Mollie Mabry 9-29-1866 [b]
Hollingsworth, S. N. to Martha P. Gray 10-2-1849
Hollins, R. T. to Maggie T. Mitchell 1-19-1863
Hollins, Saml. P. to Pamelia F. Knott? 12-12-1850 (12-19-1850)
Hollinsworth, S. G. to Mary A. Williams 8-20-1856
Hollis, Achillis to Mary Jane Hodges 4-17-1860 (4-19-1860)
Hollis, Henry to Mary E. Masters 3-4-1856
Hollis, Joseph to Mary Parish 1-16-1851
Hollis, Joseph to Mary Parrish 1-14-1851
Hollis, W. to S. E. Davidson 10-13-1866 (10-16-1866)
Hollis, William K. to Nancy J. Johnson 8-31-1847 (9-2-1847)
Hollister, McKendrie to Elenora Bigham 6-14-1864
Holmes, W. J. to Agnes Ann Allen 10-20-1846
Holt, Benj. E. to Elizabeth A. Hill? 6-17-1848 (6-18-1848)
Holt, David to Bell Cross 12-1-1866 (12-2-1866)
Holt, G. L. to Martha J. Binkley 1-8-1867 (1-10-1867)
Holt, James N. to Jane Ann Woodson 12-31-1851 (1-1-1852)
Holt, John E. to Frances R. Heathman 9-14-1848
Holt, John to R. Binkley 7-2-1862
Holt, Wm. F. to Araminter Foust 3-13-1849
Homan, B. B. to Sarepta M. Jorden 7-21-1863 (7-22-1863)
Homan, Bladen B. to Hariet E. Trice 12-17-1844
Hook, Harvey to Mary J. E. Trice 4-19-1852
Hook, Samuel to Frances Ann Trice 10-9-1848 (10-19-1848)
Hooper, Marcillus J. to Gabriella E. Holt 4-28-1860 (4-29-1860)
Hooper, W. A. to Virginia B. Bagwell 2-27-1866 (3-1-1866)
Hooser, J. H. to R. R. Whedem? 10-3-1862
Hoover, W. U. to Nannie J. Smith 3-2-1861 (3-4-1861)
Hopkins, Joseph H. to Martha Crouch 12-4-1860
Hopkins, L. D. to Mary L. Bowman 10-19-1843 (10-21-1843)
Hopson, Albert to Lucinda E. Perkins 4-17-1840
Hopson, James F. to Mary C. Kinner 11-12-1844

Hopson, James S. to Eliza J. Restner 7-21-1852
Hopson, M. S. to Judith L. Oglesby 9-6-1841
Hord, James H. to Louiza W. Whitlow 8-18-1858 (8-14?-1858)
Horde, Ezekiel to Martha Ann King 6-7-1853
Horn, C. M. to Sarah A. F. Wiley 10-29-1860 (10-30-1860)
Horn, Collin to Harriet Brown 12-21-1866 (12-25-1866) [b]
Horn, Josiah M. to Mary J. Tyer? 11-22-1843 (11-20?-1843)
Horn, Josiah to Elizabeth H. Allen 5-2-1840 (5-5-1840)
Horn, Judson to Nancy Bowers 5-2-1839 (5-3-1839)
Hosler?, Nathan to Elizabeth Carter 1-5-1853 (1-9-1853)
House, Francis Marion to Georgiann T. Allwell 10-26-1865
House, R. M. to Mary R. Barnes 5-8-1838 (5-10-1838)
Houston, Ephraim S. to Adaline Burton 10-25-1839 (10-30-1839)
Houston, Henry to Louisa Whitworth 12-14-1849
Houston, John to Nancy Whitworth 3-2-1846 (3-3-1846)
Houston, S. T. to Martha Nicholson 4-16-1849 (4-17-1849)
How, Martin to C. Williams 5-9-1865 (5-11-1865)
Howard, E. to M. A. Crusman 12-2-1851
Howard, Frank to Emma Payne 9-29-1866 [b]
Howard, Isaac P. to Mattie A. Cooly 6-20-1865 (7-4-1865)
Howard, John to Jane Newman 1-31-1842 (2-3-1842)
Howard, Martin to Sarah E. Bell 2-13-1846 (2-19-1846)
Howell, Andrew to Frances Campbell 8-1-1859 (8-2-1859)
Howell, J. W. to H. A. Donaldson 10-7-1851 (10-8-1851)
Howell, James A. to Selina C. Dunning 1-5-1853
Howell, James H. to M. J. E. McFall 3-12-1840
Howell, T. S. to Lutitia T. Campbell 7-22-1857 (7-23-1857)
Howerton, C. L. to Dorothy A. St. John 11-16-1846 (11-18-1846)
Howlett, William to Margaret Riter 1-19-1859
Hubbard, Lewis to Elizabeth Sampson 4-25-1841 (4-26-1841)
Hudson, H. J. to Elizabeth J. Hamlin 8-23-1860
Hues, R. B. to S. A. M. Rouland 10-18-1851
Hughes, James to Mary McCarty 1-12-1861
Hughs, Lewis T. to M. A. Buckhannon 11-14-1839 (11-15-1839)
Hull, W. H. to Elizabeth Jorden 6-17-1854
Hume, William P. to Jennetta C. Garvin 11-13-1844 (11-21-1844)
Humphreys, C. M. to Mrs. M. M. Lankford 6-3-1865
Humphreys, Joshua to Martha Lankford 3-14-1840 (3-17-1840)
Humphreys, Richd. H. to Maurina A. Lamaster 5-16-1843
Humphries, Richard W. to Margaret Williams 1-6-1848
Humphries, William S. to Mary Jane McCaughan 2-12-1846
Humphrys, R. E. to Mary S. Nall 8-8-1848
Humphrys, R. E. to S. H. Sevier 7-12-1847
Hunt, H. B. to M. F. Kelly 3-10-1865 (3-16-1865)
Hunt, John O. to Catharine E. Hurt 1-18-1841 (1-21-1841)
Hunt, John W. to Mary Ann H. Jones 12-18-1839 (12-24-1839)
Hunt, Michael to Sarah Rose 7-29-1843
Hunt, Thomas S. to M. E. Martin 3-25-1850 (3-28-1850)
Hunt, Thos. S. to Mrs. Sophia W. Jackson 6-25-1864 (6-30-1864)
Hunt, Wm. R. to Jane Aykes 1-1-1851 (1-2-1851)
Hunter, Abner to Mary Bell 12-2-1839 (12-5-1839)
Hunter, Allen to Martha Ann M. Walker 12-12-1846 (12-23-1846)
Hunter, Allen to Mary J. Rudolph 11-8-1848
Hunter, Thomas to Nancy McFaddin 10-25-1855 (10-28-1855)
Hurst, B. B. to Martha Barrett 9-28-1858
Hurst, J. H. to Frances Harris 12-4-1851
Hurst, W. R. to Martha Martin 6-18-1846
Hurt, William to Mary A. H. Bayliss 12-10-1853 (12-13-1853)
Huskey, George W. to Mary Morris 8-10-1858 (8-11-1858)
Hust, G. W. to Manerva E. Cox 10-5-1848
Huston, Geo. E. to L. J. Moore 5-2-1842
Hutcherson, Armsted to Ann Tyler 5-8-1866 [b]
Hutcherson, Charles W. to Martha Ann Holt 11-20-1854 (11-23-1854)
Hutcherson, James to Sally Lamaster 7-7-1858
Hutcherson, Jasper N. to Eveline L. Stansit 7-7-1858
Hutcherson, Wm. S. to Narcissa F. Fouste 5-30-1848
Hutchings, Jno. to Elizabeth Fletcher 12-13-1841 (12-14-1842)
Hutchinson, James W. to Anne Eliza Jett 10-24-1848
Hutchison, James A. to Susan A. Wills 5-11-1857 (5-14-1857)
Hutchison, Thomas to Mary Adeline Holt 8-9-1854 (8-10-1854)
Hyland, Thomas J. to Margaret Sullivan 2-26-1859 (3-6-1859)
Ingram, C. M. to Mansel P. Marlow 4-26-1857
Ingram, Thomas M. to Frances A. Bibb 8-29-1856
Irby, Nathaniel P. to Mary N. Waller 6-29-1852 (6-30-1852)
Ireland, J. E. to Emily D. Weren? 9-2-1846

Irvin, Wm. M. to Eliz. McKeage 8-27-1840
Irving, John A. to Mary Atkinson 1-14-1865
Irwin, Joseph M. to Adaline B. Beaumont 6-17-1841
Ivy, John J. to Columbia R. House 8-25-1856
Jackson, Alexander to Darthula Baxter 10-2-1850
Jackson, Andrew to Phebe Myers 9-19-1844
Jackson, Freeman to Martha A. Garrette 5-12-1864
Jackson, George to Elizabeth Mayse 3-18-1865 (may be black)
Jackson, Green P. to Mary P. O'Neal 10-3-1866 (10-4-1866)
Jackson, J. B. to Sophia Vaughn 1-9-1860 (1-10-1860)
Jackson, J. M. to Mary C. Corben 8-14-1860 (8-15-1860)
Jackson, Jas. H. to Martha J. Jones 9-20-1849
Jackson, Jas. to Elizabeth Cook 5-13-1865 (5-14-1865)
Jackson, Jessee to Susan Yarbrough 1-21-1852 (1-23-1852)
Jackson, John to E. Yarborough 6-19-1862 (6-23-1862)
Jackson, John to Winney Suggs 7-3-1856
Jackson, Joseph B. to Mahala Riley 8-14-1856
Jackson, Joseph to Mary Bradley 6-12-1850
Jackson, Josiah to Elizabeth Jackson 11-14-1863 (11-21-1864?)
Jackson, Josiah to Susan Jones 10-18-1843 (10-19-1843)
Jackson, Leander to Nancy S. Baker 3-10-1857 (3-11-1857)
Jackson, Miles to Livina Almon 3-11-1856 (2?-11-1856)
Jackson, Robert to Louzana Mitchell 10-16-1854 (11-23-1854)
Jackson, Stephen to Patsy Yarbrough 6-13-1839
Jackson, Thomas H. to Edeann T. Pierce 1-15-1861
Jackson, Thomas H. to Emma A. Staten 1-23-1855 (1-25-1855)
Jackson, Thos. H. to Mrs. S. C. Blackman 9-4-1862
Jackson, W. A. to Allice Rudolph 3-7-1865 (3-16-1865)
Jackson, William J. to Sarah Ann Owens 7-13-1859 (8-12-1859)
Jackson, William Robert to Nancy Ann Suter 3-31-1855 (4-1-1855)
Jackson, Willis to Virginia Gilbert 11-12-1861
Jackson, Wm. M. to Amanda J. Loving 10-25-1847
James, Britton to S. G. Bayair 12-25-1843
James, J. L. jr. to Eliza A. Smith 7-6-1847
James, James E. to Caroline Haggie 10-6-1859
James, John H. to Charlotte S. Neblett 3-9-1853 (3-11-1853)
James, Richard to Mildred Harbour 11-25-1841
James, W.K. to Mary Row 12-8-1851
James, William to Elizabeth Jones 11-23-1854
James, Wm. E. to Eliza J. Bailey 11-3-1864 (11-10-1864)
Jameson, George to Sally Ann Powers 12-7-1854
Jamison, George to Sally Ann Powell 12-7-1855
Janes, E. F. to Mary T. Flack 9-11-1848 (9-12-1848)
Jarman, Albert W. to Melvina E. Cobb 1-19-1853 (1-20-1853)
Jarman, Josiah to Nancy E. Rogers 7-29-1839 (7-31-1839)
Jarman, Robert S. to Margarette D. Lyles 9-10-1838 (10-?-1838)
Jarman, Wilis to Charlotte Galy 4-3-1854 (4-4-1854)
Jarrett, James to Tennessee Cross 1-13-1866 [b]
Jarvis, Edmond to Amanda Mercer 10-19-1849
Jefferson, Allen to Ann Williams 3-30-1842 (4-30-1842)
Jeminsopn, G. W. to Lorinda Grogain 9-30-1861
Jenkins, Alney? M. to Emily W. Bodine 2-17-1854
Jenkins, Champion H. to Maria Bransford 9-11-1847
Jenkins, J. T. to Z. T. Evans 1-14-1867 (1-18-1867)
Jenkins, James to Mildred Johnson 5-13-1852 (5-15-1852)
Jenkins, Jas. T. to Sarah F. Allen 6-29-1865
Jenkins, John D. to Mary E. Morris 5-10-1866
Jennett, J. R. to Mary A. M. P. Bowers 12-19-1860 (12-20-1860)
Jennings, John M. to Tennessee Outlaw 12-5-1862 (12-9-1862)
Jerdan, Anderson to Clarissa Jerdan 1-4-1867 [b]
Jessup, H. C. to Nina M. Cobb 12-27-1865
Jeter, Mathew A. to Nancy Mildred Trice 4-17-1852 (4-19-1852)
Jett, R. W. to Mary E. Crenshaw 4-12-1860
Jewell, James to Martha A. Todd 2-13-1852
Jinkins, C. H. to C. P. Ballentine 12-15-1840 (12-16-1840)
Jitt, Edward to Elizabeth Taylor 5-16-1840
Jobe, James to Elizabeth T. Stephens 11-13-1845
Joda?, Wm. to Catharine Winters 1-28-1844
Johnson, B. D. to Hellin Hollins 1-19-1863 (1-22-1863)
Johnson, B. W. to Clay Munford 12-5-1865 (12-6-1865)
Johnson, Ben to Martha Johnson 4-28-1866 (5-20-1866) [b]
Johnson, Burton to Martha McKinney 9-22-1845
Johnson, Cave to Elizabeth Brunson 2-20-1838
Johnson, Charles to Eliza Martin 11-24-1865
Johnson, E. W. to Caroline Roggers 1-11-1867 (1-13-1867) [b]

Johnson, Edward S. to Almeta Trice 7-22-1865 (7-23-1865)
Johnson, Edward S. to Editha Ann Trice 6-28-1856 (6-29-1856)
Johnson, Fauntly to Lucy Hem 11-5-1859 (11-8-1859)
Johnson, Geo. H. to M. A. McCommack 10-23-1843 (10-31-1843)
Johnson, Geo. H. to Mary A. McConnick 10-23-1843 (10-31-1843)
Johnson, George W. to Virginia M. Brodie? 7-17-1853
Johnson, Harmon F. to Anna Crank 3-22-1841 (3-25-1842)
Johnson, J. H. to Mary Chester 11-3-1855
Johnson, James C. to Frances Elizabeth Coleman 5-6-1847
   (5-14-1847)
Johnson, James T. to Ann D. Jett 9-25-1860 (9-27-1860)
Johnson, James to Mahala Johnson 4-8-1861
Johnson, John H. to Julia A. Coleman 9-24-1859 (9-25-1859)
Johnson, John T. to Rebecca Johnson 3-25-1854 (3-26-1854)
Johnson, John to Harriett Cross 6-5-1865
Johnson, Jonathan L. to Catharine W. Killibrew 11-26-1840
Johnson, Joseph T. to Louisa M. Barksdale 3-14-1854
Johnson, Mose to Cella Dennis 12-8-1866 [b]
Johnson, Nathan S. to Elizabeth J. Watson 12-1-1856
Johnson, Nelson to Ann Monford 12-26-1866 (12-28?-1866) [b]
Johnson, P. A. V. to Rosana B. Johnson 4-3-1849 (4-5-1849)
Johnson, Pascal to Jane Moore 11-13-1847
Johnson, Robt. W. to Jennie E. Drane 7-30-1860 (7-31-1860)
Johnson, Samuel J. to Mary B. McCain 1-20-1859
Johnson, Thos. E. to Ellin E. Powers 7-23-1864 (7-24-1864)
Johnson, W. L. to Sarah Thompson 11-23-1843
Johnson, W. T. to S. A. Bumpass 5-9-1857 (5-19-1857)
Johnson, William J. to Mary S. Chiles 1-2-1855 (1-4-1855)
Johnson, Wm. C. to Elizabeth Riter 3-31-1840
Joiner, Abraham to Suena Taylor 1-20-1866 (1-21-1866) [b]
Joiner, Thomas to Eliza Eaton 1-18-1843 (2-19-1843)
Joins, Burrell jr. to Mary Jane Ellis 12-28-1844
Jolly, Edwd. M. to Rebecca Brim? 12-10-1843
Jolly, Wilis to Louisa Skeggs 5-4-1856
Jones, Alfred to Delila McFerson 2-16-1857
Jones, Charles to Elenor E. Birch 10-22-1847
Jones, E. B. to Dorothy Powers 5-23-1842
Jones, Elisha J. to Mary H. Dorson 1-13-1866 (1-17-1866)
Jones, Ezekiel to Virginia Gordon 4-11-1840 (5-14-1840)
Jones, George to Lovicy Rinehart 4-5-1848
Jones, George to Martha Morris 4-11-1839
Jones, Henry to Alletta E. Cromwell 4-27-1848 (4-29-1848)
Jones, Henry to Martha Woodson 1-5-1866 [b]
Jones, Isham to Martha E. Trotter 9-2-1865 (9-4-1865)
Jones, James C. to Eliza Jones 2-6-1844
Jones, James C. to Lucy A. Johnson 2-1-1847 (2-4-1847)
Jones, James G. to Charity Morrisson 12-4-1839 (12-5-1839)
Jones, James H. to Catharine Hurst 4-20-1848
Jones, James H. to Martha Jones 2-13-1852
Jones, John H. to Finetti Shadwick 5-12-1841
Jones, John J. to Martha Jenell 12-13-1848
Jones, John L. to Hany Fall 10-23-1846
Jones, John M. to Mary Ann Lyle 1-12-1848
Jones, John T. to Sarah W. Jones 12-5-1849
Jones, John Thomas to Elizabeth W. Jones 11-10-1859
Jones, John W. to Mary W. Fort 5-13-1864 (5-18-1864)
Jones, Joseph M. to Frances H. Kendrick 4-20-1844 (5-1-1844)
Jones, Joshua Jorden to Easter Millin 8-24-1857 (8-26-1857)
Jones, Matison to Elizabeth Coon 12-23-1845
Jones, Robert J. to Mary Jane Weakley 7-20-1844 (7-25-1844)
Jones, Robert to Mary Majors 3-5-1846
Jones, Samuel C. to Mary Ann Bumpass 2-11-1858
Jones, Samuel P. to Martha Jane Harrison 12-30-1855 (12-20?-1855)
Jones, Shelby W. to Mollie Hunt 4-4-1866 (4-5-1866)
Jones, T. C. to Nancy E. Morriss 10-29-1863 (11-2-1863)
Jones, Thomas C. to Bettie Harris 9-26-1865 [b]
Jones, Thos. A. to Ethalinda(Catharine) Broddie 9-9-1846 (9-10-1846)
Jones, W. H. to T. H. Jones 8-2-1865
Jones, Willis B. to Sally Ann Steely 1-15-1847 (SB 1848?)
Jones, Willis to Susanah Jones 5-28-1850
Jones, Wm. J. to Susan W. Jones 9-3-1851
Jones?, Alsey to Doratha Lankford 1-26-1841 (1-28-1841)
Jordan, Adam to Martha Ann Farmer 10-30-1856
Jordan, John H. to Mary H. Stovall 3-10-1863 (3-14-1863)
Jorden, Robert B. to Dolly K. Horton 12-20-1858 (12-21-1858)

Jorden, West to Amelia Cook 11-17-1859
Jorden?, Saml. to Polly Hancock 12-30-1846
Jordon, Howel T. to Lucy A. Kendrick 10-25-1841 (10-28-1841)
Jordon, James Richard to Eliza C. A. Handy? 6-28-1848 (6-29-1848)
Kagle, Elijah to Nancy Midcastle 7-9-1844
Keath, John W. to Mary F. Terrell 11-17-1845
Keats, Anderson to Elizabeth Duncan 4-6-1864 (4-7-1864)
Keats, Charles Logan to Narcissa Drue Morris 5-19-1853 (5-22-1853)
Keats, Henry W. to Susan Ann Sally 2-2-1858 (2-4-1858)
Keats, Thos. G. to Jane Brantley 11-26-1862
Keel, John W. to Sarah Mays 3-17-1848 (3-19-1848)
Keel, Nathaniel to Penesa Wortham 11-5-1866
Keeler, Robert W. to Catharine Dunlap 9-4-1860 (9-13-1860)
Keesee, B. O. to Cornelia R. Peaches 7-27-1852
Keesee, John W. to Louiza Deane 2-15-1859
Keesee, P. H. to Mary E. Ussery 12-20-1855
Keesee, Robert to Annie Ogburn Howard 3-24-1866 (3-31-1866) [b]
Keesee, Thomas to Puss Gupton 7-23-1866 [b]
Keeser, Reuben C. to Judith P. Ligon 12-30-1839
Keeth, Joseph to Samuella Buck 11-24-1847 (11-25-1847)
Kellow, John to Allis Mathis 12-13-1865
Kelly, John D. to Mary Gower 5-19-1845
Kelly, John W. to Mary Lamaster 8-2-1841
Kelly, Michael to Nancy Carroll 7-23-1858 (7-24-1858)
Kelly, Peter to Mrs. Fannie Broadbent 3-30-1861
Kelly, Quince to Margaret Petters 11-8-1866 [b]
Kelly, T. to Mrs. Ann Nester 5-7-1862 (5-8-1862)
Kelly, Timothy to Mary Ford 12-9-1857 (12-14-1857)
Kelly, William M. to Ann B. White 10-10-1849
Kenady, John F. to Nancy J. Tine? 10-14-1841
Kendrick, Cager to Carolin Wood 8-16-1866 [b]
Kendrick, Green to Amanda Dinwooddie 10-30-1865 (11-2-1865) [b]
Kendrick, Henry to Henrietta Smith 1-1-1866 (with 1867) [b]
Kendrick, J. D. to F. J. Johnson 10-11-1864
Kendrick, John F. to Martha C. Evans 1-25-1854
Kendrick, Wm. A. to Harriett Jones 7-8-1865 (7-9-1865)
Kennedy, David N. to Sarah A. Bailey 11-22-1843
Kennedy, James H. to Joanna E. Corban 6-2-1856
Kennedy, Jas. L. to Sallie M. Harris 12-17-1866 (12-18-1866)
Kennedy, John to Harriett Fry 6-18-1866 [b]
Kenner, Joseph to Martha Tabb 4-29-1841
Kenner, N. B. to Mary Brantly 6-17-1858
Kephart, W. F. to Sarah E. Trundle 8-4-1866 (8-7-1866)
Kestner?, William to Polly Rineheart 4-6-1839
Kidd, Wm. H. to Alvyra Roberts 5-7-1843 (5-10-1843)
Kilband, James to Margaret Welsh 7-7-1866 (7-9-1866)
Killebrew, J. B. to Mary C. Wimberly 12-3-1857 (12-2?-1857)
Killebrew, James L. to Rachael Ann Slaughter 7-19-1859 (7-21-1859)
Kimbrew, Stephen to Arabella Gill 5-21-1866 [b]
Kimbrough, T. R. to Bettie Kimbrough 1-17-1866 (1-18-1866)
Kincaid, Jordon to Aliph Lanier 4-29-1839
King, B. F. to Mary E. Turner 12-15-1855
King, Duncan to Nancy Dailey 4-11-1839
King, Geo. to Polly Wells jr. 1-22-1844
King, J. M. to Mary J. Hoover 12-24-1840
King, Jacob L. to Martha J. Moss 12-10-1857 (12-18-1857)
King, John L. to Emily L. Gilbert 1-8-1855
King, John to Bridget Kelly 12-28-1858 (12-30-1858)
King, John to Susan Sally 1-3-1852 (1-4-1852)
King, Rufus L. to Martha A. Hausdale 12-16-1848
King, Saml. to Polly Vaughan 12-15-1842
King, William James to Ann E. Morrison 2-16-1854 (2-19-1854)
Kirk, John T. to Orlina Rudolpha 12-30-1854 (12-31-1854)
Kirkland, E. to Martha Langston 12-12-1865 (2-25-1865?)
Kirksey, John to Ann Andrews 3-3-1859
Kisee, John A. to Mary C. Edmonson 1-28-1851
Kistner, C. H. to C. T. Morgan 2-3-1863
Kistner, James to Tabitha Rinehart 10-29-1844 (10-31-1844)
Kittinger, Martin to Mary E. Kirtly 11-1-1848
Knight, Jacob to Sarah Ann Rail 9-9-1847
Knight, Wm. B. to Emily C. Dawson 3-11-1844 (3-14-1844)
Knight, Wm. to Susan Josephine Harris 8-20-1852
Knox, James to Carolina Downey 12-21-1859
Knox, Robt. H. to Sophia Jackson 9-12-1843 (9-14-1843)
Knox, W. to Jane Allensworth 6-7-1866 [b]

Kreamer, John to Sally Ann Wiggins 12-20-1845
Kyes?, Thomas to Emeline Powers 7-8-1858 (7-9-1858)
LaRue, James B. to Lucinda L. Tarpley 9-19-1861
Lacey, James T. to Elizabeth Cunningham 5-26-1851
Lackey, John W. to Sarah Harris 2-19-1843 (2-21-1843)
Lackey, Thos. to Lucy Gatewood 10-13-1848
Lacy, D. M. to Lucinda Harrison 10-25-1857
Ladd, Henry to Virginia Ousley 4-12-1855
Ladd, John W. to Lynacy Grubbs 9-17-1851
Laffoon, George W. to Mary Coker 2-18-1848
Lamb, Peter to Eliza Jane Harrison 12-26-1858
Lander, Robt. H. to P. F. Wall 8-7-1851
Landram, Marks M. to Elizabeth Pegram 8-19-1851
Lane, Isaac to Mary Givins 7-24-1849 (7-27-1849)
Langford, Wm. to Georgian Trigg 12-22-1866 [b]
Langston, G. W. to Lucy Ann Tally 1-17-1860 (1-19-1860)
Langston, John N. to Frances Thornsberry 6-28-1849
Langston, Westley T. to Martha Ann Carroll 3-29-1859 (3-30-1859)
Lanier, T. C. to Sarah M. Griffin 1-7-1856
Lankford, Charles W. to E. A. Elliott 9-2-1851 (9-3-1851)
Lankford, Griffin to Mary Shores 12-24-1852
Lankford, W.? H. to Angeline Hudgens 9-24-1846
Lankley, Joseph F. to Ann M. Key 1-26-1852
Larkin, A. N. to Louiza B. Corban 1-2-1859 (1-5-1859)
Larkin, Ebenezer E. to Mary Jane Good 7-1-1856 (7-3-1856)
Larkins, Jas. M. to Emma V. Bagwell 2-19-1866 (2-20-1866)
Lashbrook, Elberd S. to Mildred A. Wells 9-29-1850
Latham, Jacob to Susan H. Driskall 9-26-1844
Latham, John R. to K. M. Slaughter 7-21-1856
Latham, Wm. to Liddy Yates 3-7-1848
Laughran, David to Evilina Pritchard 12-20-1839 (12-25-1839)
Laurison?, William to Nancy E. Shoemaker 12-30-1852
Lawhon, Jasper N. to Nancy Farless 10-16-1851
Lawhon, Martin A. to Lucy Littlefield 12-29-1846
Lawrence, Bellefield to Syrena Reynolds 5-25-1858 (5-27-1858)
Lawrence, Munroe to Amanda A. Tanner 1-31-1847
Laws?, Lewis to Julia A. Richardson 5-28-1856 (6-29-1856)
Lawson, Leander to Augusta Jones 7-9-1866 [b]
Lay, John S. to Sarah D. Averett 4-22-1854 (4-25-1854)
Leathers, F. D. to T. C. Wry 7-30-1847 (8-1-1847)
Leavel, Benjamin to Yurena Kellis 12-26-1866 [b]
Leavell, Benjamin S. to Emma C. Beaumont? 12-3-1852
Leavell, Granvill to Matilda Gold 4-11-1866 (4-14-1866) [b]
Leavell, Preston to Patty Rives 12-29-1866 [b]
Leavell, St. Clair to Mahaly Rives 5-7-1866 [b]
Leavitt, N. L. to M. E. W. Williams 12-26-1865 (12-27-1865)
Lee, Archer to Nancy Bennett 6-24-1853 (6-28-1853)
Lee, B. D. to Arsula A. Smith 3-19-1853
Lee, Edward F. to Bethia Clemmons 8-31-1844
Lee, Ellickzander to Anny Wickley 12-30-1866 (12-31-1866) [b]
Lee, Gideon to Mary Rineheart 12-23-1843 (12-28-1843)
Lee, James B. to Mary Ann Poe 4-7-1860
Lee, Saml. to Sarah Shepherd 6-19-1838
Lee, Stephen to Edith Toler 11-18-1862
Lee, Thomas to Mary J. Morgan 2-4-1866
Leedle(Tudle?), George to Eliza Ann Hawkins 8-24-1859 (8-25-1859)
Legget, John T. to Amanda Adams 3-15-1853 (3-23-1853)
Leggett, Samuel N. to Catharine McCrary 6-1-1859
Leggett, Wm. to Jane Elizabeth Adams 1-10-1853 (1-21-1853)
Leggit, Mathew to Artimisia Rose 1-24-1859 (1-30-1859)
Leigh, Bingham S. to Sally Collishan 12-13-1843 (12-14-1843)
Leigh, Geo. W. to Angelina B. McGinty 11-5-1841
Leigh, Geo. W. to Elizabeth J. Trice 9-9-1850
Leigh, Henry to Elizabeth Peterson 2-24-1841
Lemaster, Ephraim to Mary Ann Olive 7-13-1841 (7-15-1841)
Lemay, James H. to Elizabeth Averet 6-21-1844
Lemle?, Peter to Mary Darnell 8-1-1839
Leonard, T. D. to Fredonia L. Doleney 2-26-1849
Lester, Joshua to Elizabeth A. Johnson 8-16-1849
Lester, Joshua to Louiza M. Johnson 11-14-1855 (11-15-1855)
Lester, William E. to Rosina Mildred Cherry 10-6-1859
Lett?, J. F. to Mary C. Chiles 10-5-1842
Levell, Granville to Matilda Gold 4-9-1866 (not executed) [b]
Levell, John to Sally Baynham 3-28-1866 (4-14-1866) [b]
Levell, Wash to Martha Elliott 2-24-1866 [b]

Lewis, A. R. to Fredonia Edwards 2-14-1856
Lewis, Charles M. to Elizabeth Carver 7-10-1846
Lewis, George T. to Sofronia J. Craig 9-3-1861 (9-5-1861)
Lewis, Henry to Hannah Smith 4-1-1842 (4-9-1842)
Lewis, Hiram to Amanda Harriet Robinson 5-11-1847
Lewis, Hiram to Martha Cain 6-4-1854
Lewis, James K. P. to Mary C. M. William 12-7-1863 (12-10-1863)
Lewis, James M. to E. G. Bartie 1-30-1843
Lewis, Jas. H. to Ellin Ellett 12-22-1866
Lewis, Jas. P. to Nancy J. Vaughn 6-30-1866 (7-2-1866)
Lewis, John to Rachel Outlaw 6-20-1866 (6-21-1866) [b]
Lewis, Joseph to Martha A. Skaggs 5-18-1854
Lewis, R. to E. C. T. Gill 1-15-1851
Lewis, Robert V. to Isabella Boyd 4-14-1856
Lewis, Thos. D. to Mrs. Nancy Sneed 6-1-1865 (6-11-1865)
Lewis, Willis E. to Mary Ann Thomas Craig 3-1-1858 (3-4-1858)
Liggan, David B. to Phebe Ann Sisk 10-18-1854
Ligon, David T. to Sarah L. Ligon 11-24-1859
Ligon, John B. to Demetria L. Ligon 11-13-1856
Ligon, S. M. to Nancy Rinehart 8-23-1858 (8-24-1858)
Ligon, Wesley to Hannah Furgerson 1-23-1867 (1-26-1867) [b]
Ligun?, David A. to Sarah M. G. Lockert 7-23-1846
Linch, Geo. to B. Linch 1-1-1866 [b]
Linch, Prince to Susan Crowder 1-1-1866 [b]
Lindley, W. P. to Laura Lemmons 1-13-1864 (1-14-1864)
Lindsay, M. L. to Susan C. Bearden 5-4-1857
Lindsey, James M. to Martha J. Ferguson 12-29-1841
Linebaugh, Joseph to Mary Jane Reasons 2-22-1848 (2-28-1848)
Lipford, William A. to Barbery Ann Gunn 9-4-1865 (9-6-1865)
Lisenby, Dick to Della Smith 6-23-1866 (6-24-1866) [b]
Lisenby, H. W. to Elinor Ann E. Baines 9-18-1849
Lisenby, H. W. to Sarah Jane Ferrell 10-19-1858 (10-27-1858)
Lisenby, Henry W. to Mary Jane Dyer 5-25-1847 (5-27-1847)
Lisenby, John F. to Susan E. Cruse 3-12-1859
Lisenby, William to Martha J. Booth 1-10-1854
Little, J. K. S. to Julia Ann Paris 5-11-1852
Littlefield, Jehu to Emily Ann Franklin 4-5-1858 (4-6-1858)
Lloyd, Jas. to Adeline Tucker 1-8-1866 [b]
Lockert, Charles D. to Laura E. Holland 12-9-1859 (12-22-1859)
Lockert, James W. to Sarepta S. Wilson 5-3-1852 (5-4-1852)
Locket, D. R. to Sarah E. Woodson 12-18-1850
Lockhart, Harrison C. to Catharine E. King 9-23-1854
Lockhart, Harrison C. to Cathrine E. King 9-23-1854 (9-24-1854)
Logan, Soloman to Matilda Powers 8-27-1854
Loman, John W. to Eliza A. Coffman 8-9-1850
Long, Albert G. to Mary J. Sturdevant 10-28-1855 (10-29-1855)
Long, Andrew to Frances Coward 11-12-1851
Long, John W. to Elizabeth C. Walsh 1-2-1845
Long, John to Eliza A. Wallace 6-9-1855
Long, L. F. to Louiza Jane Wilie 1-25-1854
Longmire, James H. to Mary F. Richards 8-11-1846
Loutzenheiser, William to Lydia Grymes 6-9-1854
Love?, R. to E. A. Hargrave 1-18-1844
Loving, E. T. to Louisa London 3-8-1842
Low, Wm. B. to S. H. Blanks 3-7-1848
Lowe, J. M> to Fannie E. Smith 6-26-1866 (6-27-1866)
Loyd, John to Mary E. Chasteen 11-23-1857 (11-24-1857)
Loyd, Standford to Martha Clinard 1-28-1859
Lucas, George F. to Ann L. Burney 10-13-1856 (10-15-1856)
Luck, Peyton to Elvira R. McCrane 11-9-1847 (11-10-1847)
Lucket, D. A. to Verranda W. Willis 6-4-1843
Lulre?, Wm. M. to L. C. Bradley 10-16-1851 (10-17-1851)
Lunderman, Sam to Barbery Evans 3-10-1866 (3-12-1866) [b]
Lunsford, W. J. to M. J. Davis 12-31-1847
Luson, Jno. D. to Mary J. Funk 1-16-1844
Luster, Joseph to Winney Wiggins 9-11-1841 (9-27-1841)
Luter, John to Mary M. Morrison 2-5-1841 (2-7-1841)
Lutt, Charles A. to Mary E. Duke 5-23-1851
Lyddy, Timothy to Mahala Powers 7-3-1861 (7-6-1861)
Lyle, A. J. to E. F. Martin 11-2-1841 (11-5-1841)
Lyle, Allen to Eliza Woodman 12-13-1859 (12-14-1859)
Lyle, Andrew J. to Eliza P. Sale 10-31-1856 (11-1-1856)
Lyle, Berry to Ally Trice 3-24-1855
Lyle, Ennis B. to Nancy M. Powel 2-4-1861 (2-10-1861)
Lyle, G. B. to Lucy Ann Macklin 10-26-1854

Lyle, Gideon B. to Julia A. Anglen 11-28-1843 (11-29-1843)
Lyle, Golconda to Mary Woodman 1-24-1855 (1-25-1855)
Lyle, James L. to Patsy Moore 7-30-1845
Lyle, Mastin C. to Catharine Lyle 6-4-1864
Lyle, Robert P. to Arabella A. P. Moore 8-27-1858
Lyle, Robert to Kesiah Ann Cross 2-15-1859 (3-3-1859)
Lyle, W. J. to Elizabeth M. Batem 11-22-1860
Lyle, William H. to Malinda M. McCorkle 2-7-1852 (2-15-1852)
Lyle, Wm. to Nancy Jane Bagget? (no date; with 11-1850)
Lyles, Thomas to Vina Hampton 4-7-1856
Lynch, Jas. to Frelove Alexander 8-2-1850 (8-7-1850)
Lynch, William to Martha Marlow 9-28-1840 (10-1-1840)
Lynes, Anselmo to Betty M. Trice 7-2-1848
Lynes, Thomas to Rachael Ruby Mahan 3-19-1847
Lynes, Wm. J. to Jane W. Averiette 5-3-1847 (5-4-1847)
Mabry, John E. to Malinda Davis 3-4-1847
Macklewain, P. to Amy Cherry 12-22-1865
Macklin, H. W. to Martha C. Duke 8-21-1855 (8-22-1855)
Macrae, B. W. jr. to Alice Miller 10-2-1856
Macrae, G. W. to Fannie M. Morris 9-11-1866 (9-12-1866)
Madall, James W. to Nancy E. Davis 2-17-1856 (2-27-1856)
Maddison, Richd. H. to Susan Lewis 2-16-1843
Maddox, Wm. J. to Elmira K. Pinson 5-29-1847
Madison, Richard P. to Susan Radford 1-19-1854
Magaffin, William to Anna E. Gray 8-11-1858 (8-12-1858)
Magarrin, Peter to Elizabeth Fletcher 3-1-1839
Major, James H. jr. to Judith Hunter 10-1-1842 (10-6-1842)
Major, James H. to Jane Hollis 12-25-1851
Major, R. W. to Lucy B. Abbott 3-31-1846 (4-1-1846)
Major, Robert W. to Judith H. Gupton 4-21-1842
Major, Thomas J. to Elizabeth R. Jones 11-28-1853 (11-29-1853)
Majors, James H. to Amanda Walker 10-12-1840 (10-15-1840)
Majors, James H. to Jane Hollis 9-25-1851
Malen, Bluford to Susannah E. Weakley 12-31-1846 (1-12-1847)
Maliss?, Abner to Sarah Ann Yarbrough 1-29-1853
Mallory, William to Henrietta Sawyer 2-14-1845
Malone, Robert to Nancy Lawson 11-13-1846 (11-14-1846)
Malory, Sam to Jennie Boddie 10-31-1866 [b]
Malory, William B. to Martha M. Harris 10-17-1859 (10-18-1859)
Malory, William T. to Ann Eliza Robertson 12-20-1844 (12-24-1844)
Manion, Ambrose to Nancy E. Ingram 10-11-1852
Manion, John A. to Nancy Patten 3-23-1854
Mann, Charles E. to Octavia Wolf 9-23-1839
Manning, Allen to Hilly Ford 3-17-1838
Manning, James to Eberline Gilbert 10-23-1852 (10-28-1852)
Manning, Robert to Tenny (Jenney?) Lee 12-13-1860
Manning, William to Alice James Calesham 10-6-1853 (10-7-1853)
Mansfield, John A. to Lucinda Pendleton 8-21-1845 (8-21-1844?)
Mansker, James to Jane Anderson 12-10-1844
Manson, Alex W. to Etha B. Ogburn 2-17-1866 (2-20-1866)
Manson, John P. to Martha E. Allen 2-17-1866 (2-20-1866)
Manson, Thomas H. to Sally E. Balthrop 11-23-1858
Mansons?, G. L. to Sally Wisdom 8-9-1849 (8-14-1849)
Marable, G. W. B. to E. J. Nolen 8-3-1866 (8-5-1866)
Marable, James A. to Mary E. Ogburn 12-22-1845
Marable, James A. to Mary J. Bellamy 3-25-1854 (3-28-1854)
Marable, John H. jr. to Mrs. Eudina H. Smith 11-12-1844 (11-13-1844)
Marable, John T. to M. A. Edwards 4-28-1865 (4-29-1865)
Mardis, James to Rachael Lynes 9-25-1855 (10-9-1855)
Marion?, William to Lucy Israella Ingram 12-30-1857 (12-27?-1857)
Marklin, H. G. to Rebecca J. Tomlinson 5-24-1866
Marquis, Robert to Martha P. Pool 4-25-1848
Marr, Peter N. to Eliza Margarette Buck 10-24-1840
Marsh, William to Mrs. Mary Bowls 9-12-1865 (9-13-1865)
Marshall, Benjamin T. to Eliza Jobeler? 10-16-1838 (10-18-1838)
Marshall, Berton to Martha A. Gilford 3-23-1854
Marshall, George W. to Jane Manning 10-12-1853 (10-13-1853)
Marshall, J. W. to Nancy Wales 6-21-1852 (6-22-1852)
Marshall, James W. to Mary Jane Grant 9-23-1846 (9-24-1846)
Marshall, S. R. to Sarah Ann McFall 1-24-1850
Marshall, William J. to Nancy D. J. Browning 9-20-1840 (9-21-1840)
Mart, Wm. J. to Mary J. Atkinson 12-30-1852
Martin, Albert to Elizabeth Bass 10-22-1866 [b]
Martin, Ambrose to Frances Mockbee 11-2-1842

Martin, Bradley to Adaline Ogburn 10-1-1850
Martin, Elijah to Elizabeth Powers 12-16-1840
Martin, Fred to Isabella Ogburn 3-24-1866 (3-31-1866) [b]
Martin, George D. to Susan Henry 1-15-1855
Martin, James E. to Marian Jones 10-25-1852 (12-25-1852)
Martin, James E. to Nancy Eley 4-29-1857 (5-1-1857)
Martin, James L. to Frances J. Shulas 10-9-1854 (10-10-1854)
Martin, James to Lavinia Alley 8-9-1841
Martin, James? M. to Delana L. Allen 3-19-1851
Martin, Jno. R. to M. J. Anglen 1-16-1849 (1-18-1849)
Martin, John D. to Mary J. McGee 6-5-1842 (5?-5-1842)
Martin, Madison to Malvina Harris 10-13-1840
Martin, P. D. to Margaret Voss 5-31-1850
Martin, R. B. to Agness Garrett 11-25-1845 (11-26-1845)
Martin, Richard O. to Mary Dean 3-29-1852
Martin, S. G. to Melissa M. Calesham 12-12-1859
Martin, Smith to Sally Gill 10-29-1866 [b]
Martin, Stelring N. to Almeda J. Lyle 11-26-1853
Martin, Thomas to Elizabeth Bull 9-27-1843 (9-28-1843)
Martin, William to Mary Hagie 7-22-1852
Martin, William to Sallie Beachert 11-3-1856
Massey, Walt S. to Martha A. McCallister 9-2-1847
Mather, Drury M. to Mary Elizabeth Harper 12-22-1846 (12-24-1846)
Mathews, B. to Sarah Weakly 12-28-1847 (12-30-1847)
Mathis, John W. to Harriet T. Baird 2-10-1857 (2-11-1857)
Mathis, Samuel J. to Louiza T. Morrow 12-17-1858
Matthis, Buckner to Elizabeth Jones 12-10-1841 (12-16-1841)
Mauzy, Napoleon to Agness Griffin 9-3-1840
Mavuty?, James to Arrabella Corlew 7-28-1843 (8-2-1843)
Maxey, A. B. to Moley V. Bailey 1-17-1867
May, John W. to Mary M. Morgan 3-17-1864
May, John to Ann K. Hunt 3-18-1848 (3-19-1848)
May, W. H. to Narcissa Green 11-19-1854
Mayberry, Thomas to Rebecca Mockabee 10-20-1848
Mayfield, Darby N. to Ellen Elder 11-18-1865 (12-28-1865) [b]
Mayfield, LaFayette J. to Frances A. White 12-2-1864 (12-8-1864)
Maynard, James Henry to Mary E. Massey 8-13-1840
Mays, Henry to Nely Burnett 4-21-1865 [b]
Mays, T. J. to Ruth A. McElvain 7-19-1855
Mays, W. D. to Sarah Ann Duke 6-30-1847 (7-1-1847)
McBride, Charles W. to Susan Ann Johnson 7-27-1853
McBride, William P. to Delila Claxton 7-29-1858 (7-30-1858)
McCall, Alpheus W. to Charlotte Ann Fall 4-17-1856
McCarnes, Alliner to Mary Powell 10-30-1845 (11-4-1845)
McCarroll, James E. to Susan Stevinson 8-30-1854
McCarter, Robert to Elizabeth Shepherd 11-4-1861 (11-5-1861)
McCarver, Olliver to Mary Ann Powers 8-24-1857 (8-26-1857)
McCauley, George D. to Nancy A. Allbright 10-24-1866 (10-25-1866)
McCauley, Isaac to Fanny Smith 7-21-1866 [b]
McCauley, John to Louisa Bingham 5-3-1842
McCauley, Murdock to Tennessee Jackson 12-18-1850 (12-19-1850)
McCaulley, Wilay to Mary A. Mills 1-8-1867
McClain, Hugh B. to Rhoda Ann McClanahan 10-15-1848
McClolpin?, Andrew J. to Rachel Eliza Cuisty? 9-3-1849
McClure, Frank to Carrie Finley 11-17-1866 (11-18-1866) [b]
McClure, W. C. to E. J. White 3-31-1846
McComack, James to Nancy Godsey 3-12-1861
McCorkle, Clement to Adaline Regions 2-25-1846 (2-29-1846)
McCrae, Richard K. to Pauline E. Wood 2-16-1857 (2-19-1857)
McCraw, Wm. B. to Huctus Hill 3-23-1840
McCulley, William S. to Parthenia Phillips 3-20-1866 (3-21-1866)
McCullick, Thos. to Ann Norfleet 1-23-1844
McCulloch, Thomas to Mary J. Pickering 3-12-1838
McCurdey, Murdock to Lucey Ann Jackson 1-27-1853
McCurdy, G. to Mary Ross 2-16-1847
McCurdy, Thomas S. to Martha A. McCawly 3-21-1846 (3-25-1846)
McDaniel, A. to Sue E. Barbee 12-22-1857
McDaniel, John W. to Ann E. Small 10-23-1851 (10-26-1851)
McDaniel, Wm. A. to Barbary Carter Stacks 2-22-1845 (4-2-1845)
McDermot, Robert to Nancy Griffith 9-2-1847
McDonald, Chas. to Mary Ragon 9-15-1862 (9-18-1862)
McDonnall, James to Fannie Byrne 3-4-1865
McEntire, Horace to Harriett Rinehart 4-24-1865 (4-25-1865)
McEntire, John to Winney Wiggins 3-28-1853
McEwin, John to Parnelia Powers 4-13-1859 (4-15-1859)

McFadden, Wm. R. to Emily J. Davis 2-17-1846 (2-19-1846)
McFaddin, A. V. to Nancy Herring 4-7-1846
McFaddin, George to Adaline Wilkins 11-17-1857
McFadin, David W. to Lucy W. Jackson 1-23-1845
McFerlin, Andrew J. to Martha A. Winders 1-19-1843
McFursian, George to Nancy Jones 1-9-1867 [b]
McGahee?, Samuel C. to Ann E. Driskill 4-19-1849
McGee, Benjamin F. to L. S. Davis 6-28-1842
McGee, Brunson to Mary H. Holcomb 11-21-1854
McGee, G. H. to Mary J. Buckingham 9-30-1852
McGee, Joseph N. to Ann Bristo 12-30-1857 (12-31-1857)
McGee, Wm. W. to Mary N. Malory 12-10-1849 (12-21-1849)
McGeehee, James L. to Martha Baugh 8-8-1838 (8-14-1838)
McGehehee, James O. to Marinia Landcaster 3-15-1853
McGehee, Sampson to Sarah Furguson 12-17-1841
McGehee, W. C. L. to Mary George 6-7-1848
McGinnis, James to Cynthia Seay 2-21-1860 (2-23-1860)
McGriggar, W. B. to Ruth E. Wilson 10-2-1856 (10-9-1856)
McGuire, Bernard to Pamela A. E. Coleman 3-28-1849
McGuire, Hugh to Elizabeth Baker 9-11-1847 (9-12-1847)
McGuire, Thomas to Martha Jackson 10-12-1848
McKennon, Daniel A. to Martha A. Clifton 9-23-1856
McKew, Jo to America Lancaster 12-22-1859
McKinley, Peter to Tennessee Creamer 9-26-1850
McKinney, J. M. to Martha A. Baker 11-5-1846
McKinney, James M. to Martha Tucker 2-13-1847
McKinnon, Kenneth to Amanda A. Jarrell 12-23-1851
McKinnon, Kenneth to Margaret Oldham 11-30-1858
McKoin, John G. to Mary Jane Barker 2-13-1840
McLean, David D. to Dorinda Casper 2-25-1858 (2-28-1858)
McLean, John S. to Susan P. Marr 6-29-1857 (6-30-1857)
McLean, Malcom to Elizabeth Ann Casper 7-28-1858 (7-29-1858)
McLemore, John C. to Temperance E. Davenport 10-26-1850
McMalin, Dick to Marthy Baggett 12-31-1866 (1-8-1867)
McManus, Thos. to Mary H. Jackson 8-4-1865
McMeans, J. R. to Sally E. Willis 9-1-1841
McMurphy, M. to Mary McCarty 2-23-1863
McMurray, William to Susan R. Collins 1-29-1856
McMurry, J. J. to Catharine Warden 11-19-1849 (11-20-1849)
McNeil, A. J. to M. L. Hamlet 10-2-1865 (10-6-1865)
McNeil, Henry to Virginia Miller 5-11-1854
McNeil, Samuel J. to Mary Ann Jackson 5-10-1858
McNichols, James T. to Wilmoth Terrel 10-11-1865 (10-12-1865)
McPherson, John H. to Margaret Whitacer 4-18-1861
McQuary, James A. to Mary C. Flack 1-12-1854
McQuary, Thornton to Penelopee Jackson 2-20-1865
McQueene, Michael to Ann Britt 9-2-1854
McQuerry, William S. to Martha Jane Bunting 12-27-1847
McQuerter, Reuben to Jane Cowan 6-12-1839 (6-27-1839)
McReynolds, Soloman to Bitsey Edington 1-17-1867 [b]
McReynolds, W. O. to Susanna H. Robinson 5-29-1860
McReynolds, W. S. to Mary A. Jett 9-28-1847
Meacham, James H. to Elizabeth Tolar 7-20-1852
Meek, John C. to Eliza Sears 5-1-1854
Meesman, James to Priscilla Broink? 10-14-1846 (10-22-1846)
Megarren, Charles F. to Mrs. Medora M. Fletcher 12-13-1864 (12-14-1864)
Mehlhop, John Frederick to E. L. Scott 1-29-1862
Melson, John E. to Harriet Gupton 9-27-1845 (9-28-1845)
Meneese, J. T. to Nannie(Demetria?) A. Goodwin 11-9-1859
Menifee, Samuel W. to Syrnia(Lorrania?) L. Dean 11-4-1859 (11-8-1859)
Merritt, Jas. K. M. to Elizabeth A. Chester 12-7-1865
Merriweather, James H. to Lucinda B. McClure 3-9-1840 (3-10-1840)
Merryweather, Nick to Sarah Naswerthy 1-19-1867 [b]
Metcalf, C. J. to J. P. Keesee 7-9-1860 (7-10-1860)
Metcalf, Edmond to Grace Osbern 2-9-1867 (2-16-1867) [b]
Metcalf, Joseph N. to Editha A. Allen 10-15-1866 (10-16-1866)
Metcalf, Tom to Mary Lacy 7-19-1866 [b]
Metcalf, V. M. to Ellen D. Kellibrew 12-27-1855
Metcalfe, C. W. C. to Elizabeth D. Whitfield 8-8-1838 (8-14-1838)
Micle, John C. to Lucinda L. Phillips 3-10-1857
Miles, M. M. H. to Nancy A. Jones 1-7-1851 (2-5-1851)
Miles, Nathaniel J. to Mary E. Mallory 3-24-1856 (3-25-1856)
Miles, Sam to Catharine Griggsby 2-1-1867 [b]

Miles, Thos. J. to Martha J. Smith 10-4-1850
Miller, Elcaner to Hannah Lewis 5-20-1848 (5-28-1848)
Miller, Eleanor to Dycy Bagget 5-24-1840 (5-26-1840)
Miller, J. M> to Amanda A. Balsett? 6-28-1856
Miller, John C. to Mary E. Orndorff 1-23-1855
Miller, Martin to Eliza Jones 1-11-1861
Miller, Theodore to Mary L. Johnson 9-29-1853
Miller, William L. to Melissa Petty 4-29-1853 (4-30-1853)
Mills, John to Eliza J. Kenner 11-10-1860 (11-14-1860)
Mills, Thomas to Caroline Pritchard 9-15-1842 (9-16-1842)
Milom, George T. to Sally B. Trice 10-19-1848
Mimms, Thos. S. to J. S. Taliafaro 9-15-1862
Minnis, George C. to Isabella J. Herndon 8-16-1852 (8-17-1852)
Minor, Chas. to M. J. Parchment 8-5-1866
Minor, Henry to Sally E. Wyatt 1-21-1856 (1-22-1856)
Minor, Peter to Mariah Davis 1-26-1867 (1-27-1867) [b]
Mitchel, C. T. to Malvina Blane 11-23-1850
Mitchell, Jas. to Milly Stewart 4-22-1865 [b]
Mitchell, Johnathan H. to Mrs. M. J. Wilburn 11-16-1865
Mixen, William to Susan Mixen 7-22-1858
Mixion, Allin to Mary E. Williams 12-19-1866
Mixon, John to Elizebeth Suggs 2-27-1857
Mockabee, John to Caroline Darnell 2-22-1847
Mockbee, Joseph H. to Mary E. Gray 1-29-1863
Molaney, Owen to Mary Ann Markland 10-3-1846
Monroe, J. B. to Nancy Ann Cotrell 2-10-1849 (3-1-1849)
Monroe, S. H. to Lou. F. Crockett 6-26-1860
Montgomery, William H. to Elizabeth A. Holt 4-11-1854
Moodie, F.B. to Roxana Tarwater 3-17-1863 (3-24-1863)
Moody, Abner to Quintalia E. Thweatt 12-7-1864
Moody, Guss to Nora Mathis 11-5-1866
Moody, Henry to Mrs. S. Gamble 8-5-1862 (8-7-1862)
Moody, James M. to Acenith Shelby 2-3-1856
Moody, John to Ester Ramey 9-27-1865 (9-29-1865)
Moody, L. D. to Minnie Norfleet 10-28-1865 (11-2-1865)
Moore, Albert to Lila Anderson 8-6-1866 [b]
Moore, Charles F. to Winey Kelly 2-21-1852
Moore, D. G. to Jane M. Cocke 9-15-1838
Moore, David to Martha Martin 5-26-1866 (6-4-1866) [b]
Moore, Dock to Barbary Johnson 4-8-1865 (4-9-1865) [b]
Moore, Edward D. to Susan J. Barber 6-17-1853 (6-19-1854?)
Moore, Elisha to Mrs. Martha Halsell 10-17-1861
Moore, Emmett to Bettie Rives 2-6-1867 (2-9-1867) [b]
Moore, George N. to Mary L. Gatewood 7-6-1854 (7-11-1854)
Moore, J. K. to Mary Tibbs 3-29-1866
Moore, Jno. W. to Lucy E. Ely 11-9-1849
Moore, John A. to Susan Cake 6-21-1865
Moore, John W. to Nancy S. Sturn? 2-13-1854
Moore, John to Patience A. Smith 1-8-1839
Moore, L. B. to Eliza Bryant 11-6-1838
Moore, Lewis to Sue Dillard 1-22-1862
Moore, Page to Bettie Neal 11-24-1866 (11-29-1866) [b]
Moore, Robert S. to Martha H. Alcorn 7-26-1842
Moore, Samuel A. to Sarah P. Fergerson 4-4-1845 (4-8-1845)
Moore, William to Mary E. Orton 8-4-1860 (8-20-1860)
Moore, Wm. to Mary Ann Prestley 11-24-1865 (not executed)
Morehead, Henry W. to Elizabeth Black 3-9-1838 (3-22-1838)
Morehead, Peter E. to Elizabeth D. Stanton 6-29-1845
Moreland, John A. to Margarett ----- 1-29-1839
Morgan, Cornelius E. to Acenith Stewart 6-16-1855 (6-17-1855)
Morgan, Cornelius E. to Emely C. Hogan 12-23-1848 (12-24-1848)
Morgan, J. T. to Nancy C. Ramey 12-12-1865
Morgan, J. W. W. to Mary E. Carden 7-13-1849
Morgan, James T. to Jane Hagan 1-16-1855 (1-18-1855)
Morgan, Morgan J. to Charlotte Price 6-8-1842
Morgan, Samuel H. to Mildred L. Bowling 11-4-1859 (11-8-1859)
Morgan, Wade H. to Margarett Hogan 9-20-1842 (9-22-1842)
Morgan, Wade to Mary Langford 1-26-1849 (1-28-1849)
Morgan, Wade to Rebecca Harney 4-18-1859 (4-26-1859)
Morgan, Willis to Frances Williams 4-29-1865 (4-30-1865)
Morgan, Willis to Fredonia McGehee 6-20-1843 (6-22-1843)
Morgan, Zachariah to Lavitha Mathis 7-28-1853
Morril, John D. to Margaret E. Merriweather 4-30-1845 (5-6-1845)
Morris, Chas. M. to Mary S. Brown 10-2-1862
Morris, George N. to Mary E. Mallory 11-7-1855

Morris, Gustavus to Ruth Elizabeth Broadbent 12-28-1863 (12-29-1863)
Morris, James B. to Susan Armstrong 9-1-1860
Morris, John W. to Martha Mosier 3-22-1856
Morris, John to Sarah G. Williamson 6-20-1846 (6-21-1846)
Morris, Mathew to Martha J. Binkley 2-10-1854
Morris, Nathan J. to Louvina Frances Caudle 3-5-1861
Morris, Ross to Elizabeth C. Starkey 1-1-1851
Morris, Ross to Elizabeth C. Starkey 1-1-1851 (1-5-1851)
Morris, Thos. J. to Emily J. Coon 12-17-1851
Morris, Wm. to Mary Frances Gordon 1-22-1866
Morrisett, Richard to Rhode Davidson 12-?-1838 (12-19-1838)
Morrison, Andrew to Mollie Davis 10-19-1866 (10-18?-1866) [b]
Morrison, Charles H. to Ann Hinton 10-21-1847
Morrison, Daniel to Polly Cock 6-20-1843
Morrison, James P. to Nancy J. Powers 12-30-1856
Morrison, James to Martha Jones 3-30-1842
Morrison, John L. to Sarah F. Starkey 1-3-1856
Morrison, Lewis to Eliza Rose 4-6-1865
Morrison, Robert to Mary Catherine Harris 12-12-1865 (12-14-1865)
Morrison, Thomas to Missouri Ann Trotter 1-4-1866
Morrisson, B. F. to Mary Riggens 1-14-1844
Morrisson, James M. to Mary Hail 10-23-1839 (10-26-1839)
Morrisson, James P. to Sarah M. Davidson 1-4-1839
Morrisson, James to Hannah J. McFaddin 4-5-1838 (4-9-1838)
Morrisson, William to Rosanna Gilbert 2-5-1839 (2-6-1839)
Morrow, George to Elizabeth Black 1-11-1866
Morrow, John to Mary S. Davis 1-2-1850 (SB 1851?)
Morrow, N. B. to D. P. Cherry 1-8-1859 (1-12-1859)
Morrow, Randal to Harriett Tyne 10-15-1841 (10-19-1842)
Morrow, Ransom to Almeda Caudle 7-16-1839 (7-20-1839)
Morrow, Thomas W. to Mary E. Lynes 10-25-1855
Morrow, U. L. to _____ ---- 6-24-1851
Mosely, Wm. C. to Elizabeth Jane Williams 7-16-1846
Mosley, R. D. to Bittie George McCauley 9-27-1865 (9-28-1865)
Moss, John P. to Sarah E. Robertson 4-7-1853 (4-15-1853)
Moss, John R. to Elizabeth Tramell 6-15-1863 (6-17-1863)
Moss, Protheus to Mary E. Trammel 12-12-1865 (12-14-1865)
Moss, Robert M. to Henrietta Clardin 11-11-1850
Moss, Stephen Y. to Caroline F. Gold 1-10-1840 (3-18-1840)
Moss, W. D. to Mrs. Mary F. Davis 11-30-1861 (12-1-1861)
Muir, John K. to Bettie Harris 1-1-1861 (1-2-1861)
Mulkerus, John to Maria O'Donald 7-20-1857 (7-22-1857)
Mullin, Richard to Missouri Tennessee Claxton 1-17-1859 (1-20-1859)
Murphy, Henry M. to Mary J. Franklin 12-29-1852
Murphy, James H. to Celia Ann Woodford 11-26-1846
Murphy, Lawson J. to Silvestey A. Carney 9-29-1852 (9-30-1852)
Murphy, Thos. to S. A. Welch 10-15-1844
Murphy, Willey to Jennetta Bell 1-13-1842
Murphy, Wm. D. to Susan Long 10-11-1844
Murrell, William A. to Eliza A. Cook 10-21-1846
Musgorve, M. A. to Paralee Perdue 4-10-1855
Myatt, Raleigh to Nancy J. Payne 7-28-1853
Myers, Henry H. to E. R. Outlaw 12-5-1862 (12-14-1862)
Myers, John to Martha Ann Hogan 10-7-1856
Myres, Hugh to Sally Breedon 8-21-1846 (8-23-1846)
Myres, James O. to Octavia Bullard 10-5-1857
Myres, Jno. H. to Jenetta S. Dunnivan? 9-4-1849
Myres, John A. to Martha Jenning 12-15-1858
Myres, M. A. to Mary Elizabeth Ransdale 11-3-1855
Myres, Peter to Mary J. Bustam 12-17-1845
Nalin, Johnathan T. to Margaret J. Broddus 6-13-1854
Namey?, William to Elizabeth Cavis 1-21-1847
Nance, Edward L. to Feboe A. Dorson 5-28-1853
Nance, J. P. to M. T. Trice 11-12-1862
Nanney, R. D. to Nancy Nicholson 11-21-1847 (11-21-1849?)
Nanny, Amos to Martha A. Tippet 1-11-1841 (1-19-1841)
Napier, Phillip to Emma Townson 1-1-1867 [b]
Neal, Elijah to Mary Elizabeth Bruce 11-12-1859
Neal, Richard H. to Ann R. Duff 2-9-1857 (2-10-1857)
Neblett, Allen to Belle Ann Neblett 11-11-1847
Neblett, Ben R. to Eliza N. Hatcher 1-21-1840 (1-22-1840)
Neblett, J. S. to Sue T. Orgain 1-31-1867
Neblett, James C. to Sally V. Waller 4-8-1857 (4-9-1857)
Neblett, James E. to Susan E. Rice 11-25-1856 (11-24?-1856)

Neblett, John W. to Mary T. Brodie 9-9-1844 (9-16?-1844)
Neblett, Martin to Martha Roberts 8-26-1865 [b?]
Neblett, Sterling to Eliz. P. McCauley 10-28-1843
Neblett, Sterling to Nancy Caldwell 6-19-1843
Neblett, William H. to Eliza Richardson 12-1-1845 (12-4-1845)
Neblett, Wm. L. to Mary Knott 3-4-1844
Neely, T. J. to Agness Fletcher 5-5-1857
Nelson, Henry H. to Eliza Phillips 3-14-1864
Nelson, John E. to Maria L. Moody 12-24-1860 (12-25-1860)
Nesbett, Richard Montgomery to Sophronia Powers 1-18-1855
Nesbitt, Jas. L. to Martha J. Rye 12-20-1864 (1-11-1865)
Nesbitt, Thomas to Juliann Wickham 5-2?-1838 (5-7-1838)
Neville, G. D. to Armitia Travis 11-1-1845 (11-2-1845)
Newberry, J.? M. to M. E. Martin 1-26-1851
Newell, John McCreary to Marietta Niblett 1-25-1854 (1-26-1854)
Newell, William to Ann Davis 5-2-1841 (5-12-1841)
Newhall, Henry M. to Sarah Ann White 10-15-1849
Newman, Jno. to Elizabeth Yates 10-19-1843 (10-22-1843)
Newman, Wilton to Diantia Sophronia Powers 10-30-1855
Newton, Henry to Harriet Channell 4-6-1857 (4-7-1857)
Newton, William T. to Martha Ann Hardy 4-6-1856
Niblett, John D. to Mary A. M. Harris 9-23-1856 (9-26-1856)
Niblett, John E. to Elizabeth J. Thompson 5-15-1855 (5-16-1855)
Niblett, John M. to Martha E. West 2-23-1854
Niblutt, William J. to Susan T. Harris 1-11-1860
Nichelson, John G. to Susan Wright 9-1-1855 (9-18-1855)
Nichols, Gidion A. to Mary Teasley 1-15-1840
Nichols, Westley to Fanny Parker 1-12-1846 (1-15-1846)
Nicholson, David to Mary Catharine Council 10-1-1860 (10-9-1860)
Nicholson, David to Matilda Carns 12-26-1853 (1-5-1854)
Nicholson, Gideon to Mary Barton 12-30-1852
Nicholson, John D. to Winfred Hunter 3-7-1850
Nicholson, John to Susan Nicholson 9-17-1855
Nicholson, Josiah to Priscilla Gupton 9-16-1844 (10-5-1844)
Nicholson, Major to Nancy Tippet 6-4-1845
Nicolson, James to Sarah Ann Brown 1-24-1849 (1-25-1849)
Nixon, John R. to Treacy Ann Whitfield 8-13-1853 (8-15-1853)
Noel, Walter M. to Penelope Ann Acre 3-26-1855
Nolan, Richard to Harriett Harris 7-7-1849
Nolen, Bluford to Delia Billingsly 11-22-1849
Nolen, James to Henrietta Huse 4-29-1865
Nolen, James to Sally Fletcher 2-24-1842
Nolen, Jas. to Mrs. Sarah Ann Ball 5-17-1866
Nolen, John T. to Sally Ann Horn 7-13-1858 (7-20-1858)
Nolen, Thomas to Elmira Dean 7-10-1853 (7-20-1853)
Norfleet, Knox P. to Mary E. Cuthbertson 11-24-1866 (11-28-1866)
Norflett, Henry A. to Eliza Stamper 11-19-1866 (11-22-1866)
Norris, Albert M. to Georgia Ann Adams 8-2-1849 (8-3-1849)
Norris, Ambers W. to Susanna Powell 2-28-1860
Norris, F. M. to Sallie Channel 9-17-1863
Norris, William to Mary Adams 11-18-1839 (11-19-1839)
Northington, Albert C. to Sarah E. Wade 2-6-1845 (2-12-1845)
Northington, Cordal N. to Sophia Fuqua 1-27-1858 (2-2-1858)
Northington, Egbert N. to Margaret S. Neblett 11-20-1855
Northington, Felix jr. to Susan A. Jones 6-15-1841
Northington, Saml. H. to Mary E. Carr 6-2-1845
Nothington, Dick to Hannah Powell 9-7-1866 [b]
Nothington, Solomon to Nelly Forkner 7-22-1865 [b]
Nothington, Washington to Fany Pennington 6-11-1866 [b]
Nothington?, N. L. to Nannie P. Burruss 7-20-1852
Nott, Thos. to Johnie Sullivan 11-8-1862 (11-15-1862)
Nutt, John E. to Allis Irwin 12-11-1866
Nuvell, D. S. to Mariah C. Jordan 10-31-1843 (11-1-1843)
O'Brien, John to Blanch Herring 12-19-1866
O'Brien, Michael to Nancy Jane Warren 1-17-1859 (1-20-1859)
O'Bryan, Michael to Sally Daniel 6-2-1858 (6-4-1858)
O'Donnell, P. R. to Mary Killroy 4-28-1866 (4-30-1866)
O'Neal, John to Mrs. Ellin Richardson 10-12-1861
O'Rork, Jeremiah to Martha Ann Day 1-30-1862
ODonieley, Joseph T. to Eliz. Williams 4-30-1847
ONeal, Peter to Angelina A. Smith 10-31-1843 (11-1-1843)
Oakley, Green to Elizabeth Ramsey 10-11-1845
Oats, James to Mary E. Campbell 8-7-1856
Oats?, Thos. G. to Elza Dicus 12-17-1848 (12-18-1848)
Odam, John W. to Mary E. Mosure 10-13-1853

Odam, John W. to Mary Masure 10-15-1853
Odam, Malachiah to Betty Ann Wilson 6-2-1858
Odum, John to Patsy Clark 11-6-1846 (11-7-1846)
Ogburn, James to Ann Johnson 12-21-1844 (12-22-1844)
Ogburn, M. W. to Z. A. Smith 12-17-1855
Ogburn, Thomas to Ethalinda E. Jones 9-3-1860
Oglesby, Westley to Mary A. Jenkins 7-26-1860
Ohara, Daniel to Hester Alexander 4-2-1838 (4-5-1838)
Ohara, John to Tennessee Peck 10-30-1862
Ohara, Micheal to Mary Reddan 11-11-1862 (11-15-1862)
Oldham, Elisha R. to Matilda Vaughan 2-26-1841 (3-2-1841)
Oldham, G. D. to Margarett Gray 1-22-1838? (1-23-1839)
Oldham, Geo. W. to Virginia E. Hatcher 10-9-1843
Oldham, J. M. to M. L. Woodson 7-16-1864 (7-20-1864)
Oldham, Jas. to Rachel A. Stewart 6-20-1865
Oldham, Moses to Mary Bell Lyles 7-21-1852
Oldham, Samuel Jessee to Harriet Louiza Holt 12-2-1858 (12-4-1858)
Oliphant, Saml. to Ann Russell 11-8-1865
Oneal, John to E. S. Britten 9-10-1852 (9-11-1852)
Oneal, Marmaduke D. to Margaret E. Ramey 5-26-1858
Oneal, Travis? to Nancy Hardy 1-2-1851
Oneal, Wm. to Caroline H. Moore 10-20-1841 (10-22-1841)
Orndorff, John to Caroline Farmer 10-12-1842
Orne, Richard to Elizabeth Bradbery 1-5-1846 (1-7-1846)
Orrell, James to Elizabeth Gullet 10-10-1847
Osburn, Isaac T. to Mary E. Downey 10-27-1851
Osburn, James B. to Catharine F. Whitfield 1-19-1846 (1-21-1846)
Osburn, John B. to M. B. Trice 12-30-1850 (12-31-1850)
Osburn, John to Amanda Woollard 11-27-1847
Oughton, William to Mary Johnston 3-19-1860
Ouseley, W. T. to Emma L. Parham 1-11-1854 (1-13-1854)
Outlaw, Charles to Margrett Horne 12-15-1866 [b]
Outlaw, G. R. to Martha Adkins 11-1-1843
Outlaw, James E. to Sallie E. Wall 1-3-1861
Outlaw, Jas. M. to Sarah Billingsly 2-10-1849 (2-11-1849)
Outlaw, John F. to Agnes A. Smith 9-19-1848
Outlaw, Joshua to Lucrecia Dilling 8-26-1846 (8-27-1846)
Overbee, William to Mary Jane Jones 5-19-1839
Overton, Alvin to Eliza Overton 5-15-1866 (6-3-1866) [b]
Overton, Daniel to Fannie Wilkins 6-25-1866 [b]
Overton, Robert to Manerva L. Caudle 5-7-1866 (5-8-1866) [b]
Owen, W. B. to Catharine Moore 1-21-1856
Owens, W. D. to Lavina T. Rye 3-13-1866 (3-20-1866)
Ozment, Thos. to Mrs. Elizabeth Jessup 7-16-1866 (7-17-1866)
Pace, B. H. to Martha Crotzer 9-18-1849
Pace, Benjamin to Emily Gupton 1-11-1847 (1-23-1847)
Pace, Carson to Elizabeth Farmer 12-11-1847
Pace, Geo. W. to Elizabeth King 9-16-1851 (9-18-1851)
Pace, Hardy C. to Fredonia A. Norris 6-3-1857 (6-4-1857)
Pace, James H. to Sarah Catharine Biggers 12-28-1852
Pace, Wm. H. to Judy Perdue 1-29-1842 (1-30-1842)
Pace, Wm. T. to Mrs. Ann. J. Waller 11-21-1864 (12-1-1864)
Padget, Merrill to Elizabeth Dickson 8-15-1838 (8-16-1838)
Page, Carter to Elizabeth Ann Byars 12-13-1843 (12-14-1843)
Page, J. W. to Mary E. Dawson 11-29-1866
Page, Robt. B. to Ida Lee 6-1-1866
Page, W. M. to A. J. Weakley 12-27-1854 (12-29-1854)
Pailey, Meridith to Frances Woodward 8-15-1854
Paine, John L. to Eliza J. Robb 12-14-1842 (12-22-1842)
Paizan?, Martin to Catharine Hampton 4-10-1856
Palmer, Wm. E. to Mary E. M. Manson 4-15-1840
Pannell, Morton W. to Sarah Allen 7-29-1841
Parchman, L. B. to Sarah F. Outlaw 1-15-1852
Parham, John to Mary Garth 11-17-1866 [b]
Parham, Thos. G. to Lucinda R. Grady 3-7-1843
Parish, Hudson to Henny H. Fletcher 9-17-1842
Parish, William H. to Matilda S. Howard 12-23-1859 (12-25-1859)
Parker, Geo. W. to Margarett Brockman 4-11-1849
Parker, John B. to Eliza J. Coleman 9-3?-1838 (9-6-1838)
Parker, John to Caroline Southwood 9-8-1842
Parker, Thos. to Elizabeth Wickham 8-26-1864 (8-29-1864)
Parker, W. C. to E. M. Bowers 12-26-1858
Parker, William to Catharine Allen 12-21-1846 (12-22-1846)
Parker, Willis to Elizabeth J. Cross (no date; with 6-1852)
Parker, Willis to Elizabeth Jane Cross 5-7-1852

Parr, Alexander to Mary Morrisson 9-16-1842 (9-18-1842)
Parrish, Allen H. to Mary Ann Catharine Bagwell 9-22-1852 (9-23-1852)
Parrish, M. R. to Susan R. Mathis 5-13-1852
Parton, Hugh H. to Louisa H. Johnson 10-23-1855
Pass, N. W. to Dicy Turner 7-10-1846 (7-11-1846)
Patrick, James H. to Angeline McCauley 1-8-1840 (2-6-1840)
Patterson, John William to Jane Hamlin 12-28-1856
Patterson, William to Charlotte Mathis 7-8-1848
Patterson, Wm. to Elizabeth Duncan 2-18-1860
Paxton, W. L. to L. G. Moss 3-20-1843
Payne, Dick to Margaret Jackson 4-21-1865 [b]
Payne, James E. to Harriet Jones 11-27-1845
Payne, James E. to Mary A. J. Power 1-31-1840
Payne, M. C. to Martha A. Robb 11-7-1849 (11-8-1849)
Payne, Robert S. to Susan Gold 10-24-1853 (10-27-1853)
Peacher, Joseph M. to Mrs. Fannie M. Wynns 4-20-1865
Peacher, Joseph to Mary Hill 3-5-1848
Peacock, H. to Martha McBride 3-29-1849
Pearce, Joseph to Selina Jackson 3-22-1863
Pearcy, James C. to Maryana Wright 10-18-1859
Peck, Francis to Tennessee J. Harris 2-26-1855
Pennington, David E. to Elizabeth W. Shannon 12-19-1843
Pennix, Wm. R. to Martha Bailey 10-15-1839 (10-18-1839)
Pepper, W. O. to Mary S. Eckels 4-3-1860 (4-4-1860)
Pepper, W. O. to Mildred K. Eckles 4-20-1857 (4-21-1857)
Perdew, Bennet to Elizabeth F. Abbott 9-20-1845 (9-28-1845)
Perdue, Charles to Paralee Robertson 12-24-1845 (1-2-1846)
Perdue, J. F. to N. M. Cain 1-6-1855 (1-7-1855)
Perdue, James to Amanda M. Gupton 12-25-1848
Perdue, John N. to Mary E. Lee 6-3-1848 (6-4-1848)
Perdue, John W. to Martha Pace 3-18-1848 (3-19-1848)
Perdue, Spencer to Matilda Beasley 9-3-1840 (9-20-1840)
Perham, Bosalvin C. to Mary Ware 11-8-1864
Perkins, Alfred L. to Sarah Ann Metheny 11-11-1851
Perkins, H. W. to M. J. Mansfield 3-23-1845
Perkins, Harry to Patsy Fletcher 12-27-1866 [b]
Perkins, Tom to Sarah Hester 12-28-1866 [b]
Perkins, W. to Susan Allen 3-18-1862
Perrin, Isaac M. to Louisa A. Carney 1-28-1839 (1-29-1839)
Perrin?, J. M. to F. A. E. V. Gardner 4-6-1841
Perry, Alfred to Mary C. Calvert 8-26-1849
Peterson, Isaac to Margaret A. Long 12-22-1853
Peterson, James B. to Catharine Priestley 11-22-1852
Petree, Richd. to Ann McPherson 10-11-1865 (10-13-1865) [b]
Pettus, David to Martha Ferguson 1-14-1867 (1-26-1867) [b]
Pettus, Thomas F. to Martha A. Cowherd 12-9-1839 (12-10-1839)
Pettus, William to Elizabeth Strother 2-12-1845
Petty, James H. to Harriett W. Jones 5-8-1842
Petty, John Thomas to Martha Pinson 2-25-1853 (3-9-1853)
Peyton, George to Jane Elizabeth Hill 7-22-1858
Phelps, William H. to Martha M. Caro 6-30-1840
Philips, William to Mary Elizabeth Duncan 12-7-1847
Phillip, Wm. J. to Nancy Johnson 12-7-1864
Phillips, A. J. to Ann Maria Crockett 4-11-1864 (4-24-1864)
Phillips, C. R. to Sarena R. Shelby 12-4-1861 (12-5-1861)
Phillips, Frank A. to Ella M. Lofland 2-13-1861 (2-14-1861)
Phillips, Frank to Fannie S. Plummer 8-10-1865
Phillips, George W. to Elizabeth Williams 1-28-1857 (1-29-1865(sic)
Phillips, Preston D. to Mrs. Catharine Crockett 11-20-1861
Philpot, Simeon to Lucinda A. Davis 5-29-1840 (6-3-1840)
Phipps, James L. to Almeda Phillips 5-15-1860 (5-20-1860)
Pickering, Robert H. to Alice G. Ely 1-18-1855
Pickering, Wiley P. to Emily A. Yates 1-21-1867 (1-24-1867)
Pierce, F. M. to H. F. Davis 1-18-1865
Pierce, Thomas F. to Mary C. Glenn 7-12-1860
Pigue, J. A. to Mary Brown 11-8-1855
Pile, Johnson to Lucy B. Brown 9-25-1844
Pillow, Parker B. to Amanda Hollis 4-17-1844 (4-11?-1844)
Pinson, William C. to Catharine Nicholson 9-18-1839 (9-19-1839)
Pinson, William R. to Martha Bailey 10-10-1839
Pirtle, Jno. M. to Nannie H. Rogers 3-6-1855
Pitman, M. C. to Ellen S. Ely 1-12-1858
Pitt, O. G. to Elizabeth A. Randle 1-13-1846
Plant, John W. to Ann F. Williamson 7-26-1845 (7-30-1845)

Plaster, Wm. H. to M. E. Harris 11-26-1849 (11-29-1849)
Plummer, C. B. to Mrs. M Baxter 8-11-1862
Plummer, S. to Rebecca H. Bringhurst 10-14-1851
Poe, E. G. to Julia A. Shanklin 1-12-1859
Poindexter, W. S. to E. H. Everett 6-29-1859 (7-30-1859)
Poindexter, W. S. to Mrs. Mary F. Gee 9-8-1866 (9-10-1866)
Pollard, Byard G. to Susanna C. Herndon 9-16-1844 (9-17-1844)
Pollard, J. E. to Miss Tom Harris 1-3-1867 (1-20-1867)
Pollard, Joseph H. to Eliza M. Boothe 9-19-1855
Pollard, Joseph to Frances Beville 1-26-1841
Pollard, Reuben R. to Mary E. Hatcher 4-18-1842
Pollard, Reuben T. to Nancy C. Britain 10-15-1856 (10-18-1856)
Pollard, Sandy to Harriett Fairfax 5-7-1866 (5-9-1866) [b]
Pollard, Wallace to Martha White 6-9-1865
Pollard, Wm. B. to Mary Henderson 12-7-1843
Pollock, R. M. to E. Brooks 1-8-1866
Pollock, Sanford to Mary Adams 7-13-1845
Pollock, W. M. to Leonard Fowlkes 9-8-1858
Pool, B. N. to Frances Batts 1-25-1855
Pool, Ephraim to Saprina Rutherford 4-10-1854
Pool, Henry J. to Mary Campbell 3-15-1847
Pool, R. S. P. to Elizabeth M. McConnel 10-10-1860
Pool, Russell to Parthenia Davie 12-14-1866 [b]
Poston, Benj. F. to Sallie M. Bruighurst? 5-18-1858
Pottard, George M. to Martha Young 12-15-1840 (12-23-1840)
Potter, Isaac to Nancy Edes 4-22-1844 (4-29-1844)
Powel, Barny E. to Margarette A. Macklin 4-21-1840
Powel, Daniel to Mary Angeline Perry 10-6-1840
Powel, John to Eliza Charnell 12-5-1843
Powel, Levi to Edy H. Dodd 6-11-1843
Pullom, Wiley to Rebecca Martin 1-19-1864
Powell, Hawket to Lila Myers 11-30-1865
Powell, Henry W. to Mary Chanwell 11-20-1847 (12-25-1847)
Powell, J. W. to Lucy Ann Barbee 6-2-1856
Powell, John to Martha Jett 12-19-1853 (12-20-1853)
Powell, Joseph to Rebecca Blanton 2-15-1852
Powell, Ransom to Caroline Powell 4-29-1840 (5-7-1840)
Powell, W. H. to Susan Morrison 2-4-1852
Powell, W. J. to Mary T. Sisk 8-15-1860
Powell, Wilie to Jane Martin 10-8-1847 (10-14-1847)
Powell, William to Sally Davis 1-21-1847
Powell, Wm. A. to Sarah Wilcutt 7-28-1866
Powell, Wm. G. to Nancy L. Beedin 9-15-1846 (9-16-1846)
Power, Arthur N. to E. A. Allen 1-29-1842 (2-6-1842)
Power, Saml. D. to Sarah A. Duff 11-8-1858
Power, Samuel D. to Fredonia M. Major 3-21-1853 (3-29-1853)
Power, Stephen to Mrs. Paulina Williams 3-16-1866
Powers, B. C. to Susan Martin 8-30-1841 (9-2-1841)
Powers, Cas. M. to Elizabeth Dillon 1-25-1839 (1-29-1839)
Powers, Charles R. to Malinda Edwards 11-20-1845
Powers, Francis B. to Almyra Jones 2-6-1865
Powers, Harvey J. to Caroline Ely 12-13-1860 (12-16-1860)
Powers, Henry to Sarah Ann Griffie 1-8-1856
Powers, Hiram to Lucy Terrell 8-10-1857
Powers, Jacob jr. to Margarett Johnson 1-1-1852
Powers, Jacob to Mary E. Harrison 1-3-1857 (1-6-1857)
Powers, James M. to Nancy N. Hogan 9-4-1845
Powers, Jas. Andrew to Eliza Jane Barbee 12-24-1860 (12-28-1860)
Powers, Jas. to Mariah E. Dillon 9-26-1842 (9-29-1842)
Powers, John W. to Nancy Woodleech (no date; with 1851)
Powers, John to Ella A. Lyons 2-2-1846 (2-8-1846)
Powers, John to Jane McKaughn 2-15-1839 (2-19-1839)
Powers, John to Mary Hamrick? 12-19-1859 (1-5-1859?)
Powers, Martin C. to Susan C. Jennings 1-7-1861 (1-22-1861)
Powers, Michael to Parasetta Barker 3-5-1859 (3-6-1859)
Powers, Noah J. to Nancy Farmer 12-24-1856
Powers, R. C. to E. F. Martin 12-19-1850
Powers, R. P. to Mary Nesbitt 10-31-1860
Powers, Robert to Elizabeth Crotzer 12-28-1853 (12-29-1853)
Powers, S. B. to Mary E. Williamson 12-1-1866
Powers, Thomas J. to Margaret Rogers 5-11-1856
Powers, Thompson to Nancy A. Broom 7-24-1860 (7-26-1860)
Powers, Wm. D. to Elizabeth P. Sullinger 8-7-1843
Powers, Wm. H. to Sarah Jane Smith 3-25-1851 (3-16?-1851)
Preastley, Geo. to Fannie Gordan 10-15-1865 [b]

Prentiss, Thos. F. W. to Addie S. A. Pacaud 12-4-1865 (12-5-1865)
Prescott, John C. to B. Sam? 7-8-1863
Prewett, James D. to Margaret Shelby 12-26-1853 (12-27-1853)
Prewett, John D. to Jane Certhbertson 11-14-1861 (11-17-1861)
Prewett, Thomas B. to Martha H. Brame 3-13-1845
Prewitt, William to Frances Evans 5-14-1866 (5-20-1866)
Price, Ajack to Rebecca Milam 1-26-1853 (1-27-1853)
Pride, Halcat to Mary E. Gunn 10-22-1858 (10-24-1858)
Pride, Halcot? to Ellin L. S. Collins 11-18-1856 (11-20-1856)
Pride, Jas. S. to Harriett F. Hardy 4-17-1865
Pride?, Hatcok? to Lucena M. Murphy 12-19-1840
Pritchard, William to Mary Susan Morris 11-3-1852
Pritchard, Wm. B. to Eliza Jane Morris 3-7-1838 (3-8-1838)
Pritchet, John H. to E. J. House 1-10-1843
Pritchett, Elijah to Malinda Ann Hargis 10-22-1839 (10-24-1839)
Pritchett, George to Louisa Yancey 12-13-1866 (12-14-1866) [b]
Pritchett, John J. to Catharine Clift 10-18-1850
Prockter, Edd to Winie Cole 3-12-1866 (3-15-1866) [b]
Prockter, W. H. to Delphia E. Gillum 1-19-1867 (1-21-1867)
Proctor, James H. to Louiza T. Southward 11-25-1853
Proctor, Wm. W. to Elizabeth Ann Southward 2-10-1848 (2-11-1848)
Prophit, Shepherd to Nettie Spernin 11-4-1865 (11-5-1865)
Proudfit, Wellington to Nancy Barret 11-30-1845
Provost, C. C. to Mrs. Elizabeth Nicholson 11-9-1865
Pruitt, John B. to Udora Hallyard 12-16-1853 (12-22-1853)
Pucket, Thomas E. to Martha J. Hargrave 10-9-1853 (10-13-1853)
Puckett, Harrison to Nancy Amandy 11-4-1852
Puckett, Jim to Laura Taylor 12-28-1866 (12-29-1866) [b]
Pugh, Thomas T. to Agatha A. Veall 2-1-1854 (2-2-1854)
Pugh, Wm. E. to Mary E. Walker 12-8-1853
Pullom, Geo. W. to Susan C. Hitt 8-16-1866
Purdy, George G. to Delphina Drury 9-29-1855 (9-27?-1855)
Purnell, George Washington to Hana C. Wilkins 10-27-1858
Quarles, C. L. to Sarah E. Sherrod 5-5-1852
Quarles, David to Matilda Quarles 8-2-1847 (8-5-1847)
Quarles, John to Nancy Hutcherson 10-18-1843 (10-21-1843)
Quarles, Rick to Rachel Solomon? 11-19-1843
Quarles, William J. to Rebecca R. Solomon 12-31-1844
Quarles, William J. to Rebecca R. Solomon 12-31-1844 (1-2-1845)
Quincey, Voluntine to Manna Adkins 10-29-1849
Radford, Henry to Martha Estis 9-8-1866 [b]
Radford, James M. to Martha P. Killebrew 4-5-1853 (4-7-1853)
Ragan, D. M. to Fannie W. Long 1-30-1866 (1-31-1866)
Ragsdale, J. R. to Louvice P. Averitt 9-27-1852
Ragsdale, Jas. S. to Mack Hester 10-28-1865 (11-7-1865)
Ragsdale, R. J. to Louisie? Averett 9-2-1852
Ragsdale, W. E. to A. E. Collins 11-9-1866 (11-20-1866)
Raines, James to Margarette A. McBride 12-15-1838
Ramey, B. R. to Nancy J. Rogers 1-10-1860 (1-11-1860)
Ramey, James M. to Araminta J. Davis 2-25-1857 (2-26-1857)
Ramsey, A. D. to Adaline M. Lord 5-7-1845
Ramsey, Stephen to Margaret Burnine 8-11-1853
Randel, Byack? to Aggey Medley 12-26-1866 [b]
Randell, James P. to Elizabeth Smith 11-8-1838
Randle, George H. to Elvira J. Royster 6-12-1854 (6-15-1854)
Randle, J. N. to Mary F. Johnson 12-15-1860
Randle, Sheron? to Elizabeth L. Grant 11-16-1846 (11-17-1846)
Randolph, Jessee M. to Frances S. Oglesby 10-20-1853
Ransale, D. W. to C. A. Pollard 9-15-1865 (9-17-1865)
Ransdale, John E. to Elizabeth Anderson 10-13-1866 (10-17-1866)
Ransdell, Charles M. to Mrs. Mattie Pollard 5-2-1864 (5-3-1864)
Ranson, C. W. to Mrs. L. B. Sullivan 11-8-1860
Ratliff, Noah to Eliza Ann Martin 12-28-1850
Rawlins, Thomas to Eliza C. Carter 1-7-1839 (1-10-1839)
Ray, Amos to Arena Clardy 3-13-1866 [b]
Ray, Drury to Sally Williams 3-16-1853 (3-17-1853)
Ray, James Henry to Cirena Lucey 8-25-1846
Ray, John H. to Mrs. Emma A. Jackson 1-16-1862
Ray, John to Mary Wiggins 7-7-1840
Ray, Joseph to Letecia J. Jinkins 11-6-1863 (11-10-1863)
Ray, Thomas to Mary Satterfield 11-16-1863
Razor, W. J. to Mary Jane Welsh 5-23-1859 (5-24-1859)
Read, John C. to Martha A. Outlaw 3-25-1851 (3-26-1851)
Read, Lunsford to Letitia Stewart 10-29-1844 (11-15-1844)
Reagan, John D. to George Ann Collins 1-28-1860 (1-29-1860)

Reason, James jr. to Nancy J. Morris 2-12-1842 (2-13-1842)
Reasons, James H. to Jane C. Neblett 4-18-1853
Reasons, Jessee to Margarett M. Morrisson 10-26-1843
Redman, Wm. to H. M. Trice 7-4-1849
Reed, James to Emerline Allensworth 12-29-1865 [b]
Reeder, Henry A.? to Louise J. Moore 10-17-1838 (10-18-1838)
Rees, Thomas B. D. to Sarah E. Moss 11-21-1857 (11-25-1857)
Reeser, G. S. to Mary Ann Bourne 12-7-1852
Revel, W. J. T. to Mrs. Bettie Goostree 5-24-1865
Reyan, Arthur to Telitha McCormac 4-23-1863
Reynolds, H. H. to Caroline West 4-24-1855 (4-23?-1855)
Reynolds, Henry to Mary Marcus 1-12-1855
Reynolds, John W. to Fredonia C. Hase? 9-16-1855
Reynolds, Joseph to Martha Callester 2-12-1852
Reynolds, N. C. L. to Penny? D. Cantrell 10-14-1842
Reynolds, William W. to Sallie J. Smith 10-14-1863
Rhea, Albert G. to Jane F. Stockdal 9-10-1848
Rhea, Hiram W. to Margaret Ann Furgerson 8-16-1865
Rhinehart, Abram to Mary Crotzer 12-20-1843 (12-21-1843)
Rhinehart, David to Ann Crotzer 3-14-1842
Rhinehart, Jacob to Mary Ann Hewett 12-18-1852
Rhinehart, John to Elizabeth Smith 1-12-1847 (1-14-1847)
Rhinehart, Wm. to Sally Cavender 11-1-1843 (11-2-1843)
Rice, Claybourn to Martha A. Wilson 2-3-1858 (2-14-1858)
Rice, Joshua M. to Mary J. Broaddus 5-?-1853
Rice, Samuel A. to Sarah E. Ring 1-22-1855
Rice, Westley to Mauda Beaumont 5-3-1866 [b]
Rice, William to Barbary Knott 11-2-1846
Rich, Reelinghisen to Sidney Ann Rogers 5-14-1865
Richards, A. C. to Ann Blane 1-6-1851 (1-16-1851)
Richardson, Garnet W. to Martha Edmondson 1-13-1848
Richardson, Garnet W. to Mrs. Sallie E. Organ 6-28-1864
Richardson, John T. to Sarah L. Wyatte 5-10-1845
Richardson, Nathaniel S. to Mildred Anderson 12-27-1853
Richardson, Stafford to Adaline Roberts 9-9-1865 (9-15-1865)
Richter, Otto to Lizzie Quin 1-19-1865
Ricon?, Charles to Mary A. Taylor 4-25-1859
Ridly, Thomas J. to Sarah E. Heathcoat 7-17-1853
Riggins, Chas. to Mary E. Cherry 1-13-1852
Riggins, Geo. B. to Bettie Lee 1-18-1866 (1-25-1866)
Riggins, George B. to Isabella F. Cherry 5-25-1859
Riggins, George to Rebecca Jenkins 12-27-1841 (1-3-1842)
Riggins, Henry to Luiza Low 12-25-1866 (12-27-1866) [b]
Riggins, Jackson to Mary W. Harris 12-7-1856
Riggins, John? J. to Sarah T. Buck 12-28-1858
Riggins, M. P. to Fanny Jane McHenry? 4-20-1854
Riggins, P. N. to Mary Shepard 11-21-1866 (11-22-1866)
Riggins, Peter to Ellen Carter 7-7-1866 (7-8-1866) [b]
Riggins, Reuben to Tabitha Pearson 8-17-1853
Riggins, William L. to Rachael Riggins 3-7-1859 (3-9-1859)
Riggins, William jr. to C. M. Shamwell 12-22-1853
Riggs, Jas. L. to E. C. Rogers 11-30-1843
Riggs, Jos. L. to Matilda King 11-8-1842
Riley, Robert S. to Cynthia Scott 9-24-1852
Rinehart, Jacob L. to Mary Ann Hewett 1-28-1853
Rinehart, James to Lucretia Grant 9-9-1854 (9-10-1854)
Rinehart, John B. to Rebecca A. Heflin 12-27-1856 (12-30-1856)
Rinehart, Peter to Martha Majors 12-16-1845
Rinehart, Peter to N. E. Pool 3-9-1864
Rinehart, William to Lockey Harris 2-20-1860 (2-21-1860)
Rineheart, Pleasant to Elizabeth Powers 12-18-1849 (12-20-1849)
Rippey, Jessee to Orlina Black 1-22-1852
Riter, James to Malinda Ballentine 1-4-1841 (1-6-1841)
Ritt, Benj. F. to Larini Mallory 8-4-1859 (8-7-1859)
Rivas?, James to Sarah Davis 5-24-1850 (5-25-1850)
Rives, C. J. to Ann E. Brockman 1-7-1852 (1-15-1852)
Rives, Charles A. to Ann E. Brockmon 1-7-1852
Rives, Henry A. to Eleanor P. Tillotson 4-25-1838
Rives, James T. to Rebecca A. Tamer 9-18-1841 (9-22-1841)
Rives, Jessee to Nancy H. Greenwood 4-28-1849
Rives, John W. to Lucy Moss 12-7-1841 (12-9-1841)
Rives, William V. to Lucy W. Clardy 12-1-1844
Roach, Edward C. to Mollie L. Green 12-12-1866 (12-14-1866)
Roach, James to Adaline J. Little 3-14-1842 (3-15-1842)
Roach, R. M. to Cynthia J. Pain 4-4-1865 (4-6-1865)

Roachel, James to Susan Chance 1-11-1839 (1-12-1839)
Roark, James B. to Sarah Ann Holland 4-22-1845 (4-23-1845)
Robb, Alfred E. to Ellmira E. Paine 1-14-1857
Robb, Edward C. to Evia H. Hester 12-18-1854 (12-19-1854)
Roberson, Howard to Mary Dycus 1-2-1852
Roberson, James M. to Genety Ann Robinson 1-28-1854 (1-29-1854)
Roberts, Collin D. to Martha E. Rainey 10-12-1863 (10-13-1863)
Roberts, George to Mariah West 8-29-1866 (9-8-1866) [b]
Roberts, John to Mary Ann Herring 12-5-1844
Roberts, Nelson to Susan Edmondson 8-4-1866 [b]
Roberts, R. A. to Mary C. Neblett 11-4-1841
Roberts, R. W. to Ann Eliza Neblett 6-22-1859
Roberts, Richard to Margaret C. Bagwell 5-6-1852
Roberts, Richard to Mary E. Duff 12-14-1859
Roberts, Samuel M. to Catherine Williams 3-7-1859 (3-9-1859)
Robertsen, James? L. to Martha Clift 12-14-1842
Robertson, Allen to Margaret J. Walker 2-17-1851
Robertson, Dabney C. to Hannah E. Hendrix 10-28-1857
Robertson, Eli to Eliza Jane Smithwick 5-2-1853
Robertson, George to Mary Walker 10-16-1838
Robertson, I. N. to Delila J. Ramey 9-21-1865 (9-23-1865)
Robertson, Isreal to Elizabeth Hardcastle 7-25-1848
Robertson, Robert D. to Farbary Williams 2-21-1850 (2-23-1850)
Robertson, Robert John Israel to Ann Eliza Vick 11-27-1847
    (12-2-1847)
Robertson, Robert to Mary Ann Rollins 9-9-1863
Robertson, Thomas N. to Mary A. Howell 11-24-1857
Robertson, W. T. to Harriet S. Outlaw 12-26-1865 (12-27-1865)
Robertson, William B. to Nancy Jane Carroll 8-17-1857
Robertson, Wm. A. to Delilah Rhinehart 3-31-1846 (4-8-1846)
Robins, John D. to Jane Lofland 5-4-1865
Robinson, Edmond to ———— ———— 11-28-1846
Robinson, Edmond to Sarah A. Anderson 11-28-1846 (11-29-1846)
Robinson, Edward to Sarah A. Anderon 11-28-1846 (11-29-1846)
Robinson, Isreal to Rebecca Alley 6-24-1864 (6-26-1864)
Robinson, William to Anna R. Buck 12-31-1846
Robinson, William to Annis L. Buck 11-9-1858
Rochel, James to Elizabeth Young 7-28-1849 (8-1-1849)
Rockwell, Wm. H. to Callie A. Milford 7-29-1865 (7-30-1865)
Roger, William to Sarah Gibbs 9-10-1838
Rogers, A. A. C. to Fredonia B. Walker 7-22-1845 (7-25-1845)
Rogers, Edward H. to Adelia Hardcastle 8-3-1842 (8-4-1842)
Rogers, Edward to Susannah Baker 9-27-1841
Rogers, Enoch to Elinor Amelia Crowell 2-12-1847
Rogers, Richard A. to Rosanna Lad 7-22-1860 (7-21?-1860)
Rogers, Thomas to Elizabeth Cocke 9-28-1858
Rogers, Thomas to Mrs. Nancy Waller 1-16-1862 (1-6?-1862)
Rogers, William J. to Arabella Rye 9-8-1855 (9-9-1855)
Rogers, William to Ann E. Ballentine 4-25-1853
Rogers, William to Margaret J. Spencer 6-25-1854
Roland, John to Emma Boofter? 10-13-1863
Roland, W. J. to Virginia Taylor 9-10-1862
Roland, William J. to Elizabeth Jennings 5-14-1861
Rollins, Clayton to Frances Bone 4-4-1842 (4-7-1842)
Rollins, Thomas to Rebecca Ferrell 2-13-1856
Rollo?, John A. to Rebecca Grady 12-6-1847 (12-12-1847)
Rook, John C. to Nancy Proctor 5-28-1841 (6-4-1841)
Roscoe, John to Evelina Watwood 2-7-1848
Rose, Elisha to Ophelia Bradley 3-16-1860 (3-15?-1860)
Rose, George W. to Emma Braytn 3-29-1865 (3-31-1865)
Rose, Isaac James to Rusia Catharine Sanderson 4-11-1856
Rose, James W. to Margaret E. Cartright 12-7-1846 (12-9-1846)
Rose, Wilie to Rebecca Bradly 12-8-1851 (12-11-1851)
Rose, William M. to Nancy Jones 4-16-1844 (4-15-1844)
Rose, Wormerly to Frances Jackson 1-2-1860 (1-17-1860)
Ross, Reuben C. to Frances Johnson 1-27-1849
Rosson, John to Sally J. Morrow 6-5-1848
Rosson, William R. to Ann Elizabeth Pickering 9-15-1857 (9-30-1857)
Rosson, Willis B. to Elizabeth An Pickering 10-23-1866 (10-24-1866)
Roulan, Bradly L. to Lamida? C. Edmonds 4-20-1850 (4-21-1850)
Rousy, Westley to Melica Donley 7-28-1863
Row, Elisha to Emeline Powell 5-30-1840 (6-4-1840)
Rowland, George to Frances Mays 11-14-1842
Rowland, J. E. to M. J. Paterson 9-23-1865 (9-26-1865)
Rowland, James L. to Leander T. Turner 9-14-1865 (9-17-1865)

Royster, C. G. to M. E. Neblett 11-26-1855 (11-28-1855)
Royster, George W. to Eliza M. Vaughn 12-2-1861
Rudd, Ausburn to Polly Ann Greenfield 10-13-1852
Rudd, Balbar to Mary Hightower 1-2-1851
Rudd, Richard to Lavinia Francis 4-7-1841
Rudolp, William to Lucy Wims 1-25-1853
Rudolph, Andrew to Ann E. Carter omitted with 11-1839
Rudolph, Chas. Y. to Fannie S. Rudolph 10-4-1858 (10-8-1858)
Rudolph, Cornelius R. to Catharine Powers 1-2-1854 (1-5-1854)
Rudolph, E. B. to Rachel M. Duvall 1-23-1849 (1-30-1849)
Rudolph, Eli to L. A. Crotzer 1-7-1861 (1-17-1861)
Rudolph, Elijah to Mary Ramey 5-14-1838
Rudolph, George F. L. to Adelia H. Covington 12-11-1854
    (12-12-1854)
Rudolph, James M. to Zuritha J. Winn 12-21-1853 (12-22-1853)
Rudolph, Jno. E. to Susan C. Henning 2-15-1843 (2-16-1843)
Rudolph, John E. to Lucy A. Hargis 8-9-1852 (8-11-1852)
Rudolph, Wm. H. to Elizabeth A. Lockutt 10-14-1846
Rudolph, Wm. to Maggie A. Swift 11-22-1865
Russell, A. B. to Clara H. Beaumont 11-9-1848
Russell, Henry to Patsey Weakley 11-17-1866 [b]
Russell, Silas to Sarah J. Bush 10-26-1846 (10-28-1846)
Ryan, Jeremiah to Lucinda Ann Morrison 6-13-1866
Ryan, Joseph W. to Margaret White 5-28-1855 (5-29-1855)
Ryan, Mathew to Mrs. Mary Quin 3-15-1864 (3-16-1864) [*]
Ryan, Welbern to Puss Duffill 5-5-1863
Rye, A. B. to Sarah J. Bryant 12-14-1859
Rye, H. C. jr. to N. C. Slayden 8-2-1864
Rye, James H. to Lucinda Burney 2-27-1864 (3-2-1864)
Rye, James W. to Palina L. Ligon 10-19-1859 (10-21-1850)
Rye, John R. to Mary Jane Lee 9-29-1866
Rye, Jos. F. to Hellen J. Nesbett 10-31-1864 (11-10-1864)
Rye, Thomas to Ellender Carroll 2-13-1854 (2-14-1854)
Ryon, John G. to Margaret E. Morrison 6-6-1861
Sale, Alexander F. to Trannia? J. Loftland 1-1-1853 (1-9-1853) Sale,
P. L. to Cynthia A. Grigsby 8-30-1865 (9-1-1865)
Sales, Thomas J. to Mary W. Morrison 12-11-1855 (12-20-1855)
Sallee?, Joseph M. to Matilda A. Duncurson 2-7-1838
Salmon, Patrick to Elizabeth Tanner 12-31-1860
Sampson, L.W. to Margaret Clark 11-9-1852
Sanders, Jim to Martha Marable 1-13-1866
Sanders, Wm. to Louisa Riggins 9-29-1866 (9-30-1866) [b]
Sanderson, John to Catharine Sutor 1-29-1845
Sanderson, John to Drucilla Clark 11-24-1855 (11-25-1855)
Sanderson, John to Tennessee Jones 6-15-1863
Sanford, George T. to F. E. J. Harbin? 7-26-1856
Sanford, George to Lucinda Lafoon 12-31-1841
Sappington, E. D. to P. C. Brathet 11-6-1838
Saunders, Nathaniel to Mrs. Harriet Burney 7-5-1845
Savage, Jeremiah to Mary McCauliff 6-25-1859
Sawyer, S. A. to Lucy Gray 10-5-1843
Sawyer, Wilie B. to Julia A. Clark 4-12-1847
Scaggs, Westley G. to Henrietta J. Halsey 1-2-1862 (1-3-1862)
Scales, Allen to Emeline White 2-16-1856
Scarborough, Wm. to Ellen Renner 8-12-1865 (8-13-1865)
Schmittou, J. A. L. to Nancy E. Batson 4-7-1866 (4-8-1866)
Schrodt, John H. to Ellen S. Russell 6-21-1865 (6-22-1865)
Scott, George W. to Margaret Jane Shuff 4-16-1857
Scott, James to Turgey T. Fort 2-25-1848
Scott, John B. to Manervy Ann Brock 3-21-1848
Scott, William to Rebecca Whitaker 2-9-1860
Scudder, Philander to Catharine Hicks 1-15-1846
Scudder, Saml. to Elizabeth Gilbrel 9-19-1843
Scudder, Samuel to Lucy Ann Dycus 9-1-1859 (9-3-1859)
Searcy, William to Jane Dicks 7-25-1840 (7-26-1840)
Searcy, Wm. to Lavicy Gilbert 3-27-1845
Seargeant, John B. to Emerline Cardin 1-1-1866
Seay, A. M. to Mary O. Pollard 8-24-1864 (8-28-1864)
Seay, James A. to Louisa Borne 11-22-1859 (11-24-1859)
Seay, James Benj. to Martha M. Tramell 12-14-1858 (12-16-1858)
Seay, John O. to Sarah E. E. Fletcher 9-15-1856
Seay, Joseph A. to Sarah Ann Shepherd 10-4-1856 (not executed) [*]
Seay, Joseph Alexander to Amanda Frances Burgess 12-28-1853
    (12-18?-1853)
Seay, Joseph(James?) A. to Sally Ann Threat 4-21-1858 (4-22-1858)

Seay, Noah to Mattie Stugall 12-8-1865 (12-10-1865)
Seay, Robert E. to Malissa V. Fletcher 12-19-1855 (12-20-1855) Seay,
William D. to Malinda P. Fletcher 2-11-1852
Seay, William J. to Eliza Catharine Foster 10-25-1858
Seay, Wm. F. to Louisa Seay 1-12-1865 (1-18-1865)
Seevers?, Gabriel to Elizabeth Gate 8-24-1842
Sensing, D. P. to Mary J. Forsythe 10-28-1864
Senter, George to Sarah Bayles 6-29-1839
Senter, Luke to Frances Powers 8-28-1845
Settle, Josiah W. to Elisa Emily Allensworth 10-3-1859 (10-4-1859)
Settle, W. P. to Amanda Galbrath 1-15-1852
Settle, William B. to Margaret J. Keller 9-2-1846 (9-8-1846)
Shackleford, John K. to Ellen Arnold 1-31-1857
Shamwell, William G. to Susan K. Tabb 1-15-1840
Shanahan, John to Mary Daly 6-1-1860 (6-5-1860)
Shanklin, Joseph to Maranda L. Harrison 1-27-1852
Shanklin, Robert to Lucy Creswell 1-27-1852
Shanklin, Robert to Rebecca J. Penney 4-1-1839 (4-4-1839)
Shaughnessy, Patrick to Mary Hays 12-4-1862 (12-6-1862)
Shaw, Ephram to Catha Petty 8-30-1838
Shaw, J. J. to B. A. Harned 4-30-1866
Shaw, J. W. to Martha E. Hubbard 3-22-1846
Shaw, James H. to Sarah T. Murfee 12-23-1843 (12-27-1843)
Shaw, Robert to Hatty Fletcher 12-28-1865 (12-30-1865)
Shaw, Thomas H. to Mary Clark 9-27-1862' (10-1-1862)
Shaw, Thomas J. to Emma A. Jones 5-26-1856 (5-27-1856)
Shaw, W. A. to Harritte Hise 4-27-1840
Shearron, Sterling to Angeline W. Stewart 11-25-1853 (11-30-1853)
Shelby, Even W. to Virginia A. Sallee 4-12-1841
Shelby, Isaac to Eliza Bailey 12-20-1855
Shelby, Urvin P. to Patience H. Shelby 2-26-1840
Shelby, W. H. to Sally A. Walker 9-25-1844
Shelby, Wm. to Mary Balden 7-21-1865 (1-21-1875?)
Shelton, E. M. to E. Hunt 9-15-1862 (9-16-1862)
Shelton, Francis M. to Elizabeth Burnett 4-29-1853 (5-1-1853)
Shelton, G. A. to Sarah J. Garnett 10-16-1852
Shelton, Henry C. to Mary E. Harris 2-8-1864 (2-11-1864)
Shelton, Henry C. to Mary S. Lowery 11-19-1861 (11-21-1861)
Shelton, M. C. to M. A. Madding 4-4-1860
Shelton, S. L. to Cynthia Ann Shepherd 7-6-1860
Shelton, Saml. to Martha Meacham 10-10-1839
Shelton, Samuel to Martha Ann Barbee 5-3-1855
Shelton, Thomas to Louisa Jane Nesbitt 4-11-1849 (4-13-1849)
Shelton, W. G. to Mary Ann Tuiller? 4-30-1847
Shelton, Wesley D. to Margarett A. Latham 1-18-1843
Shelton, William B. to Sarah Catharine Smith 1-27-1862
Shenerr?, Alexander C. to Margaret C. Hooper 2-22-1845
Shepherd, George G. to Nancy Toler 11-25-1855 (10?-25-1855)
Shepherd, James S. to Elizabeth E. Buckley 10-11-1853 (10-13-1853)
Shepherd, Lodwick to Margarette Toller 1-23-1840
Shepherd, Luther to Nancy Shepherd 12-16-1859
Shepherd, Samuel to Frances Brantly 11-24-1858 (11-25-1858)
Shepherd, Samuel to Margaret McClain 7-4-1853c
Shepherd, William L. to Martha Ann Marcom 8-4-1859
Sherell, Jefferon T. to Elizabeth P. Saunders 8-26-1846
Sherrod, James P. to Eliz. A. Quarles 10-12-1843
Sherwood, Jas. to Eliza Carroll 9-3-1838 (9-6-1838)
Shimoville?, William Alexander to Mary Demarius Gray 11-6-1844
    (11-8-1844)
Shird, Lias to Mathy Lewis 12-29-1866 [b]
Shirley, John T. to Virginia Ann C. Epps 9-16-1846
Shockning?, Patrick to Elizabeth M. Gray 4-29-1860
Shoemaker, Randal to Adeline (was Jane) Smith 6-5-1851
Shoemaker, William to Mary Adams 7-18-1856
Shorter, Alston H. to Patsey (col?) Weakley no date
Shote, John W. to Emily Whitsett 12-18-1857 (12-27-1857)
Shrader, Mitchel M. to Mary Hardy 8-9-1854
Shryrock, Saml. W. to Adelaid McKeage 1-30-1855
Shuff, Samuel to Missouri F. Alman 8-16-1865 (8-20-1865)
Shurff, James to Elizabeth Allison 5-19-1857 (5-14?-1857)
Shurwood, John to Rachael J. Carroll 12-9-1840
Sidney, David to Harriett Smoot 12-28-1866 (12-31-1866) [b]
Sikes, Robert to Martha Powell 4-24-1846 (4-26-1846)
Silgus, Asa to Nancy Bunlin 5-1-1856
Simmons, B. C. to Mary M. Hanna 3-22-1858

Simmons, DeMarcus G. to Sue C. Kimble 10-2-1861 (10-3-1861)
Simmons, John to Eliza J. Newman 9-8-1842
Simmons?, Johnathan to Audry Butts 2-21-1848 (3-1-1848)
Simons, A. H.? to A. D. L. Hulett 5-13-1851
Simons, Marion to Eliza Ann Bagget 9-17-1853 (9-18-1853)
Simons, R. A. to Catharine M. Gibson 4-23-1854
Simpson, John Alex to Ann Eliza Davison 1-17-1860 (1-23-1860)
Simpson, William N. to Elizabeth Ann Benham 12-25-1850
Sims, A. L. to Josephine B. Royster 10-4-1858 (12-6-1858)
Sims, Marion to Nancy Baggett 12-26-1850
Singleton, James W. to Mary E. Gafford 6-27-1857 (6-2?-1857)
Singsing, Jno. P. to Eliz. M. Allen 7-5-1845 (7-10-1845)
Sinks, Jas. to Susan Baggett 1-3-1861
Sisk, William to Mildred Sisk 3-10-1841
Sisney, Temple W. to Eliza A. Troxel 9-4-1842
Skipworth, J. C. to Cynthia Ann Jenkins 11-10-1853
Sladen, Wesley to Mary Catharine Campbell 3-3-1858 (3-4-1858)
Slaughter, A. C. to Ann Crawford 11-9-1847
Slaughter, G. H. to Amelia Bowman 10-4-1856 (10-5-1856)
Slaughter, Guilford to Emily Fauntleroy 4-6-1854 (4-15-1854)
Sliney, John to Mary Dalton 11-9-1857 (11-10-1857)
Small, Mathew to Emily Councill 2-28-1856 (4-28-1856)
Smith, A. J. to Mary E. Edwards 12-28-1841
Smith, A. R. to Mary A. C. Rudder(Rudolph?) 4-21-1853
Smith, Alexander to Paralee E. Rudolph 11-10-1857
Smith, Andrew Jackson to Elizabeth Susan Oldham 5-11-1853
Smith, B. R. to A. Brown 11-7-1866 (11-9-1866)
Smith, Benjamin to Sarah Terrell 12-30-1853
Smith, Bryan to Eliza E. Blount 9-21-1855 (9-23-1855)
Smith, Bryant to Martha Ann Elizabeth Smith 8-2-1865 (8-5-1865)
Smith, C. H. to Lucy Dabney 12-9-1856
Smith, Charles G. to Martha D. Johnson 9-28-1859
Smith, Christopher to Mary Gleason 8-31-1858 (9-1-1858)
Smith, David C. to Jane Heflin 2-11-1839 (2-14-1839)
Smith, E. D. to Elizabeth Brown 10-19-1850
Smith, E. J. to Lee Ann Davenport 12-2-1854 (12-3-1854)
Smith, E. P. to Martha N. Miles 1-3-1854
Smith, Eli to Elizabeth Tramell 8-29-1859 (9-1-1859)
Smith, Eli to Harriet Smith 1-20-1861 (2-3-1861)
Smith, Fielding to Emily C. Jelk 4-15-1846 (4-16-1846)
Smith, G. B. to E. B. Bowman 12-18-1848
Smith, G. Washington to Anna Jane McCool 12-13-1848
Smith, Geo. M. to Isabella H. Cruse 9-19-1865 (9-26-1865)
Smith, Geo. W. to Mary Walker 11-22-1866 (11-23?-1866)
Smith, Geo. to Fannie Powell 11-4-1864 (11-11-1864)
Smith, Geo. to Mary Ann Ramey 2-3-1863 (2-11-1863)
Smith, Geordin? L. to Peggy Minerva Smith 1-20-1856
Smith, George R. to Frances Jarrell 1-16-1855 (1-17-1855)
Smith, Giles R. to Lucy N. Collins 4-26-1851
Smith, Green to Sallie E. Wall 8-20-1866 (8-23-1866)
Smith, Henry to Eliza Miles 1-9-1845
Smith, Henry to Keziah Bell 4-30-1866 [b]
Smith, Henry to Mary Gupton 5-23-1843 (5-25-1843)
Smith, Hiram to Lucy C. Kelly 5-11-1863
Smith, Howell to Sarah Ann Dycus 3-30-1850 (3-31-1850)
Smith, Hugh to Nancy Foster 8-17-1865 (8-24-1865)
Smith, J. A. to Rachael M. Little 10-4-1858
Smith, Jackson to Susan Overton 12-27-1866 (12-28-1866) [b]
Smith, James M. to Martha Smith 4-7-1847
Smith, James T. to Egenarra Stephens 1-?-1859 (11-25-1852?)
Smith, James W. to Nancy Shepherd 8-5-1857 (8-6-1857)
Smith, James W. to Sarah Davis 12-1-1852
Smith, James Jackson 3-26-1845
Smith, James to Rachel Smith 4-28-1866 [b]
Smith, Jas. D. to Henrietta T. Adkins 5-14-1866
Smith, Jas. to Angeline Smith 2-2-1867 (1?-3-1867)
Smith, Jas. to Eliza Bumpas 2-26-1863 (3-25-1863)
Smith, Jessee to M. A. Moody 8-19-1862 (8-21-1862)
Smith, Jno. A. to Mary E. Layne 8-26-1843
Smith, John W. to Susan Stewart 12-22-1838
Smith, John to Frances Shepherd 11-15-1847
Smith, John to Lavenia Martin 7-6-1840
Smith, Jonas to Elizabeth Dycus 5-10-1845 (5-11-1845)
Smith, Joseph to Nancy Luke 12-21-1854
Smith, Loreol? R. to H. M> Dyer 10-12-1843 (10-13-1843)

Smith, Mark to Mary J. Pearson 10-20-1847
Smith, Melvin F. to Nancy Ann Baggett 4-25-1853 (5-1-1853)
Smith, Peter to Eliza Bryan 12-8-1841 (12-9-1841)
Smith, Richardson G. to M. L. Donaldson 12-20-1859 (12-25-1859)
Smith, Robert to Martha A. Chester 1-4-1858 (1-5-1858)
Smith, Saml. to Frances Wilson 12-26-1865 (12-7?-1865)
Smith, Thomas to Lukitty Ellin Fouse 2-15-1865 (2-16-1865)
Smith, Valentine W. to Mary L. Leigh 11-1-1859
Smith, Washington W. to Rhoda A. Jarrell 9-20-1853 (9-22-1853)
Smith, William A. to Sally Ann Baggett 7-14-1852 (7-15-1852)
Smith, William C. to Althea M. Wheatley 6-21-1854
Smith, William G. to Caroline G. Brown 1-22-1845 (1-27-1845)
Smith, William H. to Debora Carter 11-6-1853
Smith, William Henry to Serilda Knight 5-30-1858
Smith, William to Martha Clark 3-2-1856
Smith, William to Sarah J. Powell 5-14-1864 (5-15-1864)
Smith, Wm. C. to Natha A. Bell 11-28-1854 (11-29-1854)
Smith, Wm. C. to Sarah D. Edwards 2-16-1842 (2-17-1842)
Smith, Wm. M. to E. J. Smith 1-16-1843 (1-19-1843)
Smith, Wm. to Della Smith 5-2-1866 (12-30-1866) [b]
Smith?, James H. to Eugenia Fauntleroy 12-6-1859
Snell, J. J. to Lucy White 4-5-1862 (4-7-1862)
Snidly?, S. B. to M. J. Allender 8-24-1849
Snyder, Henry N. to Ann E. Hill 2-28-1848
Solomon, Jas. E. to Lavinia A. Bratton 9-6-1866
Solomon, Wm. A. to Amanda S. Barton 10-29-1861
Southal, W. H. to Mary E. Thacker 1-19-1852 (1-29-1852)
Southall, William H. to Mary E. Thacker 1-13-1851
Southward, B. W. to Manerva Myrick 8-7-1845 (8-3?-1845)
Southward, Francis M. to Rebecca Jane Ellice 12-14-1859 (12-15-1859)
Southward, Thomas J. to Ann Raines 1-12-1839 (1-13-1839)
Southwood, J. B. to Polly Powers 2-14-1856
Southwood, W. B. to Nineva Myrick 9-7-1845
Span, Preston to Rebecca Blak 10-30-1857 (10-2?-1857)
Speed, W. W. to Mary Simons? 7-12-1846
Speel, J. A. to Caroline Smith 11-30-1863
Speer, Aaron to Martha Powers 5-12-1864
Spence, Joseph to Sally A. Ogburn 4-14-1858 (4-15-1858)
Spencer, James L. to Emily J. Bundurant 4-11-1839
Spillers, Fount to Dicy Ann Winters 5-2-1866
Springfield, Wm. L. to Eliza Groves 6-18-1851 (6-24-1851)
Springs, Joseph B. to Jerusa C. Scudder 3-20-1838 (3-15?-1838)
Spurier, E. R. to Eliza J. McCauley 8-1-1866 (8-2-1866)
St. John, William J. to Virginia Bourne 1-9-1855 (1-10-1855)
Stacker, Joe to Bella Haynes 1-3-1867 (1-5-1867) [b]
Stamper, Jas. to Jane Rose 12-29-1863
Stamper, R. H. to C. Boid 6-23-1862
Stamper, Robert to Sarah Ann Jones 6-28-1847
Stanfill, J. M. to Sarah Welker 8-7-1856
Stanley, H. L. to Mollie F. Jones 9-20-1866
Staples, William to Mary C. Williams 9-22-1847
Stapp, John C. to Authusia A. Rasor 6-28-1846 (6-28-1846)
Starkey, Johnathan to Sarah A. Bellamy 10-2-1856 (10-8-1856)
Starks, James A. to Lucy S. Lofland 4-9-1858 (4-15-1858)
Staten, John T. to Nannie K. Wray 4-14-1857 (4-15-1857)
Staton, Charles W. to Adelia A. Whitfield 11-15-1865
Staton, John T. to Eliza Dicks 9-17-1864 (9-18-1864)
Stawn?, John W. to Charlott M. Spears 11-9-1850
Stegall, George to Clementine Willard 11-13-1854
Steger, William to Rozetta Hatcher 5-14-1866 [b]
Stenchfield, Joseph W. to Mary E. Ryen 12-23-1865
Stenn, Thos. L. to Mary Janie Caner 6-25-1843
Step, Vanburen to Elmanda M. Outlaw 6-20-1854 (6-22-1854)
Step, Vantreace? to Amanda M. Outlaw 6-20-1854
Stephens, J. W. B. to Malinda Brawner 2-27-1861
Stephens, James to Ann McKinnon 2-26-1858 (2-28-1858)
Stephens, William H. to Harriet Bodine 2-19-1858 (2-20-1858)
Stevenson, John B. to Mary J. Hudgens 11-8-1853
Stevenson, Miles W. to Virginia F. Lacy 7-4-1859 (7-6-1859)
Stewart, A. C. to Louise? Bush 5-30-1856 (5-31-1856)
Stewart, A. J. to Mourning L. Welker 10-10-1848
Stewart, A. to Mary Ballentine 8-19-1851 (8-30-1851)
Stewart, Antony to Nancy Snowden 1-23-1867 (2-19-1867) [b]
Stewart, Brice to Eliza McClure 10-29-1839

Stewart, George W. to Elizabeth Watson 11-22-1856
Stewart, Isam to Jane McKenels 12-26-1866 [b]
Stewart, James L. to Nancy Browning 9-19-1857
Stewart, Joel to Malinda Wilson 5-30-1838
Stewart, John to Catharine Cain 9-16-1849
Stewart, John to Elmira E. Lisenby 1-4-1867 (1-6-1867)
Stewart, Mack to Mary Britton 7-4-1866 [b]
Stewart, Richard T. to Sarah Jane Autin? 1-18-1860
Stewart, Robert W. to Laura Eveline Crewell 7-27-1865
Stewart, Saml. B. to Dora Judkins 5-2-1866
Stewart, Shelby to Mary Weakley 12-21-1841 (12-25-1841)
Stewart, Willie B. to Emily M. Stroud 11-21-1840 (11-26-1840)
Stewart, Wm. to Butchett Starks 10-5-1841
Stewat, Thomas to Margarett Anderson 10-10-1839
Stigall, J. W. to Mary S. Hannah 11-6-1865
Stiles, William to Sarah R. Lunsford 3-31-1857
Stodghill, T. J. to Amerentha P. Ashby 7-9-1860
Stokes, Andrew J. to Fannie Farmer 1-21-1867 (1-24-1867)
Stokes], Thomas H. to Mary E. Jones 9-4-1857
Stone, Isaac D. to Sarah A. E. Lockert 12-14-1846 (11?-16-1846)
Stone, M. B. to Mary Heflin 12-29-1863 (12-31-1863)
Stone, Michael B. to T. M. Allice Anderson 1-6-1853
Stone, Morgan to Mary E. Crane 8-8-1859
Stone, William F. to Miss N. Blount 12-23-1848
Stones, Able to Sarah Galbrith 12-1-1866 [b]
Story, Littleton to Elizabeth Baker 3-21-1846
Stout, Jacob V. D. to Rachel Burrough 2-13-1854 (2-15-1854)
Stratton, John H. to Virginia Lyaris? 10-19-1854
Strayhorn?, David to Mickie Priscilla Jones 1-25-1855
Strother, Thomas J. to Araminta Dozier 8-26-1858 (8-28-1858)
Stull, Leroy J. to Mollie Coyle 10-30-1865
Sugg, G. B. to P. Sugg 9-18-1862
Sugg, J. E. to M. V. Sugg 12-19-1865 (12-20-1865)
Sugg, John H. to Sarah G. Brown 12-29-1866 (12-30-1866)
Sugg, Quintus to Martha A. Rainwater 2-24-1860
Sugg, Samuel B. to Martha Baggett 4-7-1858
Sugg, Wm. R. to Lucinda Sugg 7-31-1863 (8-2-1863)
Suggs, Greenbery to Margaret J. Birdwell 7-11-1846 (7-12-1846)
Suiter, Wilkins to Mary Ann Sanderson 11-18-1854 (11-19-1854)
Sulivan, John to Nancy Yarborough 4-2-1844
Sullins, Zachariah to Elizabeth Carraway 12-13-1840 (12-14-1850)
Sullivan, Daniel to Priscilla Willis 2-23-1843
Sullivan, John to Elizabeth Luck 6-29-1859 (6-30-1859)
Sullivan, Solaman D. to Harriet Little 9-27-1856 (9-28-1856)
Sullivan, W. P. to Margaret J. May 5-31-1853
Sullivan, William M. to Lucinda B. Allensworth 12-10-1850 (12-17-1850)
Sullivan, William P. to Margaret J. Henderson 5-30-1853
Sullivant, James to Felicia Ann Cook 12-18-1858
Sullivant, Wesley to Eliza Ann Patterson 2-19-1840
Suter, Samuel to Sarah Clarke 1-15-1852
Suter, Thos. to Alcy Luallen 5-3-1864
Suter, William to L. C. Bradley 10-26-1850 (10-27-1850)
Suter, Wm. to Julia Manning 3-18-1863 (3-19-1863)
Suter?, Washington to Elizabeth Yarbrough 2-26-1842 (2-27-1842)
Sutloff, John to Mary A. E. Hester 3-6-1838 (3-13-1838)
Sutton, James to Frances Macklin 12-22-1854 (12-28-1854)
Swaney, John L. to Mrs. S. J. Winston 8-27-1860
Swett, Richard H. to Ann E. Wright 6-8-1856
Swift, Anthony to Elizabeth Smith 4-13-1864 (10-14-1864)
Swift, G. B. to Amanda Council 10-22-1866 (10-23-1866)
Swift, George H. to Adeline Martin 6-8-1859
Swift, George H. to Lucy Ann Orgain 4-28-1853 (5-3-1853)
Swift, James M. to Sarah F. Ussery 12-22-1852 (12-23-1852)
Swift, Thomas J. to Emily C. Crocker 5-21-1844
Swift, W. F. to Kate Williamson 4-9-1857
Swisher, Fredrick to Jane Bircham 3-18-1850
Swotwell, Jas. A. to Delilah Cherry 12-8-1848
Sykes, James Westley to Sarah L. Bumpas 5-23-1865
Sykes, Thomas Henry to Nancy Vaughn 7-13-1852 (7-15-1852)
Sykes, Wallen Elisha to Mary E. Jackson 9-29-1859
Sykes, Wiley to Ellin Harris 12-12-1860
Tagus?, Robert to Mary Dykes 1-15-1855 (1-21-1855)
Talar, John Thomas to Frances Jane Shepherd 10-21-1852
Taler, Wm. W. to A. F. Council (no date; with 1-1851)

Talley, G. W. to Mary Jane Talley 3-1-1852
Tally, George F. to Mary Abernathy 3-2-1861 (3-3-1861)
Tally, James P. to Louiza M. White 2-18-1847
Tally, Lennoir to Lucey C. Gerayn? 10-28-1846
Tally, Morton J. to Mary Jane White 7-10-1845
Tally, R. L. to Eliza J. McCarter 11-17-1866 (11-22-1866)
Tally, Simmons S. to Mary Elizabeth Batson 2-7-1859 (2-9-1859)
Tally, Wm. H. to Susan Ann Lea 10-15-1848
Tandy, C. M. to Mary M. Henry 10-23-1862 (10-29-1862)
Tandy, George to Nancy Mason 12-12-1865 (4-3-1866)
Tandy, James B. to Isapheny A. Blackman 7-5-1848 (8-8-1848)
Tandy, Lewis to Silvy Johnson 4-10-1866 (4-14-1866)
Tanner, John William to Bridget Maricie 1-5-1859 (1-6-1859)
Tarpley, R. B. to L. M. Smith 11-30-1865
Tarr, Saml. H. to Jennie M. Pierce 12-2-1863
Tate, James to Mary F. McDonald 1-19-1859
Tayler, Wyman to Martha Francisco 12-8-1852 (10?-8-1852)
Taylor, A. J. to Elizabeth Dinwiddie 11-26-1866 (11-27-1866)
Taylor, Albert M. to Sarah A. Morehead 7-19-1855
Taylor, Andrew J. to Mary Frances Wilson 10-12-1859
Taylor, D. W. to E. M. Dudley 12-4-1849
Taylor, Edward to Pamelia Weiring 12-29-1851
Taylor, F. M. to Margaret Lane 1-23-1860 (1-24-1860)
Taylor, James T. to Agnes Fleming 11-1-1859
Taylor, Jas. K. to Mary A. Fletcher 12-20-1864 (12-22-1864)
Taylor, Jno. B. to Rebecca Major 2-22-1844 (3-6-1844)
Taylor, John A. to Minerva Sloan 4-25-1855
Taylor, Loyd to Louisa Binkley 2-9-1867 (2-10-1867)
Taylor, Milton to Sarah R. Sims 8-13-1853
Taylor, Wm. H. to Ann Louisa Broadhead 6-19-1850 (6-20-1850)
Taylor, Wm. to Jennie Malory 1-25-1865 (1-26-1865)
Taylor, Z. M. to Eliza N. Poston 6-19-1844 (6-20-1844)
Teasley, Dempsy G. to Juda J. Chambless 1-25-1844 (2-1-1844)
Teasley, F. M. to Lucinda Weakley 12-8-1851
Teasley, Geo. W. to Nancy Pool 1-5-1851
Telford, Hugh to Julia McDaniel 4-13-1842
Tender, Isaac R. to Frances G. Walker 3-7-1865
Tenzric?, Thomas J. to Susan E. Randal 1-15-1845
Terrell, William B. to Julia Ann Allison 10-17-1848
Terrell, William B. to Julia Ann? Allison 10-17-1848 (10-19-1848)
Terrington?, Joseph B. to Julier B. Walker 2-23-1842
Terry, James to Elizabeth Logan 12-22-1840
Terry, W. W. to Mary E. Drake 9-23-1851
Terry, Westley to Leanna Rives 12-29-1866 (1-1-1867) [b]
Thacker, John Calvin to Mrs. Selina Hester 7-26-1861 (7-27-1861)
Thacker, M. L. to Narcissa Martin 1-18-1858 (1-21-1858)
Thacker, Marcus L. to Elizabeth Wilson 11-10-1855
Thacker, William M. to Tennessee L. Marion? 10-3-1857 (10-15-1857)
Tharp, Josiah to Sarah Caroline Walker 2-10-1853 (2-16-1853)
Thaxton, Francis M. to Rebecca Bobbit 1-17-1854 (1-19-1854)
Thermond, James M. to Praree H. Broddie 5-9-1859 (5-11-1859)
Therston, Sam to Mariah Martin 7-2-1866 [b]
Thom, Wm. A. to George Ann Stanton 4-7-1843 (4-14-1843)
Thom, Wm. to George Ann Stanton 4-7-1843
Thomas, Caleb to Laura Boid 5-12-1866 [b]
Thomas, E. R. N. to F. F. McGinty 2-5-1848
Thomas, George S. to Sophia Barret 12-30-1847
Thomas, J. B. to C. W. Covington 1-17-1850
Thomas, James to Virginia Jones 3-1-1854 (3-5-1854)
Thomas, John E. to Mary Caroline Ridley 7-24-1852
Thomas, Reuben to Emily H. Carmac 9-6-1854
Thomas, T. A. to Eliza McGinty 10-7-1843 (10-8-1843)
Thomas, Thomas to Biddie Anderson 12-22-1866 [b]
Thomas, W. R. to E. M. Sallee 12-11-1849
Thomason, E. W. to Victoria Reynolds 11-6-1865 (11-8-1865)
Thomason, John G. to Nancy N. Reynolds 1-14-1861 (2-20-1861)
Thompson, James E. to Sarah E. Fossey 12-27-1866
Thompson, John G. to Ellen E. Poston 5-1-1861
Thompson, Robert to Mary Reynolds 2-15-1853
Thompson, William H. to Virginia C. Burwell? 12-17-1858
Thompson, William R. to Martha A. Hunt 3-18-1840
Thompson, William to M.J. Johnson 8-4-1840
Thorn, J. T. to Nancy Martin 12-17-1860
Thorn, R. J. W. to Mary T. Mickle 12-12-1842 (12-15-1842)
Thorn, Saml. to Martha Higgins 5-3-1844 (5-4-1844)

Thorn, W. A. to Mary Staunton 2-1-1845 (2-2-1845)
Threat?, Doctor Johnathan to Mary F. Crowder 1-31-1857 (2-3-1857)
Thweat, Cath to Sarah A. Daily 2-25-1847
Thweat, John to Sally Sherfield? 12-13-1843
Thwett, Saml. W. to F. E. Seay 12-18-1862 (12-19-1862)
Tidwell, John W. to Frances Emily Smith 3-13-1858 (3-14-1858)
Tilley, F. J. to N. V. Herring 3-27-1859 (3-24?-1859)
Tims, William to Elizabeth Price 9-18-1863
Tinsley, Allanson to C. G. Fox 8-17-1843
Tinsley, B. W. to Amanda J. Mayfield 10-1-1862 (10-9-1862)
Tinsley, David R. to Victoria Ann Redford 1-9-1858 (1-12-1858)
Tinsley, John N. to Jemima Pollock 7-31-1845
Todd, Albert G. to Frances Gamblin 10-16-1859
Todd, Joshua to Martha Fox 12-24-1840
Toler, Isaah to Edith Shepherd 7-16-1838 (7-17-1838)
Toler, Robert J. to Emily E. Barbee 10-30-1856
Toler, Wm. H. to Caroline Jonal 2-21-1849
Tomlinson, David to Harriet Trice (no date; with 12-1851)
Tomlinson, William A. to Mary Dowdy 1-11-1858 (1-14-1858)
Tomlinson, William D. to Malissa J. Payne 2-18-1858 (2-21-1858)
Tomlinson, William H. to Martha S. Outlaw 4-15-1856
Torean, Geo. to Althea M. Donaldson 3-31-1863 (4-9-1863)
Torian, Westley to Olivia Watts 12-28-1866 [b]
Torides?, James to Lucinda Knight 2-2-1854
Trahem, Jas. W. to Isabella Baynham 11-14-1865 (11-15-1865)
Trainnum?, Robert C. to Sarah E. Sallee 3-18-1839
Tramel, Denis to Mary F. Chester 12-24-1866 (12-25-1866)
Tramel, Isaac to Martha Broddy 5-15-1866 [b]
Trammell, Shade to Mary Dodd 6-28-1843 (6-8?-1843)
Trammill, Shadrick to Jane Smith 8-29-1859 (8-30-1859)
Travis, Dudley to Elizabeth C. Johnson 4-3-1839
Travis, Harburt to Martha Roberts 5-22-1851
Traylor, T. H. to Amanda M. Oneal 1-9-1859 (1-10-1859)
Tribble, G. W. to Elizabeth Herendon 2-25-1863 (2-26-1863)
Trice, Edward to Martha Chissenhall 12-23-1838 (1-7-1839)
Trice, Elzy to F. Pettus 4-7-1862 (4-8-1862)
Trice, George W. to Molly E. Ward 1-7-1862
Trice, Henry F. to Frances L. Buckly 11-23-1853 (11-24-1853)
Trice, James A. to M. L. Barker 3-6-1850
Trice, James T. to Margaret J. Smith 8-16-1860
Trice, James to Mary Trice 12-29-1846
Trice, Jesse? F. to E. A. Allen 2-3-1841 (2-6-1841)
Trice, Richmond S. to Margaret J. Harris 5-6-1861
Trice, Scot to Josepheen Gray 2-7-1867 [b]
Trice, Silas W. to Mary H. Trice 9-13-1862
Trice, Vinse to Adiline Dist 12-26-1866 (1-5-1867) [b]
Trigg, Thomas S. to Elizabeth Metcalf 4-17-1845
Trimer, Geo. W. to Elizabeth J. Rives 2-1-1844
Trotter, Benjamin to Elizabeth Binwell? 12-16-1856
Trotter, Elijah to Mary Ann Dawson 2-28-1855
Trotter, Green B. to Paralee Patterson 11-12-1847 (11-14-1847)
Trotter, Jas. M. to Louisa Harris 8-11-1863 (8-12-1863)
Trotter, Jerome to Sarah E. Trotter 9-29-1866 (10-3-1866)
Trotter, John N. to Lavinia Whittington 10-10-1839
Trotter, Joseph J. to Winney Jones 10-30-1845
Trotter, Sylvanus to Elizabeth H. Lee 11-29-1865 (12-6-1865)
Trovelle, Henry to Mary Crow 9-22-1839
Tubberville, James to Mary A. Clark 11-8-1849
Tubbs, William to Mary Ann McGraw 1-18-1843
Tucker, D. P. to Lucy Ann Thompson 2-27-1848
Tucker, G. W. to Orphelia Ann Allener 6-24-1856
Tucker, Granville to Rebecca Ware 11-19-1839
Tucker, Samuel F. to Nancy E. Oaglesby 10-31-1855
Tucker, Thomas to Prissilla Tyner 11-12-1839
Tucker, Thos. W. to Mrs. Permelia A. Bryant 2-8-1864 (2-17-1864)
Turbeville, James to Mary Jane Wallace 2-13-1860
Turner, Alfred J. to Elizabeth Allen 9-6-1852
Turner, Chas. R. to Hennie C. Smith 10-12-1858 (10-13-1858)
Turner, James D. to Seighnora Smith 2-27-1855
Turner, Jas. T. to Martha E. Poore 2-24-1864
Turner, Jno. R. to Nancy Morrison 5-6-1862
Turner, John H. to Virginia M. Allen 12-11-1861
Turner, John W. to Elizabeth Richardson 3-1-1841 (3-2-1841)
Turner, John W. to Mary Eveline Richardson 8-10-1859
Turner, N. L. to Emily F. Izor 9-3-1860 (9-6-1860)

Turnley, Walker to Mary F. Cross 7-22-1865
Turnley, William H. to Amelia Ann Wisdom 10-15-1859 (10-16-1859)
Tutor, James R. to Caroline Sims 12-1-1841
Tutt, David V. to Alice J. Donley(Dulaney?) 12-22-1859
Tutt, Henry D. to Mary Wood 11-9-1864 (11-10-1864)
Tyer, Jefferson to Amanda M. Woodward 12-9-1847
Tyer, Michel to Nancy Edwards 7-15-1856 (7-16-1856)
Tyler, Grandison to Indiana Anderson 4-7-1842
Tyler, Quintus? M. to Emily B. Waller 1-12-1843
Tylor, Cain M. to Mary A. W. Haynes 11-18-1841
Tylor, William B. to Adelia Taylor 11-5-1857
Tyner, Henry R. to Rosella S. Wright 12-15-1847 (12-16-1847)
Tyner, Jas. K. to Martha Carnes 7-11-1849 (7-12-1849)
Underwood, Alexander to Elizabeth Caroline Jackson 2-11-1861
Underwood, Calvin to Amanda Baggett 8-13-1864
Underwood, Henry H. to Malvina E. Ferrill 9-13-1861
Underwood, James to Sallie A. Channel 1-9-1865 (1-12-1865)
Underwood, Lorenzo J. to Nancy C. Davis 10-27-1854
Underwood, T. S. to Sarah Headom 10-4-1854 (10-5-1854)
Underwood, William Benjamin to Olive Hodges 10-30-1858 (11-1-1858)
Ussery, John R. to America Smith 11-22-1853
Ussery, Wm. M. to Elizabeth Ann Neblett 11-23-1847 (11-25?-1847)
Vance, Calvin F. to Margaret Dabney 8-5-1856
Vandack, Jim to Betty Vollentine 12-8-1866 (12-9-1866) [b]
Vaughan, Lewis to Mary Elizabeth Barker 3-10-1851
Vaughan, Martin V. to Mary Davis 11-22-1865 (11-23-1865)
Vaughan, Richd. to Nancy Powell 1-31-1849 (2-1-1849)
Vaughn, H. C. to Mary A. G. Isbell 7-22-1840
Vaughn, J. T. to Frances A. Killebrew 10-13-1862 (10-15-1862)
Vaughn, James to Sophia Hunt 3-22-1848 (3-26-1848)
Vaughn, Lafayette to Margaret Cornell 11-14-1852
Vaughn, Lewis R. to Cordelia Ann Evans 1-27-1860 (1-29-1860)
Vaughn, W. A. to Caroline Dinwiddy 4-14-1862 (4-16-1862)
Vaughn, W. T. to L. J. Mann 9-16-1862
Vaughn, William T. to Sarah Ann Elliott 5-29-1860
Vaughn, William to Mary Frances Baker 9-7-1844
Vick, Howel to Evelina Powel 9-28-1864
Vick, John N. to Mary Jane Duke 12-11-1845 (12-18-1845)
Vick, William to Martha A. Duke 12-30-1853 (1-1-1854)
Victory, Jasper to Mary Jane Edes 4-10-1850
Viles, Ransom to Martha Luallen 5-28-1859 (6-1-1859)
Vincent, John to Tabitha Wright 10-8-1839
Vinsen, Abraham to Sarah J. Bearden 2-17-1864
Wade, Henderson to Margaret Furgurson 7-29-1847
Wade, John William to Ellen Council 2-17-1855 (2-19-1855)
Waggoner, S. T. to Elizabeth T. Koop 12-10-1840 (12-16-1840)
Wagstaff, R. W. to Mary E. Jarrell 8-24-1865
Waldroop, Antony to Jane Trice 12-10-1865 [b]
Walker, Isaac D. to Susan M. Cummins 3-21-1842 (3-17?-1842)
Walker, Jas. G. to Eudora Crowder 11-21-1864 (11-24-1864)
Walker, John to G. A. P. F. Humphries 12-10-1846 (12-23-1846)
Walker, John to Sally Batts 10-23-1847 (10-24-1847)
Walker, Richard B. to Sophronia S. Moseley 2-10-1853 (2-15-1853)
Walker, Willie M. to Aggy Coon 9-25-1841 (9-26-1841)
Walker, Willis to Mary Powell? 7-9-1849
Wall, Cincinnattus to Mary Ann Bumpas 10-15-1866
Wall, Elijah S. to Mary Jane Brown 5-6-1847
Wall, James H. to Susan Clardy 7-4-1838 (7-5-1838)
Wall, James H. to Sylvesta Adkins 3-13-1852 (3-14-1852)
Wall, Joseph W. to Susan J. Martin 1-29-1866 (1-31-1866)
Wall, Squire S. to Manervia A. Brown 9-23-1848 (9-24-1848)
Wall, Wm. to Nancy Barton 11-10-1839
Wallace, Emanuel to Martha Malory 4-16-1866 (4-17-1866) [b]
Wallace, James S. to Polly Warden 12-15-1845
Wallace, Josiah? to Mary Trice 12-18-1866 (12-28?-1866) [b]
Wallace, Levi to Malinda J. Stuart 2-9-1855
Wallace, Martin S. to Harriet T. Smith 4-26-1845 (6-9-1845)
Waller, John W. to Fredonia W. Niblett 11-5-1861 (11-6-1861)
Waller, Lewis A. to Alia J. Trice 5-12-1847
Waller, Thomas to Mary Keller 8-6-1850 (8-7-1850)
Waller, W. P. to E. Staley 9-3-1862
Waller, William P. to Nancy Jane Harris 9-16-1852
Walls, William Henry to Mary Manning 7-2-1853 (7-3-1853)
Walsh, Hiram to Mary A. McCutcheon 2-27-1849

Walsh, Hyram to Martha L. Manin? 3-6-1855
Walsh, James to Mary Sulivan 11-22-1866 (11-25-1866)
Walter, John B. to Nancy Batson 10-20-1854
Walthal, Thomas to Elizabeth Pollard 12-22-1840 (12-24-1840)
Walthall, Stephen to Mary Edwards 1-20-1866 (2-3-1866) [b]
Walther, Allen to Sarah Jane Lynes 11-24-1847
Ward, George H. to Mary Jane Wilson 10-29-1866
Ward, Jonathan R. to Zelia F. Shelby 1-28-1840
Ward, Saml. G. to L. J. Dabny 12-7-1841
Warden, Thomas to Lavica Lewis 6-4-1852
Ware, Chester to Mollie Brown 6-9-1866 [b]
Ware, R. S. to Jane Ann Norfleet 10-28-1853 (11-2-1853)
Ware?, John to Fanny Jolly 5-7-1838
Warfield, C. M. to Mary E. Hutchings 6-10-1846 (6-16-1846)
Warfield, Chas. M. to Frances Johnson 8-3-1839 (8-8-1839)
Warfield, George H. to E. J. Johnson 1-6-1848
Warfield, George W. to Polley Young 12-26-1866 [b]
Warfield, Jack to Lu Carney 12-25-1866 [b]
Warfield, Walis to Janie Johnson 12-25-1866 (12-28-1866) [b]
Warren, Robt. W. to Frances Sanders 8-8-1843
Warrick, Wm. to Jane Trice 11-21-1865 [b]
Waters, Andrew J. to Mary C. Taylor 2-12-1857
Waters, Asa to Henny Parish 12-29-1859 (SB 1858?)
Waters, Edward C. to Sarah A. Meacham 7-3-1858 (7-4-1858)
Waters, J. H. to C. J. Dodd 7-31-1858
Waters, John to Mollie Carr 1-13-1866
Waters, Joseph H. to Emily J. Epperson 12-28-1864
Watkins, Henry F. to Amand L. Wimberly 10-2-1838
Watkins, Stephen D. to Mary D. Baxter 12-13-1842 (12-20-1842)
Watson, Abner T. to Mary E. Pride 11-6-1865 (11-15-1865)
Watson, Isaac W. to Harriett E. Reynolds 9-24-1863 (10-8-1863)
Watson, Jefferson R. to Susan Bunting 2-17-1840 (2-19-1840)
Watson, Joseph to Barbary Ann Coon 11-22-1850
Watson, Robb to Nancy Spicer 6-28-1838 (7-5-1838)
Watson, Samuel to Mary J. Wyatt 5-21-1853 (5-22-1853)
Watson, T. J. to Elizabeth Ann Rudolph 1-15-1845 (1-16-1845)
Watson, Tilton to Sarah Frey 12-24-1844 (4-2-1845)
Watts, G. M. to Judith B. Shelton 1-12-1846 (1-15-1846)
Watts, Henry W. to Susan Olive Braime 5-14-1859 (5-15-1859)
Watts, Johnson D. to Eliza B. Slaughter 12-30-1854 (12-31-1854)
Watts, Warner to Eliza Medley 5-9-1866 (5-10-1866) [b]
Watwood, Alexander to Frances S. White 2-2-1842
Watwood, Elias to Martha E. Burns 11-23-1853 (11-24-1853)
Waugh, Charles to Mary Lenslley? 9-17-1839
Weakley, David to Elizabeth Pascal 4-28-1838
Weakley, Henry to Martha Drake 1-16-1866 (1-27-1866) [b]
Weakley, James M. to Elizabeth Darnell 9-12-1838 (10-10-1838)
Weakley, James Thomas to Isabella Heagan 4-21-1857 (4-22-1857)
Weakley, John C. to Elizabeth Ann Hogan 4-19-1859 (4-21-1859)
Weakley, Saml. K. to Narcissa P. Weakley 12-29-1849 (12-31-1849)
Weakley, Talin? R. to Susan M. E. Sanderlin 11-16-1853 (11-22-1853)
Weakley, William C. to Mary A. M. Birdwell 1-2-1854 (1-4-1854)
Weakly, Robert H. to Louisa Louis 8-8-1845 (8-10-1845)
Weatherford, Green W. to Martha Caroline Coleman 10-19-1852
Weatherford, Solomon to Eliza Harriss 3-12-1844
Weaver, George to Mary Ann Hogan 11-18-1848 (11-19-1848)
Weaver, Henry H. to M. A. Vaughn 4-17-1863 (4-18-1863)
Weaver, Jessee to Elizabeth Owens 4-5-1865 (4-6-1865)
Weaver, Thomas J. to Henrietta J. Collins 9-23-1851 (9-30-1851)
Webb, Benjamin to Margaret Davenport 10-25-1852 (10-28-1852)
Webster, Charles A. to Eliza Jane Minton 7-27-1858 (7-29-1858)
Weed, Osbourn to Agness D. Wright 5-21-1844
Weeks, Jas J.? to Mrs. Emily Jane Hickey 7-10-1865
Weill, John P. to F. C. Seay 6-29-1863
Welborne, Ephraim B. to Frances K. Acocke 9-30-1840
Welbourne, Munroe to Mary Jane Leason 3-28-1852
Welch, Reubin J. to Sarah Council 6-4-1860
Welker, George to Louisa Brown 1-5-1857 (1-8-1857)
Welker, Jacob G. to Clarissa F. Bryan 9-30-1859 (10-2-1859)
Welker, Joseph A. to Elizabeth W. Horn 4-21-1854 (4-23-1854)
Welker, Thomas to Mary J. King 7-14-1845 (7-17-1845)
Welker, W. T. to L. F. Stanfield 4-25-1864 (4-26-1864)
Wells, P. H. to Hardin? J. Wells 3-6-1856 (3-16-1856)
Wells, Richard T. to Martha E. Watwood 2-15-1852
Wells, W. D. to Martha Dukes 8-28-1856

Wells, Wm. H. to Mary E. Porter 5-14-1843
West, C. D. to Serena Hicks 11-12-1850
West, Doury A. to Mary E. Cowherd 8-13-1839
West, Drury H. to E. W. Dickson 5-2-1864
West, Greenberry to Margaret Patterson 11-9-1852
West, Johnson B. to Fredonia Leigh 8-22-1866 (8-26-1866)
West, Joseph B. to Mary R. Jarad 10-4-1851
Westcott, Stephen D. to Virginia R. Cooksey 6-8-1855 (6-14-1855)
Western, George to Hisler? Ann Bradley 1-29-1853
Whalen, Michael to Sally Cincannon? 3-5-1860
Whealley, H. D. to Jane M. Cammick 7-30-1853 (8-1-1853)
Wheatley, Thornton to Fanny Buckner 11-17-1866 (12-22-1866) [b]
Wheatley, W. L. to Inez Parker 9-4-1865
Wheatley, William L. to Mollie E. Harrison 12-24-1865 (12-27-1865)
Wheeler, John to Jane Whitfield 11-3-1866 (11-11-1866) [b]
Wheeler, Sanford D. to Letitia A. Mumford 1-19-1856 (1-20-1856)
Wheeler, Woodson to Amand McCartis 11-5-1866 [b]
Wheelis, Joe to Nellie Cocke 8-2-1860
Wheetly, Isaac to Hana Davis 1-1-1867 (1-2-1867) [b]
Whelen, John S. to Martha Catharine Calishaw 4-9-1852 (4-11-1852)
Wheless, Joseph to Cillanara Powers 7-12-1842
Whitacer, A. J. to Jennie Tritt 12-11-1859
Whitaker, W. A. to Rebecca McKeage 7-25-1842
White, B. to Mary Dolan 7-31-1862 (7-31-1862)
White, Charles W. to Fannie Williams 10-19-1859
White, Dallis to Jennie Martin 9-6-1866
White, George D. to Henrietta Bibb 9-4-1855 (9-6-1855)
White, James A. to Eliza Ann Presnell? 10-12-1847 (10-13-1847)
White, John C. to Henrietta J. Primett 3-9-1846
White, John C. to V. C. Wall 7-28-1862 (8-14-1862)
White, John W. to Mary C. Hester 1-3-1867
White, John to Mary Bright 7-8-1843 (7-18-1843)
White, Josiah to Jane Chappel 10-25-1839
White, Meridith R. to America B. Cabness 9-17-1844
White, Samuel R. to Rebecca A. Reeves 10-9-1854
White, Thos. to Mary White 5-19-1866 (5-20-1866) [b]
Whitefield, L. S. to Eliza J. Trice 12-3-1857
Whitehead, Abraham to Dora C. Brunt 6-17-1865 (6-18-1865)
Whitehead, Benjamin to Lucy B. Simmons 4-29-1840 (4-27?-1840)
Whitehead, S. H. to Mary A. Martin 5-13-1843
Whitfield, H. B. to Susan F. Samuels 1-22-1852 (1-29-1852)
Whitfield, James to Laura Warfield 12-27-1865 (12-26?-1865) [b]
Whitfield, Lewis to Sarah C. Williams 1-18-1842
Whitfield, N.Lewis to Sue C. Bourne 9-5-1863 (9-10-1863)
Whitfield, Needham B. to H. E. Wilcox 4-1-1843
Whitfield, Robt. D. to Susan A. Scott 12-28-1841
Whitfield, Wm. B. to Mary E. Killebrew 9-24-1849
Whitfield, Zack to Matilda Warfield 12-23-1865 (12-26-1865) [b]
Whitlock, George L. to Margaret F. Patton 10-23-1855
Whitlock, Robt. to Ann Moore 7-17-1866 [b]
Whitlow, William K. to A. A. Veal 9-13-1852
Whitmore, J. A. to Emoline Hendricks 8-22-1845
Whitworth, P.? to Eliz. An Holt 7-17-1841
Whitworth, Thomas to Martha Hogan 2-1-1840 (2-2-1840)
Whitworth, William H. to Elizabeth Person 3-18-1850 (3-22-1850)
Whobrey?, S. H. to Frances C. Younger 11-25-1851
Whuldom?, Wm. R. to Mary E. Coffman 10-10-1852
Wickham, Robert W. to Elizabeth Marsh 1-?-1859 (2-3-1859)
Wickham, S. G. to Delila Weaver 4-1-1852
Wickham, Sam to Bettie Shuff 1-5-1865 (1-8-1865)
Wicks, Johnson to Sarah Marshall 10-11-1845
Wiggins, William to Rebecca Bell 12-25-1845
Wigginton, Geo. to Eliza Wootton 6-5-1863
Wight?, Elias to Lucinda Brock 7-26-1840
Wilbourn, Munroe to Mary Outlaw 5-16-1844
Wilcox, Henry to Jennie Vance 8-17-1865 [b?]
Wilcox, John E. to Mary L. Faxon 12-6-1855
Wilder, Homer J. to A. E. Quick 4-22-1861 (4-23-1861)
Wilie, John Benjamin to Clara Jones 11-24-1858 (11-25-1858)
Wilkerson, Green to Cas Ann Humphries 3-22-1847
Wilkerson, James W. to Sarah A. Barker 9-10-1853
Wilkins, Hugh B. to Sary A. Dodd 12-17-1846
Wilkins, James J. to Luvenia Wilkins 8-10-1859
Wilkinson, H. T. to Mary C. Ligon 12-17-1863
Willard, Beverly G. to Taylor Jordan 2-19-1866 (2-27-1866)

Willard, Chas. S. to E. Beard 3-1-1862
Willeford, George S. to Elizabeth Hestor 12-20-1844 (12-22-1844)
Willerford, Geo. S. to Frances Burgess 2-21-1849 (2-25-1849)
Willhight, William to Malinda Gaines? 11-4-1847
Willhite, William to Sallie Eaton 10-9-1863
Williams, Alfred to Sarah Allen 3-11-1851
Williams, Arsmtead C. to America J. Pickering 2-23-1864
Williams, Bengamin L. J. to Nancy M. Thaxton 3-12-1855 (3-15-1855)
Williams, Benjamin R. to Elizabeth C. Laughren 7-17-1861 (7-18-1861)
Williams, Brickner K. to Elizabeth D. Hart 11-6-1844 (11-7-1844)
Williams, Charles to Fannie Carver 2-16-1860
Williams, Dr. T. F. to M. E. Newell 2-4-1867
Williams, Edmond to Isabell Ligon 12-23-1865 (12-28-1865) [b]
Williams, Edward L. to Mary Ann Dye 6-20-1840 (6-23-1840)
Williams, F. H. to Susan A. Hawkins 7-21-1853
Williams, Fedrick to Jane McFarland 11-20-1845
Williams, Francis M. to Angeline B. McCoy 3-15-1864
Williams, Henry to Adaline Grant 2-23-1864
Williams, J. B. to Ellen H. Gray 12-8-1862
Williams, J. B. to Mrs. Auriminter L. Whitfield 11-15-1865
Williams, James H. to Leonora Norfleet 1-22-1859 (1-27-1859)
Williams, James P. to Eliza Ann Lyles 3-24-1840 (3-26-1840)
Williams, Jas. A. to Mary Smith 7-7-1862 (7-13-1862)
Williams, Jas. D. to Mary Emerline Davis 11-15-1860 (11-16-1860)
Williams, John E. to Edy Ann Wiggs 11-2-1846
Williams, John J. to Fredonia R. Britt 10-8-1843
Williams, John P. to Mildred Hopson 12-12-1842 (12-13-1842)
Williams, John to Rody Trigg 3-31-1866 [b]
Williams, Joseph B. to Adaline T. Bridgewaters 10-24-1839
Williams, Latan G. to Nancy N. Johnson 8-23-1858
Williams, Lewis G. to E. D. Gray 7-16-1839
Williams, Lewis to Julia Wallace 6-18-1866 [b]
Williams, Patrick H. to Martha M. Reasons 1-19-1843 (1-20-1843)
Williams, Plummer? J. to Sarah Johnson 8-26-1856
Williams, Rhoden S. to Lockey Cane 3-27-1842 (3-31-1842)
Williams, Robert H. to Ann Williams 6-3-1853
Williams, Robert to Arabella Norfleet 4-4-1854
Williams, Roger to Mary E. S. Budwatten 12-16-1846 (12-17-1846)
Williams, Sam to Martha Townley 9-12-1865 [b?]
Williams, Thomas M. to Elizabeth J. Fielder 3-19-1856 (3-20-1856)
Williams, Thos. to Cornelia A. S. Bert 9-1-1849
Williams, W. T. to Fannie Balthrop 3-29-1864
Williams, William to Evelina Bundarant 8-31-1844 (7?-30?-1844)
Williams, Willis W. to Mary Ann Sherron 11-28-1840
Williamson, Alfred to Elizabeth V. George 12-14-1857
Williamson, B. M. to Mary A. Bowers 8-10-1857 (8-11-1857)
Williamson, John J. to Nancy Jane Pace 12-20-1858 (12-21-1858)
Williamson, P. B. to Sally Ann Barnes 4-5-1848 (4-6-1848)
Williamson, Perry B. to Sarah Neblett 11-19-1839 (11-20-1839)
Willis, Lewis R. to Sallie A. Newell 5-15-1865
Willoby, B. F. to Moriah Hackney 11-13-1846 (11-16-1846)
Wills, B. L. to Ellen Thomas 1-15-1866
Wils, William to Omzella Pollard 12-24-1866 (12-26-1866) [b]
Wilson, Garland to Elizabeth Garnett 10-27-1856
Wilson, Henry Washington to Ruthey Ellen Shrader 12-20-1853 (1-3-1854)
Wilson, J. J. to Jennie B. Moore 1-1-1866
Wilson, Jackson to Fannie Broadie 11-26-1866 (12-17-1866) [b]
Wilson, James M. to Mary Williams 10-16-1838
Wilson, James to Isbell? F. Dycus 11-22-1844 (11-28-1844)
Wilson, Jas. T. to Rosanna Fapp 3-7-1842
Wilson, John W. to Martha W. Wilson 12-1-1852
Wilson, John to Martha Ann Wheless 10-31-1838 (12-13-1838)
Wilson, Kindred to Mallissa Elliott 9-8-1866 (9-11-1866)
Wilson, Morris W. to Lucy C. Johnson 9-18-1852 (9-19-1852)
Wilson, Ned to Martha Rollins 6-15-1866 [b]
Wilson, Robt. A. to Ann Eliza Barbee 11-21-1860
Wilson, Robt. H. to Lizzie Peacher 9-8-1860 (9-11-1860)
Wilson, Thomas A. to Berrilla A. Thacker 8-26-1856
Wilson, W. H. to E. M. Johnson 4-28-1854
Wilson, William G. to Matt. F. Kelly 1-27-1859
Wilson, William to Martha P. Pooll 6-29-1838
Wilson, Young to Lucy Hardy 10-14-1861

Wimberley, Robert H. to Martha Delinia Barker 9-28-1853 (10-11-1853)
Wimberly, George S. to Judith P. Reeser 9-18-1847
Wimberly, Harrison to Elizabeth Pride 6-9-1866 [b]
Wims, John A. to Frances C. Johnson (no date; with 2-1852)
Winfree, Fleming to Hester Abner 1-13-1846
Winn, Peter to Mary E. McAllester 10-20-1853
Winn, Richd. M. to Martha Q. Highsmith 10-18-1866
Winn, W. H. to Eliza S. Rudolph 9-29-1856 (10-14-1856)
Winn, Wm. W. to Martha Brake 1-18-1839
Winsett, Frank to Mary Rose 5-22-1863
Winstead, D. B. to Valeria Johnson 10-29-1862
Winstead, John C. to Rosena Stiles 6-24-1857
Winters, L. G. to M. E. Manion 2-17-1856
Wisdom, Dick to Ann Courts? 9-24-1866 [b]
Wisdom, Limon to Irene Wilcox 5-3-1866 [b]
Wisdom, Manuel to Kitty Merryweather 5-27-1865 (6-24-1865)
Wisdom, Thomas W. to Clara Beaumont 3-6-1855
Withers, E. to Rachel Cooper 5-29-1860
Withers, John A. to Ruth A. McFadden 3-31-1840
Witt, William to Martha Martin 12-24-1853
Wood, A. S. to Bettie J. Brown 3-12-1866 (3-13-1866)
Wood, Alexander S. to Sarah Jane Fredrick 2-24-1858 (2-25-1858)
Wood, Alexander to Rhoda Bulls 6-6-1850
Wood, Dr. B. S. to M. Hellen Bowling 11-22-1866
Wood, John W. to Caroline Oneal 3-11-1858
Wood, Leander M. to Mary R. Bennett 10-11-1858 (10-13-1858)
Wood, Moses to Tabitha Copeland 8-10-1854
Wood, Wm. A. to Lucinda Brown 2-26-1843
Wood, Wm. B. to Sally Stone 2-11-1852 (3-8-1852)
Woodall, W. W. to M. H. Gupton 10-24-1866 (10-25-1866)
Woodburn, John F. to Isabell Rich 5-14-1865
Woodman, George M. to L. B. Dilworth 3-22-1855
Woodmore, T. M. to Martha J. Furlow? 8-12-1855
Woodruff, George Washington to Susan J. Gilleland 9-16-1861
Woods, Levis to Frances Caroline Bullion 10-4-1850 (10-9-1850)
Woodson, Arther T. to Margarett Walker 1-18-1850
Woodson, Jacob C. to ElizabethAnn Cooksey 4-7-1856 (4-9-1856)
Woodson, Jos. J. to Martha Strey? 12-23-1843 (12-26-1843)
Woodson, Joseph N. to Sarah J. Smith 2-15-1865 (2-16-1865)
Woodson, Peter J. to Mary A. Borders 10-5-1861
Woodson, Saml. B. to Martha J. Marshall 3-14-1866 (3-15-1866)
Woodson, Samuel B. to Mary E. Cooksey 12-22-1857
Woodson, Silas H. to Theressa A. Hooper 9-10-1856
Woodson, T. W. to Emma Hart 6-20-1855
Woodson, Thomas S. to Armindia J. Elliott 6-28-1865
Woodson, Thos. S. to A. F. Oldham 12-20-1864 (12-22-1864)
Woodson, William B. to Sarah M. Chiles 1-14-1840 (1-17-1840)
Woodward, F. to Ann Hoskins 3-3-1840
Woodward, Philip S. to Ellener Bowman 8-1-1843 (8-3-1843)
Wooldridge, John E. to Erwin C. Frazer 12-30-1853
Woolf, John to Eliza Jane McTernis 3-1-1849
Woolfolk, George W. to Catharine Hickey Christy 6-7-1855
Woolsy, T. T. to M. F. Quisenbury 8-10-1854
Wootan, Wm. R. to Nancy Smith 5-13-1849
Wooten, J. J. to Harriet Smith 12-28-1846
Wootten, A. W. to Amanda Ainsworth 6-3-1865 (6-11-1865)
Wootton, John to Martha Howerton 2-25-1839 (3-8-1839)
Word, B. F. to M. A. Majors 1-28-1864
Word, John W. to Adda E. Majors 11-2-1857 (11-3-1857)
Workman, Allen R. to Mary R. O. Kane 1-16-1865
Wortham, James to Margaret Reynolds 3-30-1866 (4-1-1866)
Worthington, Horris to Sarah R. White 5-17-1848 (5-18-1848)
Wray, James M. to Mary A. Jorden 4-9-1853 (4-10-1853)
Wright, A. C. to Mary A. C. Smith 2-12-1851 (2-13-1851)
Wright, Andrew Jackson to Mary Levina Smith 6-7-1853 (6-10-1853)
Wright, Banister to Martha Ann Bats 12-21-1852
Wright, David to Fereby S. Hopper 2-24-1845
Wright, Dixon G. to Nancy Catharine Utley 5-17-1852
Wright, E. U. E. to Ann C. Wright 7-14-1845
Wright, Geo. M. to Sarah J. Keesee 11-18-1856
Wright, J. W. to Mary M. House 8-14-1860
Wright, Silas D. to Eliza Johnson 3-21-1865
Wright, Thomas to P. A. Haggard 4-9-1856
Wright, W. D. to Eliza Smith 12-18-1844

Wyar?, William D. to Delana Pierson 7-15-1858
Wyatt(Myatt?), William to Nancy Desire? 12-11-1857 (12-14-1857)
Wyatt, Henry O. to Mary E. Richardson 11-22-1844 (11-24-1844)
Wyatt, Henry to Martha E. Harrison 4-1-1848 (4-2-1848)
Wyatt, Jas. to S. E. Matthews 11-14-1864
Wyatt, John L. to Elizabeth Jett 10-5-1857 (10-6-1857)
Wyatt, R. C. to Jennie Edmonson 11-29-1862
Wyatt, R. W. to M. C. Orgain 10-3-1862
Wyatt, Sidney to Mary A. Ragsdale 2-18-1850
Wyckoff, A. to M. A. Fletcher 3-30-1843
Wykoff, A. J. to Mary E. Bumpass 12-3-1853
Wynn, David to Mary Murphy 12-23-1865 (12-26-1865) [b]
Wynne, Edward S. to Sarah E. Bayless 12-27-1845 (12-28-1845)
Wynns, Napoleon B. to Frances Outlaw 2-10-1858 (2-11-1858)
Yancy, Thomas L. to Sarah A. Barker 11-1-1847 (11-4-1847)
Yandell, Benja. F. to M. J. Carner 1-26-1863
Yandell, L. C. to T. M. Woodruff 8-8-1865
Yarborough, Henry C. to Selina G. Jackson 9-10-1864 (9-11-1864)
Yarbrough, Charles to Melia C. Caits 9-4-1845
Yarbrough, F. Marion to Clarrissa Davis 4-22-1856 (5-1-1856)
Yarbrough, Henry C. to Elizabeth Hodge 1-21-1864 (not executed)
Yarbrough, Joseph W. to Milly Yarbrough 11-26-1850
Yarbrough, Mires to Lucy Martin 10-17-1842 (10-20-1842)
Yarbrough, Norrord to Lovisa King 7-3-1838 (7-5-1838)
Yarbrough, Samuel to Elizabeth Trotter 3-31-1847 (4-2-1847)
Yarbrough, W. A. to Mary Hunt 1-26-1851 (1-30-1851)
Yarrington, William F. to M. M. E. J. Hansbrough 2-9-1841
        (2-11-1841)
Yates, Ebinezer to Mary Crocket 6-12-1858 (6-13-1858)
Yates, Fountain to Martha Yates 5-19-1866 (5-20-1866) [b]
Yates, James G. to Sally Carry 8-17-1839 (8-18-1839)
Yates, John to Fannie Oldem 12-27-1866 (12-26?-1866) [b]
Yates, Moulton D. to Fanny E. Sleigh 9-20-1859
Yates, William H. to Hannah Blankenship 8-6-1866 (8-7-1866)
Yatman, Archey to Polley Venters 12-21-1866 [b]
Young, Chas. A. to Miss Susan R. Johnson 1-12-1852
Young, D. L. to Mary Ann Marr 10-20-1847 (10-21-1847)
Young, G. O. to Margrette Marr 7-9-1840
Young, Green? to Martha Osborn 1-20-1866 [b]
Young, Isaac N. to Nancy M. Thompson 1-7-1850
Young, J. M. to Nancy M. Thompson 6-7-1850
Young, Jas. R. to Bittie W. Warfield 2-4-1865 (2-9-1865)
Young, Pleasant J. to Emily E. Love 3-1-1847
Young, William F. to Catharine A. Caudle 12-17-1859
Young, William F. to Mary P. Shelley 11-30-1853
Zelle, William E. to Elanor B. Mathis 3-5-1849
Zimring, W. B. to Louisa E. McQuerry 1-15-1850 (1-17-1850)

----, ----- to Edmond Robinson 11-28-1846
----, Elizabeth to J. W. Harnell? 8-17-1855
----, Emiline to Jessee Carter 5-11-1843
----, Margarett to John A. Moreland 1-29-1839
----, Margarette to John W. Campbell 10-18-1838
----, _____ to U. L. Morrow 6-24-1851
Abbott, Elizabeth F. to Bennet Perdew 9-20-1845 (9-28-1845)
Abbott, Lucy B. to R. W. Major 3-31-1846 (4-1-1846)
Abbott, Mary E. T. to Henry Clay Cox 12-24-1857
Abbott, Mary to Daniel Berry 3-2-1844 (3-6-1844)
Abernathy, Mary to George F. Tally 3-2-1861 (3-3-1861)
Abner, Hester to Fleming Winfree 1-13-1846
Abney, Malinda J. to John J. Darnal 4-13-1852
Acocke, Frances K. to Ephraim B. Welborne 9-30-1840
Acre, Penelope Ann to Walter M. Noel 3-26-1855
Adams, A. F. to G. P. Bagwell 8-4-1840
Adams, Amanda to John T. Legget 3-15-1853 (3-23-1853)
Adams, Ann M. to David A. Elliott? 11-2-1853 (11-3-1853)
Adams, Catharine to Robert J. Cain 11-16-1838
Adams, Eliza to Augustus E. Hewlett 9-11-1865
Adams, Ermine P. to William F. Adams 12-11-1858 (12-12-1858)
Adams, Georgia Ann to Albert M. Norris 8-2-1849 (8-3-1849)
Adams, H. M. to Jas. A. Grant 5-12-1862
Adams, Jane Elizabeth to Wm. Leggett 1-10-1853 (1-21-1853)
Adams, Louisa to A. E. Evans 6-13-1864 (6-15-1864)
Adams, Martha J. to Jessee G. Adams 12-19-1851 (12-23-1851)
Adams, Martha to John B. Halseel 7-7-1841 (7-8-1841)
Adams, Martha to Oliver Adams 8-24-1856
Adams, Mary C. to Mark P. Gibbs 10-20-1863
Adams, Mary S. to A. G. Adams 11-18-1862 (11-20-1862)
Adams, Mary to Sanford Pollock 7-13-1845
Adams, Mary to William Norris 11-18-1839 (11-19-1839)
Adams, Mary to William Shoemaker 7-18-1856
Adkins, Henrietta T. to Jas. D. Smith 5-14-1866
Adkins, Isabella W. to George R. Harris 11-24-1855 (11-28-1855)
Adkins, Manna to Voluntine Quincey 10-29-1849
Adkins, Martha to G. R. Outlaw 11-1-1843
Adkins, Mary Adaline to George E. Boyd 8-16-1853 (9-28-1853)
Adkins, Mary C. to Samual A. Clifton 5-10-1856
Adkins, Sylvesta to James H. Wall 3-13-1852 (3-14-1852)
Agen, Ellen to Anthony Diver 5-15-1861
Ainsworth, Amanda to A. W. Wootten 6-3-1865 (6-11-1865)
Akins, Elmira to William Hill 11-17-1864
Albright, Martha to Henry Haynes 10-29-1850
Albright, Sally Ann to C. S. Hodges 6-30-1838 (7-9-1838)
Alcorn, Martha H. to Robert S. Moore 7-26-1842
Alcorn, Prudence J. to Harvey Hogg 4-24-1855
Alexander, Frelove to Jas. Lynch 8-2-1850 (8-7-1850)
Alexander, Hester to Daniel Ohara 4-2-1838 (4-5-1838)
Alexander, Mahala Jane to Richard Washington Harris 1-24-1853
Allan, Martha to Richard Daniel 1-22-1841 (2-4-1841)
Allbright, Arlean to W. T. Dowdy 9-22-1856
Allbright, Nancy A. to George D. McCauley 10-24-1866 (10-25-1866)
Allen, Agnes Ann to W. J. Holmes 10-20-1846
Allen, Barbara Ann to E. J. Edwards 8-22-1858
Allen, Barbara Ann to E. J. Edwards 9-8-1858
Allen, Bettie to Joseph Hackney 1-9-1866 [b]
Allen, Catharine to William Parker 12-21-1846 (12-22-1846)
Allen, Delana L. to James? M. Martin 3-19-1851
Allen, E. A. to Arthur N. Power 1-29-1842 (2-6-1842)
Allen, E. A. to Jesse? F. Trice 2-3-1841 (2-6-1841)
Allen, Editha A. to Joseph N. Metcalf 10-15-1866 (10-16-1866)
Allen, Eliz. M. to Jno. P. Singsing 7-5-1845 (7-10-1845)
Allen, Elizabeth H. to Josiah Horn 5-2-1840 (5-5-1840)
Allen, Elizabeth to Alfred J. Turner 9-6-1852
Allen, Fredonia to Jehu Hargrove 12-1-1857 (12-3-1857)
Allen, Lucy B. to W. P. Gill 11-26-1845
Allen, M. L. to Jas. M. Brown 8-27-1862
Allen, Martha E. to John P. Manson 2-17-1866 (2-20-1866)
Allen, Mary A. to Joseph Burgess 3-11-1843 (3-12-1843)
Allen, Mary A. to William J. Graham 5-18-1854 (5-8?-1854)
Allen, Marya to J. W. Broom 1-7-1867
Allen, Pennina to Joseph Carmack? 8-6-1854
Allen, Phebee to Therston Barker 6-19-1865
Allen, Sally M. to Andrew J. Holliday 12-19-1854

Allen, Sarah E. to John Baggett 7-11-1866 (7-12-1866)
Allen, Sarah F. to Jas. T. Jenkins 6-29-1865
Allen, Sarah R. to Benjamin C. Felts 12-29-1852
Allen, Sarah to Alfred Williams 3-11-1851
Allen, Sarah to Morton W. Pannell 7-29-1841
Allen, Sue N. to W. T. Dye 4-23-1861
Allen, Susan to W. Perkins 3-18-1862
Allen, Virginia M. to John H. Turner 12-11-1861
Allender, Lutitia F. M. to Jehu N. Cartwright 10-14-1856 (10-16-1856)
Allender, M. J. to S. B. Snidly? 8-24-1849
Allener, Orphelia Ann to G. W. Tucker 6-24-1856
Allensworth, Elisa Emily to Josiah W. Settle 10-3-1859 (10-4-1859)
Allensworth, Emerline to James Reed 12-29-1865 [b]
Allensworth, Jane to W. Knox 6-7-1866 [b]
Allensworth, Lucinda B. to William M. Sullivan 12-10-1850 (12-17-1850)
Allensworth, Vene to Sam Garrett 12-27-1866 [b]
Alley, Lavinia to James Martin 8-9-1841
Alley, Mary Ann to Joseph J. Basford 3-13-1854
Alley, Mary to Thomas Collier 1-25-1866
Alley, Rebecca to Isreal Robinson 6-24-1864 (6-26-1864)
Allin, Caroline E. H. to Horace M. Acre 9-1-1857 (9-2-1857)
Allison, Elizabeth to James Shurff 5-19-1857 (5-14?-1857)
Allison, Julia Ann to William B. Terrell 10-17-1848
Allison, Julia Ann? to William B. Terrell 10-17-1848 (10-19-1848)
Allison, Sarah J. to Edwin H. Grant 10-11-1856
Allman, Mary to Enos Harned? 3-1-1851 (3-7-1851)
Allwell, Georgiann T. to Francis Marion House 10-26-1865
Alman, Margarett C. to D. J. Hays 7-24-1851
Alman, Missouri F. to Samuel Shuff 8-16-1865 (8-20-1865)
Almon, Livina to Miles Jackson 3-11-1856 (2?-11-1856)
Almon, Mary Ann to John J. Dilling 8-1-1857 (8-6-1857)
Amandy, Nancy to Harrison Puckett 11-4-1852
Anderon, Sarah A. to Edward Robinson 11-28-1846 (11-29-1846)
Anderson, Biddie to Thomas Thomas 12-22-1866 [b]
Anderson, Clarinda to Jackson Garnett 7-?-1862 [b]
Anderson, Elizabeth to John E. Ransdale 10-13-1866 (10-17-1866)
Anderson, Indiana to Grandison Tyler 4-7-1842
Anderson, Jane to James Mansker 12-10-1844
Anderson, Lila to Albert Moore 8-6-1866 [b]
Anderson, Margarett to Thomas Stewat 10-10-1839
Anderson, Martha to John Fry 4-4-1842
Anderson, Mildred to Nathaniel S. Richardson 12-27-1853
Anderson, Rebecca to John Comparee? 10-20-1840 (10-21-1840)
Anderson, Sarah A. to Edmond Robinson 11-28-1846 (11-29-1846)
Anderson, T. M. Allice to Michael B. Stone 1-6-1853
Andrews, Ann to John Kirksey 3-3-1859
Andrews, Sally Ann to Burrell Corban 8-21-1851
Anglen, Julia A. to Gideon B. Lyle 11-28-1843 (11-29-1843)
Anglen, M. J. to Jno. R. Martin 1-16-1849 (1-18-1849)
Apperson, Virginia to Archibald M. Anderson 9-29-1838 (9-30-1838)
Armstrong, Sarah J. to John M. Crunk 11-28-1853
Armstrong, Susan to James B. Morris 9-1-1860
Arnold, Ellen to John K. Shackleford 1-31-1857
Ashby, Amerentha P. to T. J. Stodghill 7-9-1860
Ashford, Julia Ann to Hesakiah Pagril? Hart 8-30-1850 (9-5-1850)
Atcherson, Columbia Ann to John N. Combs 1-11-1861
Atkerson, Mary to John Gray 12-25-1866 (12-27-1866) [b]
Atkinson, Mary J. to Wm. J. Mart 12-30-1852
Atkinson, Mary to John A. Irving 1-14-1865
Atkinson, Quintella to Beverly Clark 8-29-1846
Autin?, Sarah Jane to Richard T. Stewart 1-18-1860
Averet, Elizabeth to James H. Lemay 6-21-1844
Averett, Anna to William Davis 7-11-1842
Averett, Louisie? to R. J. Ragsdale 9-2-1852
Averett, Sarah D. to John S. Lay 4-22-1854 (4-25-1854)
Averiette, Jane W. to Wm. J. Lynes 5-3-1847 (5-4-1847)
Averitt, Louvice P. to J. R. Ragsdale 9-27-1852
Avritt, Mary A. to J. W. Foster 5-25-1848
Aykes, Jane to Wm. R. Hunt 1-1-1851 (1-2-1851)
Bacules?, Mariah to R. N. Graves 5-13-1846
Bagget, Dycy to Eleanor Miller 5-24-1840 (5-26-1840)
Bagget, Eliza Ann to Marion Simons 9-17-1853 (9-18-1853)
Bagget, Lucy to Leander Harney 2-4-1860 (2-6-1860)
Bagget, Martha to W. F. Broom 1-1-1867 (1-3-1867)

Bagget?, Nancy Jane to Wm. Lyle (no date; with 11-1850)
Baggett, Amanda to Calvin Underwood 8-13-1864
Baggett, D. A. to A. Baggett 7-30-1862 (8-3-1862)
Baggett, Elizabeth to Hughy Burns 1-22-1844
Baggett, Elizabeth to Josiah Bagget 3-19-1860 (3-23-1860)
Baggett, Holly to John W. Bennet 7-8-1865
Baggett, Martha to David Davis 2-21-1849 (2-22-1849)
Baggett, Martha to Samuel B. Sugg 4-7-1858
Baggett, Marthy to Dick McMalin 12-31-1866 (1-8-1867)
Baggett, Mary to Luke Heal 9-11-1858 (9-12-1858)
Baggett, Nancy Ann to Melvin F. Smith 4-25-1853 (5-1-1853)
Baggett, Nancy to Marion Sims 12-26-1850
Baggett, Sallie to G. Harvey 9-17-1864
Baggett, Sally Ann to William A. Smith 7-14-1852 (7-15-1852)
Baggett, Susan to Jas. Sinks 1-3-1861
Baguel, Mary J. to Stephen T. Fortune 8-14-1857
Bagwell(Bagett?), Lizza V. to James M. Gill 11-18-1856 (11-26-1856)
Bagwell, A. V. to W. P. Guthrie 2-1-1864
Bagwell, Emma V. to Jas. M. Larkins 2-19-1866 (2-20-1866)
Bagwell, Margaret C. to Richard Roberts 5-6-1852
Bagwell, Mary Ann Catharine to Allen H. Parrish 9-22-1852
    (9-23-1852)
Bagwell, Virginia B. to W. A. Hooper 2-27-1866 (3-1-1866)
Bagwell, Virginia to James W. Drake 7-27-1859 (8-30-1859)
Bailey, Eliza J. to Wm. E. James 11-3-1864 (11-10-1864)
Bailey, Eliza to Isaac Shelby 12-20-1855
Bailey, Mahala to C. Frederick 8-5-1841
Bailey, Martha to William R. Pinson 10-10-1839
Bailey, Martha to Wm. R. Pennix 10-15-1839 (10-18-1839)
Bailey, Mary E. to Marmaduke O. Dennis 9-22-1840 (9-23-1840)
Bailey, Moley V. to A. B. Maxey 1-17-1867
Bailey, Nancy Jane to E. H. Dean 7-4-1854
Bailey, Ruthey to Calvin? Bardes 12-27-1866
Bailey, S. A. to N. Y. Cavitt 9-18-1854 (9-19-1854)
Bailey, Sarah A. to David N. Kennedy 11-22-1843
Bailey, Susan P. to T. F. Blakemore 12-18-1849 (12-19-1848?)
Bailey, Susan to Washington Hargrove 12-13-1856 (12-18-1856)
Baily, Mary Jane to William H. Bruce 6-20-1857 (6-25-1857)
Baines, Elinor Ann E. to H. W. Lisenby 9-18-1849
Baird, Emily to John Bradley 1-16-1845
Baird, Emily to Joihn Bradly 1-16-1845
Baird, Harriet T. to John W. Mathis 2-10-1857 (2-11-1857)
Baird, Jane to William Bradley 3-5-1838
Baird, Levita A. to Alexander L. Carter 5-27-1861 (5-30-1861)
Baird, Mary Ann to Larkin Bradley 2-29-1844 (3-1-1844)
Baker, Elizabeth to Hugh McGuire 9-11-1847 (9-12-1847)
Baker, Elizabeth to Littleton Story 3-21-1846
Baker, Martha A. to J. M. McKinney 11-5-1846
Baker, Mary Frances to William Vaughn 9-7-1844
Baker, Nancy S. to Leander Jackson 3-10-1857 (3-11-1857)
Baker, Patsey to Isaac Garrett 11-3-1866 [b]
Baker, Sarah Elizabeth to John H. Calesham 2-28-1854
Baker, Susannah to Edward Rogers 9-27-1841
Balden, Mary to Wm. Shelby 7-21-1865 (1-21-1875?)
Balentine, Sarah to Marcus D. Boyd 2-9-1850 (2-10-1850)
Ballentine, Ann E. to William Rogers 4-25-1853
Ballentine, C. P. to C. H. Jinkins 12-15-1840 (12-16-1840)
Ballentine, Malinda to James Riter 1-4-1841 (1-6-1841)
Ballentine, Mary to A. Stewart 8-19-1851 (8-30-1851)
Balsett?, Amanda A. to J. M> Miller 6-28-1856
Balthrop, Fannie to W. T. Williams 3-29-1864
Balthrop, Mattie J. to James Y. Carter 6-15-1858 (6-17-1858)
Balthrop, Sally E. to Thomas H. Manson 11-23-1858
Bane, Mary to John Baggett 8-17-1856
Banes, Mary to Jacob B. Hase 2-19-1844 (2-21-1844)
Barbee, Ann Eliza to Robt. A. Wilson 11-21-1860
Barbee, Eliza Jane to Jas. Andrew Powers 12-24-1860 (12-28-1860)
Barbee, Emily E. to Robert J. Toler 10-30-1856
Barbee, Lucy Ann to J. W. Powell 6-2-1856
Barbee, Martha Ann to Samuel Shelton 5-3-1855
Barbee, Martha to Geo. W. Darnel 7-23-1850 (7-24-1850)
Barbee, Sue E. to A. McDaniel 12-22-1857
Barber, Harriett to Jackson Davie 9-15-1866 (10-20-1866) [b]
Barber, Susan J. to Edward D. Moore 6-17-1853 (6-19-1854?)

Barker, Barbary Ann to A. M. Clayton 1-10-1839
Barker, Caroline E. to F. Glass 1-9-1845 (1-15-1845)
Barker, Deny to William Furgerson 1-1-1866 (4-1-1866) [b]
Barker, M. L. to James A. Trice 3-6-1850
Barker, Margaret to Jas. Fortson 1-24-1867 [b]
Barker, Martha Delinia to Robert H. Wimberley 9-28-1853
    (10-11-1853)
Barker, Mary Elizabeth to Lewis Vaughan 3-10-1851
Barker, Mary Jane to John G. McKoin 2-13-1840
Barker, Mary W. to E. Walton Barker 11-14-1860 (11-15-1860)
Barker, Nancy A. to Cyrus W. Greenfield 9-9-1856
Barker, Nancy M. to Robt. F. Ferguson 8-19-1842
Barker, Parasetta to Michael Powers 3-5-1859 (3-6-1859)
Barker, Sarah A. to James W. Wilkerson 9-10-1853
Barker, Sarah A. to Thomas L. Yancy 11-1-1847 (11-4-1847)
Barksdale, Louisa M. to Joseph T. Johnson 3-14-1854
Barksdale, Sarah V. to Frank E. Hardwick 6-23-1859
Barnes, Mary R. to R. M. House 5-8-1838 (5-10-1838)
Barnes, Sally Ann to Berry W. Andrews 12-16-1839 (12-19-1839)
Barnes, Sally Ann to P. B. Williamson 4-5-1848 (4-6-1848)
Barnett, Lucrecia to A. Garnett 12-18-1857
Barret, Nancy to Wellington Proudfit 11-30-1845
Barret, Sophia to George S. Thomas 12-30-1847
Barrett, Martha to B. B. Hurst 9-28-1858
Bartie, E. G. to James M. Lewis 1-30-1843
Bartlett, Sarah E. to Daniel R. Blair 6-19-1865
Barton, Amanda S. to Wm. A. Solomon 10-29-1861
Barton, Mary to Gideon Nicholson 12-30-1852
Barton, Mary to William L. Dwyer 11-26-1856 (11-27-1856)
Barton, Nancy to Wm. Wall 11-10-1839
Bashar, Angelina to James R. Craft 11-20-1855
Bass, Elizabeth to Albert Martin 10-22-1866 [b]
Batem, Elizabeth M. to W. J. Lyle 11-22-1860
Batheny, Elizabeth to Oscar Gupton 1-7-1840
Bats, Martha Ann to Banister Wright 12-21-1852
Batson, Mary Elizabeth to Simmons S. Tally 2-7-1859 (2-9-1859)
Batson, Nancy E. to J. A. L. Schmittou 4-7-1866 (4-8-1866)
Batson, Nancy to John B. Walter 10-20-1854
Batson, Susan to Wm. Haigue? 1-13-1851 (1-15-1851)
Batts, Frances to B. N. Pool 1-25-1855
Batts, Jane to Abner Gupton 5-18-1844 (5-19-1844)
Batts, Sally to John Walker 10-23-1847 (10-24-1847)
Baugh, Elizabeth to Frederick Gillum 3-10-1845
Baugh, Martha to James L. McGeehee 8-8-1838 (8-14-1838)
Baxter, Darthula to Alexander Jackson 10-2-1850
Baxter, Louisa to Gilbert T. Abernathy 1-2-1839 (1-8-1839)
Baxter, Mary D. to Stephen D. Watkins 12-13-1842 (12-20-1842)
Baxter, Mrs. M to C. B. Plummer 8-11-1862
Bayair, S. G. to Britton James 12-25-1843
Bayles, Sarah to George Senter 6-29-1839
Bayless, Arabella to W. J. Hart 5-1-1848 (5-4-1848)
Bayless, Fanny? to James Darnell 7-24-1841 (7-31-1841)
Bayless, Sarah E. to Edward S. Wynne 12-27-1845 (12-28-1845)
Bayliss, Lucy to William Fulkerson 8-28-1860 (8-29-1860)
Bayliss, Mary A. H. to William Hurt 12-10-1853 (12-13-1853)
Bayliss, Sarah M. to J. M. Cachett 2-17-1846 (2-19-1846)
Baynham, Isabella to Jas. W. Trahem 11-14-1865 (11-15-1865)
Baynham, Sally to John Levell 3-28-1866 (4-14-1866) [b]
Beach, Eliza to P. T. Cavellur? 2-8-1840
Beachert, Sallie to William Martin 11-3-1856
Beaime?, Caroline to James M. Bucks 11-25-1845 (11-29-1845)
Beard, E. to Chas. S. Willard 3-1-1862
Bearden, Sarah J. to Abraham Vinsen 2-17-1864
Bearden, Susan C. to M. L. Lindsay 5-4-1857
Beasley, Matilda to Spencer Perdue 9-3-1840 (9-20-1840)
Beaumont, Adaline B. to Joseph M. Irwin 6-17-1841
Beaumont, Clara H. to A. B. Russell 11-9-1848
Beaumont, Clara to Thomas W. Wisdom 3-6-1855
Beaumont, Florence to Edward H. Brittan 6-26-1865
Beaumont, Mary Ann to W. J. Castner 6-9-1842
Beaumont, Mauda to Westley Rice 5-3-1866 [b]
Beaumont?, Emma C. to Benjamin S. Leavell 12-3-1852
Beckham(Beshears?), Harriet to John Godsey 11-15-1855
    (11-25-1855)
Beedin, Nancy L. to Wm. G. Powell 9-15-1846 (9-16-1846)

Bell, Elizabeth G. to George W. Catron 5-6-1839 (5-7-1839)
Bell, Jennetta to Willey Murphy 1-13-1842
Bell, Keziah to Henry Smith 4-30-1866 [b]
Bell, M. C. to A. B. Hendrick 12-18-1862
Bell, Mary C. to Chas. M. Day 12-4-1851
Bell, Mary to Abner Hunter 12-2-1839 (12-5-1839)
Bell, Natha A. to Wm. C. Smith 11-28-1854 (11-29-1854)
Bell, Rebecca to William Wiggins 12-25-1845
Bell, Sarah E. to Martin Howard 2-13-1846 (2-19-1846)
Bell, Sophia Ann to Obediah B. Griffin 1-31-1859 (2-4-1859)
Bellamy, Mary J. to James A. Marable 3-25-1854 (3-28-1854)
Bellamy, Sarah A. to Johnathan Starkey 10-2-1856 (10-8-1856)
Bellemy, Lacy to Granderson Eldridge 1-6-1866 (1-15-1866) [b]
Benham, Elizabeth Ann to William N. Simpson 12-25-1850
Bennett, Mary R. to Leander M. Wood 10-11-1858 (10-13-1858)
Bennett, Nancy to Archer Lee 6-24-1853 (6-28-1853)
Bernan, Fanny to George Bradshaw 4-21-1865 [b]
Bert, Cornelia A. S. to Thos. Williams 9-1-1849
Bethune, Ann Eliza to Jacob B. Basford 10-14-1854 (10-19-1854)
Beville, Frances to Joseph Pollard 1-26-1841
Bibb, Frances A. to Thomas M. Ingram 8-29-1856
Bibb, Henrietta to George D. White 9-4-1855 (9-6-1855)
Biggers, Sarah Catharine to James H. Pace 12-28-1852
Bigham, Elenora to McKendrie Hollister 6-14-1864
Billingsly, Delia to Bluford Nolen 11-22-1849
Billingsly, Nancy to W. G. Black 3-11-1851
Billingsly, Sarah to Jas. M. Outlaw 2-10-1849 (2-11-1849)
Bingham, Louisa to John McCauley 5-3-1842
Binkley, Louisa to Loyd Taylor 2-9-1867 (2-10-1867)
Binkley, Martha J. to G. L. Holt 1-8-1867 (1-10-1867)
Binkley, Martha J. to Mathew Morris 2-10-1854
Binkley, R. to John Holt 7-2-1862
Binwell?, Elizabeth to Benjamin Trotter 12-16-1856
Birch, Elenor E. to Charles Jones 10-22-1847
Bircham, Eliza to William Holcomb 11-24-1854
Bircham, Jane to Fredrick Swisher 3-18-1850
Bird, Sadie J. to Charles J. Elmire 12-15-1859
Birdwell, Julian to Robert C. Chance 1-13-1846 (1-14-1846)
Birdwell, Margaret J. to Greenbery Suggs 7-11-1846 (7-12-1846)
Birdwell, Mary A. M. to William C. Weakley 1-2-1854 (1-4-1854)
Black, Clarinda to James J. Blanton 3-10-1851
Black, Elizabeth to Daniel Hodges 2-1-1840 (2-2-1840)
Black, Elizabeth to George Morrow 1-11-1866
Black, Elizabeth to Henry W. Morehead 3-9-1838 (3-22-1838)
Black, Hulda to William Davis 8-13-1851 (8-14-1851)
Black, M. A. to A. J. Fanning 10-27-1855
Black, Maria F. to Thomas Ellis 5-15-1866 (5-23-1866)
Black, Mary to Thomas Baggett 11-1-1862 (11-17-1862)
Black, Orlina to Jessee Rippey 1-22-1852
Blackman, Isapheny A. to James B. Tandy 7-5-1848 (8-8-1848)
Blackman, Mrs. S. C. to Thos. H. Jackson 9-4-1862
Blair, Sarah E. to Marcus Hodges 12-24-1866 (12-26-1866)
Blak, Rebecca to Preston Span 10-30-1857 (10-2?-1857)
Blake, Sarah C. to James Coe 10-29-1855
Blake, Susan E. to Rolf Eldridge 3-14-1859 (3-15-1859)
Blakemore, Martha L. to Jno. B. Helm 5-26-1842 (6-2-1842)
Blane, Ann to A. C. Richards 1-6-1851 (1-16-1851)
Blane, Malvina to C. T. Mitchel 11-23-1850
Blankenship, Hannah to William H. Yates 8-6-1866 (8-7-1866)
Blanks, S. H. to Wm. B. Low 3-7-1848
Blanton, Mrs. C. to G. W. Coon 12-20-1863
Blanton, Rebecca to Joseph Powell 2-15-1852
Blount, Eliza E. to Bryan Smith 9-21-1855 (9-23-1855)
Blount, Martha to William Bumpass 10-26-1857 (10-29-1857)
Blount, Miss N. to William F. Stone 12-23-1848
Boatwright, Mattie E. to A. F. Estes 5-9-1859 (1-10-1859)
Bobbit, Rebecca to Francis M. Thaxton 1-17-1854 (1-19-1854)
Bobo, Charlotte M. to W. B. Gardner 12-7-1847
Bobo, Elizabeth A. to Joseph M. Dye 5-11-1840 (5-12-1840)
Bobo, Lucinda to David Grant 7-20-1840 (7-21-1840)
Boddie, Jennie to Sam Malory 10-31-1866 [b]
Bodine, Emily W. to Alney? M. Jenkins 2-17-1854
Bodine, Harriet to William H. Stephens 2-19-1858 (2-20-1858)
Boid, C. to R. H. Stamper 6-23-1862
Boid, Laura to Caleb Thomas 5-12-1866 [b]

Bonds, Sarah Ann to John Anderson 2-26-1847? (2-28-1848)
Bone, Elizabeth to Benjamin Baggett 7-4-1849
Bone, Frances to Clayton Rollins 4-4-1842 (4-7-1842)
Boofter?, Emma to John Roland 10-13-1863
Booth, Bell to Samuel Bolton 1-24-1861
Booth, Martha J. to William Lisenby 1-10-1854
Boothe, Eliza M. to Joseph H. Pollard 9-19-1855
Borders, Mary A. to Peter J. Woodson 10-5-1861
Borne, Louisa to James A. Seay 11-22-1859 (11-24-1859)
Bourne, Fannie J. to H. E. Beech 12-15-1859 (12-22-1859)
Bourne, Mary Ann to G. S. Reeser 12-7-1852
Bourne, Sue C. to N.Lewis Whitfield 9-5-1863 (9-10-1863)
Bourne, Virginia to William J. St. John 1-9-1855 (1-10-1855)
Bowers, E. M. to W. C. Parker 12-26-1858
Bowers, Elizabeth C. to K. C. Bowers 12-19-1849 (12-24-1849)
Bowers, Elizabeth C. to Kinchen C. Bowers 12-19-1850 (12-24-1849?)
Bowers, Lucretia to Geo. Dougherty 1-29-1866 (1-31-1866)
Bowers, Mary A. M. P. to J. R. Jennett 12-19-1860 (12-20-1860)
Bowers, Mary A. to B. M. Williamson 8-10-1857 (8-11-1857)
Bowers, Nancy to Judson Horn 5-2-1839 (5-3-1839)
Bowers, Perlina to Drury Allen 7-11-1841
Bowling, M. Hellen to Dr. B. S. Wood 11-22-1866
Bowling, Mildred L. to Samuel H. Morgan 11-4-1859 (11-8-1859)
Bowling, Virginia A. to James B. Grant 2-7-1854
Bowls, Mrs. Mary to William Marsh 9-12-1865 (9-13-1865)
Bowman, Amelia to G. H. Slaughter 10-4-1856 (10-5-1856)
Bowman, E. B. to G. B. Smith 12-18-1848
Bowman, Ellener to Philip S. Woodward 8-1-1843 (8-3-1843)
Bowman, Mary L. to L. D. Hopkins 10-19-1843 (10-21-1843)
Boyd, Isabella to Robert V. Lewis 4-14-1856
Boyd, Virginia C. to William M. Finly 9-20-1859
Boyd, Wilmuth H. to Henry L. Bailey 3-22-1843
Brackett, Rebecca to Enoch Asby 11-10-1849
Bradbery, Elizabeth to Richard Orne 1-5-1846 (1-7-1846)
Bradley, Hisler? Ann to George Western 1-29-1853
Bradley, L. C. to William Suter 10-26-1850 (10-27-1850)
Bradley, L. C. to Wm. M. Lulre? 10-16-1851 (10-17-1851)
Bradley, Lockey C. to Felix G. Gilbert 6-18-1850 (not endorsed)
Bradley, Mary to Joseph Jackson 6-12-1850
Bradley, Nannie to Jas. C. Davis 4-18-1865
Bradley, Ophelia to Elisha Rose 3-16-1860 (3-15?-1860)
Bradly, Jenny to W. B. Daniel 7-6-1855
Bradly, Mary to John Cook 6-9-1857
Bradly, Rebecca to Wilie Rose 12-8-1851 (12-11-1851)
Bradshaw, Lou to John Boswell 8-7-1866 [b]
Bradshaw, Mary Frances to George Davis 4-9-1852 (4-11-1852)
Braime, Susan Olive to Henry W. Watts 5-14-1859 (5-15-1859)
Brake, Margaret to John W. Gray 1-5-1843
Brake, Martha to Wm. W. Winn 1-18-1859
Brame, Agniss to P. N. Anderon 3-23-1844
Brame, Martha H. to Thomas B. Prewett 3-13-1845
Branigan, Bridget to Edward Costello 4-21-1859
Bransford, Maria to Champion H. Jenkins 9-11-1847
Brantley, Jane to Thos. G. Keats 11-26-1862
Brantley, Prissilla to Elliott Coleman 6-29-1839 (7-1-1839)
Brantly, Elizabeth to John H. Buck 4-8-1857
Brantly, Frances to Samuel Shepherd 11-24-1858 (11-25-1858)
Brantly, Martha A. to Gillam W. Burgess 6-19-1856
Brantly, Mary C. to Henry Hickison 7-27-1855 (7-31-1855)
Brantly, Mary to N. B. Kenner 6-17-1858
Brathet, P. C. to E. D. Sappington 11-6-1838
Bratton, Lavinia A. to Jas. E. Solomon 9-6-1866
Brawner, Malinda to J. W. B. Stephens 2-27-1861
Braytn, Emma to George W. Rose 3-29-1865 (3-31-1865)
Breeden, Adelia Ann J. to George Breedin 3-25-1858
Breeden, Mary B. to William H. Breeden 11-22-1855 (10?-22-1855)
Breeden, Rhoda Caroline to L. O. Breeden 3-25-1858
Breedon, Sally to Hugh Myres 8-21-1846 (8-23-1846)
Brewers, Elizabeth to J. Collier 1-20-1851
Brickell, Almetia to Wm. V. Hackney 8-2-1850
Brickle, Jane A. to John H. Bryan 1-3-1842 (1-4-1842)
Brickle, Mary E. to Samuel Baylis 11-11-1847
Bridge, Rebecca Ann to James Bagget 5-30-1860
Bridgewaters, Adaline T. to Joseph B. Williams 10-24-1839
Bright, Mary to John White 7-8-1843 (7-18-1843)

Bright, Sally to Demsey Enniss 8-25-1838 (8-26-1838)
Brim?, Rebecca to Edwd. M. Jolly 12-10-1843
Bringhurst, Rebecca H. to S. Plummer 10-14-1851
Brinson, Mary E. to Hugh S. Garland 11-12-1839
Bristo, Ann to Joseph N. McGee 12-30-1857 (12-31-1857)
Bristow, Darcus to William Clymer 3-21-1846 (3-26-1846)
Britain, Nancy C. to Reuben T. Pollard 10-15-1856 (10-18-1856)
Britt, Ann to Michael McQueene 9-2-1854
Britt, Fredonia R. to Charles S. Hodges 7-8-1848
Britt, Fredonia R. to John J. Williams 10-8-1843
Britten, A. H. to Rev. A. J. Baird 5-8-1850
Britten, E. S. to John Oneal 9-10-1852 (9-11-1852)
Britton, Mary to Mack Stewart 7-4-1866 [b]
Broadbent, Mrs. Fannie to Peter Kelly 3-30-1861
Broadbent, Ruth Elizabeth to Gustavus Morris 12-28-1863
    (12-29-1863)
Broaddie, Medora to A. D. Fletcher 12-3-1861
Broaddus, Martha A. to Elijah Broaddus 5-31-1838
Broaddus, Mary J. to Joshua M. Rice 5-?-1853
Broadhead, Ann Louisa to Wm. H. Taylor 6-19-1850 (6-20-1850)
Broadie, Fannie to Jackson Wilson 11-26-1866 (12-17-1866) [b]
Broadmax, Fancis? to Edmond Herring 12-8-1866 [b]
Broady, Lily to Tom Broady 1-1-1867 (4-14-1867) [b]
Broady, Peggy to Henry Cordal 12-12-1866 (12-16-1866) [b]
Brock, Ellen to Jas. M. Crocket 10-7-1848
Brock, Lucinda to Elias Wight? 7-26-1840
Brock, Manervy Ann to John B. Scott 3-21-1848
Brock, Mrs. Louisa to Thos. D. Harvey 1-26-1865
Brockman, Ann E. to C. J. Rives 1-7-1852 (1-15-1852)
Brockman, Margarett to Geo. W. Parker 4-11-1849
Brockman, Mary J. to K. A. Butterworth 10-31-1850 (10-5-1850)
Brockman, Nancy C. to William M. Brickle 11-10-1864
Brockmon, Ann E. to Charles A. Rives 1-7-1852
Broddie, Ethalinda(Catharine) to Thos. A. Jones 9-9-1846 (9-10-1846)
Broddie, Praree H. to James M. Thermond 5-9-1859 (5-11-1859)
Broddis, Elizabeth to Robert Crews 5-18-1846
Broddus, Margaret J. to Johnathan T. Nalin 6-13-1854
Broddy, Martha to Isaac Tramel 5-15-1866 [b]
Brodie, Mary T. to John W. Neblett 9-9-1844 (9-16?-1844)
Brodie, Sally Ann H. B. to L. B. Boon 6-8-1841 (6-15-1841)
Brodie, Susan to James A. Boyd 1-23-1849 (1-25-1849)
Brodie?, Virginia M. to George W. Johnson 7-17-1853
Broink?, Priscilla to James Meesman 10-14-1846 (10-22-1846)
Brooking, Jane to Lewis P. Heleighty? 8-28-1847
Brooks, E. to R. M. Pollock 1-8-1866
Broom, Frances E. to Charles G. Hodges 6-17-1854 (6-22-1854)
Broom, Mary C. to James H. Hinley 9-30-1865
Broom, Nancy A. to Thompson Powers 7-24-1860 (7-26-1860)
Browder, Lucy Ann to Olander Hawkins 3-25-1865 [b]
Browder, Martha H. to Jonathan S. Baker 4-11-1853
Brown, A. to B. R. Smith 11-7-1866 (11-9-1866)
Brown, Bettie J. to A. S. Wood 3-12-1866 (3-13-1866)
Brown, Caroline G. to William G. Smith 1-22-1845 (1-27-1845)
Brown, Elizabeth to E. D. Smith 10-19-1850
Brown, Harriet to Collin Horn 12-21-1866 (12-25-1866) [b]
Brown, Louisa to George Welker 1-5-1857 (1-8-1857)
Brown, Lucinda to Wm. A. Wood 2-26-1843
Brown, Lucretia E. to Nathan Allen 6-7-1843
Brown, Lucy B. to Johnson Pile 9-25-1844
Brown, Mahala to Jessee L. Crotzer 7-28-1842
Brown, Manervia A. to Squire S. Wall 9-23-1848 (9-24-1848)
Brown, Martha C. to Leander W. Crotzer 11-13-1856
Brown, Martha to Edwin T. Hart 12-29-1853
Brown, Martha to Jno. W. Bagwell 11-30-1843 12-1-1843
Brown, Mary Ann to William M. Bagwell 9-28-1852
Brown, Mary Elizabeth to James W. Council 10-26-1858 (10-27-1858)
Brown, Mary Jane to Elijah S. Wall 5-6-1847
Brown, Mary L. to A. B. Donaho 10-4-1855
Brown, Mary S. to Chas. M. Morris 10-2-1862
Brown, Mary to J. A. Pigue 11-8-1855
Brown, Mary to Wiley F. Crotzer 10-29-1844
Brown, Mary to William Bailey 7-1-1839 (7-4-1839)
Brown, Mollie to Chester Ware 6-9-1866 [b]
Brown, Nancy to John C. Burney 12-29-1847
Brown, Sarah Ann to James Nicolson 1-24-1849 (1-25-1849)

Brown, Sarah G. to John H. Sugg 12-29-1866 (12-30-1866)
Brown, Sarah to Wilson Chumbles 1-20-1855
Brownfield, Maranda to Milton W. Holland 10-16-1842 (10-17-1842)
Browning, Nancy D. J. to William J. Marshall 9-20-1840 (9-21-1840)
Browning, Nancy to James L. Stewart 9-19-1857
Bruce, Mary Elizabeth to Elijah Neal 11-12-1859
Bruce, Rebecca to Isaac Edward 5-1-1847 (5-2-1847)
Bruighurst?, Sallie M. to Benj. F. Poston 5-18-1858
Brunson, Elizabeth to Cave Johnson 2-20-1838
Brunson, Judith B. to Thomas A. Davis 2-24-1848
Brunson, Parnelope J. to Edwin W. Hickman 9-4-1845
Brunson, Penelope J. to E. W. Hickman 9-4-1845
Brunt, Dora C. to Abraham Whitehead 6-17-1865 (6-18-1865)
Bruton, Sarah S. to John M. Hogan 4-16-1850
Bryan, Clarissa F. to Jacob G. Welker 9-30-1859 (10-2-1859)
Bryan, Eliza to Peter Smith 12-8-1841 (12-9-1841)
Bryan, Henrietta to Washington Grant 10-20-1841
Bryan, Rebecca A. to Ethanah P. Adams 10-19-1855
Bryan, Robert A. V. to Henry Dickerson 12-8-1840
Bryan, Tennessee H. to Wm. T. Bryan 10-31-1864 (11-1-1864)
Bryant, Eliza to L. B. Moore 11-6-1838
Bryant, Elizabeth Ann to Abial Cushman 12-11-1848 (12-12-1848)
Bryant, Mary J. to John Griffey 12-19-1864 (12-21-1864)
Bryant, Mary T. to Christopher Bryan 3-1-1847
Bryant, Mrs. Permelia A. to Thos. W. Tucker 2-8-1864 (2-17-1864)
Bryant, Sarah J. to A. B. Rye 12-14-1859
Buck, Angie to Saml. Brockman 8-26-1857 (8-21?-1857)
Buck, Anna R. to William Robinson 12-31-1846
Buck, Annis L. to William Robinson 11-9-1858
Buck, Eliza Margarette to Peter N. Marr 10-24-1840
Buck, Lucy B. to John W. Blanton 12-4-1851
Buck, R. to J. B. Helm 12-15-1862 (12-16-1862)
Buck, Samuella to Joseph Keeth 11-24-1847 (11-25-1847)
Buck, Sarah T. to John? J. Riggins 12-28-1858
Buckhannon, M. A. to Lewis T. Hughs 11-14-1839 (11-15-1839)
Buckhanon, Margaret to James Griffin 7-7-1845
Buckingham, Mary J. to G. H. McGee 9-30-1852
Buckle, Martha to Wm. C. Gooch 9-16-1841
Buckley, Elizabeth E. to James S. Shepherd 10-11-1853 (10-13-1853)
Buckley, Mary Ann to Richard N. Hatcher 7-29-1846 (7-30-1846)
Buckly, Frances L. to Henry F. Trice 11-23-1853 (11-24-1853)
Buckly, Mancy M. to William Louis Gardiner 5-3-1856 (5-4-1856)
Buckner, Fanny to Thornton Wheatley 11-17-1866 (12-22-1866) [b]
Buckner, Louisa A. M. to Thos. L. Cotton 5-4-1854
Budwatten, Mary E. S. to Roger Williams 12-16-1846 (12-17-1846)
Bull, Angeline to Jessee B. Hagewood 8-20-1858 (8-22-1858)
Bull, Elizabeth to Thomas Martin 9-27-1843 (9-28-1843)
Bull, Harriet to Lorn Collins 2-28-1855
Bull, Mary L. to James M. Harris 12-21-1854
Bullard, Jane C. to Saml. Commins 5-22-1848 (5-24-1848)
Bullard, Octavia to James O. Myres 10-5-1857
Bullard, Sarah P. to P. K. Dilling 7-25-1848
Bullifin, Martha J. to Richard C. George 3-5-1838
Bullion, Frances Caroline to Levis Woods 10-4-1850 (10-9-1850)
Bullock, Lucy Ann to Jessee W. Bartee 2-7-1852
Bulls, Rhoda to Alexander Wood 6-6-1850
Bumpas, Eliza to Jas. Smith 2-26-1863 (3-25-1863)
Bumpas, Mary Ann to Cincinnattus Wall 10-15-1866
Bumpas, Sarah L. to James Westley Sykes 5-23-1865
Bumpass, Mary Ann to Samuel C. Jones 2-11-1858
Bumpass, Mary E. to A. J. Wykoff 12-3-1853
Bumpass, Nancy F. to Jas. Henry Brame 1-11-1866
Bumpass, S. A. to W. T. Johnson 5-9-1857 (5-19-1857)
Bundarant, Evelina to William Williams 8-31-1844 (7?-30?-1844)
Bundurant, Emily J. to James L. Spencer 4-11-1839
Bunghurst, Mary to W. S. Garvin 10-20-1842
Bunlin, Nancy to Asa Silgus 5-1-1856
Bunting, Martha Jane to William S. McQuerry 12-27-1847
Bunting, Susan to Jefferson R. Watson 2-17-1840 (2-19-1840)
Burgess, Amanda Frances to Joseph Alexander Seay 12-28-1853
    (12-18?-1853)
Burgess, Eliza to Sampson Hart 2-15-1843 (2-16-1843)
Burgess, Frances to Geo. S. Willerford 2-21-1849 (2-25-1849)
Burgess, Virginia B. to P. C. Hambaugh? 10-5-1852
Burnes, Elizabeth to Thomas R. Clark 8-18-1848 (8-21-1848)

Burnett, Elizabeth to Francis M. Shelton 4-29-1853 (5-1-1853)
Burnett, Nely to Henry Mays 4-21-1865 [b]
Burney, Ann L. to George F. Lucas 10-13-1856 (10-15-1856)
Burney, Elizabeth C. to Nicholas E. Bagwell 12-15-1858 (12-16-1858)
Burney, Lucinda to James H. Rye 2-27-1864 (3-2-1864)
Burney, Mrs. Harriet to Nathaniel Saunders 7-5-1845
Burnine, Margaret to Stephen Ramsey 8-11-1853
Burns, Martha E. to Elias Watwood 11-23-1853 (11-24-1853)
Burns, Mary E. to Goin Harriss 12-30-1843 (12-31-1843)
Burrough, Rachel to Jacob V. D. Stout 2-13-1854 (2-15-1854)
Burruss, Nannie P. to N. L. Nothington? 7-20-1852
Burton, Adaline to Ephraim S. Houston 10-25-1839 (10-30-1839)
Burton, Ann to Jacob Hogan 4-4-1842 (4-5-1842)
Burton, Harriet to Elijah Anderson 9-4-1848
Burton?, Martha to Watson Dockry 1-31-1850 (2-5-1850)
Burwell?, Virginia C. to William H. Thompson 12-17-1858
Bush, Louise? to A. C. Stewart 5-30-1856 (5-31-1856)
Bush, Sarah J. to Silas Russell 10-26-1846 (10-28-1846)
Bustam, Mary J. to Peter Myres 12-17-1845
Butler, Eliza C. to George W. Butler 8-5-1860
Butler, Maria to John Cox 1-13-1860 (1-15-1860)
Butts, Audry to Johnathan Simmons? 2-21-1848 (3-1-1848)
Byars, Elizabeth Ann to Carter Page 12-13-1843 (12-14-1843)
Byless, Agness to Jessee G. Adams 2-8-1864 (2-15-1864)
Byrne, Fannie to James McDonnall 3-4-1865
Byrus, Sarah M. to George Grant 10-31-1839
Cabaniss, Virginia R. to William H. Herndon? 3-15-1853
Cabness, America B. to Meridith R. White 9-17-1844
Cage, Elmira E. to Henry Grant 12-26-1866 [b]
Cahill, Hannah to John Dunlavy 4-16-1855 (4-17-1855)
Cain, Catharine to John Stewart 9-16-1849
Cain, Martha to Hiram Lewis 6-4-1854
Cain, N. M. to J. F. Perdue 1-6-1855 (1-7-1855)
Cain, Sarah to J. Forsythe 7-24-1850
Caisley, Elizabeth to William O. Gordan 2-18-1843 (2-23-1843)
Caits, Melia C. to Charles Yarbrough 9-4-1845
Cake, Susan to John A. Moore 6-21-1865
Caldwell, Nancy to Sterling Neblett 6-19-1843
Calesham, Alice James to William Manning 10-6-1853 (10-7-1853)
Calesham, Elizabeth M. to Spelward? P. Evans 1-9-1860
Calesham, Melissa M. to S. G. Martin 12-12-1859
Calhoon, Lucy Melvina to Orrin Edwards 1-22-1861 (1-24-1861)
Calisham, Eliza to William E. Ellis 8-23-1853
Calishaw, Martha Catharine to John S. Whelen 4-9-1852 (4-11-1852)
Callester, Martha to Joseph Reynolds 2-12-1852
Calvert, Mary C. to Alfred Perry 8-26-1849
Cammick, Jane M. to H. D. Whealley 7-30-1853 (8-1-1853)
Campanie, Sarah to Thomas Handy 5-7-1858 (5-9-1858)
Campbell, Eliza J. to Gabriel Gillaspie 11-11-1856 (11-16-1856)
Campbell, Frances to Andrew Howell 8-1-1859 (8-2-1859)
Campbell, Lutitia T. to T. S. Howell 7-22-1857 (7-23-1857)
Campbell, Mary Catharine to Wesley Sladen 3-3-1858 (3-4-1858)
Campbell, Mary E. to James Oats 8-7-1856
Campbell, Mary to H. H. Center 9-19-1860
Campbell, Mary to Henry J. Pool 3-15-1847
Campbell, Nannie to Calep Bryan 9-21-1865 [b]
Cane, Lockey to Rhoden S. Williams 3-27-1842 (3-31-1842)
Caner, Mary Janie to Thos. L. Stenn 6-25-1843
Cantrell, Penny? D. to N. C. L. Reynolds 10-14-1842
Carden, Mary E. to J. W. W. Morgan 7-13-1849
Cardin, Emerline to John B. Seargeant 1-1-1866
Cardin, Sarah F. to John W. Faris 3-30-1864 (3-31-1864)
Carmac, Emily H. to Reuben Thomas 9-6-1854
Carneal, Nancy Jane to Lawrence Allison 1-21-1858 (1-22-1858)
Carnell, Mildred Jane to Kendal Burgess Davis 9-8-1856
Carner, M. J. to Benja. F. Yandell 1-26-1863
Carnes, Martha to Jas. K. Tyner 7-11-1849 (7-12-1849)
Carney, Cordelia to George T. Cross 3-1-1855
Carney, Julia to Saml. Hodgson 10-1-1853 (10-4-1853)
Carney, Louisa A. to Isaac M. Perrin 1-28-1839 (1-29-1839)
Carney, Lu to Jack Warfield 12-25-1866 [b]
Carney, M. E. to R. H. Carney 3-9-1861 (no return)
Carney, Mary E. to David C. Estis 12-6-1856 (12-7-1856)
Carney, Paptice to Overton Frazier 12-27-1866 (12-29-1866) [b]
Carney, Silvestey A. to Lawson J. Murphy 9-29-1852 (9-30-1852)

Carney, Winny to Thomas Butler 4-5-1856
Carns, Matilda to David Nicholson 12-26-1853 (1-5-1854)
Caro, Martha M. to William H. Phelps 6-30-1840
Carr, Caroline to B. F. Christian 11-17-1839 (11-21-1839)
Carr, Lucinda D. to Thomas Bonner 8-19-1840
Carr, Mary E. to Saml. H. Northington 6-2-1845
Carr, Mollie to John Waters 1-13-1866
Carr, Nancy to Jas. E. Franklin 10-28-1847
Carr, Sallie to James Hair 8-1-1859
Carr, Virginia to James T. Atkins 11-18-1840 (12-22-1840)
Carraway, Elizabeth to Zachariah Sullins 12-13-1840 (12-14-1850)
Carroll, Caroline to Jerry Forsythe 9-2-1857 (9-27-1857)
Carroll, Eliza to Jas. Sherwood 9-3-1838 (9-6-1838)
Carroll, Ellender to Thomas Rye 2-13-1854 (2-14-1854)
Carroll, Martha Ann to Westley T. Langston 3-29-1859 (3-30-1859)
Carroll, Mary Ann to Philip Cellighan 8-29-1848
Carroll, Nancy Jane to William B. Robertson 8-17-1857
Carroll, Nancy to Michael Kelly 7-23-1858 (7-24-1858)
Carroll, Rachael J. to John Shurwood 12-9-1840
Carry, Sally to James G. Yates 8-17-1839 (8-18-1839)
Carsly?, Martha Ann to John M. Harris 1-3-1852
Carter, Amanda F. to Benjamin Davis 4-24-1844
Carter, Ann E. to Andrew Rudolph omitted with 11-1839
Carter, Debora to William H. Smith 11-6-1853
Carter, Edline to Lemial Barker 12-24-1866 [b]
Carter, Eliza C. to Thomas Rawlins 1-7-1839 (1-10-1839)
Carter, Elizabeth to Nathan Hosler? 1-5-1853 (1-9-1853)
Carter, Ellen to Peter Riggins 7-7-1866 (7-8-1866) [b]
Carter, Julia Ann to Saml. Dougherty 10-13-1843
Cartright, Margaret E. to James W. Rose 12-7-1846 (12-9-1846)
Carver, Elizabeth to Charles M. Lewis 7-10-1846
Carver, Fannie to Charles Williams 2-16-1860
Cary, Mary to Patrick Castello 2-5-1859 (2-13-1859)
Casper, Dorinda to David D. McLean 2-25-1858 (2-28-1858)
Casper, Elizabeth Ann to Malcom McLean 7-28-1858 (7-29-1858)
Cassey, Mary Ann to Andrew Davis 5-14-1852
Catharine, Ferrid R. to Benjamin Franklin 5-18-1860
Cathey, Mrs. Nancy L. to James W. Buckingham 7-17-1865 (7-26-1865)
Catlet, Sarah Frances to John Hayden 5-15-1859
Caudle, Almeda to Ransom Morrow 7-16-1839 (7-20-1839)
Caudle, Catharine A. to William F. Young 12-17-1859
Caudle, Louvina Frances to Nathan J. Morris 3-5-1861
Caudle, Manerva L. to Robert Overton 5-7-1866 (5-8-1866) [b]
Caulder, Mrs. Margaret J. to Daniel H. Duncan 6-10-1852
Causby, Elizabeth to Wm. O. Gordon 2-18-1843
Causey, Martha to Michael Black 7-6-1840
Cavender, Sally to Wm. Rhinehart 11-1-1843 (11-2-1843)
Cavis, Elizabeth to William Namey? 1-21-1847
Cawsey, Sarah Ann to Alfred Black 10-4-1855
Certhbertson, Jane to John D. Prewett 11-14-1861 (11-17-1861)
Chambless, Juda J. to Dempsy G. Teasley 1-25-1844 (2-1-1844)
Chamless, Martha W. to Joseph J. F. Clifton 1-20-1841 (1-21-1841)
Chance, Susan to James Roachel 1-11-1839 (1-12-1839)
Channel, Sallie A. to James Underwood 1-9-1865 (1-12-1865)
Channel, Sallie to F. M. Norris 9-17-1863
Channell, Harriet to Henry Newton 4-6-1857 (4-7-1857)
Chanwell, Mary to Henry W. Powell 11-20-1847 (12-25-1847)
Chappel, Jane to Josiah White 10-25-1839
Charnell, Eliza to John Powel 12-5-1843
Chasteen, Clarissa to John Coyle 10-12-1850 (10-17-1850)
Chasteen, Mary E. to John Loyd 11-23-1857 (11-24-1857)
Cherry, Amy to P. Macklewain 12-22-1865
Cherry, D. P. to N. B. Morrow 1-8-1859 (1-12-1859)
Cherry, Delilah to Jas. A. Swotwell 12-8-1848
Cherry, Hardin to William L. Evans 9-19-1855 (9-17?-1855)
Cherry, Isabella F. to George B. Riggins 5-25-1859
Cherry, Maria L. to Aquilla Grant 2-24-1848
Cherry, Mary E. to Chas. Riggins 1-13-1852
Cherry, Rosina Mildred to William E. Lester 10-6-1859
Chesten, Sumira to Jeff Cornell 7-7-1866 [b]
Chester, Charlotte to Dan Chester 5-2-1866 [b]
Chester, Elizabeth A. to Jas. K. M. Merritt 12-7-1865
Chester, Martha A. to Robert Smith 1-4-1858 (1-5-1858)
Chester, Martha Jane to William Carnal 1-22-1858 (1-24-1858)

Chester, Mary F. to Denis Tramel 12-24-1866 (12-25-1866)
Chester, Mary to J. H. Johnson 11-3-1855
Chester, Susan to Thomas F. Dailey 11-24-1852
Childers, Sarah to William R. Ford 12-8-1848
Chiles, C. M. to R. A. Harris 1-12-1847 (1-13-1847)
Chiles, Lucy M. to John S. Goolder 8-5-1844 (8-7-1844)
Chiles, Mary C. to J. F. Lett? 10-5-1842
Chiles, Mary S. to William J. Johnson 1-2-1855 (1-4-1855)
Chiles, Queen Victoria to James M. Buck 5-19-1859 (5-20-1859)
Chiles, Sarah M. to William B. Woodson 1-14-1840 (1-17-1840)
Chilton, E. A. to Henry A. Fowlkes 9-21-1839
Chilton, Jenette J. to A. B. Harrison 3-9-1849 (3-10-1849)
Chissenhall, Martha to Edward Trice 12-23-1838 (1-7-1839)
Christy, Catharine Hickey to George W. Woolfolk 6-7-1855
Cincannon?, Sally to Michael Whalen 3-5-1860
Clardin, Henrietta to Robert M. Moss 11-11-1850
Clardy, Arena to Amos Ray 3-13-1866 [b]
Clardy, Lucy W. to William V. Rives 12-1-1844
Clardy, Mary Jane to John Dodd 2-2-1847 (2-4-1847)
Clardy, Sarah Ann to Jas. Clardy 5-21-1866 (1-16-1867) [b]
Clardy, Susan to James H. Wall 7-4-1838 (7-5-1838)
Clark, Cyntha Ann to John M. Franklin 8-4-1843
Clark, Drucilla to John Sanderson 11-24-1855 (11-25-1855)
Clark, Huldy to Benjamine Davidson 6-28-1842 (6-30-1842)
Clark, Julia A. to Wilie B. Sawyer 4-12-1847
Clark, Margaret to L.W. Sampson 11-9-1852
Clark, Martha to William Smith 3-2-1856
Clark, Mary A. to James Tubberville 11-8-1849
Clark, Mary to Harbard Barker 12-25-1866 [b]
Clark, Mary to Thomas H. Shaw 9-27-1862' (10-1-1862)
Clark, Mary to William Carrier 12-20-1858 (12-24-1858)
Clark, Mrs. Martha Ann to L. W. Bruster 6-9-1864
Clark, Nancy to J. C. Breeden 9-23-1848 (9-17?-1848)
Clark, Patsy to John Odum 11-6-1846 (11-7-1846)
Clark, Virginia T. to Charles G. Clark 1-14-1858 (1-16-1858)
Clarke, L. A. to Wm. Adwell 1-8-1861
Clarke, Sarah to Samuel Suter 1-15-1852
Claxton, Delila to William P. McBride 7-29-1858 (7-30-1858)
Claxton, Louisanna to John B. Cross 12-7-1866
Claxton, Martha Jane to Terry(Tyree) Fane 2-14-1859 (2-16-1859)
Claxton, Missouri Tennessee to Richard Mullin 1-17-1859 (1-20-1859)
Clayton, Louisa F. to William S. Dismukes 2-20-1860 (2-23-1860)
Clemmons, Bethia to Edward F. Lee 8-31-1844
Clift, Catharine to John J. Pritchett 10-18-1850
Clift, Martha to James? L. Robertsen 12-14-1842
Clifton, Harriett to Wm. W. Davis 7-20-1840 (7-22-1840)
Clifton, Huldy to Nicholas Bristoe 2-24-1848 (SB 1849?)
Clifton, Martha A. to Daniel A. McKennon 9-23-1856
Clifton, Rebecca to Miles Harris 12-23-1839 (12-26-1839)
Clinard, Martha to Standford Loyd 1-28-1859
Clinard, Mary A. to Joseph Ainsworth 7-15-1848 (7-16-1848)
Cobb, Irene (Frances?) to Francis P. Gracy 11-9-1857 (11-10-1857)
Cobb, Jane to William Goggin 3-23-1854
Cobb, Melvina E. to Albert W. Jarman 1-19-1853 (1-20-1853)
Cobb, Nina M. to H. C. Jessup 12-27-1865
Cock, Polly to Daniel Morrison 6-20-1843
Cocke, Elizabeth to Thomas Rogers 9-28-1858
Cocke, Jane M. to D. G. Moore 9-15-1838
Cocke, Mary to Benjamin Harper 10-4-1850 (10-7-1850)
Cocke, Nannie R. to Henry C. Carless 3-1-1862
Cocke, Nellie to Joe Wheelis 8-2-1860
Cocke, Sarah to Jno. Dunlavey 6-5-1844 (6-6-1844)
Coffee, Mrs. Margaret to Hugh Flannigan 4-9-1861 (4-13-1861)
Coffman, Eliza A. to John W. Loman 8-9-1850
Coffman, Mary E. to Wm. R. Whuldom? 10-10-1852
Coker, Mary to George W. Laffoon 2-18-1848
Cole, Winie to Edd Prockter 3-12-1866 (3-15-1866) [b]
Coleman, Eliza J. to John B. Parker 9-3?-1838 (9-6-1838)
Coleman, Elizabeth Ann to William E. Fletcher 11-3-1847
Coleman, Emma to Dudley E. Asberry 6-20-1865
Coleman, Frances Elizabeth to James C. Johnson 5-6-1847 (5-14-1847)
Coleman, Julia A. to John H. Johnson 9-24-1859 (9-25-1859)
Coleman, Martha Caroline to Green W. Weatherford 10-19-1852
Coleman, Pamela A. E. to Bernard McGuire 3-28-1849

Coleman, Sarah H. to Samuel Clark 9-9-1851
Collier, Emily to Sanford Bowers 10-14-1853 (10-18-1853)
Collins, A. E. to W. E. Ragsdale 11-9-1866 (11-20-1866)
Collins, Amanda to John Collins 11-7-1859
Collins, Cora G. to James K. Caudle 10-9-1858 (10-13-1858)
Collins, Edith N. to Elbert H. Harrison 5-31-1838
Collins, Eliza J. to Erastus Baine 3-25-1853 (3-27-1853)
Collins, Ellin L. S. to Halcot? Pride 11-18-1856 (11-20-1856)
Collins, George Ann to John D. Reagan 1-28-1860 (1-29-1860)
Collins, Henrietta J. to Thomas J. Weaver 9-23-1851 (9-30-1851)
Collins, Lucy N. to Giles R. Smith 4-26-1851
Collins, Mary Elizabeth to Edward Choate 10-29-1856
Collins, Mary E. to John E. Comer 2-8-1843 (2-10-1843)
Collins, Mary W. to Thomas Harper 12-28-1858 (12-29-1858)
Collins, Mary to Levi Bowe 12-20-1841 (12-23-1841)
Collins, Sally to Ellingston A. Carroll 2-21-1853 (2-24-1853)
Collins, Susan R. to William McMurray 1-29-1856
Collins, Virginia J. to Lewis T. Edwards 9-11-1865 (9-12-1865)
Collishan, Sally to Bingham S. Leigh 12-13-1843 (12-14-1843)
Comer, Sarah W. to Jno. S. Davidson 2-27-1844
Conley, Mary W. to John N. Alexander 4-11-1842
Conly, Mary to W. D. Boothe 10-3-1852
Conrad, Laura E. to Franklin S. Beaumont 11-21-1854
Conrad?, Mattie P. to Sterling F. Beaumont 5-24-1853
Cook, Amelia to West Jorden 11-17-1859
Cook, Caroline M. to Josiah S. Guardner 9-19-1848
Cook, Eliza A. to William A. Murrell 10-21-1844
Cook, Elizabeth to Jas. Jackson 5-13-1865 (5-14-1865)
Cook, Felicia Ann to James Sullivant 2-10-1858
Cook, Maggie G. to Henry A. Armstead 1-24-1867 (2-6-1867)
Cook, Mary A. to J. T. Hendrick 11-11-1852
Cooke, Mary A. to J. T. Hendrick 11-11-1852
Cooksey, Eliza F. to John W. High 12-18-1844 (12-19-1844)
Cooksey, ElizabethAnn to Jacob C. Woodson 4-7-1856 (4-9-1856)
Cooksey, Mary E. to Samuel B. Woodson 12-22-1857
Cooksey, Rebecca to G. W. Campbell 5-3-1840
Cooksey, Virginia R. to Stephen D. Westcott 6-8-1855 (6-14-1855)
Cooly, Mattie A. to Isaac P. Howard 6-20-1865 (7-4-1865)
Coon, Aggy to Willie M. Walker 9-25-1841 (9-26-1841)
Coon, Barbary Ann to Joseph Watson 11-22-1850
Coon, Elizabeth to John Barton 11-7-1847
Coon, Elizabeth to Matison Jones 12-23-1845
Coon, Emily J. to Thos. J. Morris 12-17-1851
Coon, Sarah to Isaac Durrell 8-24-1847
Cooper, Annie H. to J. C. Bead 12-11-1858 (12-12-1858)
Cooper, Martha to F. C. Gresham 2-24-1844
Cooper, Nancy to Saml. Grant 8-27-1840
Cooper, Rachel to E. Withers 5-29-1860
Copeland, Lucy S. to Richard C. Gardner 2-7-1849 (2-8-1849)
Copeland, Tabitha to Moses Wood 8-10-1854
Corban, Joanna E. to James H. Kennedy 6-2-1856
Corban, Louiza B. to A. N. Larkin 1-2-1859 (1-5-1859)
Corben, Mary C. to J. M. Jackson 8-14-1860 (8-15-1860)
Cordle, Enerline(Emily?) to Bob Cordle 1-6-1866 (10-20-1866) [b]
Cordle, Frances to Arthur Bryant 7-21-1841
Corlew, Arrabella to James Mavuty? 7-28-1843 (8-2-1843)
Corlew, Mary Jane to Nathan Gilbert 12-15-1839
Cornell, Margaret to Lafayette Vaughn 11-14-1852
Corney, Virginia to C. W. Bailey 11-26-1850
Cotrell, Nancy Ann to J. B. Monroe 2-10-1849 (3-1-1849)
Council, A. F. to Wm. W. Taler (no date; with 1-1851)
Council, Amanda to G. B. Swift 10-22-1866 (10-23-1866)
Council, Ellen to John William Wade 2-17-1855 (2-19-1855)
Council, Margaret M. to Abraham Brazer 5-17-1855
Council, Martha T. to L. J. Hensler 12-16-1854 (12-21-1854)
Council, Mary Catharine to David Nicholson 10-1-1860 (10-9-1860)
Council, Priscilla to W. P. Adkins 2-14-1859 (2-15-1859)
Council, Sarah to Reubin J. Welch 6-4-1860
Councill, Emily to Mathew Small 2-28-1856 (4-28-1856)
Counsell, Caroline to John Carroll 12-9-1840
Courts?, Ann to Dick Wisdom 9-24-1866 [b]
Covington, Adelia H. to George F. L. Rudolph 12-11-1854 (12-12-1854)
Covington, C. W. to J. B. Thomas 1-17-1850
Covington, Catharine to E. M. Clark 4-20-1843 (4-25-1843)
Cowan, Jane to Reuben McQuerter 6-12-1839 (6-27-1839)

Coward, Frances to Andrew Long 11-12-1851
Cowherd, Martha A. to Thomas F. Pettus 12-9-1839 (12-10-1839)
Cowherd, Mary E. to Doury A. West 8-13-1839
Cox, Celia Ann to Anderson Grinsted 4-27-1866 [b]
Cox, Manerva E. to G. W. Hust 10-5-1848
Cox, Mariann to Joseph G. Hall 5-28-1847
Coyle, Mollie to Leroy J. Stull 10-30-1865
Craig, Mary Ann Thomas to Willis E. Lewis 3-1-1858 (3-4-1858)
Craig, Sofronia J. to George T. Lewis 9-3-1861 (9-5-1861)
Crane, Mary E. to Morgan Stone 8-8-1859
Crank, Anna to Harmon F. Johnson 3-22-1841 (3-25-1842)
Crawford, Ann to A. C. Slaughter 11-9-1847
Creamer, Tennessee to Peter McKinley 9-26-1850
Crenshaw, Mary E. to R. W. Jett 4-12-1860
Creswell, Lucy to Robert Shanklin 1-27-1852
Crewell, Laura Eveline to Robert W. Stewart 7-27-1865
Crimmins, Catharine to John Dilling 6-17-1845 (6-18-1845)
Crocker, Emily C. to Thomas J. Swift 5-21-1844
Crocket, Catharine to F. M. Binkley 2-25-1846 (2-26-1846)
Crocket, Mary to Ebinezer Yates 6-12-1858 (6-13-1858)
Crockett, Ann Maria to A. J. Phillips 4-11-1864 (4-24-1864)
Crockett, Lou. F. to S. H. Monroe 6-26-1860
Crockett, Mrs. Catharine to Preston D. Phillips 11-20-1861
Cromwell, Alletta E. to Henry Jones 4-27-1848 (4-29-1848)
Cromwell, Lurana A. to James Harris 11-5-1847 (11-7-1847)
Cross, Bell to David Holt 12-1-1866 (12-2-1866)
Cross, Easter to John Brackingberry 8-21-1865
Cross, Elizabeth J. to Willis Parker (no date; with 6-1852)
Cross, Elizabeth Jane to Willis Parker 5-7-1852
Cross, Harriett to John Johnson 6-5-1865
Cross, Kesiah Ann to Robert Lyle 2-15-1859 (3-3-1859)
Cross, Mary F. to Walker Turnley 7-22-1865
Cross, Tennessee to James Jarrett 1-13-1866 [b]
Crotzer, Ann to David Rhinehart 3-14-1842
Crotzer, Delila to A. Fite 4-16-1845 (4-17-1845)
Crotzer, Elizabeth to Robert Powers 12-28-1853 (12-29-1853)
Crotzer, L. A. to Eli Rudolph 1-7-1861 (1-17-1861)
Crotzer, Martha to B. H. Pace 9-18-1849
Crotzer, Mary to Abram Rhinehart 12-20-1843 (12-21-1843)
Crouch, Martha to Joseph H. Hopkins 12-4-1860
Crouse, Jane to Henry Fortsone 10-31-1866 (12-24-1866) [b]
Crow, Mary to Abner J. Gupton 7-12-1866
Crow, Mary to Henry Trovelle 9-22-1839
Crowder, Elizabeth to Robt. H. Edmonson 11-12-1864 (12-1-1864)
Crowder, Eudora to Jas. G. Walker 11-21-1864 (11-24-1864)
Crowder, Martha to W. H. Eldridge 11-25-1862
Crowder, Mary F. to Doctor Johnathan Threat? 1-31-1857 (2-3-1857)
Crowder, Susan to Prince Linch 1-1-1866 [b]
Crowell, Elinor Amelia to Enoch Rogers 2-12-1847
Crown?, Lilevant to William Barton 9-6-1854
Crunk, Susan to James Harned 3-21-1858
Cruse, Isabella H. to Geo. M. Smith 9-19-1865 (9-26-1865)
Cruse, Susan E. to John F. Lisenby 3-12-1859
Crusman, M. A. to E. Howard 12-2-1851
Cuisty?, Rachel Eliza to Andrew J. McClolpin? 9-3-1849
Culbertson, Elizabeth to James H. Hester 7-14-1842
Cummings, Elizabeth to Wm. H. Dillins 11-10-1846 (11-11-1846)
Cummins, Sarah E. to William E. Bullard 8-13-1855 (8-14-1855)
Cummins, Susan M. to Isaac D. Walker 3-21-1842 (3-17?-1842)
Cunningham, Elizabeth to James T. Lacey 5-26-1851
Curtis, Mary to Cyrus Cook 1-30-1866 [b]
Curtis, Sarah M. to Jas. H. Harris 9-12-1848
Custer, Mary J. to J. J. Hensley 11-3-1854
Cuthbertson, Mary E. to Knox P. Norfleet 11-24-1866 (11-28-1866)
Dabney, Almyra R. to John F. Hews 8-8-1838
Dabney, George Frances to Louis Dabney 1-20-1853
Dabney, Lucy to C. H. Smith 12-9-1856
Dabney, Margaret to Calvin F. Vance 8-5-1856
Dabney, Mary to Henry Criner 8-18-1866 [b]
Dabny, L. J. to Saml. G. Ward 12-7-1841
Dailey, Nancy to Duncan King 4-11-1839
Daily, Sarah A. to Cath Thweat 2-25-1847
Dalton, Bridget to Thomas Gibbons 11-9-1857
Dalton, Catharine to John Cannell? 12-12-1857 (12-13-1857)
Dalton, Mary to John Sliney 11-9-1857 (11-10-1857)

Daly, Mary Ann to Samuel F. Allen 12-10-1844 (12-12-1844)
Daly, Mary to John Shanahan 6-1-1860 (6-5-1860)
Damron, Mary to John Bonds 5-31-1851
Dancy, Charlotte M. to Ilas? M. Fort 12-4-1854 (12-6-1854)
Dancy, Eliza P. to Josiah W. Fort 10-1-1853
Daniel, Martha Ann to William Hay 1-13-1859
Daniel, Sally to Michael O'Bryan 6-2-1858 (6-4-1858)
Darnel, Emily E. to Bartley Barbee 1-21-1850
Darnell, Caroline to John Mockabee 2-22-1847
Darnell, Elizabeth to James M. Weakley 9-12-1838 (10-10-1838)
Darnell, Frances E. to A. L. Cherry 1-3-1867 (1-11-1867)
Darnell, Mary to Peter Lemle? 8-1-1839
Darnell, Rebecca to Richard Cravens 1-8-1846
Darnell, Zerilda to Gersham Cravens 10-14-1845
Davenport, Lee Ann to E. J. Smith 12-2-1854 (12-3-1854)
Davenport, Margaret to Benjamin Webb 10-25-1852 (10-28-1852)
Davenport, Temperance E. to John C. McLemore 10-26-1850
Davidson, Elizabeth A. to Elisha R. Harrison 4-3-1850 (4-4-1850)
Davidson, Huldy to Liftnot? Crocket 8-2-1849 (8-5-1849)
Davidson, L. J. to Jno. D. Clark 9-15-1849 (9-16-1849)
Davidson, Nancy G. to A. D. Fitz Gerald 12-26-1866 (12-29-1866)
Davidson, Rhode to Richard Morrisett 12-?-1838 (12-19-1838)
Davidson, S. E. to W. Hollis 10-13-1866 (10-16-1866)
Davidson, Sarah L. to W. J. Harrison 1-23-1851
Davidson, Sarah M. to James P. Morrisson 1-4-1839
Davie, Lennia to Levi Chester 7-23-1842 (7-26-1842)
Davie, Parthenia to Russell Pool 12-14-1866 [b]
Davie, Saphrona A. to A. F. Davie 5-13-1850
Davie, Sarah A. to Daniel Gold 11-5-1858
Davie, Sarah to Buck Davie 1-6-1866 (10-20-1866) [b]
Davis, Allis to Chas. Britton 7-28-1866 (7-19?-1866) [b]
Davis, Angeline to Joseph E. Flowers 1-27-1848
Davis, Ann to William Newell 5-2-1841 (5-12-1841)
Davis, Araminta J. to James M. Ramey 2-25-1857 (2-26-1857)
Davis, Arminda to David jr. Elbert 1-25-1844
Davis, Clarrissa to F. Marion Yarbrough 4-22-1856 (5-1-1856)
Davis, Eliza to John Baggett 10-1841 (10-7-1841)
Davis, Emily J. to Wm. R. McFadden 2-17-1846 (2-19-1846)
Davis, H. F. to F. M. Pierce 1-18-1865
Davis, Hana to Isac Wheetly 1-1-1867 (1-2-1867) [b]
Davis, L. S. to Benjamin F. McGee 6-28-1842
Davis, Lucinda A. to Simeon Philpot 5-29-1840 (6-3-1840)
Davis, Lutitia to David jr. Elliott 1-13-1846
Davis, M. J. to W. J. Lunsford 12-31-1847
Davis, Mahaly Elizabeth to Henry Delp 12-29-1860 (12-31-1860)
Davis, Malinda to John E. Mabry 3-4-1847
Davis, Mariah to Peter Minor 1-26-1867 (1-27-1867) [b]
Davis, Mary Emerline to Jas. D. Williams 11-15-1860 (11-16-1860)
Davis, Mary S. to John Morrow 1-2-1850 (SB 1851?)
Davis, Mary to Martin V. Vaughan 11-22-1865 (11-23-1865)
Davis, Mollie to Andrew Morrison 10-19-1866 (10-18?-1866) [b]
Davis, Mrs. Mary F. to W. D. Moss 11-30-1861 (12-1-1861)
Davis, Nancy C. to Lorenzo J. Underwood 10-27-1854
Davis, Nancy E. to James W. Madall 2-17-1856 (2-27-1856)
Davis, Nancy to William Grinson? 10-5-1840 (10-8-1840)
Davis, Sally to William Powell 1-21-1847
Davis, Sarah C. to John S. E. Foster 9-11-1865 (9-14-1865)
Davis, Sarah to James Rivas? 5-24-1850 (5-25-1850)
Davis, Sarah to James W. Smith 12-1-1852
Davison, Ann Eliza to John Alex Simpson 1-17-1860 (1-23-1860)
Davison, Caroline T. to John H. Heathman 1-21-1854
Dawson, Emily C. to Wm. B. Knight 3-11-1844 (3-14-1844)
Dawson, Lafayett Ann to John M. Hill 5-27-1852
Dawson, Mary Ann to Elijah Trotter 2-28-1855
Dawson, Mary E. to J. W. Page 11-29-1866
Dawson, Sarah to James C. Hester 12-6-1858 (12-9-1858)
Day, Martha Ann to Jeremiah O'Rork 1-30-1862
Dean, Elizabeth J. to Francis G. Bingham 6-4-1853
Dean, Elmira to Thomas Nolen 7-10-1853 (7-20-1853)
Dean, Martha L. to Marcus M. Greene 1-31-1852 (2-1-1852)
Dean, Mary to Richard O. Martin 3-29-1852
Dean, Secile to J. O. Breedin 12-19-1863
Dean, Syrnia(Lorrania?) L. to Samuel W. Menifee 11-4-1859 (11-8-1859)
Deane, Louiza to John W. Keesee 2-15-1859

Denney, Prussia to John H. Atkins 8-17-1852
Dennis, Cella to Mose Johnson 12-8-1866 [b]
Dennison, Dorothy A. to Joseph Chilton 2-22-1850
Desire?, Nancy to William Wyatt(Myatt?) 12-11-1857 (12-14-1857)
Dickinson, Amanda to Jo. C. Coleman 5-7-1866 (5-8-1866) [b]
Dicks, Christina G. to Lewis A. Diffenderffer 1-17-1854
Dicks, Eliza to John T. Staton 9-17-1864 (9-18-1864)
Dicks, Elvira to David? Cook 1-14-1867 [b]
Dicks, Jane to William Searcy 7-25-1840 (7-26-1840)
Dicks, Jerusha R. to John J. Hagood 12-13-1856 (12-14-1856)
Dickson, E. W. to Drury H. West 5-2-1864
Dickson, Elizabeth to Merrill Padget 8-15-1838 (8-16-1838)
Dickson, Frances to Charles Givans 1-16-1867 (1-26-1867) [b]
Dicus, Elza to Thos. G. Oats? 12-17-1848 (12-18-1848)
Dillard, Sallie to John W. Hester 6-8-1857
Dillard, Sue to Lewis Moore 1-22-1862
Dilling, Delila T. to Robert J. Alman 12-29-1853
Dilling, Lucrecia to Joshua Outlaw 8-26-1846 (8-27-1846)
Dilling, Mary A. to John H. Boswell 8-14-1863 (8-16-1863)
Dilling, Nancy C. to James D. Bowers 6-9-1856 (6-10-1856)
Dillon, Elizabeth to Cas. M. Powers 1-25-1839 (1-29-1839)
Dillon, Mariah E. to Jas. Powers 9-26-1842 (9-29-1842)
Dilworth, L. B. to George M. Woodman 3-22-1855
Dinwiddie, Elizabeth to A. J. Taylor 11-26-1866 (11-27-1866)
Dinwiddie, Louisa Frances to David S. Griffey 1-16-1854
Dinwiddie, Sallie B. to Thos. Herndon 1-11-1866 (1-14-1866)
Dinwiddy, Caroline to W. A. Vaughn 4-14-1862 (4-16-1862)
Dinwooddie, Amanda to Green Kendrick 10-30-1865 (11-2-1865) [b]
Dist, Adiline to Vinse Trice 12-26-1866 (1-5-1867) [b]
Dobson, Janetta to John Harrold 3-24-1840
Dodd, C. J. to J. H. Waters 7-31-1858
Dodd, Edy H. to Levi Powel 6-11-1843
Dodd, Ellen to Wm. Haddock 2-21-1850
Dodd, Mary to Shade Trammell 6-28-1843 (6-8?-1843)
Dodd, Sary A. to Hugh B. Wilkins 12-17-1846
Dolan, Catharine to Michael Baker 7-24-1854 (7-26-1854)
Dolan, Mary to B. White 7-31-1862 (7-31-1862)
Dolan, Mrs. Amelia to J. C. Gardner 4-29-1863
Doleney, Fredonia L. to T. D. Leonard 2-26-1849
Donaldson, Althea M. to Geo. Torean 3-31-1863 (4-9-1863)
Donaldson, H. A. to J. W. Howell 10-7-1851 (10-8-1851)
Donaldson, M. L. to Richardson G. Smith 12-20-1859 (12-25-1859)
Donaldson, Z. H. to B. W. Boatwright 9-24-1860 (9-28-1860)
Donaldson, Zilpha to Robt. J. Blaksey 6-13-1850
Donalson, Amanda J. to Thomas Davis 7-3-1852 (7-4-1852)
Donley(Dulaney?), Alice J. to David V. Tutt 12-22-1859
Donley, Melica to Westley Rousy 7-28-1863
Donnolly, Maria A. to Jehu P. Fritt 1-31-1858
Dorety, Elizabeth to John D. Carneel? 5-6-1854 (5-7-1854)
Dority, Mary to John Becley? 12-11-1858
Dorne?, Mary to John Clifford 4-19-1858
Dorson, Feboe A. to Edward L. Nance 5-28-1853
Dorson, Mary H. to Elisha J. Jones 1-13-1866 (1-17-1866)
Dortch, Ann L. to Wm. M. Finley 4-3-1849
Dortch, Annie to Wm. L. Chilton 4-27-1847
Dortch, Maina D. to Joshua Cobb 1-18-1843
Dortch, Nancy to John B. Bailey 10-8-1845
Doss, Mary Jane to James A. J. Cotton 9-3-1851 (9-4-1851)
Doughran, Julia to William Ellis 1-8-1845 (1-9-1845)
Dowdy, Mary to William A. Tomlinson 1-11-1858 (1-14-1858)
Downey, Carolina to James Knox 12-21-1859
Downey, Mary E. to Isaac T. Osburn 10-27-1851
Downing, Letitia L. to Edwin C. Hickman 8-18-1864
Dozier, Araminta to Thomas J. Strother 8-26-1858 (8-28-1858)
Drake, Martha to Henry Weakley 1-16-1866 (1-27-1866) [b]
Drake, Mary E. to W. W. Terry 9-23-1851
Drane, Jennie E. to Robt. W. Johnson 7-30-1860 (7-31-1860)
Driskall, Susan H. to Jacob Latham 9-26-1844
Driskell, Elizabeth to Bannister W. Hogan 10-30-1840
Driskell, M. H. to G. W. Driskell 8-26-1849
Driskill, Ann E. to Samuel C. McGahee? 4-19-1849
Driver?, Mary J. to James Franziers? 7-17-1851 (7-27-1851)
Drury, Delphina to George G. Purdy 9-29-1855 (9-27?-1855)
Dudley, E. M. to D. W. Taylor 12-4-1849
Dudley, Frances to James E. Franklin 6-4-1840

Duff, Ann R. to Richard H. Neal 2-9-1857 (2-10-1857)
Duff, Mary E. to Richard Roberts 12-14-1859
Duff, Sarah A. to Saml. D. Power 11-8-1858
Duffill, Puss to Welbern Ryan 5-5-1863
Duke, Frances D. to G. W. Booker 10-22-1839 (10-23-1839)
Duke, Henrietta to C. J. Gupton 9-17-1866 (12-20-1866)
Duke, Martha A. to William Vick 12-30-1853 (1-1-1854)
Duke, Martha C. to H. W. Macklin 8-21-1855 (8-22-1855)
Duke, Mary E. to Charles A. Lutt 5-23-1851
Duke, Mary Jane to John N. Vick 12-11-1845 (12-18-1845)
Duke, Sarah Ann to W. D. Mays 6-30-1847 (7-1-1847)
Dukes, Martha to W. D. Wells 8-28-1856
Duncan, Atalantus G. to E. C. Dycas 4-30-1849 (5-1-1849)
Duncan, Elizabeth to Anderson Keats 4-6-1864 (4-7-1864)
Duncan, Elizabeth to Wm. Patterson 2-18-1860
Duncan, Marona to John Baker 12-4-1839 (12-5-1839)
Duncan, Mary Elizabeth to William Philips 12-7-1847
Duncan, Matilda to Elisha P. Green 7-11-1839 (7-26-1839)
Duncan, Melissa to Thomas Brake 6-3-1856
Duncurson, Matilda A. to Joseph M. Sallee? 2-7-1838
Dunlap, Catharine to Robert W. Keeler 9-4-1860 (9-13-1860)
Dunlap, Nannie S. to B. W. Coward 4-18-1864 (4-20-1864)
Dunning, Gabriella to Jas. W. Brown 12-31-1866
Dunning, Selina C. to James A. Howell 1-5-1853
Dunning, Susan E. to Samuel H. Canseter 9-21-1856 (9-26-1856)
Dunnivan?, Jenetta S. to Jno. H. Myres 9-4-1849
Durham, Margaret to James Durham 10-10-1860
Durrett, Susan Ann to D. A. Elliott 9-11-1858 (9-16-1858)
Duvall, Rachel M. to E. B. Rudolph 1-23-1849 (1-30-1849)
Dycus, Amanda to Gilliam W. Burgess 9-20-1859
Dycus, Catharine H. to Rewben N. Dawson 12-21-1844 (12-22-1844)
Dycus, Cathrine A. to Henry Allen 9-27-1847
Dycus, Elizabeth to John T. Fletcher 1-14-1856
Dycus, Elizabeth to Jonas Smith 5-10-1845 (5-11-1845)
Dycus, Isbell? F. to James Wilson 11-22-1844 (11-28-1844)
Dycus, Lucy Ann to Samuel Scudder 9-1-1859 (9-3-1859)
Dycus, Mary to Howard Roberson 1-2-1852
Dycus, Nancy J. to Ambrose Evans 4-8-1839
Dycus, Sarah Ann to Howell Smith 3-30-1850 (3-31-1850)
Dye, Mary Ann to Edward L. Williams 6-20-1840 (6-23-1840)
Dyer, H. M> to Loreol? R. Smith 10-12-1843 (10-13-1843)
Dyer, Martha to Richard Audy 4-20-1856
Dyer, Mary Jane to Henry W. Lisenby 5-25-1847 (5-27-1847)
Dykes, Mary to Robert Tagus? 1-15-1855 (1-21-1855)
Eads, Mary to James Hemet? 11-20-1845
Easley, Fredonia to John Dority 9-21-1865
Eason, Selia Dilmoth to Jas. L. Henson 6-8-1865
Eaton, Eliza to Thomas Joiner 1-18-1843 (2-19-1843)
Eaton, Sallie to William Willhite 10-9-1863
Eberly, Nancy Caroline to William A. Edwards 2-3-1846
Eckels, Mary S. to W. O. Pepper 4-3-1860 (4-4-1860)
Eckles, Mildred K. to W. O. Pepper 4-20-1857 (4-21-1857)
Edes, Mary Jane to Jasper Victory 4-10-1850
Edes, Nancy to Isaac Potter 4-22-1844 (4-29-1844)
Edington, Bitsey to Soloman McReynolds 1-17-1867 [b]
Edington, Edie to Tom Coleman 12-26-1866 (12-29?-1866) [b]
Edmington, Hariett to Alexr. Byars 4-3-1843 (4-6-1843)
Edmonds, Lamida? C. to Bradly L. Roulan 4-20-1850 (4-21-1850)
Edmondson, Martha to Garnet W. Richardson 1-13-1848
Edmondson, Susan to Nelson Roberts 8-4-1866 [b]
Edmonson, Jennie to R. C. Wyatt 11-29-1862
Edmonson, Mary C. to John A. Kisee 1-28-1851
Edwards, Charlotte to Elijah Averett 3-19-1852
Edwards, Eliza J. to Chas. W. Hall 2-28-1866 (3-1-1866)
Edwards, Fredonia to A. R. Lewis 2-14-1856
Edwards, M. A. to John T. Marable 4-28-1865 (4-29-1865)
Edwards, Malinda to Charles R. Powers 11-20-1845
Edwards, Margaret to Barrett Herring 1-2-1866
Edwards, Mary E. to A. J. Smith 12-28-1841
Edwards, Mary to Stephen Walthall 1-20-1866 (2-3-1866) [b]
Edwards, Nancy to Michel Tyer 7-15-1856 (7-16-1856)
Edwards, Sarah D. to Wm. C. Smith 2-16-1842 (2-17-1842)
Eison?, Julia Ann to Jas. N. Dearing 8-22-1860 (8-23-1860)
Elder, Ellen to Darby N. Mayfield 11-18-1865 (12-28-1865) [b]
Eldridge, Bettie M. to Aristotle Eldridge 5-10-1859

Eley, Nancy to James E. Martin 4-29-1857 (5-1-1857)
Ellebrue, Elizabeth to Harrold P. Carney 4-9-1838
Ellesson, Dilila A. to Edward Good 7-18-1840 (7-23-1840)
Ellett, Ellin to Jas. H. Lewis 12-22-1866
Ellice, Rebecca Jane to Francis M. Southward 12-14-1859 (12-15-1859)
Elliott, Armindia J. to Thomas S. Woodson 6-28-1865
Elliott, E. A. to Charles W. Lankford 9-2-1851 (9-3-1851)
Elliott, Luisa to A. J. Bartee 4-3-1854 (4-4-1854)
Elliott, Mallissa to Kindred Wilson 9-8-1866 (9-11-1866)
Elliott, Martha to Wash Levell 2-24-1866 [b]
Elliott, Mary J. to Thomas A. Haynes 5-9-1850 (5-14-1850)
Elliott, Rebecca M. to B. J. Crowder 10-8-1845 (10-9-1845)
Elliott, Sarah Ann to J. H. Blair (no date; with 3-1852)
Elliott, Sarah Ann to William T. Vaughn 5-29-1860
Ellis, Lucy J. to E. H. Beaumont 10-17-1858 (10-19-1858)
Ellis, Martha to John Ferrill 8-24-1852 (8-26-1852)
Ellis, Mary Ann to Wm. Brooks 9-26-1838 (9-27-1838)
Ellis, Mary Jane to Burrell jr. Joins 12-28-1844
Ellis, Mary to Wm. Martin Burkes 11-25-1844
Ellis, Nancy to Benjamin Ferrill 8-6-1842 (8-7-1842)
Ellison, Mary to M. H. Eaker 5-28-1848
Ely, Alice G. to Robert H. Pickering 1-18-1855
Ely, Amanda to Ferdinand F. Fox 5-9-1861
Ely, Caroline to Harvey J. Powers 12-13-1860 (12-16-1860)
Ely, Ellen S. to M. C. Pitman 1-12-1858
Ely, Lucy E. to Jno. W. Moore 11-9-1849
Epperson, Emily J. to Joseph H. Waters 12-28-1864
Epps, Virginia Ann C. to John T. Shirley 9-16-1846
Estis, Martha to Henry Radford 9-8-1866 [b]
Evans, Barbery to Sam Lunderman 3-10-1866 (3-12-1866) [b]
Evans, Catharine M. to Jehu R. Brisendine 6-8-1854
Evans, Cordelia Ann to Lewis R. Vaughn 1-27-1860 (1-29-1860)
Evans, Frances to William Prewitt 5-14-1866 (5-20-1866)
Evans, Martha C. to John F. Kendrick 1-25-1854
Evans, Mary to David Gillaspy 5-29-1840 (6-4-1840)
Evans, Z. T. to J. T. Jenkins 1-14-1867 (1-18-1867)
Everett, E. H. to W. S. Poindexter 6-29-1859 (7-30-1859)
Everett, Lucinda to Zak Harris 4-25-1845
Everette, Dilly to William Clifton 9-2-1854
Ewing, Sarah M. to Thomas B. Bailey 7-20-1846
Ezel, Amanda to Edward J. Griffin 10-13-1853
Fain, Cynthia to Dabney Hagwood 1-2-1841 (1-3-1841)
Fairfax, Harriett to Sandy Pollard 5-7-1866 (5-9-1866) [b]
Fall, Charlotte Ann to Alpheus W. McCall 4-17-1856
Fall, Hany to John L. Jones 10-23-1846
Fantelroy, Mattie to George W. Harrison 12-23-1865 [b]
Fapp, Rosanna to Jas. T. Wilson 3-7-1842
Farless, Nancy to Jasper N. Lawhon 10-16-1851
Farley, C. T. to Thomas B. Hill 3-18-1841 (3-8?-1841)
Farmer, Caroline to John Orndorff 10-12-1842
Farmer, Elizabeth to Calvin L. Geter 8-21-1856
Farmer, Elizabeth to Carson Pace 12-11-1847
Farmer, Elizabeth to Thomas Bearden 5-18-1844 (5-21-1844)
Farmer, Fannie to Andrew J. Stokes 1-21-1867 (1-24-1867)
Farmer, Martha Ann to Adam Jordan 10-30-1856
Farmer, Martha C. to William Hart 8-3-1844 (8-4-1844)
Farmer, Nancy to Noah J. Powers 12-24-1856
Farmer, Rebecca E. to Washington D. Buckly]8-10-1857
Farmer, Sally to William Bearden 5-19-1845
Farmer, Sarah Ann to Adam M. Harrison 2-19-1849
Faro?, Margaret to Willis Hardy 10-8-1845 (10-9-1845)
Fauntleroy, Emily to Guilford Slaughter 4-6-1854 (4-15-1854)
Fauntleroy, Eugenia to James H. Smith? 12-6-1859
Fauntleroy, Joanna B. to Jackson Allensworth 3-2-1854
Fauntleroy, Mary E. to J. T. Garnett 1-8-1844 (1-16-1844)
Faxon, Lucy Alice to James Glascock 2-25-1858
Faxon, Mary L. to John E. Wilcox 12-6-1855
Feelix, Emeline to Peter G. Herring 12-20-1840
Felden, Rebecca H. to Frank Couget? 4-20-1865
Fergerson, Sarah P. to Samuel A. Moore 4-4-1845 (4-8-1845)
Ferguson, Clarissa to Isham W. Baker 7-1-1853
Ferguson, Martha J. to James M. Lindsey 12-29-1841
Ferguson, Martha to David Pettus 1-14-1867 (1-26-1867) [b]
Ferrell, Harriet Angeline to David F. Crouch 9-14-1859 (9-15-1859)

Ferrell, Mary Luella to George H. Dyer 10-19-1858 (10-21-1858)
Ferrell, Rebecca to Thomas Rollins 2-13-1856
Ferrell, Sarah Jane to H. W. Lisenby 10-19-1858 (10-27-1858)
Ferrill, Malvina E. to Henry H. Underwood 9-13-1861
Fielder, Elizabeth J. to Thomas M. Williams 3-19-1856 (3-20-1856)
Fields, Ally J. to W. J. Barbee 12-27-1856 (12-28-1856)
Fields, Bettie Ann to W. J. Barbee 10-23-1862 (12-4-1862)
Finley, Carrie to Frank McClure 11-17-1866 (11-18-1866) [b]
Fips, Malissa to Thomas Ellis 11-24-1852 (11-25-1852)
Fips, Mary Ann to John T. Berk 5-13-1861
Flack, Mary C. to James A. McQuary 1-12-1854
Flack, Mary T. to E. F. Janes 9-11-1848 (9-12-1848)
Fleming, Agnes to James T. Taylor 11-1-1859
Fletcher, Agness to T. J. Neely 5-5-1857
Fletcher, Cathern to John P. Hester 12-18-1855 (12-25-1855)
Fletcher, Elizabeth to Jno. Hutchings 12-13-1841 (12-14-1842)
Fletcher, Elizabeth to Peter Magarrin 3-1-1839
Fletcher, Ellen to John H. Adams 9-17-1849 (9-19-1849)
Fletcher, Hatty to Robert Shaw 12-28-1865 (12-30-1865)
Fletcher, Henny H. to Hudson Parish 9-17-1842
Fletcher, M. A. to A. Wyckoff 3-30-1843
Fletcher, Malinda P. to William D. Seay 2-11-1852
Fletcher, Malissa V. to Robert E. Seay 12-19-1855 (12-20-1855)
Fletcher, Mary A. to Jas. K. Taylor 12-20-1864 (12-22-1864)
Fletcher, Mrs. Medora M. to Charles F. Megarren 12-13-1864 (12-14-1864)
Fletcher, Patsy to Harry Perkins 12-27-1866 [b]
Fletcher, Priscilla Jane to William J. Hart 10-25-1844 (10-29-1844)
Fletcher, Sally to James Nolen 2-24-1842
Fletcher, Sarah E. E. to John O. Seay 9-15-1856
Fletcher, Virginia to William O. Hester 12-29-1855 (1-3-1856)
Fletcher, Winniford to Evan B. Blair 12-17-1840
Ford, Elizabeth to R. S. Bradbury 12-23-1846 (12-24-1846)
Ford, Hilly to Allen Manning 3-17-1838
Ford, Mary Ann to James Bradshaw 12-20-1847
Ford, Mary to Timothy Kelly 12-9-1857 (12-14-1857)
Ford, Sarah to Eli G. Dupree 8-26-1844
Ford, Sidney to John Connors 1-27-1859 (1-28-1859)
Forkner, Nelly to Solomon Nothington 7-22-1865 [b]
Forston, Lucy B. to John P. Bowling 11-3-1859 (11-8-1859)
Forsythe, Mary J. to D. P. Sensing 10-28-1864
Fort, Harriett to Wiley Fort 10-22-1866 [b]
Fort, Jack Ann to Joseph H. Fort 11-3-1849
Fort, Jinnie to Daniel Bruer 12-26-1866 (12-27-1866) [b]
Fort, Lucy to Wm. Buras 1-5-1867 (1-6-1867) [b]
Fort, Lydia to Jake Baldrey 9-15-1866 (9-22-1866) [b]
Fort, Mary G. to J. W. Battle 7-23-1856 (7-24-1856)
Fort, Mary W. to John W. Jones 5-13-1864 (5-18-1864)
Fort, Turgey T. to James Scott 2-25-1848
Fortner, Ann C. to William J. Broomfield 5-3-1854
Fortson, Amanda to G. W. Carmack 8-11-1849
Fortson, Elizabeth to D. H. Grant 10-16-1858 (10-19-1858)
Fortson, Frances C. to J. M. Durrett 1-21-1839 (1-24-1839)
Fossey, Sarah E. to James E. Thompson 12-27-1866
Foster, Augusta R. to James L. Diamond 3-11-1856 (3-13-1856)
Foster, Eliza Catharine to William J. Seay 10-25-1858
Foster, Marthy Ann to John Blaw(Balaw?) 5-22-1857
Foster, Mary J. to William H. Edmondson 1-19-1859 (1-30-1859)
Foster, Mary M. to S.? B. Boon 3-31-1843
Foster, Nancy to Hugh Smith 8-17-1865 (8-24-1865)
Fouse, Lukitty Ellin to Thomas Smith 2-15-1865 (2-16-1865)
Foust, Araminter to Wm. F. Holt 3-13-1849
Foust, Nancy Ann to David Heflin 9-20-1845 (9-25-1845)
Fouste, Margaret J. to John Cocke 9-1-1853
Fouste, Narcissa F. to Wm. S. Hutcherson 5-30-1848
Fowler, Rebecca to David Cooper 11-19-1843
Fowlkes, Leonard to W. M. Pollock 9-8-1858
Fowlkes, Ophelia to Joseph H. Billingsley 5-14-1866 (5-10?-1866)
Fox, C. G. to Allanson Tinsley 8-17-1843
Fox, Eliza to Henry Fox 1-19-1867 [b]
Fox, Martha to Joshua Todd 12-24-1840
Fox, Mary Malinda to William Hatcher 11-7-1853 (11-8-1853)
Francis, Lavinia to Richard Rudd 4-7-1841
Francisco, Martha to Wyman Tayler 12-8-1852 (10?-8-1852)
Francisco, Sarah to James Edlin 12-29-1842

Franklin, Emily Ann to Jehu Littlefield 4-5-1858 (4-6-1858)
Franklin, Mary J. to Henry M. Murphy 12-29-1852
Frazer, Erwin C. to John E. Wooldridge 12-30-1853
Frazier, Elizabeth to A. H. Cooper? 6-1-1849 (6-3-1849)
Frazier, Elizabeth to William Bruce 6-19-1845
Frazier, Mary S. to Saml. Enniss 4-27-1842 (5-5-1842)
Fredrick, Sarah Jane to Alexander S. Wood 2-24-1858 (2-25-1858)
Frey, Sarah to Tilton Watson 12-24-1844 (4-2-1845)
Fritt, Mariah to Samuel W. Evans 10-11-1853
Fritts, M. to Wm. Bayless 10-14-1862 (10-16-1862)
Fry, Harriett to John Kennedy 6-18-1866 [b]
Fulcher, Unity W. to Wm. W. Fulcher 10-30-1848 (11-2-1848)
Funk, Mary J. to Jno. D. Luson 1-16-1844
Funk, Nancy to Jacob Brown 10-28-1846
Fuqua, Sophia to Cordal N. Northington 1-27-1858 (2-2-1858)
Furgerson, Elizabeth S. to Albert G. Branham 3-1-1848 (3-2-1848)
Furgerson, Hannah to Wesley Ligon 1-23-1867 (1-26-1867) [b]
Furgerson, Margaret Ann to Hiram W. Rhea 8-16-1865
Furgurson, Margaret to Henderson Wade 7-29-1847
Furguson, Lucy to James S. Carpenter 4-14-1838
Furguson, Sarah to Sampson McGehee 12-17-1841
Furlow?, Martha J. to T. M. Woodmore 8-12-1855
Gafford, Mary E. to James W. Singleton 6-27-1857 (6-2?-1857)
Gagle, America to Allen Baggett 8-15-1865 (8-16-1865)
Gaines?, Malinda to William Willhight 11-4-1847
Galbraith, Chanie to Anthony Elder 1-14-1867 (1-19-1867) [b]
Galbrath, Amanda to W. P. Settle 1-15-1852
Galbreth, Ellen P. to Wm. T. Dortch 12-11-1860
Galbrith, Sarah to Able Stones 12-1-1866 [b]
Galey, Mary J. to Abner N. Hesler 10-20-1853
Galy, Charlotte to Wilis Jarman 4-3-1854 (4-4-1854)
Gamble, Mrs. S. to Henry Moody 8-5-1862 (8-7-1862)
Gamble?, Mary to John R. Hagwood 7-15-1840 (7-16-1840)
Gamblin, Frances to Albert G. Todd 10-16-1859
Gant, Rebecca L. to Salem P. Cipe 5-12-1852
Gardner, Bittie to Isaac Burton 9-8-1866 [b]
Gardner, F. A. E. V. to J. M. Perrin? 4-6-1841
Garland, Elizabeth C. to Henry A. Cole 11-11-1846
Garland, Lucy Ann to James N. Dortch 12-16-1841
Garland, Mary E. to William A. Forbes 12-26-1853 (12-29-1853)
Garnet, Mary Thomas to Samuel Hite 9-22-1856
Garnett, Elizabeth to Garland Wilson 10-27-1856
Garnett, Sarah J. to G. A. Shelton 10-16-1852
Garrett, Agness to R. B. Martin 11-25-1845 (11-26-1845)
Garrette, Martha A. to Freeman Jackson 5-12-1864
Garth, Mary to John Parham 11-17-1866 [b]
Garvin, Jennetta C. to William P. Hume 11-13-1844 (11-21-1844)
Gate, Elizabeth to Gabriel Seevers? 8-24-1842
Gatewood, Lucy to Thos. Lackey 10-13-1848
Gatewood, Mary L. to George N. Moore 7-6-1854 (7-11-1854)
Gee, Mrs. Mary F. to W. S. Poindexter 9-8-1866 (9-10-1866)
Geeler?, Sarah C. to T. J. Coffman 6-3-1856
George, Ann E. to Thos. J. Cocke 11-17-1845 (11-18-1845)
George, Elizabeth V. to Alfred Williamson 12-14-1857
George, Mary to W. C. L. McGehee 6-7-1848
Gepton, Sarah to Benj. Batts 1-3-1851
Gerayn?, Lucey C. to Lennoir Tally 10-28-1846
Gibbs, Julia to John L. N. Baker 1-24-1843 (1-25-1843)
Gibbs, M. A. to Isaiah R. Emmet 12-13-1840
Gibbs, Polly to Enoch Bradley 10-12-1839 (10-20-1839)
Gibbs, Sarah to William Roger 9-10-1838
Gibson, Catharine M. to R. A. Simons 4-23-1854
Gibson, Mollie E. to Harry Gordan 9-5-1865
Gilbert, Demarius to Francis H. Averitt 3-3-1843
Gilbert, Eberline to James Manning 10-23-1852 (10-28-1852)
Gilbert, Emily L. to John L. King 1-8-1855
Gilbert, Lavicy to Wm. Searcy 3-27-1845
Gilbert, Mary Ann to William C. Burchett 2-14-1843
Gilbert, Nancy C. to Jefferson Bryant 2-26-1842 (3-1-1842)
Gilbert, Rosanna to William Morrisson 2-5-1839 (2-6-1839)
Gilbert, Tennessee to James P. Green 12-11-1845
Gilbert, Virginia to Willis Jackson 11-12-1861
Gilbrel, Elizabeth to Saml. Scudder 9-19-1843
Gilcres?, Elizabeth to R. T. Coffey 12-24-1840
Giles, Martha to John C. Furguson 12-21-1840

Gilford, Martha A. to Berton Marshall 3-23-1854
Gill, Arabella to Stephen Kimbrew 5-21-1866 [b]
Gill, E. C. T. to R. Lewis 1-15-1851
Gill, Sally to Smith Martin 10-29-1866 [b]
Gillam, F. J. to D. G. Harrelson 11-20-1862 (11-23-1862)
Gilleland, Susan J. to George Washington Woodruff 9-16-1861
Gillis, Cindarella to William C. Burchett 4-11-1839
Gillum, Delphia E. to W. H. Prockter 1-19-1867 (1-21-1867)
Givins, Mary to Isaac Lane 7-24-1849 (7-27-1849)
Glass, Mrs. C. E. to George S. Atkins 11-27-1860
Glay?, Frances E. to Peter Downs 4-26-1855
Gleason, Mary to Christopher Smith 8-31-1858 (9-1-1858)
Glenn, Martha to Wm. A. Gipson 12-1-1845 (12-2-1845)
Glenn, Mary C. to Thomas F. Pierce 7-12-1860
Glenn, Mary to Richd. D. Fortson 9-6-1843
Glenn, Virginia G. to Sterling Brewer 9-4-1844 (9-5-1844)
Godsey, Nancy to James McComack 3-12-1861
Goggin, Mary to John W. Gilmore 11-13-1866 (11-14-1866)
Goggins, Janie to James S. Carpenter 9-25-1840 (9-27-1840)
Gold, Caroline F. to Stephen Y. Moss 1-10-1840 (3-18-1840)
Gold, Lizzie A. to S. W. Barbee 6-3-1865 (6-6-1865)
Gold, Matilda to Granvill Leavell 4-11-1866 (4-14-1866) [b]
Gold, Matilda to Granville Levell 4-9-1866 (not executed) [b]
Gold, Susan to Robert S. Payne 10-24-1853 (10-27-1853)
Goley, Fane A. to Richard Bridgewater 11-11-1847
Golsen, Amy to Joseph Gibbs 12-25-1865
Gooch, Sarah E. to Josiah R. Edger 5-31-1865 (6-6-1865)
Good, Mary Jane to Ebenezer E. Larkin 7-1-1856 (7-3-1856)
Goode, Elizabeth Jane to John H. Goode 2-11-1850
Goodman, Adaline to Waner Burnes 1-2-1867 [b]
Goodman, Sarah Ann to G. L. Harris 4-4-1856
Goodwin, Nannie(Demetria?) A. to J. T. Meneese 11-9-1859
Goostree, Mrs. Bettie to W. J. T. Revel 5-24-1865
Gordan, Fannie to Geo. Preastley 10-15-1865 [b]
Gordon, Mary Frances to Wm. Morris 1-22-1866
Gordon, Virginia to Ezekiel Jones 4-11-1840 (5-14-1840)
Gossett, Eliza Jane to Benjamin H. Been 3-11-1847
Gower, Mary to John D. Kelly 5-19-1845
Grady, Lucinda R. to Thos. G. Parham 3-7-1843
Grady, Martha to Jack Bryan 12-8-1866 (12-9-1866) [b]
Grady, Mattie to Richard Adams 12-27-1865
Grady, Rebecca to John A. Rollo? 12-6-1847 (12-12-1847)
Graham, Frances J. to Wm. C. Carter 10-12-1848
Graham, Sallie Ann to Bartley Epley 6-20-1866
Grant, Adaline to Henry Williams 2-23-1864
Grant, Charlott to Luke H. Furguson 11-4-1845
Grant, Charlotte to John Cooksey 5-2-1838 (5-3-1838)
Grant, E. J. to G. G. Hinch 9-27-1845 (9-28-1845)
Grant, Eliza Marian to Thelbert Covington 1-26-1860
Grant, Elizabeth L. to Sheron? Randle 11-16-1846 (11-17-1846)
Grant, Jane S. to James H. Bowling 3-17-1852
Grant, Louiza J. to David M. Brown 8-26-1857
Grant, Lucretia to James Rinehart 9-9-1854 (9-10-1854)
Grant, Mary Jane to James W. Marshall 9-23-1846 (9-24-1846)
Grant, Mary Marisee? to Green Shelton Brown 6-12-1857 (8-2-1857)
Grant, Mary to George C. Halliburton 12-16-1840
Grant, Mary to William Armonett 7-16-1840
Grant, Narcissa to B. N. Green 2-1-1842 (2-3-1842)
Gray, Abigil Matilda to E. H. Cobles 9-3-1848
Gray, Anna E. to William Magaffin 8-11-1858 (8-12-1858)
Gray, E. D. to Lewis G. Williams 7-16-1839
Gray, Elizabeth M. to Patrick Shockning? 4-29-1860
Gray, Ellen H. to J. B. Williams 12-8-1862
Gray, Josepheen to Scot Trice 2-7-1867 [b]
Gray, Lucy to S. A. Sawyer 10-5-1843
Gray, Margaret to William Combs 10-20-1858 (10-23-1858)
Gray, Margarett to G. D. Oldham 1-22-1838? (1-23-1839)
Gray, Martha P. to S. N. Hollingsworth 10-2-1849
Gray, Mary Demarius to William Alexander Shimoville? 11-6-1844
    (11-8-1844)
Gray, Mary E. to Joseph H. Mockbee 1-29-1863
Gray, Mary to Thomas M. Boardman 1-6-1859
Green, Elizabeth to Robert E. Green 4-5-1849
Green, Mollie L. to Edward C. Roach 12-12-1866 (12-14-1866)
Green, Narcissa to W. H. May 11-19-1854

Greenfield, Polly Ann to Ausburn Rudd 10-13-1852
Greenhill, Martha J. to Young Barbee 10-20-1859 (10-21-1859)
Greenwood, Catharine to W. R. Cassel? 11-15-1854
Greenwood, Nancy H. to Jessee Rives 4-28-1849
Griffie, Sarah Ann to Henry Powers 1-8-1856
Griffin, Agness to Napoleon Mauzy 9-3-1840
Griffin, Amanda to William Chapman 3-25-1859 (3-26-1859)
Griffin, Sarah C. to Hector M. Grand 3-4-1847
Griffin, Sarah M. to T. C. Lanier 1-7-1856
Griffith, Nancy to Robert McDermot 9-2-1847
Griggsby, Catharine to Sam Miles 2-1-1867 [b]
Grigsby, Cynthia A. to P. L. Sale 8-30-1865 (9-1-1865)
Grimes, Mrs. Nancy E. to James Clark 12-2-1846
Grimes, Viola to Geo. B. Cherry 12-22-1866 (12-23-1866)
Grinsted, Mary to Joseph Hatcher 7-21-1865 (7-25-1865)
Grizzard, Mrs. Lou to Wm. H. Grizzard 11-22-1864
Grogain, Lorinda to G. W. Jeminsopn 9-30-1861
Groves, Eliza to Wm. L. Springfield 6-18-1851 (6-24-1851)
Groves, Sevanna to Geo W. Groves 10-17-1859
Grubbs, Lynacy to John W. Ladd 9-17-1851
Grymes, Lydia to William Loutzenheiser 6-9-1854
Gueran, Mariah to George Abernathy 6-23-1866 [b]
Gullet, Elizabeth to James Orrell 10-10-1847
Gunn, Barbery Ann to William A. Lipford 9-4-1865 (9-6-1865)
Gunn, Mary E. to Halcat Pride 10-22-1858 (10-24-1858)
Gupton, Amanda M. to James Perdue 12-25-1848
Gupton, Emily to Benjamin Pace 1-11-1847 (1-23-1847)
Gupton, Harriet to John E. Melson 9-27-1845 (9-28-1845)
Gupton, Judith H. to Robert W. Major 4-21-1842
Gupton, M. H. to W. W. Woodall 10-24-1866 (10-25-1866)
Gupton, Martha J. to James Coon 1-11-1856 (2-11-1856)
Gupton, Mary to Henry Smith 5-23-1843 (5-25-1843)
Gupton, Priscilla to Josiah Nicholson 9-16-1844 (10-5-1844)
Gupton, Puss to Thomas Keesee 7-23-1866 [b]
Gustin, Martha N. to Ephram S. Hausben? 12-12-1850
Hackary?, Elizabeth C. to Richd. A. Hatcher 4-12-1842
Hackney, Drusilla to Benjamin B. Hackney 4-1-1855
Hackney, Harriet F. to Jos. J. W. Evans 12-20-1856 (12-21-1856)
Hackney, Moriah to B. F. Willoby 11-13-1846 (11-16-1846)
Haflin, Frances to James W. Dupree 10-15-1840
Hagan, Jane to James T. Morgan 1-16-1855 (1-18-1855)
Haggard, Darthuna to John J. Harris 3-27-1856
Haggard, P. A. to Thomas Wright 4-9-1856
Haggie, Caroline to James E. James 10-6-1859
Hagie, Mary to William Martin 7-22-1852
Hail, Mary to James M. Morrisson 10-23-1839 (10-26-1839)
Hale, Arinda to John B. Cain 1-23-1850
Hale, Martha Ann to Thomas H. Clark 1-12-1853
Hale, Paralee A. to James M. Hale 7-10-1856
Hall, Arinda to John B. Cain (no date; SB 1-20-1851?)
Hall, Elizabeth to David Harrison 12-13-1843
Halliburton, Elizabeth G. to Hugh A. Current 3-31-1859
Halliburton, Sarah F. to Marcellus Griffey 8-24-1865
Hallyard, Udora to John B. Pruitt 12-16-1853 (12-22-1853)
Halsell, Mrs. Martha to Elisha Moore 10-17-1861
Halsey, Henrietta J. to Westley G. Scaggs 1-2-1862 (1-3-1862)
Halyard, Sallie B. to John J. Adams 11-3-1863 (11-5-1863)
Ham, Elizabeth to Peter Buckhannon 9-14-1855 (9-15-1855)
Hambleton, Mary to Alfred M. Flyn 11-19-1840
Hambleton, Sarah Jane to Leigh Chisenhall 3-11-1852
Hamlet, M. L. to A. J. McNeil 10-2-1865 (10-6-1865)
Hamlet, Margaret A. to David Halliburton 9-21-1865 (10-21-1865)
Hamlin, Elizabeth J. to H. J. Hudson 8-23-1860
Hamlin, Jane to John William Patterson 12-28-1856
Hammond, Harriett C. to Chas. B. Hammond 8-4-1866 (8-5-1866)
Hampton, Catharine to Martin Paizan? 4-10-1856
Hampton, Jane to William Thomas Foster 6-1-1857
Hampton, Vina to Thomas Lyles 4-7-1856
Hamrick?, Mary to John Powers 12-19-1859 (1-5-1859?)
Hancock, Kate L. to T. H. Covington 5-30-1864
Hancock, Nancy L. to Wilie Cathey 10-12-1859 (10-13-1859)
Hancock, Polly to Saml. Jorden? 12-30-1846
Hancock, Susan F. to John R. Blake 10-22-1851 (10-23-1851)
Hancocke, Mary E. to Obadiah Broomfield 1-21-1840 (1-23-1840)
Handy?, Eliza C. A. to James Richard Jordon 6-28-1848 (6-29-1848)

Hankins, Rutha to David A. Harrison 1-2-1860 (1-5-1860)
Hanna, Mary M. to B. C. Simmons 3-22-1858
Hannah, Mary S. to J. W. Stigall 11-6-1865
Hansborough, Northana to John E. Duff 1-22-1859 (1-28-1859)
Hansbrough, M. M. E. J. to William F. Yarrington 2-9-1841 (2-11-1841)
Harbin?, F. E. J. to George T. Sanford 7-26-1856
Harbour, Mildred to Richard James 11-25-1841
Hardcastle, Adelia to Edward H. Rogers 8-3-1842 (8-4-1842)
Hardcastle, Elizabeth to Isreal Robertson 7-25-1848
Hardeman, Angeline to Jeremiah sr. Hendricks 11-23-1854
Harden, Jane to Wm. Curtis 12-22-1866 (12-23-1866)
Hardin, Nancy to John W. Buckhannon 3-28-1858
Harding, Arieller S. to Charles W. Franklin 12-16-1854 (12-18-1854)
Hardison, Mary E. to Phillip S. Hardison 12-6-1858
Hardwick, Minerva to Bardett H. Hall 12-8-1853
Hardy, Harriett F. to Jas. S. Pride 4-17-1865
Hardy, Lucy to Young Wilson 10-14-1861
Hardy, Lynda to Jessee Darnell 11-3-1856 (11-6-1856)
Hardy, Martha Ann to William T. Newton 4-6-1856
Hardy, Mary to Mitchel M. Shrader 8-9-1854
Hardy, Nancy to Travis? Oneal 1-2-1851
Hargis, Lucy A. to John E. Rudolph 8-9-1852 (8-11-1852)
Hargis, Malinda Ann to Elijah Pritchett 10-22-1839 (10-24-1839)
Hargrave, E. A. to E. R. Love? 1-18-1844
Hargrave, Martha J. to Thomas E. Pucket 10-9-1853 (10-13-1853)
Harkman?, Hester An to H. Banister 3-27-1851
Harned, B. A. to J. J. Shaw 4-30-1866
Harney, Catharine to John Dinneen 7-29-1865 (7-30-1865)
Harney, Rebecca to James R. Cochran 10-18-1853 (10-20-1853)
Harney, Rebecca to Wade Morgan 4-18-1859 (4-26-1859)
Harper, Martha to Wm. D. Carlin 10-14-1847
Harper, Mary Elizabeth to Drury M. Mather 12-22-1846 (12-24-1846)
Harrid, Ethalinda to Joseph L. Griffin 3-1-1852 (3-2-1852)
Harris, Bettie to John K. Muir 1-1-1861 (1-2-1861)
Harris, Bettie to Thomas C. Jones 9-26-1865 [b]
Harris, Easter to John Dick 12-16-1866 [b]
Harris, Eliza Ann to B. W. Hale 3-8-1849
Harris, Elizabeth C. to Jessee G. Adams 12-13-1857
Harris, Elizabeth J. to Ferdanand E. Balthrop 10-7-1864 (10-9-1864)
Harris, Elizabeth to David H. Harper 12-22-1853
Harris, Ellin to Wiley Sykes 12-12-1860
Harris, Frances to J. H. Hurst 12-4-1851
Harris, Harriett to John Heathcock 7-9-1849
Harris, Harriett to Richard Nolan 7-7-1849
Harris, Julia Ann to Lemuel Cherry 12-22-1855
Harris, Leanie to William A. Hamilton 3-5-1853 (3-6-1853)
Harris, Lockey to William Rinehart 2-20-1860 (2-21-1860)
Harris, Louisa to Jas. M. Trotter 8-11-1863 (8-12-1863)
Harris, Lucinda to Alfred Eatherly 12-12-1848
Harris, M. E. to Wm. H. Plaster 11-26-1849 (11-29-1849)
Harris, Malinda to Stephen Gibbs 1-15-1840 (1-20-1840)
Harris, Malvina to Madison Martin 10-13-1840
Harris, Margaret J. to Richmond S. Trice 5-6-1861
Harris, Martha E. to John W. Anglin 12-12-1855
Harris, Martha M. to William B. Malory 10-17-1859 (10-18-1859)
Harris, Mary A. M. to John D. Niblett 9-23-1856 (9-26-1856)
Harris, Mary C. to John M. Bowers 10-10-1851 (10-12-1851)
Harris, Mary Catherine to Robert Morrison 12-12-1865 (12-14-1865)
Harris, Mary E. to Henry C. Shelton 2-8-1864 (2-11-1864)
Harris, Mary E. to John P. Hainsworth 1-24-1857 (1-25-1857)
Harris, Mary S. to J. W. Hamid 12-27-1858 (12-29-1858)
Harris, Mary W. to Jackson Riggins 12-7-1856
Harris, Miss Tom to J. E. Pollard 1-3-1867 (1-20-1867)
Harris, Nancy Jane to William P. Waller 9-16-1852
Harris, Permelia F. to Wm. H. Broom 11-17-1863
Harris, Rosa Ann to Thomas Bell 1-10-1850 (1-17-1850)
Harris, Sallie M. to Jas. L. Kennedy 12-17-1866 (12-18-1866)
Harris, Sarah F. to William Broadbent 5-1-1849
Harris, Sarah Jane to James M. Harris 12-14-1858 (11?-14-1858)
Harris, Sarah to John W. Lackey 2-19-1843 (2-21-1843)
Harris, Susan Josephine to Wm. Knight 8-20-1852
Harris, Susan T. to William J. Niblutt 1-11-1860
Harris, Tennessee J. to Francis Peck 2-26-1855
Harrison, Ann to Benedict H. Hobbs 12-19-1839 (12-25-1839)

Harrison, Eliza Jane to Peter Lamb 12-26-1858
Harrison, Hester Ann to Robt. T. Cain 9-16-1849
Harrison, Lucinda to D. M. Lacy 10-25-1857
Harrison, Maranda L. to Joseph Shanklin 1-27-1852
Harrison, Martha E. to Henry Wyatt 4-1-1848 (4-2-1848)
Harrison, Martha Jane to Samuel P. Jones 12-30-1855 (12-20?-1855)
Harrison, Mary E. to Jacob Powers 1-3-1857 (1-6-1857)
Harrison, Mary J. to David H. Harrison 5-19-1844
Harrison, Mollie E. to William L. Wheatley 12-24-1865 (12-27-1865)
Harrison, Patsey to Henry Fletcher 9-8-1866 (9-15-1866) [b]
Harriss, Eliza to Solomon Weatherford 3-12-1844
Harriss, Mary to R. W. Blackwell 1-17-1851 (1-22-1851)
Hart, Elizabeth D. to Brickner K. Williams 11-6-1844 (11-7-1844)
Hart, Emma to T. W. Woodson 6-20-1855
Harvey, Lucy J. to W. A. J. Biter 10-18-1864
Harvey, Martha P. to William N. Grimes 9-25-1852 (9-29-1852)
Harvey, Mary Elizabeth to James W. Charlton 2-23-1847 (2-25-1847)
Harvey, Mary to James S. Bergie 1-28-1849 (1-30-1849)
Harvey, Rebecca Frances to Nelson Davis 7-15-1856 (7-17-1856)
Hase?, Fredonia C. to John W. Reynolds 9-16-1855
Hasley, Tennie A. to Joseph Dashner 1-6-1866
Hatcher, Eliza N. to Ben R. Neblett 1-21-1840 (1-22-1840)
Hatcher, Kitty to Berry Gupton 5-30-1866 (5-31-1866) [b]
Hatcher, Mary E. to Reuben R. Pollard 4-18-1842
Hatcher, Rozetta to William Steger 5-14-1866 [b]
Hatcher, Virginia E. to Geo. W. Oldham 10-9-1843
Hatsell, Lucy Ann to Hezekiah Duncan 10-9-1858 (10-12-1858)
Hausdale, Martha A. to Rufus L. King 12-16-1848
Hawkins, Eliza Ann to George Leedle(Tudle?) 8-24-1859 (8-25-1859)
Hawkins, Susan A. to F. H. Williams 7-21-1853
Hayes, Liza Ann to Oliver Bagget 2-21-1856
Hayes, Margaret to Cornelius Dinnun 3-12-1860
Haynes, Angaline C. to David H. Armstrong 7-9-1853 (7-10-1853)
Haynes, Bella to Joe Stacker 1-3-1867 (1-5-1867) [b]
Haynes, Elizabeth M. to Edwin H. Eldridge 10-26-1854 (10-27-1854)
Haynes, Mary A. W. to Cain M. Tylor 11-18-1841
Hays, Mary to Patrick Shaughnessy 12-4-1862 (12-6-1862)
Head, Frances to Garland Chiles 4-16-1847
Head, Lucy A. to A. B. Herrin 1-22-1852
Headom, Sarah to T. S. Underwood 10-4-1854 (10-5-1854)
Heagan, Isabella to James Thomas Weakley 4-21-1857 (4-22-1857)
Heathcoat, Sarah E. to Thomas J. Ridly 7-17-1853
Heathcock, Fredonia to John Cevils? 6-17-1854 (6-18-1854)
Heathman, Frances R. to John E. Holt 9-14-1848
Heflin, Agness to Reuben Harrison 5-14-1846
Heflin, Delphina A. to Elisha B. Harrison 2-5-1851
Heflin, Jane to David C. Smith 2-11-1839 (2-14-1839)
Heflin, Mary to M. B. Stone 12-29-1863 (12-31-1863)
Heflin, Rebecca A. to John B. Rinehart 12-27-1856 (12-30-1856)
Hellem, Harrett to Albert Coward 12-27-1866 (12-31-1866) [b]
Helling, Susan Mildred to George Cherry 2-11-1848
Hem, Lucy to Fauntly Johnson 11-5-1859 (11-8-1859)
Henderson, Margaret J. to William P. Sullivan 5-30-1853
Henderson, Mary to R. J. Coleman 10-28-1860
Henderson, Mary to Wm. B. Pollard 12-7-1843
Henderson, Nancy C. to John W. Gambel 4-11-1858
Hendricks, Emoline to J. A. Whitmore 8-22-1845
Hendrix, Hannah E. to Dabney C. Robertson 10-28-1857
Hennessy, Bridget to Peter Connors 9-1-1855
Henning, Susan C. to Jno. E. Rudolph 2-15-1843 (2-16-1843)
Henry, Mary M. to C. M. Tandy 10-23-1862 (10-29-1862)
Henry, Mary to Antony Garret 10-27-1866 [b]
Henry, Susan to George D. Martin 1-15-1855
Herendon, Elizabeth to G. W. Tribble 2-25-1863 (2-26-1863)
Herndon, Isabella J. to George C. Minnis 8-16-1852 (8-17-1852)
Herndon, Susanna C. to Byard G. Pollard 9-16-1844 (9-17-1844)
Herring, Ann to H. J. Davis 11-1-1838
Herring, Blanch to John O'Brien 12-19-1866
Herring, Elizabeth to John C. Byrd 2-25-1839 (2-26-1839)
Herring, Florence to John W. Faxon 2-22-1866
Herring, Mary Ann to John Roberts 12-5-1844
Herring, N. V. to F. J. Tilley 3-27-1859 (3-24?-1859)
Herring, Nancy to A. V. McFaddin 4-7-1846
Herring, Rosann to Spencer Gill 12-25-1866 [b]
Hester, Bettie to Hamilton Cornell 3-29-1866 (4-3-1866)

Hester, C. A. to M. E. Frasier 7-18-1859 (7-17?-1859)
Hester, Della to Charles Edwards 12-28-1866 [b]
Hester, Evia H. to Edward C. Robb 12-18-1854 (12-19-1854)
Hester, Mack to Jas. S. Ragsdale 10-28-1865 (11-7-1865)
Hester, Mary A. E. to John Sutloff 3-6-1838 (3-13-1838)
Hester, Mary C. to John W. White 1-3-1867
Hester, Mary J. to Henry F. Carter 5-3-1842 (5-5-1842)
Hester, Mrs. Selina to John Calvin Thacker 7-26-1861 (7-27-1861)
Hester, Pemelia R. to Jas. M. Dunlap 2-1-1867 (2-6-1867)
Hester, Sarah to Tom Perkins 12-28-1866 [b]
Hestor, Elizabeth to George S. Willeford 12-20-1844 (12-22-1844)
Hewett, Elizabeth to Gerry Farmer 12-7-1846 (12-8-1846)
Hewett, Mary Ann to Jacob L. Rinehart 1-28-1853
Hewett, Mary Ann to Jacob Rhinehart 12-18-1852
Hickey, Mrs. Emily Jane to Jas J.? Weeks 7-10-1865
Hicks, Catharine to Philander Scudder 1-15-1846
Hicks, Serena to C. D. West 11-12-1850
Higgins, Martha to Saml. Thorn 5-3-1844 (5-4-1844)
Higgins, Sarah to Daniel Coleman 1-23-1853
Highsmith, Martha Q. to Richd. M. Winn 10-18-1866
Hightower, Mary to Balbar Rudd 1-2-1851
Hill, Ann E. to Henry N. Snyder 2-28-1848
Hill, Eliza to James Collins 12-23-1844
Hill, Fanny H. to Francis J. Hall 1-12-1852 (1-13-1852)
Hill, Huctus to Wm. B. McCraw 3-23-1840
Hill, Jane Elizabeth to George Peyton 7-22-1858
Hill, Martha A. to Elijah Fletcher 11-9-1859
Hill, Mary to Joseph Peacher 3-5-1848
Hill, Sarah E. to George B. Bush 12-25-1852 (12-30-1852)
Hill?, Elizabeth A. to Benj. E. Holt 6-17-1848 (6-18-1848)
Hinson, F. M. to Joseph C. Gold 9-4-1855 (8?-12-1855)
Hinton, Ann to Charles H. Morrison 10-21-1847
Hise, Harritte to W. A. Shaw 4-27-1840
Hiter, Harriett E. to Andrew H. Ewing 11-14-1858 (11-15-1858)
Hiter, Hellen M. to John P. Alexander 12-29-1841
Hitt, Susan C. to Geo. W. Pullom 8-16-1866
Hobbs, Elizabeth to Hardin Board 10-18-1860
Hobbs, Nancy Mary to Washington L. Fuqua 9-15-1847
Hodge, Elizabeth to Abraham Baggett 9-13-1865 (9-17-1865)
Hodge, Elizabeth to Henry C. Yarbrough 1-21-1864 (not executed)
Hodges, Leona to Jessee Baggett 8-6-1860 (8-14-1860)
Hodges, Mary Jane to Achillis Hollis 4-17-1860 (4-19-1860)
Hodges, Mary to William Bagget 11-17-1859 (11-18-1859)
Hodges, Olive to William Benjamin Underwood 10-30-1858 (11-1-1858)
Hodges, Sarah W. to Charles T. Doughton 12-29-1846
Hodges, Telitha E. to P. M. Hodges 4-1-1865 (4-2-1865)
Hogan, Amanda to Joseph Davis Burney 12-6-1858 (12-8-1858)
Hogan, Elizabeth Ann to John C. Weakley 4-19-1859 (4-21-1859)
Hogan, Emely C. to Cornelius E. Morgan 12-23-1848 (12-24-1848)
Hogan, Margarett to Wade H. Morgan 9-20-1842 (9-22-1842)
Hogan, Martha Ann to John Myers 10-7-1856
Hogan, Martha to Thomas Whitworth 2-1-1840 (2-2-1840)
Hogan, Mary Ann to George Weaver 11-18-1848 (11-19-1848)
Hogan, N. J. to B. Bayless 8-12-1848
Hogan, Nancy N. to James M. Powers 9-4-1845
Hogel, Matilda H. to Jas. S. Harper 8-4-1849 (8-10-1849)
Holcomb, Mary H. to Brunson McGee 11-21-1854
Holcomb, Rebecca J. to Jas. M. Hilton 8-11-1863
Holland, Laura E. to Charles D. Lockert 12-9-1859 (12-22-1859)
Holland, Sarah Ann to James B. Roark 4-22-1845 (4-23-1845)
Hollins, Hellin to B. D. Johnson 1-19-1863 (1-22-1863)
Hollis, Amanda to Parker B. Pillow 4-17-1844 (4-11?-1844)
Hollis, Jane to James H. Major 12-25-1851
Hollis, Jane to James H. Majors 9-25-1851
Hollist, Susan to James M. Faren 8-19-1863
Holliway, Zilpha to James B. Halyard 1-22-1842
Holloway, Mary to John B. Heel 1-16-1840
Holt, Eliz. An to P.? Whitworth 7-17-1841
Holt, Elizabeth A. to William H. Montgomery 4-11-1854
Holt, Gabriella E. to Marcillus J. Hooper 4-28-1860 (4-29-1860)
Holt, Harriet Louiza to Samuel Jessee Oldham 12-2-1858 (12-4-1858)
Holt, Jane to James M. Davis 11-15-1847 (11-18-1847)
Holt, Martha Ann to Charles W. Hutcherson 11-20-1854 (11-23-1854)
Holt, Mary Adeline to Thomas Hutchison 8-9-1854 (8-10-1854)

Holt, Mary J. to Wm. T. Grant 10-24-1849
Holt, Sarah L. to John Garvis? 9-15-1850
Homen, Bettie V. to Jas. C. Donaldson 10-25-1865 (10-26-1865)
Hooper, Emerline C. to Joseph D. Brown 8-29-1864 (8-30-1864)
Hooper, Isabella to Frank Fort 8-17-1866 [b]
Hooper, Margaret C. to Alexander C. Shenerr? 2-22-1845
Hooper, Theressa A. to Silas H. Woodson 9-10-1856
Hoover, Mary J. to J. M. King 12-24-1840
Hopper, Pereby S. to David Wright 2-24-1845
Hopson, Henrietta to John T. Allensworth 5-8-1861
Hopson, Mildred to John P. Williams 12-12-1842 (12-13-1842)
Horn, E. C. P. to J. J. W. H. Fletcher 12-10-1850 (12-12-1850) Horn,
Elizabeth W. to Joseph A. Welker 4-21-1854 (4-23-1854)
Horn, Narcissa W. to Wm. D. Blanks 9-23-1849
Horn, Sally Ann to John T. Nolen 7-13-1858 (7-20-1858)
Horne, Margrett to Charles Outlaw 12-15-1866 [b]
Horton, Dolly K. to Robert B. Jorden 12-20-1858 (12-21-1858)
Hoskins, Ann to F. Woodward 3-3-1840
Hoskins, Margaret V. to James F. Holland 10-27-1858
Hott, Huldy to Henry Clifton 5-4-1840 (5-7-1840)
House, Columbia R. to John J. Ivy 8-25-1856
House, E. J. to John H. Pritchet 1-10-1843
House, Martha to Edward H. Green 1-24-1860
House, Mary M. to J. W. Wright 8-14-1860
Howard, Annie Ogburn to Robert Keesee 3-24-1866 (3-31-1866) [b]
Howard, Madosa C. to Charles M. Brown 4-15-1858
Howard, Matilda S. to William H. Parish 12-23-1859 (12-25-1859)
Howard, Sarah E. to Wm. H. Colley 6-9-1849
Howell, Mary A. to Thomas N. Robertson 11-24-1857
Howerton, Martha to John Wootton 2-25-1839 (3-8-1839)
Hubbard, Martha E. to J. W. Shaw 3-22-1846
Hudgens, Angeline to W.? H. Lankford 9-24-1846
Hudgens, Mary J. to John B. Stevenson 11-8-1853
Hudson, Rebecca W. to C. H. Batsford 12-28-1860 (12-30-1860)
Hulett, A. D. L. to A. H.? Simons 5-13-1851
Humphreys, M. A. to Benj. H. Brown 8-1-1843 (8-5-1843)
Humphries, Cas Ann to Green Wilkerson 3-22-1847
Humphries, G. A. P. F. to John Walker 12-10-1846 (12-23-1846)
Hunley, Siscia B. to Thos. E. Fulkerson 9-29-1852
Hunt, Ann K. to John May 3-18-1848 (3-19-1848)
Hunt, E. to E. M. Shelton 9-15-1862 (9-16-1862)
Hunt, Martha A. to William R. Thompson 3-18-1840
Hunt, Mary J. to G. W. Allsbrooks 9-25-1848 (9-26-1848)
Hunt, Mary to W. A. Yarbrough 1-26-1851 (1-30-1851)
Hunt, Mollie to Shelby W. Jones 4-4-1866 (4-5-1866)
Hunt, Sophia to James Vaughn 3-22-1848 (3-26-1848)
Hunter, Elizabeth C. to John Black 3-30-1844 (4-3-1844)
Hunter, Judith to James H. jr. Major 10-1-1842 (10-6-1842)
Hunter, Martha Ann to W. T. Harris 1-12-1850 (3-27-1850)
Hunter, Mary Ann to Westly Tally Harris 2-5-1845 (4-2-1845)
Hunter, Mary to Cooper Gupton 8-4-1845 (8-6-1845)
Hunter, Prissilla to David Counsell 2-15-1841 (2-18-1841)
Hunter, Virginia F. to Henry N. Gamell 5-3-1852
Hunter, Winfred to John D. Nicholson 3-7-1850
Hurst, Catharine to James H. Jones 4-20-1848
Hurt, Catharine E. to John O. Hunt 1-18-1841 (1-21-1841)
Hurt, Sarah A. to John T. Fouste 1-4-1855 (1-5-1855)
Huse, Henrietta to James Nolen 4-29-1865
Hutcherson, Eliza B. to Thomas Foust 9-21-1850 (9-26-1850)
Hutcherson, Elizabeth to Jacob P. Albright 3-27-1848
Hutcherson, Nancy to James Higgins 3-28-1853 (3-30-1853)
Hutcherson, Nancy to John Quarles 10-18-1843 (10-21-1843)
Hutcherson, Sarah Ann to Finney? L. Evans 3-17-1853
Hutchings, Adline to N. H. Belcher 5-8-1842 (5-23-1842)
Hutchings, Mary E. to C. M. Warfield 6-10-1846 (6-16-1846)
Hutchins, Olevia to James E. Brame 12-19-1859
Hutchinson, Tennessee to Geo. W. Grant 1-8-1848
Ingram, Lucy Israella to William Marion? 12-30-1857 (12-27?-1857)
Ingram, Nancy E. to Ambrose Manion 10-11-1852
Irwin, Allis to John E. Nutt 12-11-1866
Isbell, Charity to James Basford 7-6-1846 (7-23-1846)
Isbell, Mary A. G. to H. C. Vaughn 7-22-1840
Izer, J. C. A. to J. H. Farmer 1-8-1847 (1-9-1847)
Izor, Emily F. to N. L. Turner 9-3-1860 (9-6-1860)
Jackson, Elizabeth Caroline to Alexander Underwood 2-11-1861

Jackson, Elizabeth to B. F. Fox? 1-2-1843 (1-3-1843)
Jackson, Elizabeth to Josiah Jackson 11-14-1863 (11-21-1864?)
Jackson, Frances to Wormerly Rose 1-2-1860 (1-17-1860)
Jackson, Jemima to Billy Corbin 9-20-1866 (10-6-1866) [b]
Jackson, Lucey Ann to Murdock McCurdey 1-27-1853
Jackson, Lucy W. to David W. McFadin 1-23-1845
Jackson, Margaret to Dick Payne 4-21-1865 [b]
Jackson, Martha to Thomas McGuire 10-12-1848
Jackson, Mary A. to James Smith 3-26-1845
Jackson, Mary Ann to Elijah Davis 9-12-1842
Jackson, Mary Ann to Samuel J. McNeil 5-10-1858
Jackson, Mary E. to Wallen Elisha Sykes 9-29-1859
Jackson, Mary H. to Thos. McManus 8-4-1865
Jackson, Mrs. Emma A. to John H. Ray 1-16-1862
Jackson, Mrs. Sophia W. to Thos. S. Hunt 6-25-1864 (6-30-1864)
Jackson, Penelopee to Thornton McQuary 2-20-1865
Jackson, Selina G. to Henry C. Yarborough 9-10-1864 (9-11-1864)
Jackson, Selina to Joseph Pearce 3-22-1863
Jackson, Sophia to Robt. H. Knox 9-12-1843 (9-14-1843)
Jackson, Tennessee to Murdock McCauley 12-18-1850 (12-19-1850)
James, Amanda to Wm. Bailey 2-27-1866
Jarad, Mary R. to Joseph B. West 10-4-1851
Jarman, Ellen to Owen Brook 9-12-1859
Jarman, Lurana(Susanna?) to Wade Breeden 6-28-1859 (6-29-1859)
Jarman, Mrs. Ann to James Brown 7-27-1865
Jarrell, Amanda A. to Kenneth McKinnon 12-23-1851
Jarrell, Frances to George R. Smith 1-16-1855 (1-17-1855)
Jarrell, Mary E. to R. W. Wagstaff 8-24-1865
Jarrell, Rhoda A. to Washington W. Smith 9-20-1853 (9-22-1853)
Jarrell, Silvy to Sam Bradley 3-31-1866 (4-14-1866) [b]
Jelk, Emily C. to Fielding Smith 4-15-1846 (4-16-1846)
Jenell, Martha to John J. Jones 12-13-1848
Jenkins, Arabella A. to C. H. Dunn 12-7-1859 (12-8-1859)
Jenkins, Cynthia Ann to J. C. Skipworth 11-10-1853
Jenkins, Emma M. to Jas. M. Dale 9-4-1866
Jenkins, Mary A. to Westley Oglesby 7-26-1860
Jenkins, Rebecca to George Riggins 12-27-1841 (1-3-1842)
Jenkins, Tennessee B. to John C. Gillum 8-11-1863 (8-12-1863)
Jenning, Martha to John A. Myres 12-15-1858
Jennings, Elizabeth to William J. Roland 5-14-1861
Jennings, Susan C. to Martin C. Powers 1-7-1861 (1-22-1861)
Jerdan, Clarissa to Anderson Jerdan 1-4-1867 [b]
Jessup, Mrs. Elizabeth to Thos. Ozment 7-16-1866 (7-17-1866)
Jeter, Georgeann to Samuel Bradshaw 7-13-1856
Jeter, Mary Jane to Samuel Bradshaw 6-30-1852
Jett, Ann D. to James T. Johnson 9-25-1860 (9-27-1860)
Jett, Anne Eliza to James W. Hutchinson 10-24-1848
Jett, Elizabeth to John L. Wyatt 10-5-1857 (10-6-1857)
Jett, Martha to John Powell 12-19-1853 (12-20-1853)
Jett, Mary A. to W. S. McReynolds 9-28-1847
Jett, Melvile to William H. Cooksey 7-5-1854 (7-6-1854)
Jett, Mrs. E. A. to W. D. Halliberton 1-28-1861 (1-29-1861)
Jinkins, Letecia J. to Joseph Ray 11-6-1863 (11-10-1863)
Jobeler?, Eliza to Benjamin T. Marshall 10-16-1838 (10-18-1838)
Johnson, Ann to James Ogburn 12-21-1844 (12-22-1844)
Johnson, Barbary to Dock Moore 4-8-1865 (4-9-1865) [b]
Johnson, E. H. to Jessee Gilbert 2-21-1863 (2-22-1863)
Johnson, E. J. to George H. Warfield 1-6-1848
Johnson, E. M. to W. H. Wilson 4-28-1854
Johnson, Eliza to Silas D. Wright 3-21-1865
Johnson, Elizabeth A. to Joshua Lester 8-16-1849
Johnson, Elizabeth C. to Dudley Travis 4-3-1839
Johnson, Elizabeth to John A. Dancy 2-16-1857 (2-17-1857)
Johnson, Emily Jane to William J. Hickerson 11-17-1856 (11-18-1856)
Johnson, F. J. to J. D. Kendrick 10-11-1864
Johnson, Frances C. to John A. Wims (no date; with 2-1852)
Johnson, Frances to Chas. M. Warfield 8-3-1839 (8-8-1839)
Johnson, Frances to Reuben C. Ross 1-27-1849
Johnson, Janie to Walis Warfield 12-25-1866 (12-28-1866) [b]
Johnson, Juddie to Dock Black 4-14-1866 [b]
Johnson, Julia A. to M. Hartman 12-31-1862 (1-3-1863)
Johnson, Julia Ann to Chesley Bridgewater 4-20-1849
Johnson, Louisa H. to Hugh H. Parton 10-23-1855
Johnson, Louiza M. to Joshua Lester 11-14-1855 (11-15-1855)
Johnson, Lucy A. to James C. Jones 2-1-1847 (2-4-1847)

Johnson, Lucy C. to Morris W. Wilson 9-18-1852 (9-19-1852)
Johnson, M.J. to William Thompson 8-4-1840
Johnson, Mahala to James Johnson 4-8-1861
Johnson, Margarett to Jacob jr. Powers 1-1-1852
Johnson, Margarette to William Gowans 11-21-1839
Johnson, Martha A. M. to Wm. A. Baily 8-3-1846 (8-22-1846)
Johnson, Martha D. to Charles G. Smith 9-28-1859
Johnson, Martha M. to Albert M. Covington 1-4-1855
Johnson, Martha to Ben Johnson 4-28-1866 (5-20-1866) [b]
Johnson, Martha to James T. Gradey 3-1-1861 (3-5-1861)
Johnson, Mary C. to James Crosier 11-3-1849 (11-4-1849)
Johnson, Mary E. to John Duncan 11-21-1861 (11-27-1861)
Johnson, Mary Elizabeth to Thomas S. Hayes 2-17-1856
Johnson, Mary F. to J. N. Randle 12-15-1860
Johnson, Mary L. to Theodore Miller 9-29-1853
Johnson, Matilda to Jas. Anderson 5-21-1866 [b]
Johnson, Mildred to Green Buster 8-10-1865 [b]
Johnson, Mildred to James Jenkins 5-13-1852 (5-15-1852)
Johnson, Miss Susan R. to Chas. A. Young 1-12-1852
Johnson, Mrs. Julia V. A. E. to George W. Evans 11-2-1866
     (11-6-1866)
Johnson, Nancy J. to William K. Hollis 8-31-1847
     (9-2-1847)
Johnson, Nancy N. to Latan G. Williams 8-23-1858
Johnson, Nancy to Wm. J. Phillip 12-7-1864
Johnson, Rebecca to John T. Johnson 3-25-1854 (3-26-1854)
Johnson, Rosana B. to P. A. V. Johnson 4-3-1849 (4-5-1849)
Johnson, Sarah to Plummer? J. Williams 8-26-1856
Johnson, Selina to Abram Fulkerson 1-28-1862
Johnson, Silvy to Lewis Tandy 4-10-1866 (4-14-1866)
Johnson, Susan Ann to Charles W. McBride 7-27-1853
Johnson, Valeria to D. B. Winstead 10-29-1862
Johnston, Mary to William Oughton 3-19-1860
Joiner, Frances A. to Adam Eaton 9-23-1843 (10-24-1843)
Jolly, Fanny to John Ware? 5-7-1838
Jonal, Caroline to Wm. H. Toler 2-21-1849
Jones, Almyra to Francis B. Powers 2-6-1865
Jones, Amberlin? to William Ballentine 7-9-1853
Jones, Augusta to Leander Lawson 7-9-1866 [b]
Jones, Belle M. to George Hoffman 7-21-1862
Jones, Clara to John Benjamin Wilie 11-24-1858 (11-25-1858)
Jones, Eliza to James C. Jones 2-6-1844
Jones, Eliza to Leftridge Crockett 9-15-1844
Jones, Eliza to Martin Miller 1-11-1861
Jones, Elizabeth H. to Uriah B. Clark 8-22-1861
Jones, Elizabeth N. to Joseph Bumpass 12-31-1850
Jones, Elizabeth P. to D. J. Allensworth 8-17-1848
Jones, Elizabeth R. to Thomas J. Major 11-28-1853 (11-29-1853)
Jones, Elizabeth W. to John Thomas Jones 11-10-1859
Jones, Elizabeth to A. J. Binkley 1-10-1861
Jones, Elizabeth to B. F. Bryan 1-13-1855 (1-16-1855)
Jones, Elizabeth to Buckner Matthis 12-10-1841 (12-16-1841)
Jones, Elizabeth to William James 11-23-1854
Jones, Emma A. to Thomas J. Shaw 5-26-1856 (5-27-1856)
Jones, Ethalinda E. to Thomas Ogburn 9-3-1860
Jones, G. A. to H. W. Gray 12-13-1864 (not executed)
Jones, Harriet A. to Thos. Gupton 12-15-1851 (12-18-1851)
Jones, Harriet to James E. Payne 11-27-1845
Jones, Harriett W. to James H. Petty 5-8-1842
Jones, Harriett to Wm. A. Kendrick 7-8-1865 (7-9-1865)
Jones, Jane to Josephus Collins 7-11-1864
Jones, Lucy D. to Samuel Bumpass 10-20-1845
Jones, Marian to James E. Martin 10-25-1852 (12-25-1852)
Jones, Martha A. to Certain T. Halsiel 2-25-1840 (2-27-1840)
Jones, Martha C. to John Harris 4-8-1856 (4-6?-1856)
Jones, Martha J. to Jas. H. Jackson 9-20-1849
Jones, Martha to James H. Jones 2-13-1852
Jones, Martha to James Morrison 3-30-1842
Jones, Mary Ann H. to John W. Hunt 12-18-1839 (12-24-1839)
Jones, Mary Ann to Samuel Buckly 8-8-1857 (8-9-1857)
Jones, Mary E. to Thomas H. Stokes] 9-4-1857
Jones, Mary Elam to Charles B. Faulkner 8-5-1856
Jones, Mary J. to John Bumpass 12-19-1850 (12-18?-1850)
Jones, Mary Jane to William Overbee 5-19-1839
Jones, Mickie Priscilla to David Strayhorn? 1-25-1855

Jones, Mollie F. to H. L. Stanley 9-20-1866
Jones, Nancy A. to M. M. H. Miles 1-7-1851 (2-5-1851)
Jones, Nancy to George McFursian 1-9-1867 [b]
Jones, Nancy to William M. Rose 4-16-1844 (4-15-1844)
Jones, Piety Rebecca to James Braxton Coleman 11-27-1860
Jones, Rebecca to A. F. Hall 7-20-1850 (7-21-1850)
Jones, S. E. to James M. Glascock 3-22-1845
Jones, Sarah Ann to Robert Stamper 6-28-1847
Jones, Sarah W. to John T. Jones 12-5-1849
Jones, Sarah to William Baker 3-10-1848
Jones, Susan A. to Felix jr. Northington 6-15-1841
Jones, Susan M. to Martin W. Bryan 4-30-1866 (5-1-1866)
Jones, Susan W. to Wm. J. Jones 9-3-1851
Jones, Susan to Josiah Jackson 10-18-1843 (10-19-1843)
Jones, Susanah to Willis Jones 5-28-1850
Jones, T. H. to W. H. Jones 8-2-1865
Jones, Tennessee to John Sanderson 6-15-1863
Jones, Virginia to James Thomas 3-1-1854 (3-5-1854)
Jones, Winney to Joseph J. Trotter 10-30-1845
Jordan, Mariah C. to D. S. Nuvell 10-31-1843 (11-1-1843)
Jordan, Mary H. to J. T. Ennis 4-1-1865
Jordan, Taylor to Beverly G. Willard 2-19-1866 (2-27-1866)
Jorden, Elizabeth to W. H. Hull 6-17-1854
Jorden, Mary A. to James M. Wray 4-9-1853 (4-10-1853)
Jorden, Sarepta M. to B. B. Homan 7-21-1863 (7-22-1863)
Jourdan, Elizabeth B. to William H. Gelay 2-12-1859 (2-15-1859)
Jourdon, Demarius to John Burnett 3-13-1846 (3-15-1846)
Judkins, Dora to Saml. B. Stewart 5-2-1866
Justice, Rebecca to William S. Fielder 3-5-1853
Justis, Susan E. to Joseph W. Burton 12-28-1850 (12-30-1850)
Kacy, Margarett to F. S. Ford 3-25-1843 (3-29-1843)
Kane, Mary R. O. to Allen R. Workman 1-16-1865
Keats, Mary to Elisha Duncan 1-12-1858
Keats, Virginia P. to S. F. Ferrill 3-1-1865 (3-5-1865)
Keesee, J. P. to C. J. Metcalf 7-9-1860 (7-10-1860)
Keesee, Sarah J. to Geo. M. Wright 11-18-1856
Keller, Margaret J. to William B. Settle 9-2-1846 (9-8-1846)
Keller, Mary to Thomas Waller 8-6-1850 (8-7-1850)
Kellibrew, Ellen D. to V. M. Metcalf 12-27-1855
Kellis, Yurena to Benjamin Leavel 12-26-1866 [b]
Kelly, Ada B. to J. H. Hirch 1-23-1863 (2-3-1863)
Kelly, Ann E. to William L. Harding 1-9-1856
Kelly, Bridget to John King 12-28-1858 (12-30-1858)
Kelly, Lucy C. to Hiram Smith 5-11-1863
Kelly, M. F. to H. B. Hunt 3-10-1865 (3-16-1865)
Kelly, Mary Lucy to William Weldon Harris 2-7-1855 (2-8-1855)
Kelly, Matt. F. to William G. Wilson 1-27-1859
Kelly, Winey to Charles F. Moore 2-21-1852
Kendrick, Elizabeth C.? to James P. Greene 5-21-1851 (6-3-1851)
Kendrick, Frances H. to Joseph M. Jones 4-20-1844 (5-1-1844)
Kendrick, Lucy A. to Howel T. Jordon 10-25-1841 (10-28-1841)
Kendrick, Silla to Ambrose Dawson 3-5-1866 (3-8-1866) [b]
Kennedy, Kate to Dock Drane 5-18-1866 (5-28-1866) [b]
Kenner, Eliza J. to John Mills 11-10-1860 (11-14-1860)
Kerr, Elizabeth W. to M. H. Clark 7-29-1861
Kerr, Lucinda to Isaac Carroll 5-21-1839
Kerr, Martha N. to Samuel M. Anderson 4-24-1859 (4-26-1859)
Kestner, Catharine to George Grant 8-21-1860
Key, Ann M. to Joseph F. Lankley 1-26-1852
Killebrew, Easter to Chas. Green 10-20-1866 (10-27-1866) [b]
Killebrew, Frances A. to J. T. Vaughn 10-13-1862 (10-15-1862)
Killebrew, Frances J. to Jno. M. Carter 11-2-1841
Killebrew, Martha P. to James M. Radford 4-5-1853 (4-7-1853)
Killebrew, Mary E. to Wm. B. Whitfield 9-24-1849
Killebrew, Mary S. to William Cayce 4-11-1839
Killebrew, Rody to Henry Gill 9-25-1865 (10-28-1865)
Killebrew, Sarah W. to L. F. Chilton 10-15-1851
Killibrew, Catharine W. to Jonathan L. Johnson 11-26-1840
Killibrew, S. H. to E. R. Herring 6-28-1855 (7-1-1855)
Killroy, Mary to P. R. O'Donnell 4-28-1866 (4-30-1866)
Kimble, Sue C. to DeMarcus G. Simmons 10-2-1861 (10-3-1861)
Kimbrough, Bettie to T. R. Kimbrough 1-17-1866 (1-18-1866)
King, Bridgett to Daniel Carney 1-24-1859 (1-25-1859)
King, Catharine E. to Harrison C. Lockhart 9-23-1854
King, Cathrine E. to Harrison C. Lockhart 9-23-1854 (9-24-1854)

King, Elizabeth to Geo. W. Pace 9-16-1851 (9-18-1851)
King, Louiza to Joseph Gee 1-18-1854
King, Lovisa to Norrord Yarbrough 7-3-1838 (7-5-1838)
King, M. G. to J. T. Albright 1-7-1861 (1-15-1861)
King, Martha Ann to Ezekiel Horde 6-7-1853
King, Martha Ann to William Gargus 7-12-1865
King, Mary J. to Thomas Welker 7-14-1845 (7-17-1845)
King, Mary to Benjamin F. Bartlett 4-14-1845 (4-15-1845)
King, Matilda to Jos. L. Riggs 11-8-1842
King, Susannah to C. J. Cromwell 10-11-1843
Kinies?, Julian to John Bowe? 1-31-1846
Kinner, Mary C. to James F. Hopson 11-12-1844
Kinser, Dicy to John C. Brown 2-22-1845
Kirk, Margarett to Arthur Bryan 10-26-1850 (10-1?-1850)
Kirtley, Catharine to Bluford Calvert 11-20-1846
Kirtly, Mary E. to Martin Kittinger 11-1-1848
Kissebech, Mary to James M. Gay 9-8-1852
Kistner, Nancy Jane to John E. Grant 10-28-1854 (11-1-1854)
Kistnor, Mary Ann to Jas. K. Polk Heflin 2-27-1861
Knight, Easter to William Harris 3-21-1859
Knight, Lucinda to James Torides? 2-2-1854
Knight, Serilda to William Henry Smith 5-30-1858
Knott, Barbary to William Rice 11-2-1846
Knott, Mary to Wm. L. Neblett 3-4-1844
Knott?, Pamelia F. to Saml. P. Hollins 12-12-1850 (12-19-1850)
Koop, Elizabeth T. to S. T. Waggoner 12-10-1840 (12-16-1840)
Kyle, Dosia to Fletcher Epley 12-6-1866
Lacy, Bettie H. to Benjamin W. Doward 6-17-1861 (6-20-1861)
Lacy, Elizabeth to Charles W. Cavanah 11-16-1847
Lacy, Mary to Tom Metcalf 7-19-1866 [b]
Lacy, Octavia to Charles H. Balton(Ballow?) 7-25-1864 (7-27-1864)
Lacy, S. E. to J. W. Davidson 11-16-1863
Lacy, Virginia F. to Miles W. Stevenson 7-4-1859 (7-6-1859)
Lad, Rosanna to Richard A. Rogers 7-22-1860 (7-21?-1860)
Lad, Susan to James Butler 7-31-1856
Lafoon, Lucinda to George Sanford 12-31-1841
Laird, Martha to Francis Freil 7-30-1857
Laird, Mary A. E. to J. A. Dodson 9-20-1849
Laird, Mary to William H. Eldridge 1-5-1858 (1-6-1858)
Laird, Virginia G. to Charles T. Faulkerson 10-6-1859
Lake, Drusilla to L. B. Edds? 5-9-1853
Lamaster, Mary to John W. Kelly 8-2-1841
Lamaster, Maurina A. to Richd. H. Humphreys 5-16-1843
Lamaster, Sally to James Hutcherson 7-7-1858
Lambuth, Elizabeth to Jas. W. Durrett 10-23-1849
Lancaster, America to Jo McKew 12-22-1859
Landcaster, Marinia to James O. McGeehee 3-15-1853
Lander, Gracy L. to Orlander E. Davis 1-31-1852
Landram, Jessie to George P. Allensworth 11-2-1863
Lane, Hariet Caroline to George Abbott 3-12-1846 (3-13-1846)
Lane, Margaret to F. M. Taylor 1-23-1860 (1-24-1860)
Lane, Sarah M.' to Edward Epperson 12-2-1852
Langford, Mary to Wade Morgan 1-26-1849 (1-28-1849)
Langston, Emily F. to Peter Frick 12-14-1847 (12-15-1847)
Langston, Margaret J. to Wm. A. Calder 11-7-1839
Langston, Martha to E. Kirkland 12-12-1865 (2-25-1865?)
Langston, Mary to John Herrington 10-8-1845 (10-9-1845)
Langston, Rebecca to Jacob Frick 1-5-1852 (1-6-1852)
Lanier, Aliph to Jordon Kincaid 4-29-1839
Lankford, Doratha to Alsey Jones? 1-26-1841 (1-28-1841)
Lankford, Martha to Joshua Humphreys 3-14-1840 (3-17-1840)
Lankford, Mrs. M. M. to C. M. Humphreys 6-3-1865
Lasetter, Elizabeth to Wm. W. Groom 9-9-1848 (9-10-1848)
Latham, Frances E. to Allen Dorrington 3-17-1848
Latham, Margarett A. to Wesley D. Shelton 1-18-1843
Latham, Nancy A. to Jessee Bresner? 8-24-1847
Laughran, Elizabeth F. to James T. Caldwell 11-8-1850
Laughren, Elizabeth C. to Benjamin R. Williams 7-17-1861 (7-18-1861)
Lawson, Nancy to Robert Malone 11-13-1846 (11-14-1846)
Lay, Eliza Ann to Peter J. Averitt 8-27-1853
Layne, Mary E. to Jno. A. Smith 8-26-1843
Lea, Susan Ann to Wm. H. Tally 10-15-1848
Leach, Mary L. to A. L. Duerson 1-29-1852
Leason, Mary Jane to Munroe Welbourne 3-28-1852

Leavell, Dianah to Geo. Hackney 8-29-1866 [b]
Leavell, Elizabeth to Henry Elder 12-11-1865
Lee, Bettie to Geo. B. Riggins 1-18-1866 (1-25-1866)
Lee, Clarrinda F. to Mathew A. Barnes 4-5-1859 (4-7-1859)
Lee, Elizabeth H. to Sylvanus Trotter 11-29-1865 (12-6-1865)
Lee, Ida to Robt. B. Page 6-1-1866
Lee, Lucy Ann to James H. Black 10-16-1846 (11-5-1846
Lee, Lucy Jane to Allen Hamlin 9-13-1860 (9-15-1860)
Lee, M. J. to B. F. Grant 8-9-1862 (8-13-1862)
Lee, Mary E. to John N. Perdue 6-3-1848 (6-4-1848)
Lee, Mary Jane to John R. Rye 9-29-1866
Lee, Sarah A. to Saml. P. Hodges 12-14-1865 (12-20-1865)
Lee, Tenny (Jenney?) to Robert Manning 12-13-1860
Leet, Sarah to James Hardis 11-11-1863 (11-12-1863)
Leigh, Emeline to Saml. Heart 2-15-1843 (2-24-1843)
Leigh, Fredonia to Johnson B. West 8-22-1866 (8-26-1866)
Leigh, Mary Ann to James H. Flack 3-3-1842
Leigh, Mary J. to John M. Hart 3-11-1844 (3-14-1844)
Leigh, Mary L. to Valentine W. Smith 11-1-1859
Leigh, Nancy A. to Wm. F. Ferrell 3-24-1860 (3-29-1860)
Lemay, Rebecca Ann to Thos. H. Averet 9-11-1845
Lemmons, Laura to W. P. Lindley 1-13-1864 (1-14-1864)
Lemons, Mary J. to Benjamin F. Davidson 10-28-1858 (10-29-1858)
Lemons, Susan to Wm. C. Chandler 5-6-1865 (5-7-1865)
Lenslley?, Mary to Charles Waugh 9-17-1839
Leonard, Bridget to Michael Bennet 7-16-1859 (7-17-1859)
Levell, Siller to Sam Cook 2-24-1866 [b]
Lewis, Cordelia H. to John C. Bowers 11-15-1853 (11-20-1853)
Lewis, Dicy Adaline to William R. Anderson 6-11-1853 (6-12-1853)
Lewis, Eliza Jane to Elijah Duncan 12-10-1853 (12-12-1853)
Lewis, Elizabeth to John Bailey 10-9-1845
Lewis, Hannah to Elcaner Miller 5-20-1848 (5-28-1848)
Lewis, Lavica to Thomas Warden 6-4-1852
Lewis, Mary M. to Wm. Ellitt 1-17-1866
Lewis, Mathy to Lias Shird 12-29-1866 [b]
Lewis, Susan to Richd. H. Maddison 2-16-1843
Liggon, Georgian to Ambrose Clark 12-27-1865 (12-29-1865)
Ligon, Demetria L. to John B. Ligon 11-13-1856
Ligon, Isabell to Edmond Williams 12-23-1865 (12-28-1865) [b]
Ligon, Judith P. to Reuben C. Keeser 12-30-1839
Ligon, Mary C. to H. T. Wilkinson 12-17-1863
Ligon, Mary G. to Wm. H. Fort 8-30-1847
Ligon, Palina L. to James W. Rye 10-19-1859 (10-21-1850)
Ligon, Sarah L. to David T. Ligon 11-24-1859
Liles, Elizabeth to Charles Hiser 7-9-1853
Linch, B. to Geo. Linch 1-1-1866 [b]
Lindly, Sarah to George Graham 12-29-1852
Linsey, Angeline to Thos. Adams 2-1-1847
Lisenby, Elmira E. to John Stewart 1-4-1867 (1-6-1867)
Lisenby, Sally to Joseph Barnes 9-10-1855 (10-10-1855)
Litteral, Eliza to Robert Holland 11-11-1855
Little, Adaline J. to James Roach 3-14-1842 (3-15-1842)
Little, Frances to Alford Bearden 3-11-1839
Little, Harriet to Solaman D. Sullivan 9-27-1856 (9-28-1856)
Little, M. E. Taylor to Jno. Barnwell 12-27-1843
Little, Rachael M. to J. A. Smith 10-4-1858
Littlefield, Lucy to Martin A. Lawhon 12-29-1846
Littlepage, Susan to Saml. Carlyle 9-6-1843
Lockert, M. F. to James M. Berniss? 10-16-1849 (10-19-1849)
Lockert, Sarah A. E. to Isaac D. Stone 12-14-1846 (11?-16-1846)
Lockert, Sarah M. G. to David A. Ligun? 7-23-1846
Lockhert, Maggie to Henry M. Doak 8-28-1866
Lockutt, Elizabeth A. to Wm. H. Rudolph 10-14-1846
Lofland, Ella M. to Frank A. Phillips 2-13-1861 (2-14-1861)
Lofland, Jane to John D. Robins 5-4-1865
Lofland, Lucy S. to James A. Starks 4-9-1858 (4-15-1858)
Loftland, Trannia? J. to Alexander F. Sale 1-1-1853 (1-9-1853)
Logan, Elizabeth to James Terry 12-22-1840
London, Louisa to E. T. Loving 3-8-1842
Long, Eliza to James Brunty 6-5-1848
Long, Elizabeth J. to Jones H. Bancroft 1-28-1860 (1-29-1860)
Long, F. E. to T. L. Cook 2-21-1859 (2-22-1859)
Long, Fannie W. to D. M. Ragan 1-30-1866 (1-31-1866)
Long, Margaret A. to Isaac Peterson 12-22-1853
Long, Martha C. to Joel Gresham 1-9-1852

Long, Susan to Wm. D. Murphy 10-11-1844
Lord, Adaline M. to A. D. Ramsey 5-7-1845
Louis, Louisa to Robert H. Weakly 8-8-1845 (8-10-1845)
Love, Carian B. to Robert A. Anderson 7-29-1839 (8-1-1839)
Love, Emily E. to Pleasant J. Young 3-1-1847
Lovicy, May to Wm. Browning 2-14-1848
Loving, Amanda J. to Wm. M. Jackson 10-25-1847
Low, Luiza to Henry Riggins 12-25-1866 (12-27-1866) [b]
Lowe, Matt T. to Danl. D. Allen 3-14-1866
Lowery, Mary S. to Henry C. Shelton 11-19-1861 (11-21-1861)
Luallen, Alcy to Thos. Suter 5-3-1864
Luallen, Martha to Ransom Viles 5-28-1859 (6-1-1859)
Lucey, Cirena to James Henry Ray 8-25-1846
Luck, Bettie to John Goff 8-1-1865 (8-3-1865)
Luck, Elizabeth to John Sullivan 6-29-1859 (6-30-1859)
Luke, Mary A. to Jno. T. Dauson 11-8-1843
Luke, Nancy to Joseph Smith 12-21-1854
Lunsford, Sarah R. to William Stiles 3-31-1857
Lyaris?, Virginia to John H. Stratton 10-19-1854
Lyle, Almeda J. to Stelring N. Martin 11-26-1853
Lyle, Catharine to Mastin C. Lyle 6-4-1864
Lyle, Julia to Franklin Dougton 7-29-1844
Lyle, Louisa A. to James C. Allen 6-1-1852
Lyle, Lucy J. to J. W. Attaway 11-18-1865 (11-21-1865)
Lyle, Mary Ann to John M. Jones 1-12-1848
Lyle, Mary B. to J. W. R. Altaway 3-29-1858 (3-30-1858)
Lyle, Mary E. to James R. Cravens 12-5-1865
Lyle, Rebecca Elizabeth to Burrel Briant 7-16-1853
      (7-17-1853)
Lyle, Sarepta A. to C. J. Hiter 2-15-1866
Lyles, Dora to John A. Gholson 5-21-1860
Lyles, Eliza Ann to James P. Williams 3-24-1840 (3-26-1840)
Lyles, Margarette D. to Robert S. Jarman 9-10-1838 (10-?-1838)
Lyles, Mary Bell to Moses Oldham 7-21-1852
Lynes, Frances to Jno. H. Hinton 10-1-1840
Lynes, Mary E. to Thomas W. Morrow 10-25-1855
Lynes, Rachael to James Mardis 9-25-1855 (10-9-1855)
Lynes, Sarah Jane to Allen Walther 11-24-1847
Lynn, America to Joel Goodall 7-2-1853
Lynn, Elizabeth to James Heathman 10-4-1841 (10-6-1841)
Lynn, H. M. to W. T. Hargrave 10-6-1851
Lynn, Margaret C. to C. N. Carney 5-6-1848 (5-7-1848)
Lyons, Ella A. to John Powers 2-2-1846 (2-8-1846)
Maar?, Eveline to Benjamine Barnett 10-26-1849 (10-29-1849)
Mabry, Dora to Chas. Barrett 11-24-1865
Mabry, Mollie to Chas. Holliman 9-29-1866 [b]
Mackelroy, Nancy A. to John J. Erwin 10-22-1864 (10-23-1864)
Mackley, Mary B. to Hartwell D. Hogwood 3-24-1853 (3-30-1853)
Macklin, Frances to James Sutton 12-22-1854 (12-28-1854)
Macklin, Lucy Ann to G. B. Lyle 10-26-1854
Macklin, Margarette A. to Barny E. Powel 4-21-1840
Madden, M. V. to John G. Gregory 7-9-1855 (7-8?-1855)
Madding, M. A. to M. C. Shelton 4-4-1860
Maddox, Hester Ann to R. D. Gray 5-22-1854
Madison, Eliza Mildred to Thomas L. Beacun? 5-20-1845
Maham, Catharine to George W. Davis 8-24-1854
Mahan, Rachael Ruby to Thomas Lynes 3-19-1847
Major, Fredonia M. to Samuel D. Power 3-21-1853 (3-29-1853)
Major, Rebecca to Jno. B. Taylor 2-22-1844 (3-6-1844)
Majors, Adda E. to John W. Word 11-2-1857 (11-3-1857)
Majors, M. A. to B. F. Word 1-28-1864
Majors, Martha to Peter Rinehart 12-16-1845
Majors, Mary to Robert Jones 3-5-1846
Majors, Prudence to John Beardin 12-13-1841 (12-15-1841)
Makes, Martha to Jas. Gupton 1-5-1851
Mallory, Elizabeth to Nathan Hester 1-18-1844 (1-21-1844)
Mallory, Frances J. to James D. Bowers 9-9-1850
Mallory, Larini to Benj. F. Ritt 8-4-1859 (8-7-1859)
Mallory, Mary E. to George N. Morris 11-7-1855
Mallory, Mary E. to Nathaniel J. Miles 3-24-1856 (3-25-1856)
Mallory, Sally Rebecca to Henry Grimes 12-18-1855 (11?-11?-1855)
Malone, Julia Ann to Jackson Munroe Conrad 12-25-1854
      (12-27-1854)
Malone, Winny to Thomas Geleen? 4-2-1849
Malory, Jennie to Wm. Taylor 1-25-1865 (1-26-1865)

Malory, Martha to Emanuel Wallace 4-16-1866 (4-17-1866) [b]
Malory, Mary N. to Wm. W. McGee 12-10-1849 (12-21-1849)
Manin?, Martha L. to Hyram Walsh 3-6-1855
Maning, Alitha to Henry Fox 8-25-1864 (8-24?-1864)
Maning, Elizabeth to Felix G. Gilbert 3-6-1851
Manion, M. E. to L. G. Winters 2-17-1856
Manlove, Virginia to William R. Bringhurst 1-17-1867
Mann, L. J. to W. T. Vaughn 9-16-1862
Mann, Louisa to Joseph Barons? 9-7-1846 (9-8-1846)
Mann, Mrs. Martha to L. B. Fite 8-13-1866 (8-15-1866)
Manning, Ivy J. to Rizen Connally 2-4-1844 (Blve SB 1842)
Manning, Jane to George W. Marshall 10-12-1853 (10-13-1853)
Manning, Julia to Wm. Suter 3-18-1863 (3-19-1863)
Manning, Mary to William Henry Walls 7-2-1853 (7-3-1853)
Manning, Ruth A. to Edwd. B. Halsul 9-25-1842
Mansfield, M. J. to H. W. Perkins 3-23-1845
Manson, Ellen V. to E. R. Dabney 12-18-1856
Manson, Martha S. to Asaph H. Alsup 11-4-1854 (11-8-1854)
Manson, Mary E. M. to Wm. E. Palmer 4-15-1840
Marable, Ann J. to Danel Hilman 4-14-1840 (4-16-1840)
Marable, Cara T. C. to Thomas Y. Dickson 1-9-1854
Marable, Martha to Jim Sanders 1-13-1866
Marable, Rena to Watson Barker 12-1-1866 (12-18-1866) [b]
Marcom, Martha Ann to William L. Shepherd 8-4-1859
Marcus, Mary to Henry Reynolds 1-12-1855
Maricie, Bridget to John William Tanner 1-5-1859 (1-6-1859)
Marion?, Tennessee L. to William M. Thacker 10-3-1857 (10-15-1857)
Markland, Mary Ann to Owen Molaney 10-3-1846
Marlow, Mansel P. to C. M. Ingram 4-26-1857
Marlow, Martha to William Lynch 9-28-1840 (10-1-1840)
Marr, Margrette to G. O. Young 7-9-1840
Marr, Mary Ann to D. L. Young 10-20-1847 (10-21-1847)
Marr, Susan P. to John S. McLean 6-29-1857 (6-30-1857)
Marrymire, Hannah to Joseph Cahal 5-6-1848 (5-8-1848)
Marsh, C. to Oliver Davis 8-23-1862 (9-4-1862)
Marsh, Elizabeth to Robert W. Wickham 1-?-1859 (2-3-1859)
Marshall, Martha J. to Saml. B. Woodson 3-14-1866 (3-15-1866)
Marshall, Sarah A. to Thos. H. Albright 8-18-1852
Marshall, Sarah to Johnson Wicks 10-11-1845
Martin, Adeline to George H. Swift 6-8-1859
Martin, Araminda D. to Wilton C. Barksdale 9-7-1852
Martin, E. F. to A. J. Lyle 11-2-1841 (11-5-1841)
Martin, E. F. to R. C. Powers 12-19-1850
Martin, Eliza Ann to Noah Ratliff 12-28-1850
Martin, Eliza to Charles Johnson 11-24-1865
Martin, Jane to Wilie Powell 10-8-1847 (10-14-1847)
Martin, Jennie to Dallis White 9-6-1866
Martin, L. J. to John W. Henderson 5-11-1854
Martin, Laura E. to E. jr. Ensly 10-10-1860
Martin, Lavenia to John Smith 7-6-1840
Martin, Lucinda to John C. Dowdy? 7-28-1849 (8-2-1849)
Martin, Lucy to Mires Yarbrough 10-17-1842 (10-20-1842)
Martin, M. E. to J.? M. Newberry 1-26-1851
Martin, M. E. to Thomas S. Hunt 3-25-1850 (3-28-1850)
Martin, M. M. to Joshua Elder 11-27-1849
Martin, Margaret G. to G. W. Harole? 6-24-1845
Martin, Margarett to Jas. H. Gossett 8-31-1861
Martin, Mariah to Sam Therston 7-2-1866 [b]
Martin, Martha to David Moore 5-26-1866 (6-4-1866) [b]
Martin, Martha to Jessee Edes 3-31-1842 (3-30?-1842)
Martin, Martha to W. R. Hurst 6-18-1846
Martin, Martha to William Witt 12-24-1853
Martin, Mary A. to S. H. Whitehead 5-13-1843
Martin, Matilda to Josh Edmondson 9-22-1866 (9-23-1866) [b]
Martin, Nancy to J. T. Thorn 12-17-1860
Martin, Narcissa to M. L. Thacker 1-18-1858 (1-21-1858)
Martin, Rebecca to Wiley Powel 1-19-1864
Martin, Susan J. to Joseph W. Wall 1-29-1866 (1-31-1866)
Martin, Susan to B. C. Powers 8-30-1841 (9-2-1841)
Mash, Elizabeth to Henry Fortson 12-10-1844
Mason, Mary Jane to R. S. H. Beam 8-21-1855 (8-22-1855)
Mason, Nancy to George Tandy 12-12-1865 (4-3-1866)
Massey, Louisa E. to William C. Harelson 11-10-1853
Massey, Mary E. to James Henry Maynard 8-13-1840
Massey, Rincy to Charles Carneal 4-30-1866 (5-3-1866) [b]

Masters, Mary E. to Henry Hollis 3-4-1856
Masure, Mary to John W. Odam 10-15-1853
Mathews, Malinda to Absalom Ezel 8-16-1851
Mathews, Martha A. to Jas. R. Harris 4-20-1865
Mathis, Allis to John Kellow 12-13-1865
Mathis, Charlotte to William Patterson 7-8-1848
Mathis, Elanor B. to William E. Zelle 3-5-1849
Mathis, Elizabeth to John L. Daniel 12-6-1847 (12-9-1847)
Mathis, Lavitha to Zachariah H. Morgan 7-28-1853
Mathis, Nora to Guss Moody 11-5-1866
Mathis, Rebeca Mariah to Josephus N. Blackford 3-1-1861 (3-6-1861)
Mathis, Susan R. to M. R. Parrish 5-13-1852
Mathus, Eliza J. to Sampson C. Harris 4-4-1849 (4-5-1849)
Matthews, S. E. to Jas. Wyatt 11-14-1864
Maxey, Nancy to Benjamin B. Bearden 8-24-1853 (8-25-1853)
May, Margaret J. to W. P. Sullivan 5-31-1853
Mayfield, Amanda J. to B. W. Tinsley 10-1-1862 (10-9-1862)
Mayfield, Catharine J. to F. L. Garland 2-9-1852
Mays, Frances to George Rowland 11-14-1842
Mays, Sarah to John W. Keel 3-17-1848 (3-19-1848)
Mayse, Elizabeth to George Jackson 3-18-1865 (may be black)
McAddams, Elizabeth A. to Leroy S. Harrell 11-2-1848
McAllester, Mary E. to Peter Winn 10-20-1853
McBride, Margarett Ann to Thomas W. Davis 5-14-1856
McBride, Margarette A. to James Raines 12-15-1838
McBride, Martha to H. Peacock 3-29-1849
McBride?, Mary Ann to Wm. M. Griffey 2-18-1848
McCain, Mary B. to Samuel J. Johnson 1-20-1859
McCallister, Martha A. to Walt S. Massey 9-2-1847
McCallister, S. A. to Jessee Hester 12-24-1862 (12-25-1862)
McCarter, Eliza J. to R. L. Tally 11-17-1866 (11-22-1866)
McCartis, Amand to Woodson Wheeler 11-5-1866 [b]
McCarty, Hellen to Dennis Cartland 7-21-1860
McCarty, Mary to James Hughes 1-12-1861
McCarty, Mary to M. McMurphy 2-23-1863
McCaughan, Mary Jane to William S. Humphries 2-12-1846
McCauley, Angeline to James H. Patrick 1-8-1840 (2-6-1840)
McCauley, Bittie George to R. D. Mosley 9-27-1865 (9-28-1865)
McCauley, Eliz. P. to Sterling Neblett 10-28-1843
McCauley, Eliza J. to E. R. Spurier 8-1-1866 (8-2-1866)
McCauley, Mary to Charles Buckhanan 12-6-1866 (5-9-1867)
McCauley, Sarah G. to Jones Gray 1-6-1849
McCauley, Susannah to James M. Drummonds 9-8-1841 (9-9-1841)
McCauliff, Mary to Jeremiah Savage 6-25-1859
McCawly, Martha A. to Thomas S. McCurdy 3-21-1846 (3-25-1846)
McClain, Margaret to Samuel Shepherd 7-4-1853e
McClanahan, Rhoda Ann to Hugh B. McClain 10-15-1848
McCleral, Jenett to Wm. Farquehar 1-2-1849
McClure, Eliza to Brice Stewart 10-29-1839
McClure, Lucinda B. to James H. Merriweather 3-9-1840 (3-10-1840)
McComac, Nepsiarm to Isaac Brazier 7-27-1860
McComes, Jane to John Cornell 12-8-1866 (1-3-1867) [b]
McComes, Manie to Bob Brown 12-8-1866 (12-24-1866) [b]
McCommack, M. A. to Geo. H. Johnson 10-23-1843 (10-31-1843)
McConnel, Elizabeth M. to R. S. P. Pool 10-10-1860
McConnick, Mary A. to Geo. H. Johnson 10-23-1843 (10-31-1843)
McCool, Anna Jane to G. Washington Smith 12-13-1848
McCool, Catharine to Jacob Dittner 9-20-1838
McCorkle, Malinda M. to William H. Lyle 2-7-1852 (2-15-1852)
McCormac, Telitha to Arthur Reyan 4-23-1863
McCormick, Martha to Alford Eatherly 7-29-1843 (8-17-1843)
McCoy, Angeline B. to Francis M. Williams 3-15-1864
McCrae, Martha to George W. Cooper 4-4-1859 (4-5-1859)
McCrane, Elvira R. to Peyton Luck 11-9-1847 (11-10-1847)
McCrary, Catharine to Samuel N. Leggett 6-1-1859
McCraw, Martha J. to William F. Greenwood 4-1-1849
McCurdy, Molly to Cary Abernathy 4-26-1865 [b]
McCutcheon, Mary A. to Hiram Walsh 2-27-1849
McCutchin, Sally V. to Samuel D. Delany 12-15-1838 (12-19-1838)
McDaniel, Ellen to William H. Gilbert 11-2-1857
McDaniel, Eunice to William Adams 1-18-1859
McDaniel, Gertrude H. to Charles M. Herter? 2-18-1854
McDaniel, Julia to Hugh Telford 4-13-1842
McDaniel, Mariah L. to Wm. D. Edwards 3-9-1840 (3-10-1840)
McDaniel, Martha to Vincent Gray 7-27-1843

McDonald, Mary F. to James Tate 1-19-1859
McDougle, Clarrissa to John Gold 3-24-1845 (4-15-1845)
McDougle, Rachael to Henry Blair 1-21-1853 (1-28-1853)
McElvain, Ruth A. to T. J. Mays 7-19-1855
McFadden, Jane P. to George A. Edwards 3-6-1841 (3-7-1841)
McFadden, Ruth A. to John A. Withers 3-31-1840
McFaddin, Hannah J. to James Morrisson 4-5-1838 (4-9-1838)
McFaddin, Nancy to Thomas Hunter 10-25-1855 (10-28-1855)
McFall, Liziebeth to Henry Eagily? 12-18-1866 [b]
McFall, M. J. E. to James H. Howell 3-12-1840
McFall, Sarah Ann to S. R. Marshall 1-24-1850
McFarland, Jane to Fedrick Williams 11-20-1845
McFarlin, Jane to Asbure Clifton 8-23-1843 (8-25-1843)
McFerson, Delila to Alfred Jones 2-16-1857
McGee, Louisiana to Thomas F. Edmondson 11-29-1854
McGee, Mary J. to John D. Martin 6-5-1842 (5?-5-1842)
McGee, Matild H. to James Adams 6-27-1852
McGehee, Fredonia to Willis Morgan 6-20-1843 (6-22-1843)
McGehee, Sally to Thomas Haysley? 8-1-1839
McGinty, Angelina B. to Geo. W. Leigh 11-5-1841
McGinty, Eliza to T. A. Thomas 10-7-1843 (10-8-1843)
McGinty, F. F. to E. R. N. Thomas 2-5-1848
McGowan, E. P. to John B. Allen 12-18-1866 (12-21-1866)
McGowan, Jane to James C. Dunn 5-30-1860 (6-4-1860)
McGraw, Mary Ann to William Tubbs 1-18-1843
McHenry?, Fanny Jane to M. P. Riggins 4-20-1854
McKaughn, Jane to John Powers 2-15-1839 (2-19-1839)
McKeage, Adelaid to Saml. W. Shryrock 1-30-1855
McKeage, Eliz. to Wm. M. Irvin 8-27-1840
McKeage, Rebecca to W. A. Whitaker 7-25-1842
McKean, Ann Eliza to Green B. Hill 1-5-1848 (1-6-1848)
McKenels, Jane to Isam Stewart 12-26-1866 [b]
McKinney, Martha to Burton Johnson 9-22-1845
McKinnon, Ann to James Stephens 2-26-1858 (2-28-1858)
McLane, Ann to Andrew Cowans 3-27-1850
McMordie, Mary E. to Wm. H. Davis 1-23-1849
McNeal, Laura to Jack Dye 9-15-1866 [b]
McNeal, Virginia to Sam Bolin 12-18-1866 (12-26-1866)
McNeil, Eliza to Solomon Crotzer 2-13-1855
McNeil, Harriet F. to Thomas F. Channen 4-22-1854 (4-25-1854)
McNeil, Rachael Winniford to Andrew Jackson Hamlet 2-13-1855 (2-14-1855)
McPherson, Ann to Richd. Petree 10-11-1865 (10-13-1865) [b]
McQuerry, Louisa E. to W. B. Zimring 1-15-1850 (1-17-1850)
McQuery, Lucy Jane to Josiah Carneal 8-13-1853 (8-16-1853)
McTernis, Eliza Jane to John Woolf 3-1-1849
Meacham, Martha to Saml. Shelton 10-10-1839
Meacham, Mary to John Galey 9-1-1850
Meacham, Mary to W. T. Furgerson 5-31-1851 (6-1-1851)
Meacham, Sarah A. to Edward C. Waters 7-3-1858 (7-4-1858)
Mear?, Mrs. N. to George Hickman 11-13-1866 (11-15-1866)
Medley, Aggey to Byack? Randel 12-26-1866 [b]
Medley, Eliza to Warner Watts 5-9-1866 (5-10-1866) [b]
Menefee, Elizabeth to Nolley W. Elkins 11-1-1857 (11-8-1857)
Mercer, Amanda to Edmond Jarvis 10-19-1849
Merrit, Mary to R. A. Allen 7-5-1851
Merriweather, Lucy to Major Baker 8-31-1865 [b?]
Merriweather, Margaret E. to John D. Morril 4-30-1845 (5-6-1845)
Merriweather, Mary Walker to Darwin Bell 12-28-1857
Merriweather, Nancy M. to John D. Furguson 3-1-1848 (3-2-1848)
Merryweather, Kitty to Manuel Wisdom 5-27-1865 (6-24-1865)
Metcalf, Elizabeth to Thomas S. Trigg 4-17-1845
Metheny, Sarah Ann to Alfred L. Perkins 11-11-1851
Meyers, Mary E. to R. L. Brillane? 3-21-1860 (3-23-1860)
Mickle, Mary Martha to William Hicks 1-19-1856 (1-20-1856)
Mickle, Mary T. to R. J. W. Thorn 12-12-1842 (12-15-1842)
Mickle, Sarah A. to George W. Clanton 10-24-1854
Midcastle, Nancy to Elijah Kagle 7-9-1844
Milam, Mary to James Edes 4-30-1840
Milam, Rebecca to Ajack Price 1-26-1853 (1-27-1853)
Miles, Eliza to Henry Smith 1-9-1845
Miles, Martha N. to E. P. Smith 1-3-1854
Miles, Mary Elizabeth to James Appleton 1-8-1861 (1-9-1861)
Miles, Sarah E. to Johnathan Fambrough 12-20-1853
Miles, Tabitha to John Brock 11-14-1848

Milford, Callie A. to Wm. H. Rockwell 7-29-1865 (7-30-1865)
Miller, Ada to Jas. Ferriman 12-5-1865 (12-6-1865)
Miller, Alice to B. W. jr. Macrae 10-2-1856
Miller, Frances E. to John W. Bear 12-16-1845
Miller, Maranda to Thomas Cocke 10-23-1857
Miller, Martha A. to John S. Hart 7-27-1843
Miller, Sallie to John F. Forsythe 5-16-1864
Miller, Virginia to Henry McNeil 5-11-1854
Millin, Easter to Joshua Jorden Jones 8-24-1857 (8-26-1857)
Mills, M. E. to T. L. Bishop 6-27-1852
Mills, Maney to Henry? J. Buckle 12-17-1845 (12-18-1845)
Mills, Mary A. to Wiley McCaulley 1-8-1867
Minton, Eliza Jane to Charles A. Webster 7-27-1858 (7-29-1858)
Mitchell, Louzana to Robert Jackson 10-16-1854 (11-23-1854)
Mitchell, Maggie T. to R. T. Hollins 1-19-1863
Mitchell, Susan to Eli Burns 4-11-1838 (4-12-1838)
Mitchell, Virginia to John T. Gregory 12-31-1856
Mixan, Sarah to David Brigham 7-15-1852
Mixen, Susan to William Mixen 7-22-1858
Mockabee, Rebecca to Thomas Mayberry 10-20-1848
Mockbee, Frances to Ambrose Martin 11-2-1842
Mockbee, Louisa to James Bridges 5-4-1861 (5-8-1861)
Mockbee, Mary D. to William H. Duke 11-30-1858
Mockibee, Nancy A. to J. L. Grimes 11-6-1848
Moe?, Susan E. to William Boyd 1-17-1848
Monford, Ann to Nelson Johnson 12-26-1866 (12-28?-1866) [b]
Monroe, Elizabeth W. to John Bryant 1-19-1852 (1-22-1852)
Monroe, Nancy to John Bryant 5-1-1847 (5-9-1847)
Monys?, America Ann to Hezekiah P. Hart 11-26-1845
Moody, Caroline M. to John Grigg 1-10-1852 (1-11-1852)
Moody, M. A. to Jessee Smith 8-19-1862 (8-21-1862)
Moody, Maria L. to John E. Nelson 12-24-1860 (12-25-1860)
Moor, Elizabeth to Nicholas Fields 7-?-1851
Moor, Sarah to Joseph Crafton 7-12-1852
Moore, Amanda W. to Charles M. Dancy 7-11-1855
Moore, Ann to Robt. Whitlock 7-17-1866 [b]
Moore, Arabella A. P. to Robert P. Lyle 8-27-1858
Moore, Caroline H. to Wm. Oneal 10-20-1841 (10-22-1841)
Moore, Catharine to W. B. Owen 1-21-1856
Moore, Henrietta to James Fletcher 3-6-1843
Moore, Jane to Pascal Johnson 11-13-1847
Moore, Jennie B. to J. J. Wilson 1-1-1866
Moore, L. J. to Geo. E. Huston 5-2-1842
Moore, Louise J. to Henry A.? Reeder 10-17-1838 (10-18-1838)
Moore, Martha to George T. Boller 9-1-1839
Moore, Mary Isabella to Benjamin F. Coulter 5-7-1856
Moore, Mary L. to Thomas Brashears 2-24-1858
Moore, Milly to Clay Cross 11-16-1865
Moore, Nannie C. to Peter J. Hiatt 7-14-1863
Moore, Patsy to James L. Lyle 7-30-1845
Moore, Siloia to Charles Anderson 7-28-1866 [b]
Moore, Sophy to Henry Clardy 5-21-1866 [b]
Moore, Susan A. to G. W. Bartee 8-4-1852
More, Susan P. to Thomas W. Corlew 10-3-1844
Morehead, Nancy Jane to Jessee W. Holeman 11-7-1857
Morehead, Sarah A. to Albert M. Taylor 7-19-1855
Morgan, C. T. to C. H. Kistner 5-2-1863
Morgan, Margarette to James Hogan 12-10-1838
Morgan, Mary J. to Thomas Lee 2-4-1866
Morgan, Mary M. to John W. May 3-17-1854
Morm, Caroline S. to Wm. S. Buckner 4-28-1849
Morris, Eliza Jane to Wm. B. Pritchard 3-7-1838 (3-8-1838)
Morris, Elizabeth to Hezekiah P. Hart 6-23-1842
Morris, Fannie M. to G. W. Macrae 9-11-1866 (9-12-1866)
Morris, Lucy Ann to William Cross? 9-1-1853
Morris, Maria E. to Joshua Collier 7-1-1856 (7-4-1856)
Morris, Martha to George Jones 4-11-1839
Morris, Mary E. to John D. Jenkins 5-10-1866
Morris, Mary L. to Thos. M. Barker 12-28-1866
Morris, Mary Susan to William Pritchard 11-3-1852
Morris, Mary to George W. Huskey 8-10-1858 (8-11-1858)
Morris, Nancy B. to A. Drewry 9-2-1845
Morris, Nancy J. to James jr. Reason 2-12-1842 (2-13-1842)
Morris, Narcissa Drue to Charles Logan Keats 5-19-1853 (5-22-1853)
Morris, Rebecca D. to William Haris 2-11-1847 (2-25-1847)

Morris, Sallie to Robert C. Harding 8-30-1859 (9-7-1859)
Morris, Virginia to W. B. Batson 9-20-1854 (9-21-1854)
Morrison, Ann E. to William James King 2-16-1854 (2-19-1854)
Morrison, Ellen to John Flinn? 11-11-1854 (11-16-1854)
Morrison, Jennie L. to Josiah H. Brown 10-13-1866 (10-18-1866)
Morrison, Lucinda Ann to Jeremiah Ryan 6-13-1866
Morrison, Luticia to William H. Barnett 5-12-1861
Morrison, Margaret E. to John G. Ryon 6-6-1861
Morrison, Mary M. to John Luter 2-5-1841 (2-7-1841)
Morrison, Mary W. to Thomas J. Sales 12-11-1855 (12-20-1855)
Morrison, Mrs. Sallie F. to Elijah T. Hagood 12-28-1865
Morrison, N. to James H. Brown 12-20-1866
Morrison, Nancy to Jno. R. Turner 5-6-1862
Morrison, Nannie to Jack Fowler 2-8-1866
Morrison, Susan Elizabeth to James J. Hamlett 2-1-1855
Morrison, Susan to W. H. Powell 2-4-1852
Morriss, Nancy E. to T. C. Jones 10-29-1863 (11-2-1863)
Morriss, Sylvestie C. to Lemuel K. Adkins 7-25-1839 (7-27-1839)
Morrisson, Charity to James G. Jones 12-4-1839 (12-5-1839)
Morrisson, Margarett M. to Jessee Reasons 10-26-1843
Morrisson, Mary to Alexander Parr 9-16-1842 (9-18-1842)
Morrow, Jane B. to Henry M. Brown 9-11-1844
Morrow, Louiza T. to Samuel J. Mathis 12-17-1858
Morrow, Margaret E. to Peter F. Belamy 10-1-1858 (10-7-1858)
Morrow, Sally J. to John Rosson 6-5-1848
Morrow, Sarah Frances to J. J. Bailey 4-17-1861 (4-18-1861)
Morrow, Susan to Robt. H. Edmonson 2-7-1862 (2-9-1862)
Morse, Phebe to Henry Gold 1-4-1866 [b]
Moseley, Eliz. B. to James W. Anderon 3-38-1844
Moseley, Sophronia S. to Richard B. Walker 2-10-1853 (2-15-1853)
Mosely, Nancy J. to G. W. Gosset 12-18-1851 (12-23-1851)
Mosely, Nancy to Adam Henitsman 12-9-1846 (12-11-1846)
Mosier, Elizabeth A. to James R. Farmer 9-18-1861
Mosier, Martha to John W. Morris 3-22-1856
Moss, Elizabeth A. to Wm. A. Farrell 1-4-1865 (1-5-1865)
Moss, L. G. to W. L. Paxton 3-20-1843
Moss, Lucy to John W. Rives 12-7-1841 (12-9-1841)
Moss, Martha J. to Jacob L. King 12-10-1857 (12-18-1857)
Moss, Sarah E. to Thomas B. D. Rees 11-21-1857 (11-25-1857)
Moss, Susan H. to Samuel D. Buckhannon 10-13-1846 (10-22-1846)
Mosure, Mary E. to John W. Odam 10-13-1853
Mosure, Mary M. P. to J. H. Claxton 6-15-1864 (6-27-1864)
Mowrer?, Mary to Henry Baggett 5-26-1851 (5-21?-1851)
Mulcaster, Mary to A. J. Davis 3-13-1848 (3-19-1848)
Muller, Bridget to James L. Clackston 1-23-1861 (1-24-1861)
Mumford, Letitia A. to Sanford D. Wheeler 1-19-1856 (1-20-1856)
Mumford, Sarah to T. Y. Farmer 1-23-1851
Munford, Clay to B. W. Johnson 12-5-1865 (12-6-1865)
Murfee, Sarah T. to James H. Shaw 12-23-1843 (12-27-1843)
Murphey, Mrs. Mary to Martin Crame? 6-13-1864 (6-18-1864)
Murphy, Catharine to Thos. Dargan 9-10-1860
Murphy, Lucena M. to Hatcok? Pride? 12-19-1840
Murphy, Mary to David Wynn 12-23-1865 (12-26-1865) [b]
Murray, Hannah P. to John Conroy 9-6-1864
Myatt, Catharine A. L. to Josiah P. Dailey 3-13-1843 (3-15-1843)
Myers, Lila to Hawket Powell 11-30-1865
Myers, Mary E. to Wilis J. Hagan 4-23-1856
Myers, Nannie to D. J. Dingman 5-3-1866
Myers, Phebe to Andrew Jackson 9-19-1844
Myres, Nancy J. to Joshua Crotzer 2-6-1851
Myrick, Manerva to B. W. Southward 8-7-1845 (8-3?-1845)
Myrick, Nineva to W. B. Southwood 9-7-1845
Nall, Mary S. to R. E. Humphrys 8-8-1848
Nanry, Nancy to John Batts 5-16-1846 (5-17-1846)
Nash, Lizzy to M. Figuer 2-11-1848
Naswerthy, Sarah to Nick Merryweather 1-19-1867 [b]
Neal, Bettie to Page Moore 11-24-1866 (11-29-1866) [b]
Neblett, Ann Eliza to R. W. Roberts 6-22-1859
Neblett, Belle Ann to Allen Neblett 11-11-1847
Neblett, C. V. to William Edmondson 12-23-1846 (12-24-1846)
Neblett, Charlotte S. to John H. James 3-9-1853 (3-11-1853)
Neblett, Eliza Ann to Benjamin Hatcher 9-15-1842
Neblett, Elizabeth Ann to Wm. M. Ussery 11-23-1847 (11-25?-1847)
Neblett, Ellen to Hart Grant 10-13-1866 (10-14-1866) [b]
Neblett, Jane C. to James H. Reasons 4-18-1853

Neblett, M. A. to S. A. Caldwell 4-27-1858 (4-28-1858)
Neblett, M. E. to Benj. F. Harris 1-17-1860 (1-18-1860)
Neblett, M. E. to C. G. Royster 11-26-1855 (11-28-1855)
Neblett, Margaret S. to Egbert N. Northington 11-20-1855
Neblett, Mary C. to R. A. Roberts 11-4-1841
Neblett, S. L. to C. A. Brodie 6-21-1842 (6-23-1842)
Neblett, Sally V. to James D. Harrisson 11-28-1839
Neblett, Sarah to Perry B. Williamson 11-19-1839 (11-20-1839)
Neblett, Susan to Henry M. Dudley 9-13-1843
Neblett, Virginia C. to Wm. L. Dillard 1-22-1848 (1-27-1848)
Nelson, Rebecca to Robert H. Clynard 7-14-1855 (7-16-1855)
Nesbett, Hellen J. to Jos. F. Rye 10-31-1864 (11-10-1864)
Nesbit, Elizabeth(Frances?) to John Henry Armistead 12-17-1859
    (12-18-1859)
Nesbitt, Louisa Jane to Thomas Shelton 4-11-1849 (4-13-1849)
Nesbitt, Mary to R. P. Powers 10-31-1860
Nesbitt, Susan to James Adkins 11-11-1850
Nester, Mrs. Ann to T. Kelly 5-7-1862 (5-8-1862)
Nevell, Mrs. Annet to Phillip Crotzer 5-27-1864
Newel, Eliza to William Dayly 4-24-1857 (4-25-1857)
Newell, M. E. to Dr. T. F. Williams 2-4-1867
Newell, Sallie A. to Lewis R. Willis 5-15-1865
Newman, Eliza J. to John Simmons 9-8-1842
Newman, Jane to John Howard 1-31-1842 (2-3-1842)
Newson, Louvany to Allen M. Harris 1-1-1859 (1-2-1859)
Niblett, Fredonia W. to John W. Waller 11-5-1861 (11-6-1861)
Niblett, Marietta to John McCreary Newell 1-25-1854 (1-26-1854)
Niblett, Susan to Joel Bayliss 11-20-1847
Nichol, Milly to Jim Meredy Haynes 12-28-1866 (12-30-1866) [b]
Nichols, Virginia to John Byrd 4-18-1854
Nicholson, Catharine to William C. Pinson 9-18-1839 (9-19-1839)
Nicholson, Elizabeth to Wm. Hairston 1-2-1847 (1-7-1847)
Nicholson, Martha to S. T. Houston 4-16-1849 (4-17-1849)
Nicholson, Mary to Abner Gupton 2-7-1846 (2-12-1846)
Nicholson, Mrs. Elizabeth to C. C. Provost 11-9-1865
Nicholson, Nancy to R. D. Nanney 11-21-1847 (11-21-1849?)
Nicholson, Susan to John Nicholson 9-17-1855
Nickle, Mary J. to Albert E. Blake 9-9-1855
Niel, Missourie to M. Harrison 3-16-1845
Nolen, E. J. to G. W. B. Marable 8-3-1866 (8-5-1866)
Nolen, Matilda to Adam Dickson 11-13-1844 (11-14-1844)
Nolen, Sophie J. to Ambrose Coleman 11-30-1866 (12-16-1866)
Norfleet, Ann to Thos. McCullick 1-23-1844
Norfleet, Arabella to Robert Williams 4-4-1854
Norfleet, Jane Ann to R. S. Ware 10-28-1853 (11-2-1853)
Norfleet, Leonora to James H. Williams 1-22-1859 (1-27-1859)
Norfleet, Manerva Ann to Wm. G. M. Campbell 4-20-1843
    (4-26-1843)
Norfleet, Minnie to L. D. Moody 10-28-1865 (11-2-1865)
Norflett, Katy to Saml. Harbin 5-5-1866 [b]
Norris, Fredonia A. to Hardy C. Pace 6-3-1857 (6-4-1857)
Northington, Sally Ann to Robt. D. Bellemy 10-28-1839 (10-30-1839)
Norwood, Susan to Presley Hinton 8-28-1844
O'Donald, Maria to John Mulkerus 7-20-1857 (7-22-1857)
O'Neal, Mary P. to Green P. Jackson 10-3-1866 (10-4-1866)
Oaglesby, Nancy E. to Samuel F. Tucker 10-31-1855
Odam, Mary Jane to William Dyles 4-9-1851
Odoniley, J. S. to Jacob Anderson 1-4-1842
Ogburn, Adaline to Bradley Martin 10-1-1850
Ogburn, Etha B. to Alex W. Manson 2-17-1866 (2-20-1866)
Ogburn, F. H. to John C. Acre 9-14-1859 (9-21-1859)
Ogburn, Isabella to Fred Martin 3-24-1866 (3-31-1866) [b]
Ogburn, Mary E. to James A. Marable 12-22-1845
Ogburn, Sally A. to Joseph Spence 4-14-1858 (4-15-1858)
Ogburn, Sarah Ann to Robt. B. Gordon 9-19-1840 (9-27-1840)
Ogg, Virginia E. to T. F. M. Ford 12-20-1858 (12-23-1858)
Oglesby, Frances S. to Jessee M. Randolph 10-20-1853
Oglesby, Judith L. to M. S. Hopson 9-6-1841
Oharram, Fredonia to John Caudle 12-28-1859 (12-29-1859)
Oldem, Fannie to John Yates 12-27-1866 (12-26?-1866) [b]
Oldham, A. F. to Thos. S. Woodson 12-20-1864 (12-22-1864)
Oldham, Elizabeth Susan to Andrew Jackson Smith 5-11-1853
Oldham, M. J. to Benj. K. Gold 9-17-1860 (9-18-1860)
Oldham, M. L. to W. D. Clardy 2-1-1847
Oldham, Malinda Adelina to Moses C. Ford 1-17-1859 (1-18-1859)

Oldham, Margaret to Kenneth McKinnon 11-30-1858
Oldham, Sarah D. to Willis Cook 5-21-1858
Olive, Mary Ann to Ephraim Lemaster 7-13-1841 (7-15-1841)
Oneal, Amanda M. to T. H. Traylor 1-9-1859 (1-10-1859)
Oneal, Caroline to John W. Wood 3-11-1858
Oneal, Mary to George W. Ford 12-10-1853 (12-11-1853)
Oneal, Sarah to Geo. Bradberry 1-17-1846 (1-18-1846)
Oneal, Vilet to Antony Garland 8-26-1865 [b?]
Oneel, Nancy Jane to Jarvis? B. Davis? 4-13-1859 (4-15-1859)
Orenduff, Amanda to James Hatcher 6-11-1865
Orgain, Elizabeth S. to A. J. Allen 5-24-1852
Orgain, Lucy Ann to George H. Swift 4-28-1853 (5-3-1853)
Orgain, M. C. to R. W. Wyatt 10-3-1862
Orgain, Minerva E. to Benjamine Edmondson 5-13-1851
Orgain, Sue T. to J. S. Neblett 1-31-1867
Organ, Mrs. Sallie E. to Garnet W. Richardson 6-28-1864
Organ, N. Virginia to Saml. F. Allen 11-14-1863
Orndorff, Mary E. to John C. Miller 1-23-1855
Orton, Mary E. to William Moore 8-4-1860 (8-20-1860)
Osbern, Grace to Edmond Metcalf 2-9-1867 (2-16-1867) [b]
Osborn, Martha to Green? Young 1-20-1866 [b]
Osbourn, Mary Jane to Bailey F. Allen 12-24-1845 (12-25-1845)
Osburn, Mollie E. to D. A. Bentley 12-17-1866
Ousley, Virginia to Henry Ladd 4-12-1855
Outlaw, Amanda M. to Vantreace? Step 6-20-1854
Outlaw, E. R. to Henry H. Myers 12-5-1862 (12-14-1862)
Outlaw, Elmanda M. to Vanburen Step 6-20-1854 (6-22-1854)
Outlaw, Frances to Napoleon B. Wynns 2-10-1858 (2-11-1858)
Outlaw, Harriet S. to W. T. Robertson 12-26-1865 (12-27-1865)
Outlaw, Martha A. to John C. Read 3-25-1851 (3-26-1851)
Outlaw, Martha S. to William H. Tomlinson 4-15-1856
Outlaw, Mary to Munroe Wilbourn 5-16-1844
Outlaw, Nancy to George W. Butler 11-18-1865
Outlaw, Rachel to John Lewis 6-20-1866 (6-21-1866) [b]
Outlaw, Sarah F. to L. B. Parchman 1-15-1852
Outlaw, Tennessee to John M. Jennings 12-5-1862 (12-9-1862)
Overton, Eliza to Alvin Overton 5-15-1866 (6-3-1866) [b]
Overton, Julia to Payton Cordle 5-14-1866 (5-20-1866) [b]
Overton, Susan to Jackson Smith 12-27-1866 (12-28-1866) [b]
Owens, Elizabeth to Jessee Weaver 4-5-1865 (4-6-1865)
Owens, Rutha A. to Adam? H. Fambrough? 9-9-1853 (9-11-1853)
Owens, Sarah Ann to William J. Jackson 7-13-1859 (8-12-1859)
Owsley, Mary Ann to Diskin Baker 4-29-1865
Pacaud, Addie S. A. to Thos. F. W. Prentiss 12-4-1865 (12-5-1865)
Pace, Martha to John W. Perdue 3-18-1848 (3-19-1848)
Pace, Nancy Jane to John J. Williamson 12-20-1858 (12-21-1858)
Pace?, Sally to Dudley Breedlove 1-2-1855
Page, Lidia to E. N. Gupton 6-15-1844 (6-20-1844)
Page, Mary Ann to Joseph C. Borden 5-18-1844 (5-19-1844)
Page, Mrs. Harriett V. to Lewis E. Evans 5-12-1865 (5-23-1865) Pain,
Cynthia J. to R. M. Roach 4-4-1865 (4-6-1865)
Paine, Ellmira E. to Alfred E. Robb 1-14-1857
Palmo, Lucy to Junius Carter 5-15-1865 [b]
Parchment, M. J. to Chas. Minor 8-5-1866
Parchment, Sarah F. to Thomas Collins 4-8-1855
Pardue, Elizabeth to Wm. Clifton 9-10-1849 (9-11-1849)
Parham, Emma L. to W. T. Ouseley 1-11-1854 (1-13-1854)
Parham, Henrietta C. to Thomas H. Flowers 6-29-1859 (6-22?-1859)
Parham, Mary R. to S. H. Boles 7-12-1848 (7-13-1848)
Parham, Virginia A. to Joseph G. Guynn 10-20-1856
Paris, Julia Ann to J. K. S. Little 5-11-1852
Parish, Henny to Asa Waters 12-29-1859 (SB 1858?)
Parish, Luella A. C. Chiles 1-17-1864
Parish, Mary to Joseph Hollis 1-16-1851
Parker, Annie to W. A. Donaldson 11-22-1865
Parker, Fanny to Westley Nichols 1-12-1846 (1-15-1846)
Parker, Inez to W. L. Wheatley 9-4-1865
Parker, Louisana to James B. Cross 2-5-1856 (4-5-1856)
Parker, Louisiana to James Cockran 7-25-1844
Parkerson, Mary to B. N. W. Brickell 6-21-1859 (6-23-1859)
Parks, Henrietta to Henry Gipson 6-1-1866 [b]
Parmer, Betsey to Tom Davis 8-2-1866 [b]
Parrish, Mary to Joseph Hollis 1-14-1851
Parrish, Mrs. L. A. to Dr. W. J. Castner 12-26-1865
Parrish, Mrs. Matilda H. to B. F. Coleman 6-13-1865 (6-15-1865)

Parson, Ellen to Granderson Grimes 9-19-1849 (9-18?-1849)
Pascal, Elizabeth to David Weakley 4-28-1838
Pass, Frances to Robert Clark 9-29-1863
Paterson, M. J. to J. E. Rowland 9-23-1865 (9-26-1865)
Patrick, Emma to N. E. Bagwell 10-18-1866
Patten, Nancy to John A. Manion 3-23-1854
Patterson, Eliza Ann to Wesley Sullivant 2-19-1840
Patterson, Elizabeth E. W. to Anthony Dinnen? 3-27-1838
Patterson, Elizabeth to Anthony Dinning 9-20-1848 (10-1-1848)
Patterson, Margaret to Greenberry West 11-9-1852
Patterson, Matilda to George Hamins? 6-8-1854
Patterson, Paralee to Green B. Trotter 11-12-1847 (11-14-1847)
Patterson, Susan to William Haywood 4-14-1838
Patterson, Tennessee A. to Berton Harnon 8-2-1865
Patton, Margaret F. to George L. Whitlock 10-23-1855
Payne, Emma to Frank Howard 9-29-1866 [b]
Payne, Jeraldine to Nicholas Thomas Hamilton 7-21-1856 (7-22-1856)
Payne, Malissa J. to William D. Tomlinson 2-18-1858 (2-21-1858)
Payne, Nancy J. to Raleigh Myatt 7-28-1853
Payne, Shelton to George J. Dyer 2-21-1850
Peacher, Frances to Joseph H. Crowder 7-2-1866 (7-3-1866)
Peacher, Jane F. to John Ballard 3-20-1845
Peacher, Lizzie to Robt. H. Wilson 9-8-1860 (9-11-1860)
Peacher, Sarah Ann to George S. Harrison 6-11-1860
Peaches, Ann Rebecca to William H. Crowder 1-17-1854
Peaches, Cornelia R. to B. O. Keesee 7-27-1852
Pearce, Mary Ann to W. H. Bailey 11-15-1855
Pearson, Mary J. to Mark Smith 10-20-1847
Pearson, Tabitha to Reuben Riggins 8-17-1853
Peck, Tennessee to John Ohara 10-30-1862
Pegram, Elizabeth to Marks M. Landram 8-19-1851
Pendleton, Lucinda to John A. Mansfield 8-21-1845 (8-21-1844?)
Pendleton, Nancy R. to Benjamin F. Acock 9-3-1850
Penney, Rebecca J. to Robert Shanklin 4-1-1839 (4-4-1839)
Pennington, Fany to Washington Nothington 6-11-1866 [b]
Pennington, Irene J. to Wm. G. Bond 11-24-1866 (11-25-1866)
Perdue, Judy to Wm. H. Pace 1-29-1842 (1-30-1842)
Perdue, Paralee to M. A. Musgorve 4-10-1855
Perkins, Lucinda E. to Albert Hopson 4-17-1840
Perry, Mary Angeline to Daniel Powel 10-6-1840
Person, Elizabeth to William H. Whitworth 3-18-1850 (3-22-1850)
Peterson, Elizabeth to Henry Leigh 2-24-1841
Petree, Malindy to Cyrus Groom 1-?-1867 [b]
Petters, Margaret to Quince Kelly 11-8-1866 [b]
Pettus, Ellen to Zebedee F. Derrick? 7-20-1859
Pettus, F. to Elzy Trice 4-7-1862 (4-8-1862)
Pettus, Nannie to Benjamin Higgins 10-19-1866 [b]
Pettus, Sarah E. to Richard Grinstall? 5-8-1839 (5-9-1839)
Petty, Catha to Ephram Shaw 8-30-1838
Petty, Catharine to William Dyson 3-11-1847
Petty, Melissa to William L. Miller 4-29-1853 (4-30-1853)
Philip, Mary A. to R. P. Bowling 4-10-1850
Phillips, Almeda to James L. Phipps 5-15-1860 (5-20-1860)
Phillips, Eliza to Henry H. Nelson 3-14-1864
Phillips, Lucinda L. to John C. Micle 3-10-1857
Phillips, Martha to William Free 2-11-1839 (2-14-1839)
Phillips, Mary M. to Robert A. H. Burden 12-15-1857
Phillips, Parthenia to William S. McCulley 3-20-1866 (3-21-1866)
Phipps, Mary Ann to J. T. Burk 11-11-1862 (11-12-1862)
Pickering, America J. to Arsmtead C. Williams 2-23-1864
Pickering, Ann Elizabeth to William R. Rosson 9-15-1857 (9-30-1857)
Pickering, Elizabeth An to Willis B. Rosson 10-23-1866 (10-24-1866)
Pickering, Judy C. to Geo. Elliott 7-9-1841
Pickering, Mary F. to Wm. G. Elliott 10-5-1865 (10-6-1865)
Pickering, Mary J. to Thomas McCulloch 3-12-1838
Pickering, Nancy to Thomas Cage 4-1-1844 (4-2-1844)
Pierce, Edeann T. to Thomas H. Jackson 1-15-1861
Pierce, Elizabeth to Thomas Clark 11-30-1857 (12-1-1857)
Pierce, Jennie M. to Saml. H. Tarr 12-2-1863
Pierson, Delana to William D. Wyar? 7-15-1858
Pinson, Elmira K. to Wm. J. Maddox 5-29-1847
Pinson, Harriett to William Frazier 1-14-1840 (1-17-1840)
Pinson, Martha to John Thomas Petty 2-25-1853 (3-9-1853)
Pitman, Elizabeth W. to Oswell Brockman 10-7-1844
Platt, Isabella to Denis T. Driscoll 8-12-1861 (8-13-1861)

Plummer, Fannie S. to Frank Phillips 8-10-1865
Poe, Mary Ann to James B. Lee 4-7-1860
Poindexter, Martha to Lewis Carney 10-6-1866 [b]
Pollard, C. A. to D. W. Ransdale 9-15-1865 (9-17-1865)
Pollard, Elizabeth to Thomas Walthal 12-22-1840 (12-24-1840)
Pollard, Margaret F. to John L. Carroll 7-31-1852 (8-1-1852)
Pollard, Mary M. to George P. Boston 9-16-1844 (9-18-1844)
Pollard, Mary O. to A. M. Seay 8-24-1864 (8-28-1864)
Pollard, Mrs. Mattie to Charles M. Ransdell 5-2-1864 (5-3-1864)
Pollard, Omzella to William Wils 12-24-1866 (12-26-1866) [b]
Pollard, Susan A. to John B. Apperson 3-12-1846
Pollock, Jemima to John N. Tinsley 7-31-1845
Pool, Martha Ann P. to Robert Marquis 4-25-1848
Pool, Martha to Thomas Batts 1-7-1855
Pool, Mary Ann to James L. Bright 7-20-1844 (7-31-1844)
Pool, N. E. to Peter Rinehart 3-9-1864
Pool, Nancy to Geo. W. Teasley 1-5-1851
Pooll, Martha P. to William Wilson 6-29-1838
Poore, Aliney E. to Moses Crozer 4-27-1843 (5-4-1843)
Poore, Martha E. to Jas. T. Turner 2-24-1864
Porter, Mary Ann to Joel Harney 5-6-1854 (6-1-1854)
Porter, Mary E. to Wm. H. Wells 5-14-1843
Poston, Adaline W. to John F. Curts 11-17-1842
Poston, Eliza N. to Z. M. Taylor 6-19-1844 (6-20-1844)
Poston, Ellen E. to John G. Thompson 5-1-1861
Potter, Luana to William Davidson 2-18-1841
Powel, Evelina to Howel Vick 9-28-1864
Powel, Nancy M. to Ennis B. Lyle 2-4-1861 (2-10-1861)
Powell, Caroline to Ransom Powell 4-29-1840 (5-7-1840)
Powell, Caroline to Wesley Baggett 4-3-1839
Powell, Emeline to Elisha Row 5-30-1840 (6-4-1840)
Powell, Fannie to Geo. Smith 11-4-1864 (11-11-1864)
Powell, Hannah to Dick Nothington 9-7-1866 [b]
Powell, Lucy Ann to John H. Colesham 1-4-1855
Powell, Malinda to Henry Baggett 2-29-1844
Powell, Manerva to Elisha J. Charnell 1-22-1849 (1-23-1849)
Powell, Martha to Robert Sikes 4-24-1846 (4-26-1846)
Powell, Mary to Alliner McCarnes 10-30-1845 (11-4-1845)
Powell, Mary to Harvell Baggett 1-29-1844
Powell, Nancy to Richd. Vaughan 1-31-1849 (2-1-1849)
Powell, Sally Ann to George Jamison 12-7-1855
Powell, Sarah J. to William Smith 5-14-1864 (5-15-1864)
Powell, Susanna to Ambers W. Norris 2-28-1860
Powell?, Mary to Willis Walker 7-9-1843
Power, Martha A. to Abner Gupton 9-14-1841 (10-5-1841)
Power, Mary A. J. to James E. Payne 1-31-1840
Powers, C. F. to J. M. Garland 12-15-1845 (12-17-1845)
Powers, Catharine to Cornelius R. Rudolph 1-2-1854 (1-5-1854)
Powers, Cillanara to Joseph Wheless 7-12-1842
Powers, Diantia Sophronia to Wilton Newman 10-30-1855
Powers, Dorothy to E. B. Jones 5-23-1842
Powers, Eliza Ann to John M. Britt 7-20-1849 (7-22-1849)
Powers, Elizabeth to Elijah Martin 12-16-1840
Powers, Elizabeth to James Bagget 3-10-1852 (3-14-1852)
Powers, Elizabeth to Pleasant Rineheart 12-18-1849 (12-20-1849)
Powers, Elizabeth to Thomas Grimes 3-11-1840
Powers, Ellin E. to Thos. E. Johnson 7-23-1864 (7-24-1864)
Powers, Emeline to Thomas Kyes? 7-8-1858 (7-9-1858)
Powers, Frances to Luke Senter 8-28-1845
Powers, G. A. to J. M. Harvey 4-27-1860 (4-20?-1860)
Powers, Mahala to Timothy Lyddy 7-3-1861 (7-6-1861)
Powers, Margaret to Aaron Crotzer 10-21-1843 (10-22-1843)
Powers, Martha Elizabeth to Isham Breeden 12-10-1852 (12-14-1852)
Powers, Martha J. to Joseph Breeden 7-9-1864 (7-13-1864)
Powers, Martha to Aaron Speer 5-12-1864
Powers, Martha to James G. Dowdy 4-10-1848 (4-12-1848)
Powers, Mary Ann to Olliver McCarver 8-24-1857 (8-26-1857)
Powers, Mary to A. J. Hamrick 9-10-1860 (5?-12-1860)
Powers, Matilda to Soloman Logan 8-27-1854
Powers, Nancy J. to James P. Morrison 12-30-1856
Powers, Parnelia to John McEwin 4-13-1859 (4-15-1859)
Powers, Polly to J. B. Southwood 2-14-1856
Powers, Sally Ann to George Jameson 12-7-1854
Powers, Sarah J. to William D. Calisham 6-16-1856 (6-17-1856)
Powers, Sophronia to Richard Montgomery Nesbett 1-18-1855

Powers, Susan to Joseph Davison 1-20-1860 (2-1-1860)
Pratt, Mary F.? to Joseph M. Boyd 8-14-1851
Presnell?, Eliza Ann to James A. White 10-12-1847 (10-13-1847)
Prestley, Mary Ann to Wm. Moore 11-24-1865 (not executed)
Prewitt, Mar. Elizabeth to John Darnell 8-23-1866 (8-24-1866)
Price, Charlotte to Morgan J. Morgan 6-8-1842
Price, Elizabeth to William Tims 9-18-1863
Price, Mary Ann to George W. Bumpass 1-12-1854
Price, Miriam H. to Liland B. Henderson 9-1-1852
Price, Nancy(Mary?) to Allen Corneal 6-25-1857
Price, P. N. to A. W. Cain 12-8-1854
Pride, Elizabeth to Harrison Wimberly 6-9-1866 [b]
Pride, Mary E. to Abner T. Watson 11-6-1865 (11-15-1865)
Priestley, Catharine to James B. Peterson 11-22-1852
Primett, Henrietta J. to John C. White 3-9-1846
Primm, Sarah M. to James W. Griffin 6-19-1860 (6-21-1860)
Prince, Caroline M. to W. F. Clark 10-22-1862 (10-23-1862)
Prince, Mariah M to John C. Calhound 11-16-1859
Pritchard, Caroline to Thomas Mills 9-15-1842 (9-16-1842)
Pritchard, Eliza to William Corlew 2-14-1842 (2-16-1842)
Pritchard, Evilina to David Laughran 12-20-1839 (12-25-1839)
Pritchett, Mary E. to Robert C. Carr 2-15-1855
Proctor, Jane to Lewis Ellis 12-3-1839 (12-4-1839)
Proctor, Nancy to John C. Rook 5-28-1841 (6-4-1841)
Purkerson, Emily L. to Jas. H. Dyer 1-23-1861 (1-24-1861)
Quarles, Eliz. A. to James P. Sherrod 10-12-1843
Quarles, Lucy M. to Z. Britton 6-9-1866 (6-17-1866) [b]
Quarles, Matilda to David Quarles 8-2-1847 (8-5-1847)
Quick, A. E. to Homer J. Wilder 4-22-1861 (4-23-1861)
Quin, Lizzie to Otto Richter 1-19-1865
Quin, Mrs. Mary to Mathew Ryan 3-15-1864 (3-16-1864) [*]
Quisenbury, M. F. to T. T. Woosly 8-10-1854
Radford, Susan to Richard P. Madison 1-19-1854
Ragon, Mary to Chas. McDonald 9-15-1862 (9-18-1862)
Ragsdale, Ann to William Bradberry 11-19-1839
Ragsdale, Mary A. to Sidney Wyatt 2-18-1850
Rail, Sarah Ann to Jacob Knight 9-9-1847
Raines, Ann to Thomas J. Southward 1-12-1839 (1-13-1839)
Rainey, Martha E. to Collin D. Roberts 10-12-1863 (10-13-1863)
Rainwater, Martha A. to Quintus Sugg 2-24-1860
Rainwaters, Elizabeth to Samuel Eades 12-30-1847
Rainwaters, Harriet to Jas. Baggett 12-20-1862 (12-25-1862)
Ramey, Delila J. to I. N. Robertson 9-21-1865 (9-23-1865)
Ramey, Ester to John Moody 9-27-1865 (9-29-1865)
Ramey, Margaret E. to Marmaduke D. Oneal 5-26-1858
Ramey, Mary Ann to Geo. Smith 2-3-1863 (2-11-1863)
Ramey, Mary E. to Thomas Y. Dixon 11-17-1857 (11-18-1857)
Ramey, Mary to Elijah Rudolph 5-14-1838
Ramey, Nancy C. to J. T. Morgan 12-12-1865
Ramsey, Elizabeth to Green Oakley 10-11-1845
Randal, Susan E. to Thomas J. Tenzric? 1-15-1845
Randle, Elizabeth A. to O. G. Pitt 1-13-1846
Randle, Lucie A. to Isaac S. Atkins 11-18-1863
Ransdale, Elizabeth to Stephen Cocke 11-30-1853 (12-7-1853)
Ransdale, Mary Elizabeth to M. A. Myres 11-3-1855
Rasey, Mary A. to Daniel D. Allen 1-18-1850
Rasor, Authusia A. to John C. Stapp 6-28-1846 (6-28-1846)
Ratcliff, Margaret to Charles P. Bacon 12-17-1844
Ratliff, Eliza to John Falkner 11-16-1866 [b]
Read, Indiana J. to Johnathan Eatherly 3-19-1844
Reasons, Amanda M. to Thomas E. Davis 4-15-1847 (5-6-1847)
Reasons, Martha M. to Patrick H. Williams 1-19-1843 (1-20-1843)
Reasons, Mary Jane to Joseph Linebaugh 2-22-1848 (2-28-1848)
Redd?, Eliza to Joseph W. Council 11-12-1838 (11-16-1838)
Reddan, Mary to Micheal Ohara 11-11-1862 (11-15-1862)
Redford, Victoria Ann to David R. Tinsley 1-9-1858 (1-12-1858)
Reeser, Judith P. to George S. Wimberly 9-18-1847
Reeves, Rebecca A. to Samuel R. White 11-9-1854
Reeves, Sarah F. to Gabriel J. Davis 2-13-1860 (2-14-1860)
Regions, Adaline to Clement McCorkle 2-25-1846 (2-29-1846)
Renner, Ellen to Wm. Scarborough 8-12-1865 (8-13-1865)
Rensils(Walthal?), Mary to Wm. H. Haslett 1-15-1867 (1-19-1867) [b]
Restner, Eliza J. to James S. Hopson 7-21-1852
Reynolds, Charlotte to David M. Dorris 9-28-1865
Reynolds, Elizabeth to John D. Dolan 6-8-1852

Reynolds, Ellen to David F. Garrell 4-4-1853
Reynolds, Harriett E. to Isaac W. Watson 9-24-1863 (10-8-1863)
Reynolds, Margaret to James Wortham 3-30-1866 (4-1-1866)
Reynolds, Mary J. to Wm. P. Adkins 12-17-1851 (12-25-1851)
Reynolds, Mary to Robert Thompson 2-15-1853
Reynolds, Mary to Stephen Brandon 8-21-1855
Reynolds, Nancy N. to John G. Thomason 1-14-1861 (2-20-1861)
Reynolds, Syrena to Bellefield Lawrence 5-25-1858 (5-27-1858)
Reynolds, Victoria to E. W. Thomason 11-6-1865 (11-8-1865)
Rhinehart, Delilah to Wm. A. Robertson 3-31-1846 (4-8-1846)
Rice, Martha A. to Upton Edmondson 9-14-1853 (9-17-1853)
Rice, Susan E. to James E. Neblett 11-25-1856 (11-24?-1856)
Rich, Isabell to John F. Woodburn 5-14-1865
Richards, Mary F. to James H. Longmire 8-11-1846
Richardson, Eliza G. to W. S. Bryant 8-4-1845 (8-6-1845)
Richardson, Eliza to William H. Neblett 12-1-1845 (12-4-1845)
Richardson, Elizabeth to John W. Turner 3-1-1841 (3-2-1841)
Richardson, Julia A. to Lewis Laws? 5-28-1856 (6-29-1856)
Richardson, Mary E. to Henry O. Wyatt 11-22-1844 (11-24-1844)
Richardson, Mary Eveline to John W. Turner 8-10-1859
Richardson, Mrs. Ellin to John O'Neal 10-12-1861
Ridley, Mary Caroline to John E. Thomas 7-24-1852
Riggens, Mary to B. F. Morrisson 1-14-1844
Riggins, Louisa to Wm. Sanders 9-29-1866 (9-30-1866) [b]
Riggins, Lucintha to John Reuben Chisenhall 10-20-1858 (10-21-1858)
Riggins, Minerva to John Goughf 3-28-1858? (3-28-1859)
Riggins, Rachael to William L. Riggins 3-7-1859 (3-9-1859)
Riggins, Sarah A. to Joseph A. Calesham 1-12-1854
Right, Mary J. to Donal J. Allen 3-12-1849 (3-13-1849)
Riley, Mahala to Joseph B. Jackson 8-14-1856
Rinehart, Harriett to Horace McEntire 4-24-1865 (4-25-1865)
Rinehart, Lovicy to George Jones 4-5-1848
Rinehart, Nancy to S. M. Ligon 8-23-1858 (8-24-1858)
Rinehart, Sarah Ann to Joshua Crow 9-8-1859
Rinehart, Tabitha to James Kistner 10-29-1844 (10-31-1844)
Rineheart, Mary to Gideon Lee 12-23-1843 (12-28-1843)
Rineheart, Polly to William Kestner? 4-6-1839
Ring, Sarah E. to Samuel A. Rice 1-22-1855
Riter, Elizabeth to Wm. C. Johnson 3-31-1840
Riter, Margaret to William Howlett 1-19-1859
Ritter, Susan to William Harris 10-27-1866 [b]
Rives, Bettie to Emmett Moore 2-6-1867 (2-9-1867) [b]
Rives, Catharine V. to George D. Griffey 11-12-1861 (11-21-1861)
Rives, Elizabeth J. to Geo. W. Trimer 2-1-1844
Rives, Elizabeth to G. E. Brown 4-12-1849
Rives, Leanna to Westley Terry 12-29-1866 (1-1-1867) [b]
Rives, Mahaly to St. Clair Leavell 5-7-1866 [b]
Rives, Patty to Preston Leavell 12-29-1866 [b]
Rives, Susan M. to Thos. Adams 4-29-1850
Roark, Margaret Jane to Thornbury A. Bonds 10-6-1841 (10-7-1841)
Robb, Eliza J. to John L. Paine 12-14-1842 (12-22-1842)
Robb, Martha A. to M. C. Payne 11-7-1849 (11-8-1849)
Roberson, Mary C. to John S. Christian 10-17-1851
Roberts, Adaline to Stafford Richardson 9-9-1865 (9-15-1865)
Roberts, Alvyra to Wm. H. Kidd 5-7-1843 (5-10-1843)
Roberts, Beedie H. to John Edmondson 12-1-1846 (12-2-1846)
Roberts, Frances E. to James A. Grant 6-26-1850 (6-27-1850)
Roberts, Lucy Ann to Robert Edmondson 10-19-1842
Roberts, Martha to Harburt Travis 5-22-1851
Roberts, Martha to Martin Neblett 8-26-1865 [b?]
Robertson, Ann Eliza to William T. Malory 12-20-1844 (12-24-1844)
Robertson, Henrietta M. to George S. Barnett 9-13-1858 (9-16-1858)
Robertson, Paralee to Charles Perdue 12-24-1845 (1-2-1846)
Robertson, Sarah E. to John P. Moss 4-7-1853 (4-15-1853)
Robinson, Amanda Harriet to Hiram Lewis 5-11-1847
Robinson, Genety Ann to James M. Roberson 1-28-1854 (1-29-1854)
Robinson, Isabella J. to A. M. Gilliam 5-29-1847 (5-31-1847)
Robinson, Susanna H. to W. O. McReynolds 5-29-1860
Rocke, Catharine F. to A. H. Cromwell 2-8-1842 (2-9-1842)
Roger, Mahulda to Jno. Higgins 12-30-1843
Rogers, Ann to Ephraim Edmondson 12-23-1865
Rogers, E. C. to Jas. L. Riggs 11-30-1843
Rogers, Elizabeth M. to Charles M. Briggs 1-19-1848
Rogers, Fannie to William Bell 11-22-1866 [b]
Rogers, Harriett to James B. Dilling 6-11-1841 (6-13-1841)

Rogers, Margaret to Thomas J. Powers 5-11-1856
Rogers, Mary to Thornton Gorham 9-14-1865 (10-15-1865) [b?]
Rogers, Nancy E. to Josiah Jarman 7-29-1839 (7-31-1839)
Rogers, Nancy J. to B. R. Ramey 1-10-1860 (1-11-1860)
Rogers, Nannie H. to Jno. M. Pirtle 3-6-1855
Rogers, Sidney Ann to Reelinghisen Rich 5-14-1865
Roggers, Ann to John Brown 12-26-1866 [b]
Roggers, Caroline to E. W. Johnson 1-11-1867 (1-13-1867) [b]
Rollins, Henrietta to Sidney Hannah 5-16-1866 [b]
Rollins, Lizzie to Abraham Herndon 12-15-1866 [b]
Rollins, Martha to Ned Wilson 6-15-1866 [b]
Rollins, Mary Ann to Robert Robertson 9-9-1863
Rollow, Ann L. to W. D. Adams 4-2-1852 (4-4-1852)
Rollow, Mary Ann to David S. Dickinson 12-19-1851
Rose, Artimisia to Mathew Leggit 1-24-1859 (1-30-1859)
Rose, Cordelia A. to Robert Davis 4-15-1865 (4-16-1865)
Rose, Eliza to Lewis Morrison 4-6-1865
Rose, Jane to Archibald N. Hagy 11-22-1860
Rose, Jane to Jas. Stamper 12-29-1863
Rose, Martha J. to Aron W. Bose 1-2-1867 (1-8-1867)
Rose, Mary to Frank Winsett 5-22-1863
Rose, Sarah to Michael Hunt 7-29-1843
Ross, Catharine to Owen W. Herring 1-20-1840
Ross, M. A. to N. R. Dudly 12-12-1849 (12-13-1849)]
Ross, Mary L. A. E. to John R. Acre 12-22-1853
Ross, Mary to G. McCurdy 2-16-1847
Ross, Virginia to L. T. Blankenship 11-9-1852
Rouland, S. A. M. to R. B. Hues 10-18-1851
Row, Mary to W.K. James 12-8-1851
Royster, Elvira J. to George H. Randle 6-12-1854 (6-15-1854)
Royster, Josephine B. to A. L. Sims 10-4-1858 (12-6-1858)
Rudder(Rudolph?), Mary A. C. to A. R. Smith 4-21-1853
Rudolph, Allice to W. A. Jackson 3-7-1865 (3-16-1865)
Rudolph, Eliza S. to W. H. Winn 9-29-1856 (10-14-1856)
Rudolph, Elizabeth Ann to T. J. Watson 1-15-1845 (1-16-1845)
Rudolph, Fannie S. to Chas. Y. Rudolph 10-4-1858 (10-8-1858)
Rudolph, Henrietta A. to Joseph L. Herring 12-18-1854 (12-21-1855?)
Rudolph, Jane to A. Hankins 3-14-1862
Rudolph, Margaret J. to William H. Crouch 8-18-1846
Rudolph, Mary J. to Allen Hunter 11-8-1848
Rudolph, Paralee E. to Alexander Smith 11-10-1857
Rudolph, Sarah to Zumroll Grymes 9-14-1843
Rudolpha, Orlina to John T. Kirk 12-30-1854 (12-31-1854)
Russel, Hannah C. to Ira E. Easley 10-31-1839
Russell, Ann to Saml. Oliphant 11-8-1865
Russell, Ellen S. to John H. Schrodt 6-21-1865 (6-22-1865)
Russell, Mary to James Emmery 5-17-1847
Russell, Nancy L. to J. R. Gamble 1-10-1861
Rutherford, Elizabeth to W. C. Cheatham 2-26-1858
Rutherford, Harriett to Jordan Griffey 5-19-1866 [b]
Rutherford, Lucy J. to Wm. Anderson 2-27-1844
Rutherford, Saprina to Ephraim Pool 4-10-1854
Rye, Arabella to William J. Rogers 9-8-1855 (9-9-1855)
Rye, E. A. to J. R. Blake 12-16-1862
Rye, Lavina T. to W. D. Owens 3-13-1866 (3-20-1866)
Rye, Martha J. to Jas. L. Nesbitt 12-20-1864 (1-11-1865)
Rye, Pamela to Francis Broom 1-29-1839 (1-30-1839)
Rye, Sarah Ann to Wilie Davison 5-30-1846
Ryen, Mary E. to Joseph W. Stenchfield 12-23-1865
Sadler, Martha Ann to Thomas H. Guynn 9-5-1859 (9-8-1859)
Sale, Eliza P. to Andrew J. Lyle 10-31-1856 (11-1-1856)
Sale, Mary M. to P. Bowling 10-29-1866
Sallee, E. M. to W. R. Thomas 12-11-1849
Sallee, Sarah E. to Robert C. Trainnum? 3-18-1839
Sallee, Virginia A. to Even W. Shelby 4-12-1841
Sally, Susan Ann to Henry W. Keats 2-2-1858 (2-4-1858)
Sally, Susan to John King 1-3-1852 (1-4-1852)
Sam?, B. to John C. Prescott 7-8-1863
Samford, Margarett E. to Walter L. Bradley 1-7-1852
Sampson, Elizabeth to Lewis Hubbard 4-25-1841 (4-26-1841)
Sampson, Matilda to Henry Harris 1-4-1856
Sampson, Matilda to Henry Harris 9-29-1852
Sampson, Theresa to John Donley 10-23-1862 (10-24-1862)
Samuels, Susan F. to H. B. Whitfield 1-22-1852 (1-29-1852)
Sanderfer, Martha Ann to John L. Cheshire 7-8-1853

Sanderlin, Susan M. E. to Talin? R. Weakley 11-16-1853 (11-22-1853)
Sanders, Frances to Robt. W. Warren 8-8-1843
Sanders, Mary A. to Isaac Bellemy 1-6-1866 (1-15-1866) [b]
Sanderson, Mary Ann to Wilkins Suiter 11-18-1854 (11-19-1854)
Sanderson, Rusia Catharine to Isaac James Rose 4-11-1856
Satterfield, Mary to Thomas Ray 11-16-1863
Saunders, Agnes J. to Sterling Brewer 10-3-1839
Saunders, Elizabeth P. to Jefferon T. Sherell 8-26-1846
Sawyer, Alice to Maynham H. Alexander 12-19-1859 (12-20-1859)
Sawyer, Henrietta to William Mallory 2-14-1845
Sawyer, Mary to William E. Alexander 12-29-1857 (1-1-1858)
Scale, Tamilin to James Davidson 12-24-1845
Scale?, Sarah to John Bisby 2-27-1847
Scholds, Mahala to John C. Herrington 6-22-1854 (6-28-1854)
Scott, Cynthia to Robert S. Riley 9-24-1852
Scott, E. L. to John Frederick Mehlhop 1-29-1862
Scott, Elizabeth to Richard Baker 6-17-1854 (6-23-1854)
Scott, Fannie to Ben C. Epperson 10-4-1866 (10-5-1866)
Scott, Martha L. to Francis M. Drake 7-20-1857 (7-21-1857)
Scott, Susan A. to Robt. D. Whitfield 12-28-1841
Scott, Susan to James Gitt 11-25-1840
Scudder, Claussa to Jos. Cuthbertson 1-6-1842
Scudder, Jerusa C. to Joseph B. Springs 3-20-1838 (3-15?-1838)
Scudder, Martha E. to Wm. R. Coyle 3-27-1848 (3-30-1848)
Searcey, Harriett to Thomas Bodine 3-34-1843
Sears, Eliza to John C. Meek 5-1-1854
Seay, Cynthia to James McGinnis 2-21-1860 (2-23-1860)
Seay, F. C. to John P. Weill 6-29-1863
Seay, F. E. to Saml. W. Thwett 12-18-1862 (12-19-1862)
Seay, Louisa to Wm. F. Seay 1-12-1865 (1-18-1865)
Seay, Mary E. to S. G. Fletcher 12-22-1863 (12-23-1863)
Seay, Mary E. to Wm. D. Coleman 10-21-1850
Seay, Mary J. to Wm. H. Ellis 12-28-1864 (12-30-1864)
Seay, Virginia to Andrew J. Fortner 12-27-1853 (12-28-1853)
Seebree, Martha E. to Samuel Blackman 6-21-1847 (6-23-1847)
Self, Jane to Abner Clifer? 3-27-1856
Senserey, Mary Catharine to John C. Blankenship 9-11-1844 (CTF
     says 1845)
Sensing, Amelia to Archibald M. Anderson 11-24-1840
Seray, Lucy A. to Geo. W. Armstrong 6-1-1863
Settle, Catharine C. to John W. Cockrul 11-30-1842
Settle, Mary to J. C. Harelson 7-24-1848
Sevier, S. H. to R. E. Humphrys 7-12-1847
Shaddock, Paulina to Mathew Biggs 4-3-1847 (4-18-1847)
Shaddock, Paulina to Mathew Biggs 5-3-1848 (5-5-1848)
Shadwick, Finetti to John H. Jones 5-12-1841
Shamwell, C. M. to William jr. Riggins 12-22-1853
Shamwell, Emily to Joseph B. Clardy 10-7-1841
Shanklin, Elizabeth J. to Jessee J. Anderson 11-27-1863
Shanklin, Julia A. to E. G. Poe 1-12-1859
Shannon, Elizabeth W. to David E. Pennington 12-19-1843
Shelby, Acenith to James M. Moody 2-3-1856
Shelby, Margaret to James D. Prewett 12-26-1853 (12-27-1853)
Shelby, Mary Z. to Joel Gilbert 1-26-1863 (1-29-1863)
Shelby, Patience H. to Urvin P. Shelby 2-26-1840
Shelby, Sarena R. to C. R. Phillips 12-4-1861 (12-5-1861)
Shelby, Zelia F. to Jonathan Ward 1-28-1840
Shelley, Mary P. to William F. Young 11-30-1853
Shelton, Elizabeth J. to Daniel A. Carson 12-30-1846
Shelton, Georgian P. to John N. Handlin 3-12-1864 (3-15-1864)
Shelton, Judith B. to G. M. Watts 1-12-1846 (1-15-1846)
Shelton, Margarette to Charles Brantley 9-14-1838 (9-18-1838)
Shelton, Martha to Richard Averet 9-16-1856 (9-17-1856)
Shelton, Mary J. to Jarret Averett 12-18-1858 (12-21-1858)
Shepard, Mary to P. N. Riggins 11-21-1866 (11-22-1866)
Shephard, Frankie to L. W. Evans 1-1-1859 (1-2-1859)
Shepherd, Clara to Robert Forgerson 4-27-1844
Shepherd, Cynthia Ann to S. L. Shelton 7-6-1860
Shepherd, Edith to Isaah Toler 7-16-1838 (7-17-1838)
Shepherd, Elizabeth to Robert McCarter 11-4-1861 (11-5-1861)
Shepherd, Frances Jane to John Thomas Talar 10-21-1852
Shepherd, Frances to John Smith 11-15-1847
Shepherd, Jane to Wm. Greenfield 9-1-1845
Shepherd, Lucinda to David D. Buckhannon 11-22-1852 (11-25-1852)
Shepherd, Martha to William Chisenhall 3-15-1856 (3-16-1856)

Shepherd, Mary A. to William Edwards 2-11-1843
Shepherd, Mary Ann to Andrew Chaudron? 1-2-1839 (1-3-1839)
Shepherd, Nancy to James W. Smith 8-5-1857 (8-6-1857)
Shepherd, Nancy to Luther Shepherd 12-16-1859
Shepherd, Sarah Ann to Joseph A. Seay 10-4-1856 (not executed) [*]
Shepherd, Sarah to John Hays 2-28-1866 (3-4-1866) [b]
Shepherd, Sarah to Saml. Lee 6-19-1838
Shepherd, Serilda D. to William F. Addison 1-15-1860
Sherfield?, Sally to John Thweat 12-13-1843
Sheridan, Jane to A. C. Brumbaugh 10-26-1854
Sheridan, Mary to Patric Buck 7-2-1857 (7-15-1857)
Sherrod, Sarah E. to C. L. Quarles 5-5-1852
Sherron, Mary Ann to Willis W. Williams 11-28-1840
Shoemaker, Nancy E. to William Laurison? 12-30-1852
Shores, Mary to Griffin Lankford 12-24-1852
Shrader, Ruthey Ellen to Henry Washington Wilson 12-20-1853
   (1-3-1854)
Shuff, Bettie to Sam Wickham 1-5-1865 (1-8-1865)
Shuff, Julia Ann to Jos. H. Davis 12-28-1863
Shuff, Margaret Jane to George W. Scott 4-16-1857
Shuff, Sarah to Dominerkous L. Davis 6-4-1858 (6-6-1858)
Shulas, Frances J. to James L. Martin 10-9-1854 (10-10-1854)
Sidner, Ann to Leon? Barten 1-3-1867 (1-4-1867) [b]
Simery, Alatha A. to John A. Catlutt 3-28-1839
Simmons, Lucinda to W. B. Campbell? 6-27-1847
Simmons, Lucy B. to Benjamin Whitehead 4-29-1840 (4-27?-1840)
Simons, Catharine to Jeremiah Creamer 5-9-1846
Simons, Eliza Ann to Edward Calvin 1-3-1848 (7-3-1848)
Simons?, Mary to W. W. Speed 7-12-1846
Sims, Caroline to James R. Tutor 12-1-1841
Sims, Josephine to David Carney 8-6-1866 (8-7-1866) [b]
Sims, Sarah R. to Milton Taylor 8-13-1853
Sinks, Sarah Jane to Thomas Baggett 8-11-1855
Sisk, M. E. to Isah L. Fox 8-16-1851
Sisk, Mary T. to W. J. Powell 8-15-1860
Sisk, Mildred to William Sisk 3-10-1841
Sisk, Phebe Ann to David B. Liggan 10-18-1854
Skaggs, Martha A. to Joseph Lewis 5-18-1854
Skeggs, Louisa to Wilis Jolly 5-4-1856
Skinner, Mary to Jos. M. Farley 2-19-1851? (yr omitted)
Slaughter, Eliza B. to Johnson D. Watts 12-30-1854 (12-31-1854)
Slaughter, K. M. to John R. Latham 7-21-1856
Slaughter, Kizie to Robert Derrit 1-1-1867 (1-5-1867) [b]
Slaughter, Rachael Ann to James L. Killebrew 7-19-1859 (7-21-1859)
Slayden, N. C. to H. C. jr. Rye 8-2-1864
Sleigh, Ann E. to James Andrews 10-6-1858 (10-7-1858)
Sleigh, Fanny E. to Moulton D. Yates 9-20-1859
Sloan, Minerva to John A. Taylor 4-25-1855
Slye, Georg E. to Jas. Andrews 8-11-1865 (8-12-1865)
Small, Ann E. to John W. McDaniel 10-23-1851 (10-26-1851)
Smith, Adeline (was Jane) to Randal Shoemaker 6-5-1851
Smith, Agnes A. to John F. Outlaw 9-19-1848
Smith, Allena to Wm. Channel 1-6-1851 (1-9-1851)
Smith, America to John R. Ussery 11-22-1853
Smith, Angelina A. to Peter ONeal 10-31-1843 (11-1-1843)
Smith, Angeline to Jas. Smith 2-2-1867 (1?-3-1867)
Smith, Ann Eliza to Henry W. Adderhold 3-7-1860
Smith, Arabella Jane to L. C. Capps 10-4-1858
Smith, Arsula A. to B. D. Lee 3-19-1853
Smith, Caroline to J. A. Speel 11-30-1863
Smith, Caroline to William Cooper 9-4-1850
Smith, Chaney to Jim Bell 8-24-1866 [b]
Smith, Della to Dick Lisenby 6-23-1866 (6-24-1866) [b]
Smith, Della to Wm. Smith 5-2-1866 (12-30-1866) [b]
Smith, E. J. to Wm. M. Smith 1-16-1843 (1-19-1843)
Smith, Eastes to Gholston Clark 12-25-1866 (12-26-1866) [b]
Smith, Eliza A. to J. L. jr. James 7-6-1847
Smith, Eliza to Francis W. Bond 6-17-1852
Smith, Eliza to W. D. Wright 12-18-1844
Smith, Elizabeth to Anthony Swift 4-13-1864 (10-14-1864)
Smith, Elizabeth to James P. Randell 11-8-1838
Smith, Elizabeth to John Rhinehart 1-12-1847 (1-14-1847)
Smith, Elizabeth to Wm. Darnell 4-1-1844
Smith, Emerline to Bill Broaddie 2-7-1866 (2-18-1866) [b]
Smith, Fannie E. to J. M> Lowe 6-26-1866 (6-27-1866)

Smith, Fanny to Isaac McCauley 7-21-1866 [b]
Smith, Frances Emily to John W. Tidwell 3-13-1858 (3-14-1858)
Smith, Frances to William Gafford 9-1-1859
Smith, Frances to William H. Heathman 1-4-1855
Smith, Hannah to Henry Lewis 4-1-1842 (4-9-1842)
Smith, Harriet T. to Martin S. Wallace 4-26-1845 (6-9-1845)
Smith, Harriet to Eli Smith 1-20-1861 (2-3-1861)
Smith, Harriet to J. J. Wooten 12-28-1846
Smith, Hennie C. to Chas. R. Turner 10-12-1858 (10-13-1858)
Smith, Henrietta to Henry Kendrick 1-1-1866 (with 1867) [b]
Smith, Jane to George Barbee 8-30-1855
Smith, Jane to Shadrick Trammill 8-29-1859 (8-30-1859)
Smith, Josephine to R. H. Frazier 4-23-1860 (4-24-1860)
Smith, L. M. to R. B. Tarpley 11-30-1865
Smith, Laressa to J. Westley Baggett 2-4-1856 (2-7-1856)
Smith, Louisa to Dempsey Burton 11-3-1856 (11-6-1856)
Smith, Margaret J. to James T. Trice 8-16-1860
Smith, Margarett E. to W. H. Anderon 10-3-1843 (10-5-1843)
Smith, Martha A. to Joseph H. Allen 11-30-1861 (12-1-1861)
Smith, Martha Ann Elizabeth to Bryant Smith 8-2-1865 (8-5-1865)
Smith, Martha J. to Thos. J. Miles 10-4-1850
Smith, Martha to James M. Smith 4-7-1847
Smith, Martha to Robert Allen 10-4-1839 (10-10-1839)
Smith, Marthy Ann to G. W. Denny 1-5-1867 (1-8-1867)
Smith, Mary A. C. to A. C. Wright 2-12-1851 (2-13-1851)
Smith, Mary D. to William Griffey 1-14-1858 (1-16-1858)
Smith, Mary Levina to Andrew Jackson Wright 6-7-1853 (6-10-1853)
Smith, Mary M. to Thomas W. Chandler 1-1-1856
Smith, Mary to Bazel Edwards 12-24-1839 (12-15-1839)
Smith, Mary to Jas. A. Williams 7-7-1862 (7-13-1862)
Smith, Mary to Leroy Holland 10-2-1844 (10-3-1844)
Smith, Mary to R. C. Allen 9-23-1851 (9-22?-1851)
Smith, Mary to Thos. H. Allen 11-23-1861 (11-24-1861)
Smith, Mollie M. to Robt. B. Adkins 11-30-1865 (12-5-1865)
Smith, Mrs. Eudina H. to John H. jr. Marable 11-12-1844
   (11-13-1844)
Smith, Nancy H. to R. N. Foust 11-20-1866 (11-22-1866)
Smith, Nancy J. to Thompson W. Anglin 6-10-1846 (6-11-1846)
Smith, Nancy to Adam Bradley 10-4-1866] (10-5-1866) [b]
Smith, Nancy to Rily Brown 7-19-1849
Smith, Nancy to Wm. R. Wootan 5-13-1849
Smith, Nannie J. to W. U. Hoover 3-2-1861 (3-4-1861)
Smith, Patience A. to John Moore 1-8-1839
Smith, Peggy Minerva to Geordin? L. Smith 1-20-1856
Smith, Rachael to Andrew Jackson Ford 8-24-1854
Smith, Rachel to Andrew Jackson Ford 8-24-1854
Smith, Rachel to James Smith 4-28-1866 [b]
Smith, Rachel to Jas. Crotzer 1-11-1849 (1-18-1849)
Smith, Rebecca A. to Benson W. Dye 2-24-1852 (2-26-1852)
Smith, Rusia A. to Jas. G. Guren 12-27-1865 (12-28-1865)
Smith, Sallie J. to William W. Reynolds 10-14-1863
Smith, Sarah Catharine to William B. Shelton 1-27-1862
Smith, Sarah J. to Joseph N. Woodson 2-15-1865 (2-16-1865)
Smith, Sarah Jane to Wm. H. Powers 3-25-1851 (3-16?-1851)
Smith, Sarah R. to Robert J. Baily 12-13-1857 (1-7-1858)
Smith, Seighnora to James D. Turner 2-27-1855
Smith, Z. A. to M. W. Ogburn 12-17-1855
Smithwick, Eliza Jane to Eli Robertson 5-2-1853
Smittoe, Keziah to M. Drummond 7-24-1866
Smoot, Harriett to David Sidney 12-28-1866 (12-31-1866) [b]
Sneed, Elizabeth to George W. Elliott 4-3-1865 (4-11-1865)
Sneed, Mrs. Nancy to Thos. D. Lewis 6-1-1865 (6-11-1865)
Snellings, Mary Jane to Parin T. Gibbs 1-6-1847 (1-8-1847)
Snowden, Nancy to Antony Stewart 1-23-1867 (2-19-1867) [b]
Solomon, Rebecca R. to William J. Quarles 12-31-1844
Solomon, Rebecca R. to William J. Quarles 12-31-1844 (1-2-1845)
Solomon?, Rachel to Rick Quarles 11-19-1843
Southard, Louvina to Jno. Brown? 12-20-1855
Southward, Elizabeth Ann to Wm. W. Proctor 2-10-1848 (2-11-1848)
Southward, Louiza T. to James H. Proctor 11-25-1853
Southwood, Caroline to John Parker 9-8-1842
Southwood, Winna to John Brown 12-19-1855 (12-20-1855)
Spears, Charlott M. to John W. Stawn? 11-9-1850
Speed?, Sarah to Henry Hinson 8-20-1840
Speer, E. J. to N. B. Adams 8-30-1857 (8-30-1856?)

Spencer, Margaret J. to William Rogers 6-25-1854
Spernin, Nettie to Shepherd Prophit 11-4-1865 (11-5-1865)
Spicer, Nancy to Robb Watson 6-28-1838 (7-5-1838)
Spurrier, Amanda J. to James Emmery 3-15-1854
St. John, Dorothy A. to C. L. Howerton 11-16-1846 (11-18-1846)
Stacks, Barbary Carter to Wm. A. McDaniel 2-22-1845 (4-2-1845)
Stagner, Mary to James Hester 1-27-1841 (1-28-1841)
Stailey, Mary to Maxwell Hodges 6-3-1850 (6-4-1850)
Staley, E. to W. P. Waller 9-3-1862
Staley, Mary to John jr. Brooks 12-27-1847 (12-29-1847)
Stamper, Eliza to Henry A. Norflett 11-19-1866 (11-22-1866)
Stanfield, L. F. to W. T. Welker 4-25-1864 (4-26-1864)
Stansit, Eveline L. to Jasper N. Hutcherson 7-7-1858
Stanton, Elizabeth D. to Peter E. Morehead 6-29-1845
Stanton, George Ann to Wm. A. Thom 4-7-1843 (4-14-1843)
Stanton, George Ann to Wm. Thom 4-7-1843
Starkey, E. to Jas. Basford 8-25-1862 (9-2-1862)
Starkey, Elizabeth C. to Ross Morris 1-1-1851
Starkey, Elizabeth C. to Ross Morris 1-1-1851 (1-5-1851)
Starkey, Mary to Plesant E. Cocke 12-6-1860
Starkey, Sarah F. to John L. Morrison 1-3-1856
Starks, Butchett to Wm. Stewart 10-5-1841
Starks, E. to B. J. Anderon 9-19-1841
Staten, Emma A. to Thomas H. Jackson 1-23-1855 (1-25-1855)
Staton, Addie to Alfred Dunlop 12-22-1866 [b]
Staunton, Mary to W. A. Thorn 2-1-1845 (2-2-1845)
Stearn, Pricilla H. to Levi Cooper 2-22-1851 (2-23-1851)
Steel, Mary Jane to Tom Beaumont 6-26-1866 [b]
Steel, Salina H. to Samuel F. Allen 2-8-1860 (2-9-1860)
Steely, Sally Ann to Willis B. Jones 1-15-1847 (SB 1848?)
Stegall, Elizabeth A. to Thomas Harris 8-1-1858
Stephens, Amanda to W. R. Brown 12-15-1859
Stephens, Egenarra to James T. Smith 1-?-1859 (11-25-1852?)
Stephens, Elizabeth T. to James Jobe 11-13-1845
Stephens, Margaret to Absalom Davison 3-23-1847 (3-25-1847)
Stephens, Mary E. to John W. Hill 1-17-1859
Stephens, Supprana Jane to Frederick Grimes 5-5-1851
Stevinson, Susan to James E. McCarroll 8-30-1854
Steward, C. M. to T. E. C. Eatherly 7-28-1845
Stewart, Acenith to Cornelius E. Morgan 6-16-1855 (6-17-1855)
Stewart, Angeline W. to Sterling Shearron 11-25-1853 (11-30-1853)
Stewart, C. M. to T. H. Etherly 7-25-1845 (8-11-1845)
Stewart, Letitia to Lunsford Read 10-29-1844 (11-15-1844)
Stewart, Milly to Jas. Mitchell 4-22-1865 [b]
Stewart, Nancy to Charles J. Collier 9-13-1839
Stewart, Prudence to Michael Black 5-23-1846 (5-24-1846)
Stewart, Rachel A. to Jas. Oldham 6-20-1865
Stewart, Susan to John W. Smith 12-22-1838
Stiles, Rosena to John C. Winstead 6-24-1857
Stockdal, Jane F. to Albert G. Rhea 9-10-1848
Stocker, Amy to William Hawkins 11-30-1866 (12-2-1866) [b]
Stokes, Eveline to A. J. Hightower 10-14-1855
Stone, Mary E. to Thos. Dorety 7-21-1851
Stone, Nancy to Wm. N.? Hester 12-6-1841
Stone, Sally to Wm. B. Wood 2-11-1852 (3-8-1852)
Stovall, Ellen to Henry Bell 8-29-1865 [b?]
Stovall, Mary H. to John H. Jordan 3-10-1863 (3-14-1863)
Strader, Elizabeth to James Greenwood 11-15-1854
Strey?, Martha to Jos. J. Woodson 12-23-1843 (12-26-1843)
Strother, Elizabeth to William Pettus 2-12-1845
Stroud, Emily M. to Willie B. Stewart 11-21-1840 (11-26-1840)
Stuart, Malinda J. to Levi Wallace 2-9-1855
Stugall, Mattie to Noah Seay 12-8-1865 (12-10-1865)
Sturdevant, Mary J. to Albert G. Long 10-28-1855 (10-29-1855)
Sturn?, Nancy S. to John W. Moore 2-13-1854
Sugg, Lucinda to Wm. R. Sugg 7-31-1863 (8-2-1863)
Sugg, M. V. to J. E. Sugg 12-19-1865 (12-20-1865)
Sugg, P. to G. B. Sugg 9-18-1862
Suggs, Elizebeth to John Mixon 2-27-1857
Suggs, Winney to John Jackson 7-3-1856
Sulivan, Mary to James Walsh 11-22-1866 (11-25-1866)
Sullinger, Elizabeth P. to Wm. D. Powers 8-7-1843
Sullivan, Johnie to Thos. Nott 11-8-1862 (11-15-1862)
Sullivan, Margaret to Thomas J. Hyland 2-26-1859 (3-6-1859)
Sullivan, Mrs. L. B. to C. W. Ranson 11-8-1860

Suter, Nancy Ann to William Robert Jackson 3-31-1855 (4-1-1855)
Sutor, Catharine to John Sanderson 1-29-1845
Sutor, Mary E. to Joseph J. Clark 3-9-1850 (3-10-1850)
Sutton, Elizabeth to Isaac Beardune 9-2-1849
Sutton, Ellen to August Batterman 3-29-1854
Swader, Caroline C. to John E. Armstrong 1-9-1861 (1-10-1861)
Swasey, Nancy to Isaac Hanna 9-14-1842
Swift, Maggie A. to Wm. Rudolph 11-22-1865
Swingle?, Ann to B. P. Bowling 10-1-1844 (10-2-1844)
Sydnor, Lucy Ann to Stephen J. Hatsell 11-12-1850
Tabb, Martha to Joseph Kenner 4-29-1841
Tabb, Susan K. to William G. Shamwell 1-15-1840
Taler, Sarah Ann to Joseph J. Elleatt 11-9-1851
Taler?, Ellen F. to Robt. Barbee 2-24-1851
Taliafaro, J. S. to Thos. S. Mimms 9-15-1862
Talley, Mary Jane to G. W. Talley 3-1-1852
Talley, Rebecca P. to Hugh Dunlop 2-17-1852 (2-18-1852)
Tally, Elizabeth J. to Silas M. Cherry 12-17-1846
Tally, Emily to Gilbert T. Abernathy 12-14-1853 (12-15-1853)
Tally, Josephine to W. C. Barksdale 10-17-1853 (10-20-1853)
Tally, Lucy Ann to G. W. Langston 1-17-1860 (1-19-1860)
Tally, Maria to Theodore Buntin 8-27-1854
Tally, Mary A. to Jessee E. Hill 12-13-1841
Tally, Mary Jane to John Carneal 2-27-1854
Tally, Sarah G. to Andrew Abernathy 2-20-1860 (2-22-1860)
Tally, Terrell to William F. Carnell 10-5-1857
Tamer, Rebecca A. to James T. Rives 9-18-1841 (9-22-1841)
Tanner, Amanda A. to Munroe Lawrence 1-31-1847
Tanner, Elizabeth to Patrick Salmon 12-31-1860
Tap, Sarah Jane to John Daniel 8-22-1859
Tariann, Sarah to William Blackwell 2-4-1852 (2-5-1852)
Tarpley, Lucinda L. to James B. LaRue 9-19-1861
Tarwater, Roxana to F.B. Moodie 3-17-1863 (3-24-1863)
Tate, Mary to Marion G. Carney 1-5-1846 (1-16-1846)
Tate, Virginia C. to A. J. W. Bryan 1-13-1850 (1-15-1850)
Tatum, Frances to Rhodeham Easley? 9-11-1838
Taucker, Sarah to James E. Hinson 6-12-1842
Taylor, Adelia to William B. Tylor 11-5-1857
Taylor, Eliza to D. C. Claxton 8-1-1849
Taylor, Elizabeth H. to James G. Dailey 9-17-1853 (9-18-1853)
Taylor, Elizabeth to Edward Jitt 5-16-1840
Taylor, Laura to Jim Puckett 12-28-1866 (12-29-1866) [b]
Taylor, Mary A. to Charles Ricon? 4-25-1859
Taylor, Mary C. to Andrew J. Waters 2-12-1857
Taylor, Narcissa J. to Jno. J. Hays 12-2-1856
Taylor, Suena to Abraham Joiner 1-20-1866 (1-21-1866) [b]
Taylor, Virginia to W. J. Roland 9-10-1862
Teasley, Aquilla to James Frazer 7-16-1842 (7-21-1842)
Teasley, Lucrecia to James P. Hagwood 8-1-1854
Teasley, Lucy H. to M. M. Chambless 12-19-1843 (12-21-1843)
Teasley, Mary to Gidion A. Nichols 1-15-1840
Teasly, Hester Ann to James Frazier 12-21-1846
Terrel, Wilmoth to James T. McNichols 10-11-1865 (10-12-1865)
Terrell, Ann to Mathew Harris 5-25-1841
Terrell, E. S. to Jas. B. Deadman 2-8-1844
Terrell, Lucy to Hiram Powers 8-10-1857
Terrell, Mary F. to John W. Keath 11-17-1845
Terrell, Sarah to Benjamin Smith 12-30-1853
Terrell, Sarah to Robert Baily 5-25-1858 (5-26-1858)
Terrell, Susan R. to Nathan Gamble 10-24-1857 (10-25-1857)
Terry', Sarah to William Bruden 7-22-1857 (7-23-1857)
Thacker, Berrilla A. to Thomas A. Wilson 8-26-1856
Thacker, Elizabeth to Thomas Edmondson 7-3-1859
Thacker, Margaret to Wiley Harris 8-19-1865 (8-20-1865)
Thacker, Mary E. to W. H. Southal 1-19-1852 (1-29-1852)
Thacker, Mary E. to William H. Southall 1-13-1851
Thacker, Virginia C. to Hugh L. Foster 11-24-1846
Thackston, Lucy to Edward Frambrough 2-12-1840 (3-5-1840)
Thaxton, Nancy M. to Benjamin L. J. Williams 3-12-1855 (3-15-1855)
Thomas, Elizabeth H. to James F. Cummins 11-15-1855
Thomas, Elizabeth to P. Q.? Allinsworth 6-23-1844
Thomas, Ellen to B. L. Wills 1-15-1866
Thomas, Jane to James Carver 12-3-1838
Thomas, Josephine to James Gordin 5-8-1849 (5-13-1849)
Thomas, M. C. to C. B. Cherry 11-13-1860

Thomas, Mariah T. to Wm. Buckhannon 7-13-1846 (7-14-1846)
Thomas, Martha E. to John Blane 4-22-1861 (4-25-1861)
Thomas, Sarah to Thomas Cayce 5-12-1851 (5-15-1851)
Thomas, Virginia to F. M. Dilling 2-9-1866
Thompson, Caroline to Wm. L. Foster 3-10-1842
Thompson, Elizabeth J. to John E. Niblett 5-15-1855 (5-16-1855)
Thompson, Lucy Ann to D. P. Tucker 2-27-1848
Thompson, Mary E. to Thomas J. Adams 3-3-1857
Thompson, Nancy M. to Isaac N. Young 1-7-1850
Thompson, Nancy M. to J. M. Young 6-7-1850
Thompson, Rebecca A. to Stephen Cocke 6-13-1839
Thompson, Sarah to W. L. Johnson 11-23-1843
Thorn, Nancy H. to Wm. J. Bright 9-25-1851
Thorn, Tennessee to Isaac Haynes 5-4-1856 (5-2?-1856)
Thornsberry, Frances to John N. Langston 6-28-1849
Thornton, Sarah E. to William Doughton 12-26-1843
Threat, Sally Ann to Joseph(James?) A. Seay 4-21-1858 (4-22-1858)
Thweatt, Quintalia E. to Abner Moody 12-7-1864
Tibbs, Mary to J. K. Moore 3-29-1866
Tidwell, Elizabeth to Thomas Gunning 5-23-1861
Tillotson, Eleanor P. to Henry A. Rives 4-25-1838
Tilman, Rebecca E. to John P. Hancock 9-30-1852
Tine, Susannah to G. B. Dycus 9-22-1841
Tine?, Nancy J. to John F. Kenady 10-14-1841
Tinsley, Ann to Robert M. Crockett 10-2-1854 (10-4-1854)
Tinsley, Betsey A. to Tery L. Fane 2-28-1865
Tinsley, Mary to Pleasant Crews 11-21-1848 (11-23-1848)
Tippet, Martha A. to Amos Nanny 1-11-1841 (1-19-1841)
Tippet, Nancy to Major Nicholson 6-4-1845
Todd, Martha A. to James Jewell 2-13-1852
Todd, Mrs. Elizabeth W. to Wm. F. Clark 6-6-1866 (6-7-1866)
Tolar, Elizabeth to James H. Meacham 7-20-1852
Tolar, Emily to John Dougherty 2-28-1843 (3-2-1843)
Tolar, Louisa to Alford Darnell 2-28-1843 (3-2-1843)
Toler, Edith to Stephen Lee 11-18-1862
Toler, Ellin Frances to George M. Chisenhall 2-12-1861
Toler, Fredonia to Thornsberry Anderson 1-29-1848 (1-30-1848)
Toler, Margaret J. to Samuel Fuqua 2-18-1858 (2-19-1858)
Toler, Nancy to George G. Shepherd 11-25-1855 (10?-25-1855)
Toller, Margarette to Lodwick Shepherd 1-23-1840
Tolliver, Mary to Frederick Carneal 4-3-1866 [b]
Tomerlin, Mary M. to Lemuel C. Glenn 2-4-1858
Tomlinson, Rebecca J. to H. G. Marklin 5-24-1866
Tompkins, Eliza Jane to Robert Fort 1-29-1855
Toone, Sarah A. to Samuel R. Blankenship 6-22-1856
Townley, Martha to Sam Williams 9-12-1865 [b?]
Townson, Emma to Phillip Napier 1-1-1867 [b]
Tramell, Elizabeth to Eli Smith 8-29-1859 (9-1-1859)
Tramell, Elizabeth to John R. Moss 6-15-1863 (6-17-1863)
Tramell, Martha M. to James Benj. Seay 12-14-1858 (12-16-1858)
Trammel, Jane to Wm. C. Glover 11-17-1863
Trammel, Mary E. to Protheus Moss 12-12-1865 (12-14-1865)
Travis, Armitia to G. D. Neville 11-1-1845 (11-2-1845)
Travis, Carrenia to Jacob Wesley Cigar? 7-3-1855 (7-4-1855)
Trice, Alla J. to Lewis A. Waller 5-12-1847
Trice, Ally to Berry Lyle 3-24-1855
Trice, Almeta to Edward S. Johnson 7-22-1865 (7-23-1865)
Trice, Betty M. to Anselmo Lynes 7-2-1848
Trice, Editha Ann to Edward S. Johnson 6-28-1856 (6-29-1856)
Trice, Eliza A. to J. F. Alsup 6-14-1858 (6-15-1858)
Trice, Eliza J. to L. S. Whitefield 12-3-1857
Trice, Elizabeth J. to Geo. W. Leigh 9-9-1850
Trice, Frances Ann to Samuel Hook 10-9-1848 (10-19-1848)
Trice, Frances M. to William J. Barbee 12-20-1854
Trice, H. M. to Wm. Redman 7-4-1849
Trice, Hariet E. to Bladen B. Homan 12-17-1844
Trice, Harriet to David Tomlinson (no date; with 12-1851)
Trice, Henrietta E. to T. W. Jr. Atkinson 1-25-1847
Trice, Jane to Antony Waldroop 12-10-1865 [b]
Trice, Jane to Wm. Warrick 11-22-1865 [b]
Trice, Laurana J. to James M. Crabtree 8-5-1847
Trice, Lora J. to John T. Dycus 3-3-1866 (3-6-1866)
Trice, M. B. to John B. Osburn 12-30-1850 (12-31-1850)
Trice, M. T. to J. P. Nance 11-12-1862
Trice, Malord? to W. J. Barbee 1-2-1849

Trice, Manerva to Jackson Dist 12-26-1866 (1-5-1867) [b]
Trice, Margaret to W. H. Andrews 8-4-1858 (8-6-1858)
Trice, Mary Ann M. to Abner Cain Barbee 12-21-1846 (12-24-1846)
Trice, Mary H. to Silas W. Trice 9-13-1862
Trice, Mary J. E. to Harvey Hook 4-19-1852
Trice, Mary to James Trice 12-29-1846
Trice, Mary to Josiah? Wallace 12-18-1866 (12-28?-1866) [b]
Trice, Nancy Mildred to Mathew A. Jeter 4-17-1852 (4-19-1852)
Trice, Sally B. to George T. Milom 10-19-1848
Trice, Susannah to William P. Barbee 12-21-1844 (12-23-1844)
Trigg, Fannie to R. A. Barnes 1-16-1861 (1-17-1861)
Trigg, Georgian to Wm. Langford 12-22-1866 [b]
Trigg, Rody to John Williams 3-31-1866 [b]
Trigg, Susan to Demsey Collins 7-31-1866 [b]
Tritt, Jennie to A. J. Whitacer 12-11-1859
Trotter, Elizabeth to Samuel Yarbrough 3-31-1847 (4-2-1847)
Trotter, Martha E. to Isham Jones 9-2-1865 (9-4-1865)
Trotter, Missouri Ann to Thomas Morrison 1-4-1866
Trotter, Sarah E. to Jerome Trotter 9-29-1866 (10-3-1866)
Troville, Mary C. to James C. Bailey 3-20-1844
Troxel, Eliza A. to Temple W. Sisney 9-4-1842
Truax, Sarah M. to Thomas Bell 6-4-1846 (6-10-1846)
Trundle, Sarah E. to W. F. Kephart 8-4-1866 (8-7-1866)
Tubbs, Sarah to John Chester 12-22-1858 (12-23-1858)
Tuck, Sarah to Jacob Farmer 2-27-1847
Tucker, Adeline to Jas. Lloyd 1-8-1866 [b]
Tucker, Emelia to Claborn Elliott 10-6-1866 (10-18-1866) [b]
Tucker, Martha to James M. McKinney 2-13-1847
Tucker, Martha to Thompson Gibson 12-29-1845
Tucker, Mrs. Sarah to Emery S. Ball 4-28-1865 (4-29-1865)
Tuiller?, Mary Ann to W. G. Shelton 4-30-1847
Turner, Ann to Bartlett Elder 9-25-1866 [b]
Turner, Dicy to N. W. Pass 7-10-1846 (7-11-1846)
Turner, Leander T. to James L. Rowland 9-14-1865 (9-17-1865)
Turner, Martha Jane to Hugh Collier 1-4-1854
Turner, Mary E. to B. F. King 12-15-1855
Turner, Sarah E. to Zachariah Hobbs, 7-11-1842
Tyer?, Mary J. to Josiah M. Horn 11-22-1843 (11-20?-1843)
Tyler, Ann to Armsted Hutcherson 5-8-1866 [b]
Tyne, Harriett to Randal Morrow 10-15-1841 (10-19-1842)
Tyner, Prissilla to Thomas Tucker 11-12-1839
Tyre, Rebecca to Thomas H. Averett 11-1-1853
Tyre, Tabitha E. to Thos. H. Haris 2-24-1847 (2-25-1847)
Tyson, Elizabeth A. to William A. Haynes 11-1-1858
Underwood, Mary to John Baggett 12-17-1863
Underwood, Sarah to William Bagget 4-9-1850
Ussery, Mary E. to P. H. Keesee 12-20-1855
Ussery, Sarah F. to James M. Swift 12-22-1852 (12-23-1852)
Utley, Nancy Catharine to Dixon G. Wright 5-17-1852
Vance, Amanda to Nelson Bellemy 1-6-1866 (1-15-1866) [b]
Vance, Jennie to Henry Wilcox 8-17-1865 [b?]
Vance, Mary R. to Joseph M. Fauntleroy 6-17-1857 (6-18-1857)
Vance, Tabitha A. to James Daugherty 10-17-1865 (10-21-1865)
Vanhook, Elizabeth S. to Wm. Gowans 5-16-1848
Vaughan, Cynthia B. to Elisha D. Gillam 3-13-1851
Vaughan, Elizabeth J. to Wilson H. Himes? 2-4-1851
Vaughan, Matilda to Elisha R. Oldham 2-26-1841 (3-2-1841)
Vaughan, Polly to Saml. King 12-15-1842
Vaughn, Eliza M. to George W. Royster 12-2-1861
Vaughn, Elizabeth to Charles Madison Anderson 1-27-1852
Vaughn, Lucretia to Thomas Davis 12-22-1840 (12-26-1840)
Vaughn, Lucy Ann to Wm. T. Berpo 11-4-1865 (11-7-1865)
Vaughn, M. A. to Henry H. Weaver 4-17-1863 (4-18-1863)
Vaughn, Margaret Elizabeth to Aaron Griffey 10-13-1857 (10-14-1857)
Vaughn, Nancy J. to Jas. P. Lewis 6-30-1866 (7-2-1866)
Vaughn, Nancy to Thomas Henry Sykes 7-13-1852 (7-15-1852)
Vaughn, Sarah A. to M. S. Bourland 6-2-1852
Vaughn, Sarah to John R. Harris 2-21-1860 (2-22-1860)
Vaughn, Sarah to Thomas W. Bunting 2-9-1847 (2-11-1847)
Vaughn, Sophia to J. B. Jackson 1-9-1860 (1-10-1860)
Veal, A. A. to William K. Whitlow 9-13-1852
Veall, Agatha A. to Thomas T. Pugh 2-1-1854 (2-2-1854)
Venable, Sarah A. to A. V. Elam 1-6-1842
Venters, Polley to Archey Yatman 12-21-1866 [b]

Ventress, F. J. to Jonathan Gossett 8-22-1856
Vick, Ann Eliza to Robert John Israel Robertson 11-27-1847 (12-2-1847)
Vicks, Catharine to William B. Harper 6-26-1845
Vollentine, Betty to Jim Vandack 12-8-1866 (12-9-1866) [b]
Voss, Margaret to P. D. Martin 5-31-1850
Vuaghn, Zilphia Ann to John D. Furgerson 3-16-1857 (3-17-1857)
Wade, Catharine to Wm. Harrison 1-4-1848
Wade, J. B. to L. L. Campbell 4-2-1866
Wade, Sarah E. to Albert C. Northington 2-6-1845 (2-12-1845)
Waggoner, Sally Ann to Thomas Cope 9-10-1845
Wales, Nancy to J. W. Marshall 6-21-1852 (6-22-1852)
Walker, Amanda to James H. Majors 10-12-1840 (10-15-1840)
Walker, Elvirie W. to Arthar Harris 4-26-1842
Walker, Frances G. to Isaac R. Tender 3-7-1865
Walker, Fredonia B. to A. A. C. Rogers 7-22-1845 (7-25-1845)
Walker, Julier B. to Joseph B. Terrington? 2-23-1842
Walker, Margaret J. to Allen Robertson 2-17-1851
Walker, Margarett to Arther T. Woodson 1-18-1850
Walker, Martha Ann M. to Allen Hunter 12-12-1846 (12-23-1846)
Walker, Mary E. to Wm. E. Pugh 12-8-1853
Walker, Mary to Geo. W. Smith 11-22-1866 (11-23?-1866)
Walker, Mary to George Robertson 10-16-1838
Walker, Nancy M. to William Higgie 10-8-1845 (10-9-1845)
Walker, Nancy to Mathew T. Gray 10-2-1845
Walker, Sally A. to W. H. Shelby 9-25-1844
Walker, Sarah Caroline to Josiah Tharp 2-10-1853 (2-16-1853)
Walker, Sarah Elizabeth to Albert Charles 5-5-1865
Walker, Solila to Edward Edwards 3-23-1849
Wall, Arabella to J. W. Elliott 11-23-1866
Wall, F. to Joseph Brame 3-18-1863 (3-25-1863)
Wall, Frances E. to Joseph J. Bowers 1-7-1845
Wall, Mary J. to L.R. Bagwell 11-19-1859 (11-20-1859)
Wall, P. F. to Robt. H. Lander 8-7-1851
Wall, Sallie E. to Green Smith 8-20-1866 (8-23-1866)
Wall, Sallie E. to James E. Outlaw 1-3-1861
Wall, V. C. to John C. White 7-28-1862 (8-14-1862)
Wallace, Eliza A. to John Long 6-9-1855
Wallace, Julia to Lewis Williams 6-18-1866 [b]
Wallace, Mary Jane to James Turbeville 2-13-1860
Waller, Bella to Charles Barnum 8-16-1860
Waller, Emily B. to Quintus? M. Tyler 1-12-1843
Waller, Mary N. to Nathaniel P. Irby 6-29-1852 (6-30-1852)
Waller, Mrs. Ann. J. to Wm. T. Pace 11-21-1864 (12-1-1864)
Waller, Mrs. Nancy to Thomas Rogers 1-16-1862 (1-6?-1862)
Waller, Sally V. to James C. Neblett 4-8-1857 (4-9-1857)
Walls, Mary Ann to Drew S. Fletcher 3-10-1846
Walsh, Elizabeth C. to John W. Long 1-2-1845
Walthal, Henrietta to Burwell R. Burchett 2-10-1857
Walthall, Martha Ann to Madison W. Corkieff 1-31-1854
Ward, Molly E. to George W. Trice 1-7-1862
Ward, Phenaty to Joel Bruce 1-2-1843 (1-5-1843)
Warden, Catharine to J. J. McMurry 11-19-1849 (11-20-1849)
Warden, Martha Ann to Abraham Basquit 8-20-1850
Warden, Martha Ann to Malden Doughson 9-22-1845 (9-24-1845)
Warden, Polly to James S. Wallace 12-15-1845
Ware, Mary to Bosalvin C. Perham 11-8-1864
Ware, Mildred S. to Thomas M. Boardman 11-19-1861
Ware, Rebecca to Granville Tucker 11-19-1839
Warfield, A. E. to George R. Browder 9-5-1850
Warfield, Ann B. to James R. Grady 1-9-1839 (1-16-1839)
Warfield, Bittie W. to Jas. R. Young 2-4-1865 (2-9-1865)
Warfield, Joyce P. to Jacob Duguid 1-18-1858 (1-19-1858)
Warfield, Laura to James Whitfield 12-27-1865 (12-26?-1865) [b]
Warfield, Matilda to Zack Whitfield 12-23-1865 (12-26-1865) [b]
Warfield, Susan to Osbern Hiter 8-31-1865 [b?]
Warfield, Virginia S. to Thomas E. Browder 12-23-1856
Warren, Nancy Jane to Michael O'Brien 1-17-1859 (1-20-1859)
Warring, Ellen to William E. Graham 5-19-1844
Waters, Catharine to Robt. Dorch 12-23-1865 (12-25-1865)
Waters, Mary to Edmund P. Halay 5-21-1853
Watkins, Amanda L. to R. H. Ally 1-23-1845
Watson, Elizabeth J. to Nathan S. Johnson 12-1-1856
Watson, Elizabeth to George W. Stewart 11-22-1856
Watson, Matilda to Jeremiah Hinly? 10-22-1847

Watts, Martha A. to David W. Hackney 12-11-1856
Watts, Olivia to Westley Torian 12-28-1866 [b]
Watts, Sallie to S. H. Dickinson 5-14-1866
Watwood, Evelina to John Roscoe 2-7-1848
Watwood, Martha E. to Richard T. Wells 2-15-1852
Weakley, A. J. to W. M. Page 12-27-1854 (12-29-1854)
Weakley, Elizabeth to Haywood Bearden 6-7-1850
Weakley, Lucinda to F. M. Teasley 12-8-1851
Weakley, Mary Jane to Robert J. Jones 7-20-1844 (7-25-1844)
Weakley, Mary to Shelby Stewart 12-21-1841 (12-25-1841)
Weakley, Narcissa P. to Saml. K. Weakley 12-29-1849 (12-31-1849)
Weakley, Patsey (col?) to Alston H. Shorter no date
Weakley, Patsey to Henry Russell 11-17-1866 [b]
Weakley, Susannah E. to Bluford Malen 12-31-1846 (1-12-1847)
Weakly, Polly to Prestly Bishop 9-26-1848
Weakly, Sarah to B. Mathews 12-28-1847 (12-30-1847)
Weatherford, Jennie to Jerry Ganes 7-28-1866 [b]
Weatherford, M. to J. T. Darden 4-10-1862
Weaver, Delila to S. G. Wickham 4-1-1852
Weiring, Pamelia to Edward Taylor 12-29-1851
Welch, S. A. to Thos. Murphy 10-15-1844
Welker, Mourning L. to A. J. Stewart 10-10-1848
Welker, Phebe Ann to Alford G. Bledsoe 12-25-1839
Welker, Sarah J. to W. R. Brown 2-7-1852 (2-9-1852)
Welker, Sarah to J. M. Stanfill 8-7-1856
Wells jr., Polly to Geo. King 1-22-1844
Wells, Elizabeth to Isaac R. Deshong 3-9-1865
Wells, Hardin? J. to P. H. Wells 3-6-1856 (3-16-1856)
Wells, Mary Ann to B. M. Clifton 7-28-1853 (7-25?-1853)
Wells, Mary Jane to Drury Easley 9-1-1846
Wells, Mildred A. to Elberd S. Lashbrook 9-29-1850
Welsh, Margaret to James Kilband 7-7-1866 (7-9-1866)
Welsh, Mary Jane to W. J. Razor 5-23-1859 (5-24-1859)
Weren?, Emily D. to J. E. Ireland 9-2-1846
West, Amanda to Jerry Box 10-29-1866 [b]
West, Caroline to H. H. Reynolds 4-24-1855 (4-23?-1855)
West, Mariah to George Roberts 8-29-1866 (9-8-1866) [b]
West, Martha E. to John M. Niblett 2-23-1854
West, Mary Jane to Albert Grace 2-25-1858
Westzell, Catharine to Alexander H. Ashley 12-26-1856
Wetherford, Susan Ann to Richard H. Coleman 10-12-1852 (10-19-1852)
Whatley, Melvina to John J. Buckner 5-6-1855
Wheatley, Althea M. to William C. Smith 6-21-1854
Wheatley, Nannie S. to Robert E. Gibbons 12-18-1858
Whedem?, R. R. to J. H. Hooser 10-3-1862
Wheeler, Mrs. Margaret to G. W. Bagwell 5-3-1865
Wheless, Martha Ann to John Wilson 10-31-1838 (12-13-1838)
Whitacer, Margaret to John H. McPherson 4-18-1861
Whitaker, Rebecca to William Scott 2-9-1860
White, Ann B. to William M. Kelly 10-10-1849
White, E. J. to W. C. McClure 3-31-1846
White, Emeline to Allen Scales 2-16-1856
White, Frances A. to LaFayette J. Mayfield 12-2-1864 (12-8-1864)
White, Frances S. to Alexander Watwood 2-2-1842
White, Janie to Alfred Black 2-7-1855
White, Louiza M. to James P. Tally 2-18-1847
White, Lucy to J. J. Snell 4-5-1862 (4-7-1862)
White, Margaret to Joseph W. Ryan 5-28-1855 (5-29-1855)
White, Martha to Wallace Pollard 6-9-1865
White, Mary Ann to E. B. Halsel 9-15-1853
White, Mary Jane to Morton J. Tally 7-10-1845
White, Mary to Thos. White 5-19-1866 (5-20-1866) [b]
White, Sarah Ann to Henry M. Newhall 10-15-1849
White, Sarah R. to Horris Worthington 5-17-1848 (5-18-1848)
White, Susan Jane to George Washington Chester 2-4-1858 (2-6-1858)
White, Susan to Wm. M. Bryant 11-5-1846
White, Susanna to Asa Everett 9-15-1859
Whitenton, Susanah W. to Thomas G. Hargrove 12-5-1851 (12-7-1851)
Whitfield, Adelia A. to Charles W. Staton 11-15-1865
Whitfield, Catharine F. to James B. Osburn 1-19-1846 (1-21-1846)
Whitfield, Elizabeth D. to C. W. C. Metcalfe 8-8-1838 (8-14-1838)
Whitfield, Jane to John Wheeler 11-3-1866 (11-11-1866) [b]
Whitfield, Mrs. Auriminter L. to J. B. Williams 11-15-1865

Whitfield, Treacy Ann to John R. Nixon 8-13-1853 (8-15-1853)
Whitledge, Nancy B. to John S. Carr 5-9-1844
Whitlow, Louiza W. to James H. Hord 8-18-1858 (8-14?-1858)
Whitsett, Emily to John W. Shote 12-18-1857 (12-27-1857)
Whittaker, Harriet J. to Joseph E. Braddus 3-21-1853 (3-22-1853)
Whittington, Lavinia to John N. Trotter 10-10-1839
Whitworth, Louisa to Henry Houston 12-14-1849
Whitworth, Martha Ann to Absalom Davison 10-13-1840 (10-18-1840)
Whitworth, Nancy to John Houston 3-2-1846 (3-3-1846)
Whuldom, E. A. to John W. Henderson 12-18-1845
Wickham, Elizabeth to Benjamin Blackford 9-13-1838 (9-18-1838)
Wickham, Elizabeth to Thos. Parker 8-26-1864 (8-29-1864)
Wickham, Juliann to Thomas Nesbitt 5-2?-1838 (5-7-1838)
Wickley, Anny to Ellickzander Lee 12-30-1866 (12-31-1866) [b]
Wicks, Narcissa E.? to William P. Hampton 8-3-1860
Wickum, Sarah to John K. Griffin 3-20-1851
Wiggins, Mary to John Ray 7-7-1840
Wiggins, Sally Ann to John Kreamer 12-20-1845
Wiggins, Winney to John McEntire 3-28-1853
Wiggins, Winney to Joseph Luster 9-11-1841 (9-27-1841)
Wiggs, Edy Ann to John E. Williams 11-2-1846
Wilburn, Mrs. M. J. to Johnathan H. Mitchell 11-16-1865
Wilcox, H. E. to Needham B. Whitfield 4-1-1843
Wilcox, Irene to Limon Wisdom 5-3-1866 [b]
Wilcox, Margaret to Samuel H. Gill 11-30-1861
Wilcox, Virginia G. to Simon B. Herring 6-2-1853
Wilcutt, Sarah to Wm. A. Powell 7-28-1866
Wiley, Sarah A. F. to C. M. Horn 10-29-1860 (10-30-1860)
Wilie, Louiza Jane to L. F. Long 1-25-1854
Wilie, Mary A. to George H. Coleman 2-23-1859 (2-24-1859)
Wilkins, Adaline to George McFaddin 11-17-1857
Wilkins, Fannie to Daniel Overton 6-25-1866 [b]
Wilkins, Hana C. to George Washington Purnell 10-27-1858
Wilkins, Luvenia to James J. Wilkins 8-10-1859
Wilkins, Mary Ellen to Thomas Bayless 5-20-1859 (5-23-1859)
Wilkinson, Martha to Leonard G. Faxon 11-25-1854
Willard, Clementine to George Stegall 11-13-1854
William, Mary C. M. to James K. P. Lewis 12-7-1863 (12-10-1863)
Williams, A. M. to Stephen C. Batson 12-8-1840 (12-11-1840)
Williams, Adeline Minerva to Harman Abney 11-30-1847 (12-2-1847)
Williams, Amanda F. to John Cole 10-30-1865
Williams, Ann to Allen Jefferson 3-30-1842 (4-30-1842)
Williams, Ann to Robert H. Williams 6-3-1853
Williams, C. to Martin How 5-9-1865 (5-11-1865)
Williams, Catherine to Samuel M. Roberts 3-7-1859 (3-9-1859)
Williams, Cathrine to John Dortch 12-25-1866 (12-26-1866) [b]
Williams, Eliz. to Joseph T. ODonieley 4-30-1847
Williams, Elizabeth Jane to Wm. C. Mosely 7-16-1846
Williams, Elizabeth to George W. Phillips 1-28-1857 (1-29-1865(sic)
Williams, Fannie to Charles W. White 10-19-1859
Williams, Farbary to Robert D. Robertson 2-21-1850 (2-23-1850)
Williams, Frances to Willis Morgan 4-29-1865 (4-30-1865)
Williams, Harriett to Phillip E. Drane 4-17-1839
Williams, Lucena to John M. Britt 7-9-1841 (7-11-1841)
Williams, M. E. W. to N. L. Leavitt 12-26-1865 (12-27-1865)
Williams, Malissa E. to David L. Boyd 3-15-1859 (3-17-1859)
Williams, Manerva to R. Gold 10-23-1866 (10-24-1866) [b]
Williams, Margaret to Richard W. Humphries 1-6-1848
Williams, Mary A. to S. G. Hollinsworth 8-20-1856
Williams, Mary C. to William Staples 9-22-1847
Williams, Mary E. to Allin Mixion 12-19-1866
Williams, Mary to James M. Wilson 10-16-1838
Williams, Mattie to Hugh Dunlop 5-15-1865 (5-17-1865)
Williams, Mildred W. to Chas. M. Grant 1-9-1850
Williams, Mildred W. to H. M. Adcock 1-14-1853 (1-18-1853)
Williams, Mrs. Paulina to Stephen Power 3-16-1866
Williams, Sally Ann to Joseph M. Dyce? 1-27-1854
Williams, Sally to Drury Ray 3-16-1853 (3-17-1853)
Williams, Sarah Ann to John A. Cope 9-11-1849
Williams, Sarah C. to Lewis Whitfield 1-18-1842
Williams, Vicey B. to John Boon 9-25-1847 (9-26-1847)
Williamson, Ann F. to John W. Plant 7-26-1845 (7-30-1845)
Williamson, Kate to W. F. Swift 4-9-1857
Williamson, Mary E. to S. B. Powers 12-1-1866
Williamson, Sarah G. to John Morris 6-20-1846 (6-21-1846)

Williamson, Virginia A. to Michael Everson 11-29-1857
Willis, Manerva to Thomas Holland 5-11-1848
Willis, Priscilla to Daniel Sullivan 2-23-1843
Willis, Sally E. to J. R. McMeans 9-1-1841
Willis, Verranda W. to D. A. Lucket 6-4-1843
Wills, Margaret to Samuel Hobbs 4-24-1865 [b]
Wills, Susan A. to James A. Hutchison 5-11-1857 (5-14-1857)
Wilson, A. L. to J. R. Fletcher 6-5-1866
Wilson, Betty Ann to Malachiah Odam 6-2-1858
Wilson, Elizabeth to Marcus L. Thacker 11-10-1855
Wilson, Frances to Saml. Smith 12-26-1865 (12-7?-1865)
Wilson, Hester Ann to John Barbee 5-9-1853 (5-10-1853)
Wilson, Malinda to Joel Stewart 5-30-1838
Wilson, Martha A. to Claybourn Rice 2-3-1858 (2-14-1858)
Wilson, Martha W. to John W. Wilson 12-1-1852
Wilson, Mary Frances to Andrew J. Taylor 10-12-1859
Wilson, Mary Jane to George H. Ward 10-29-1866
Wilson, Mary Jane to Henry Boid 11-28-1866 (12-2-1866) [b]
Wilson, Mrs. Anni Maria to William Brunt 8-26-1865
Wilson, Ruth E. to W. B. McGriggar 10-2-1856 (10-9-1856)
Wilson, Sarepta S. to James W. Lockert 5-3-1852 (5-4-1852)
Wimberly, Amand L. to Henry F. Watkins 10-2-1838
Wimberly, Delinia M. to Finis Ewing 10-14-1858
Wimberly, Elizabeth D. to John T. Bellemy 7-24-1861
Wimberly, Mary C. to J. B. Killebrew 12-3-1857 (12-2?-1857)
Wims, Lucy to William Rudolp 1-25-1853
Wind, Elmina to Wm. Arminett 2-5-1851 (2-6-1851)
Winders, Martha A. to Andrew J. McFerlin 1-19-1843
Winn, Semanthia L. to Lemuel S. Brawner 2-8-1864
Winn, Zuritha J. to James M. Rudolph 12-21-1853 (12-22-1853)
Winston, Mrs. S. J. to John L. Swaney 8-27-1860
Winters, Catharine to Wm. Joda? 1-28-1844
Winters, Dicy Ann to Fount Spillers 5-2-1866
Wisdom, Amelia Ann to William H. Turnley 10-15-1859 (10-16-1859)
Wisdom, D. P. to George W. Bradley 9-22-1845 (9-24-1845)
Wisdom, R. W. to Wm. D. Bayer 7-10-1847 (7-13-1847)
Wisdom, Sally to G. L. Mansons? 8-9-1849 (8-14-1849)
Witherspoon, Laura A. to James Harrelson 4-7-1845
Witt, Mary A. W. to Edward J. Davis 4-4-1866
Witty, Sarah S. to Thomas J.? Cofer 7-26-1858 (7-29-1858)
Wolf, Octavia to Charles E. Mann 9-23-1839
Wood, Ann to Stephen Broddie 7-27-1866 (8-1-1866) [b]
Wood, Carolin to Cager Kendrick 8-16-1866 [b]
Wood, Catharine G. to Charles Ferrel 2-10-1855 (2-11-1855)
Wood, Mary to Henry D. Tutt 11-9-1864 (11-10-1864)
Wood, Mrs. Nannie to C. C. Carlisle 8-4-1866 (8-7-1866)
Wood, Pauline E. to Richard K. McCrae 2-16-1857 (2-19-1857)
Woodford, Celia Ann to James H. Murphy 11-26-1846
Woodleech, Nancy to John W. Powers (no date; with 1851)
Woodman, Eliza to Allen Lyle 12-13-1859 (12-14-1859)
Woodman, Mary to Golconda Lyle 1-24-1855 (1-25-1855)
Woodruff, Martha to Asahel Chappel 7-28-1849
Woodruff, T. M. to L. C. Yandell 8-8-1865
Woodson, C. H. to Henry Hobson 3-25-1841
Woodson, Jane Ann to James N. Holt 12-31-1851 (1-1-1852)
Woodson, M. L. to J. M. Oldham 7-16-1864 (7-20-1864)
Woodson, Martha to Henry Jones 1-5-1866 [b]
Woodson, Sarah E. to D. R. Locket 12-18-1850
Woodson, Susan to Fredrick jr. Bayly 1-3-1855
Woodward, Amanda M. to Jefferson Tyer 12-9-1847
Woodward, Fanny to Solomon Gupton 1-29-1866 [b]
Woodward, Frances to Meridith Pailey 8-15-1854
Woodward, Mira A. S. to Isaiah B. Dilworth 8-20-1855
Woollard, Amanda to John Osburn 11-27-1847
Wooten, Eliza R. to Andrew J. Fletcher 12-22-1857 (12-23-1857)
Wootton, Eliza to Geo. Wigginton 6-5-1863
Word, K. M. to J. R. Henderson 11-23-1851
Word, Kitty M. to James Robert Henderson 11-23-1851 (11-24-1851)
Workman, Marth L. A. to L. S. Collins 1-16-1865
Wortham, Penesa to Nathaniel Keel 11-5-1866
Wray, Elizabeth to John Clark 4-13-1848
Wray, Nannie K. to John T. Staten 4-14-1857 (4-15-1857)
Wright, Agness D. to Osbourn Weed 5-21-1844
Wright, Ann C. to E. U. E. Wright 7-14-1845
Wright, Ann E. to Richard H. Swett 6-8-1856

Wright, Eliza to Thomas Basford 12-19-1853 (12-22-1853)
Wright, Margaret to John N. Hagart? 2-14-1853
Wright, Mary J. to James M. Baggett 12-12-1865
Wright, Mary R. to J. Q. A. Bell 3-23-1846
Wright, Maryana to James C. Pearcy 10-18-1859
Wright, Rosella S. to Henry R. Tyner 12-15-1847 (12-16-1847)
Wright, Susan to John G. Nichelson 9-1-1855 (9-18-1855)
Wright, Tabitha to John Vincent 10-8-1839
Wry, T. C. to F. D. Leathers 7-30-1847 (8-1-1847)
Wyatt, Elizabeth to Hiram Davis 2-12-1850
Wyatt, Mary J. to Samuel Watson 5-21-1853 (5-22-1853)
Wyatt, Sally E. to Henry Minor 1-21-1856 (1-22-1856)
Wyatt, Sarah E. F. to David A. Harris 2-7-1858 (2-4?-1858)
Wyatte, Sarah L. to John T. Richardson 5-10-1845
Wynn, Martha Jane to James M. Brown 9-16-1851
Wynn, Sarah to Augustus Barbee 10-21-1845 (10-24-1844?)
Wynns, Mrs. Fannie M. to Joseph M. Peacher 4-20-1865
Yancey, Louisa to George Pritchett 12-13-1866 (12-14-1866) [b]
Yancy, Lucy to Alexander Coleman 7-5-1866 [b]
Yancy, Piety to John R. Barber 2-8-1867 (2-12-1867)
Yarborough, E. to John Jackson 6-19-1862 (6-23-1862)
Yarborough, Eliza to Isham Harris 5-18-1864
Yarborough, Nancy to John Sulivan 4-2-1844
Yarbrough, Elizabeth to Washington Suter? 2-26-1842 (2-27-1842)
Yarbrough, J. A. to C. C. Cocke 12-11-1855
Yarbrough, Jane to H. O. Bumpass 12-19-1844
Yarbrough, Milly to Joseph W. Yarbrough 11-26-1850
Yarbrough, Patsy to Stephen Jackson 6-13-1839
Yarbrough, Sarah Ann to Abner Maliss? 1-29-1853
Yarbrough, Susan to Jessee Jackson 1-21-1852 (1-23-1852)
Yarrell, Louisa to Welkins E. Duke 11-15-1853
Yates, Almira G. to U. J. Holland 6-10-1843 (6-13-1843)
Yates, E. M. to James W. Cunningham 9-3-1843
Yates, Elizabeth to Jno. Newman 10-19-1843 (10-22-1843)
Yates, Emily A. to Wiley P. Pickering 1-21-1867 (1-24-1867)
Yates, Jemima J. W. to Joseph R. Edgar 5-11-1846 (5-13-1846)
Yates, Liddy to Wm. Latham 3-7-1848
Yates, Martha to Fountain Yates 5-19-1866 (5-20-1866) [b]
Young, Ann Baxter to Benjn. Connel 8-15-1866 (12-1-1866) [b]
Young, Elizabeth to James Rochel 7-28-1849 (8-1-1849)
Young, M. J. to H. R. Burnley 8-15-1866
Young, Martha to George M. Pottard 12-15-1840 (12-23-1840)
Young, Mary J. to S. L. Garrard 12-4-1843 (12-12-1843)
Young, Polley to George W. Warfield 12-26-1866 [b]
Young, Sarah A. to A. E. Fergason 9-13-1849
Young, Sarah R. to J. H. Farley 9-4-1856 (9-8-1856)
Younger, Frances C. to S. H. Whobrey? 11-25-1851
Zellers, Arabella to Charles J. Ferrels 1-16-1853